F. Livesey
Professor and Head of School of Econo...
Preston Polytechnic

G. K. Pople and P. J. Davies
Lecturers in the Faculty of Law,
University of Manchester

The organisation in its environment

Volume 1

Longman
London and New York

Longman Group Limited London

Associated companies, branches and representatives throughout the world

Published in the United States of America by Longman Inc., New York

© Longman Group Limited 1980

First published 1980

British Library Cataloguing in Publication Data

Livesey, Frank
   The organisation in its environment.
   Vol. 1. – (Longman business education series).
   1. Industry – Social aspects
   I. Title   II. Pople, G K   III. Davies, P J
   338.7   HD60   79-40206

   ISBN 0-582-41185-8

Printed in Great Britain by
Richard Clay (The Chaucer Press) Ltd, Bungay, Suffolk

Longman Business Education Series

Series Editor:
J. H. Clifford, B.Sc. Econ.

Books to be published for BEC General Level Modules:
Business calculations   J. O. Bird and A. J. C. May
World of work   Millie Pincott
Communicating with people at work   Peter Little

Books to be published for BEC National Level Modules:
People and communication   S. H. Burton
The organisation in its environment Volume 2
F. Livesey, G. K. Pople and P. J. Davies

Contents

Series Editor's Foreword

The introduction of the BEC courses has provided a challenge for all colleges by asking them to reconsider what objectives a business course might have, the content involved and the way it can best be presented to students. Integration of subject matter is not as new or as difficult as the vociferous anti-BEC lobby would suggest and many who have given much thought to their teaching in the past have been crossing subject boundaries for some time.

Now it is everyone's turn and to help colleagues in preparing and developing their own materials, Longman introduce their new Business Education Series. This is not an attempt to provide answers to all the questions the BEC courses have raised. It is accepted that no series could provide a perfectly designed package of fully integrated material; developing integrated schemes of work is the job of lecturers. Rather, the aims of the Series are:

(i)   to bring together blocks of subject matter, closely related to the BEC modules;
(ii) to present it in a possible teaching order;
(iii) to highlight areas where integration might be fruitful;
(iv) to support integration and participative teaching through the various suggestions on assignments.

BEC has published its own explanatory notes on assignments and the authors in the Series have noted these in their preparation, attempting to provide:

(a) the requested variety (short exercises, essays, reports, case studies, projects);
(b) the desired balance (acquiring, reinforcing, understanding, interpreting and analysing knowledge and skills);
(c) a variable form ('offering materials, tasks and a set of relationships that draw tasks and information together in a comprehensive way').

In this volume the team of authors is led by that experienced writer on economic affairs, Professor Frank Livesey. They move gradually through a carefully argued case, examining why it is worth studying organisations, their accountability, form, objectives and policies before considering the legal rules of contract within which most business transactions take place. The field is then widened to consider the market and within this the relative position of firm and consumer both in economic and legal terms. The volume concludes by discussing the economic issues and legal obligations that exist when various types of resources are being allocated.

Each chapter is supported by a range of assignment materials varying from the short class exercise to the extended case study; all seek to enliven theory and help students apply principles to the realities of the world of work. Suggestions on possible solutions are provided in the Lecturers' Manual. It is unlikely that, on first attempt and writing before the courses are fully underway, the assignments will prove ideal. However, by careful consideration and use, lecturers should find them a useful addition to their own stock of materials in breaking up long sections of class exposition, in encouraging participative teaching and in providing follow-up work to be done outside college. As more experience is gained we would be pleased to hear from colleges as to ways in which the Series may be improved.

J. H. Clifford

Preface

This is the first of two volumes covering the syllabus for the BEC National level double module, *The Organisation in its Environment*. BEC have indicated that although students are expected to tackle the full syllabus, they might approach it in a different order from that in which it appears in the course specification. We have in fact deviated from this order only when we thought that there were very good reasons for doing so, as explained below.

The relationship between the two approaches is most easily seen by comparing the order of our chapters with that of the BEC general objectives:

Chapter	General objective
1	A
2	C
3–4	A
5–8	B
9–13	J (learning objectives J 1–3)
14	F
15	D
16–18	G
19–22	J (learning objective J 4)
23–29	E

Chapters 1 to 8 relate to the three general objectives concerned with The Organisation, and we have made only a minor change of order, bringing forward objective C.

We then make a more important change, in that we deal in Chapters 9 to 13 with the first three parts of objective J (J1–3). These are concerned with various aspects of contract law and we thought it appropriate to discuss them at this stage because many of the policies discussed in Chapters 7 and 8 involve the organisation in contractual relationships. We also felt that this would 'encourage the student to bring together and relate academic disciplines as contributors to the analysis and solution of business problems', one of the BEC aims.

The next block of Chapters, 14 to 18, deal with objectives F and G, the first two of the objectives concerned with The Organisation, its Markets, Customers and Clients. This block, and specifically Chapter 15, also deals with objective D, which is concerned with The Organisation and Demographic Factors. We delay our consideration of this objective until this stage because we feel that demographic change should be considered, as far as is possible, together with the other factors that influence demand (objective G – Chapter 16).

We then deal in Chapters 19 to 22 with a further part of objective J (J4), which is concerned with the legal protection afforded to consumers. The justification for advancing this part of objective J is basically the same as previously. The policies that we have discussed in the prior chapters affect consumers, and the relationships that arise between organisations and consumers are subject to legal controls.

Finally we deal with the whole of objective E, which is concerned with The Organisation and Its Resources. This means that we discuss the organisation's policies (Chapters 7, 8 and 14 to 18) before we discuss how it acquires the resources needed to carry out these policies. There seems little to choose between this and the reverse order of presentation.

Finally we should point out that objective H and the final parts of objective J (J5 and 6) will be dealt with in Volume 2. Although it was felt to be appropriate to prepare two volumes for a double module, there did not appear to be any obvious natural break. It seemed that objective H, 'assess the importance of domestic and overseas trade to the United Kingdom', could have been dealt with after G. However it fits just as well with objective L3, 'analyse the main components of the National Income' and so will be discussed together with that topic in Volume 2, so as to improve the balance of the length of the two volumes.

Similarly J5 and J6 could have been dealt with either after J4 (Volume 1) or with K2 (Volume 2); once again it is discussed in the second volume so as to improve the balance.

In view of the emphasis placed by BEC on assignments we have included several assignment at the end of each chapter. Suggestions as to how these assignments might be tackled, and which assignments might form part of the assessment programme, are contained in the Lecturers' Manual.

Acknowledgements

We are grateful to the following for permission to reproduce copyright material:

Butterworths & Co (Publishers) Ltd for an extract from 'Re Brocklehurst 1978, 1, A11, ER 767' and an extract from 'Photo Productions Ltd v. Securicor 1978, 3, A11, ER 146'; Cambridge University Press for a table from the article 'Dynamic Demand Functions: Some Econometric Results' by R. Stone and O. H. Rowe in *Economic Journal* 1958; The Financial Times for information extracted from various articles in the following issues of *The Financial Times* 16 November 1977; 19 December 1977; 26 January 1978; 18 July 1978; 20 July 1978; 16 September 1978 and 6 October 1978; Her Majesty's Stationery Office for the use of data based on HMSO publications for our population tables, by permission of the Controller of Her Majesty's Stationery Office; The Incorporated Council of Law Reporting for England and Wales for an extract from 'Rose and Frank Co v. J. R. Crompton & Brothers Ltd 1923, 2, K.B. 261'.

Whilst every effort has been made to trace the owners of copyright, in a few cases this has proved impossible and we take this opportunity to offer our apologies to any authors whose rights may have been unwittingly infringed.

1 Why organisations?

Introduction

From the moment that an individual is born he (or she) becomes a member of an organisation – the family. Five or six years later he becomes a member of another organisation – a school. In a further ten to fifteen years, when he starts work, he usually becomes a member of the type of organisation with which we are mainly concerned in this book – either a business or an administrative organisation. This may be a small private company, a large multi-national, the civil service, a local authority and so forth. During, and indeed after, his working life a person may, of course, be a member of other organisations – some connected with his work, e.g. a trade union – others concerned with his leisure activities, e.g. a church, golf club or photographic society.

It can be seen, then, that a person may belong to many different kinds of organisation. But these organisations all have one thing in common, namely that they utilise resources – human and material – in an attempt to achieve particular objectives.

The reasons for the formation of organisations

Most organisations are formed because this makes it easier to acquire and utilise resources for the benefit of members. To illustrate this point let us consider a group of people who wish to play cricket on a piece of land which is not being used for any other purpose. They might arrange to turn up with their equipment on one Saturday afternoon in the hope of being able to have a game. However, this hope might be frustrated either because another group of people with the same idea arrive before them or because the pitch is found to be unsuitable, perhaps because it is uneven or the grass is too long. (They might also be frustrated by the weather, but we ignore that possibility here.)

If they were sufficiently keen they might be able to overcome the second disadvantage – at least to a certain extent – by cutting the grass, and rolling out the bumps. However, the ground would no doubt then become more attractive to other groups, and they might find it even harder to get a game of cricket than previously. A more satisfactory solution might, therefore, be to form an

1

organisation, a cricket club, which could buy or rent the land, prepare it for cricket and ensure that it was available for use as and when required.

In order to obtain these benefits members would, of course – either directly or via their subscriptions – have to provide the equipment and the labour needed to prepare the pitch, fence it and so forth. Clearly the club will not be formed unless the (potential) members feel that the benefits exceed the cost.

This principle – that the benefits of participating in an organisation should exceed, or at least equal, the costs – underlies 'membership' of most organisations. There are, however, exceptions.

In some cases the benefit of membership may not be perceived by the member and his participation must be forced: for example, a number of schoolchildren would almost certainly leave school before they do, but for the State's decision that education up to the age of 16 is compulsory. In other cases there may, in fact, be no direct benefit for the individual. During war-time one might be forced to join one of the armed services (with the consequent possibility of being injured or killed). The benefit of an individual's membership of such a body does not accrue to him but to society at large.

However, these are exceptions to the general rule, noted above, that a person will participate in an organisation only if the benefits of doing so at least equal the costs.

The objectives of organisations

Some organisations specify their objectives – and policies designed to achieve these objectives – more precisely and in a more formal manner than others. Companies frequently lay down detailed objectives as part of a written plan covering their activities over a forthcoming period, say a year, whereas it would be unusual for families to do so.

However this distinction is not always clear-cut. On the one hand families may sometimes draw up a very precise plan for meeting a particular objective. For example, if they wish to acquire a new car in time for their next holiday they may need to prepare a budget of income and expenditure in order to ensure that they save sufficient money. On the other hand, although business organisations may regularly specify objectives relating to such things as the volume of sales, level of profits and number of employees, these formal objectives incorporate only part, and probably a very small part, of the objectives of the individuals who comprise the organisation.

The objectives of sub-organisations

This may occur because the organisation is so large that it is impossible to obtain information about all the objectives of each person. An attempt to overcome this problem is often made by creating smaller organisations – which we will call sub-organisations – to represent particular groups of people or interests. Employees may be represented by trade unions, shareholders by the Board of Directors, the sales department by the sales manager or director, and so forth. Since the number of sub-organisations is very much smaller than the number of people represented, it becomes easier to take account of different objectives.

However, this can only be a partial solution to the problem of size, since it is extremely unlikely that each sub-organisation will perfectly reflect the objectives of all of the people it represents. Consider a trade union which is negotiating new work schedules and rates of pay. Some of its members may prefer a fast work-rate and high wages while others prefer a slower work-rate and lower wages. It is impossible for the union to satisfy both. Similarly if the Board of Directors has to decide whether to undertake a large investment project which will depress profits this year but lead to higher profits in future years, it will be impossible to satisfy both those investors who want the highest possible return from their shares this year and those who would prefer to obtain higher returns in future years. Moreover, even if each of the sub-organisations – trade union, Board of Directors, etc. – perfectly reflected the objectives of each of its members, it is likely that conflicts would arise between these sub-organisations, between these various sets of objectives. The various ways in which organisations seek to resolve these conflicts are discussed in Chapter 5.

Summary and conclusions

Organisations of any kind have resources which they utilise in order to achieve objectives. These objectives are influenced by both internal factors – the objectives of the members of the organisation – and external factors such as government policy, the requirements of consumers and legislation (all discussed in later chapters).

In this volume we are mainly concerned with the objectives and policies of business organisations and especially the producers of goods and services, rather than with administrative or other types of organisation. We begin to focus our attention on business organisations in Chapter 4. But first we examine in Chapters 2 and 3 the accountability of different types of organisation, and their contribution to the working of a mixed economy.

Assignments

1.1

List the major resources of the following organisations: (a) a family; (b) a professional football club; (c) a trade union (d) a farmer; (e) a company manufacturing washing machines; (f) a research laboratory; (g) an advertising agency.

1.2

Outline the major objectives of the Board of Directors of a professional football club, the footballers employed by the club and the members of the supporters club, and discuss the circumstances in which the interests of these three groups might conflict.

1.3

What do you understand to be the objectives of the college at which you are studying? Indicate how you would gather information which would help you to give a more complete answer to this question.

1.4

Compare and contrast a large branch of a supermarket chain with a small 'corner shop' run by the owner, with respect to; (*a*) the resources of the two shops; and (*b*) the objectives of the people in charge of the shops. (The sources of your information should be specified.)

1.5

'The benefits of participating in an organisation should at least equal the costs.' Discuss the application of this principle to membership of the student union of your college for; (*a*) those students who pay their own membership fees; (*b*) those students whose membership fees are paid by the local authority.

2 The accountability and contribution of organisations in a mixed economy

Introduction

In the last chapter we showed that organisations are formed to facilitate the acquisition and use of resources in the desire to achieve certain objectives. We also showed that these objectives may reflect the individual objectives of the members of the organisation. In attempting to make possible the achievement of such objectives the organisation may, then, be accountable to its members. In the following sections we shall discuss the organisation's accountability to its members and also to non-participants. We shall notice that accountability is not always voluntary. We shall use the term to encompass not only self-imposed restraints on the organisation's activities designed to ensure furtherance of the objectives of individuals but also that form of compliance with the objectives of others which is enforced by legal sanction.

Factors affecting the accountability of an organisation

The accountability of an organisation will depend to a large extent upon whether or not the organisation:

1. is an employer;
2. supplies goods or services to consumers or to other organisations;
3. supplies other inputs to another organisation;
4. acquires finance from non-participants.

Although in one respect our non-commercial cricket club is responsible to its members (it must, at least to some extent, be faithful to their individual objectives) its accountability is rather limited. As a general rule we can see that the more of the features mentioned above apply to an organisation the more extensive will be its accountability, in the sense both that it will be responsible to more groups and also that its accountability will be more strict. Let us look briefly at each of the features in turn.

(*a*) If an organisation is an employer it has obligations to its workers relating to hours and conditions of work, safety and hygiene, the procedures to

5

be observed in cases of dismissal, etc. Some of these obligations are prescribed by law, some are the result of negotiations between the employer and workers' representatives (especially the trade unions) and some are voluntarily undertaken by the employer in the belief that they contribute to good industrial relations.

(b) If an organisation supplies goods and services to consumers or to another organisation it will wish to meet its customers' requirements – in terms of the quality of its products, delivery dates, etc. – in order to retain its existing customers and win new ones. It may be that the obligations are less voluntary. For example, it may be vital to a firm which has ordered machinery or raw materials that they arrive by an agreed date because they will be required for that firm's operations at that time. A buyer may insist on the inclusion in the contract of supply of goods an agreed damages clause whereby the supplier agrees to pay a certain amount of compensation for late delivery. Consumers may find it difficult to come to such individualised arrangements with a firm, however, and Parliament has seen fit to introduce in recent years a substantial amount of legislation designed to protect consumers. Thus suppliers to consumers may find that they have a wider range of accountability even than that they have specifically agreed.

(c) As noted in the previous paragraph, one organisation, a manufacturer, may supply goods which are inputs to the business of another organisation and so incur obligations.

(d) Organisations may acquire finance from a wide range of sources, some of which are outside the firm (e.g. banks, finance houses). Whether the source of the finance is internal (as it is when money is raised from shareholders who are members of the firm) or external, the organisation is accountable in various ways to the institutions or individuals providing the finance.

Thus the degree of accountability of the organisation will vary in accordance with these various features (and perhaps some others). To take two extreme examples: a family is accountable to far fewer groups than the large public company which has thousands of employees, many shareholders and which produces a wide range of products. As we noted above, accountability is often (though by no means always) legal in the sense that it is enforced by the law. We discuss in later chapters the detailed provisions of the law which impinge on organisations. As a preparation for that discussion we must now outline the major features of the legal framework.

The legal framework of accountability

Civil and criminal law

To most people law means crime and criminals and what goes on inside the Old Bailey or magistrates' courts. This could not be farther from the whole story. While there is a large body of law specifying criminal offences and the sanctions for breach of them there is another larger body of law, civil law, which also renders individuals and organisations accountable for their actions.

We must look at the nature of these two forms of legal liability in more detail. Whereas a person who commits a criminal offence is then liable to punishment (e.g. imprisonment or a fine), a person who is in breach of the civil law may be the subject of proceedings which may lead to his being ordered to compensate (usually by way of damages) the party that has suffered loss as a result of his actions. It is impossible to decide from the *nature* of his act whether someone is in breach of the criminal or civil law. The distinction lies rather *in the consequences of the action*. The same act can often give rise to both criminal and civil consequences. If, for instance, a car driver speeds the wrong way down a one-way street and hits a car coming in the opposite direction he may be prosecuted for the criminal offence of dangerous driving and he may be sued by the driver of the other car for the damage done to his vehicle. Again, a restaurant which serves infected meat may be prosecuted by the local authority for breach of a criminal offence and may also be sued by any customers who suffer food poisoning.

Where a criminal offence has been committed it is usually a State body (like the police or the local authority) which intervenes to prosecute. In the case of breach of the civil law, however, it is up to the victim to take action himself.

The real distinction, between the criminal and civil law, however, lies not in the nature of the action nor the mode of initiation of court proceedings but the different consequences of the court finding. In the case of a criminal offence it will be punishment; in the case of breach of the civil law it will usually be having to pay compensation.

Contract and tort

As far as the civil law is concerned we shall be mainly concerned in this volume with two important areas: the law of contract and the law of tort.

The *law of contract* is concerned with agreements which have legal consequences. This area of the law is obviously very important when considering the relations between organisations and their clients, customers and suppliers. The *law of tort* is concerned with 'wrongs' (the Latin word 'tortus' meant twisted or wrung and came to mean wrong) which arise independently of any agreement between the parties. Thus if someone suffers a wrong because of another's failure to keep a legally recognised agreement we shall have to look to the law of contract to discover what (if anything) he can do. If the wrong is unconnected with any agreement the law of tort may provide a remedy. The most important tort is the tort of negligence. We shall examine this and other torts in later chapters.

Forms of liability

It is commonly thought that legal liability (both criminal and civil) applies only to someone who is at fault or morally responsible in some sense. As a general rule this is deficient in at least three ways.

1. It is possible to be in breach of the law without having committed the crime or wrong intentionally or even carelessly. Many criminal offences are offences of *strict liability*, that is, they may be committed even though there was no intention to commit them and even though they did not result from carelessness. An Act of Parliament may state, for example, that it is an offence to carry on a particular business without a licence and that this will be an offence

regardless of whether a person knew, or even could be expected to know, whether a licence was required. There are parallels in civil law. If a person contracts to deliver goods on a particular date and fails to do so he may be in breach of contract even though this was due to no fault on his part. He may have been let down by a supplier or by a strike by his work-force but unless he had the foresight to make provision in the contract for this sort of eventuality he may be liable for breach. A quite considerable number of wrongs and offences which organis-ations are likely to commit are of this strict nature.

2. The civil law is concerned not so much with punishing the guilty as compensating the injured. Thus slight carelessness which might be thought not to be reprehensible at all or at least not greatly reprehensible might result in a liability to pay a large amount of compensation. Let us imagine the case of an employee permanently and seriously disabled by an accident caused by a dangerous piece of machinery which his employer has failed properly to ensure is safe. If the employee sues he will be able to recover damages to compensate him for his pain and suffering, his medical expenses and earnings both already and prospectively lost. The latter sums will be calculated according to the injured person's present earnings and his prospects for the future – factors totally irrelevant to the blameworthiness of the omission of the employer.

3. Many aspects of the civil law are concerned with *loss distribution*. There is an underlying idea that the person or organisation who should be made to bear the expenses occasioned by actions or omissions is that one who/which is most easily able to bear (or to arrange to bear) the loss. This explains some rules of law which impose strict liability. This idea, however, accounts for other rules, too, including that which imposes on an employer liability for the tortious actions of an employee in the course of his employment. The liability of employers is called *vicarious liability*: it is imposed on employers irrespective of whether they (as opposed to their workers) are at fault. Although there has been much debate as to the true reason for this rule it is no coincidence that the employer is very often in a better position than the employee to bear, either from his own resources or through insurance, the financial cost of the employee's carelessness. The importance of insurance is considerable. The availability of insurance to (and the likelihood of its having been taken out by) a party clearly influences the imposition on him by a court of legal liability.

Sources of law

We have seen that law is comprised of civil and criminal laws and that there are a variety of forms of legal liability. We look next at the sources of law, the two most important of which are legislation and case-law.

1. Legislation

Legislation is the law made by Parliament which is set out in *Acts of Parliament (or Statutes)*. Each Parliament can, in theory at least, make any new laws that it likes and can repeal any laws made by a previous Parliament. Parliament can also alter the law as made by the courts by passing an Act.

In recent years there has been a great growth in the volume of legislation affecting the activities of business organisations, much of it seeking to protect those who have to deal with organisations, such as employees and customers. Many Acts of Parliament are very detailed and complex. In spite of their complexity, however, many of the finer details are often not set out in statutes. Instead powers are given by the Act to other persons to make regulations and orders which, when made, themselves have the force of law. Local authorities are often empowered to make by-laws and similar powers are sometimes also given to public corporations (like British Rail) or to Government Ministers. The orders and regulations so made are known as *subordinate legislation*: many are what lawyers call statutory instruments. These have the same force of law as a statute provided that they are made within the powers conferred in the 'enabling' Act.

2. Case-law

Case-law is the law laid down by the judges in the courts. Many of the principles of English law have been developed by the courts when they have decided disputes. From very early on in the development of the law the courts have made law by following decisions made in earlier cases and by developing the law by analogy when the problem is not precisely the same as that decided in the earlier cases. The way to understanding how case-law operates as a source of law lies in the operation of the *doctrine of precedent*.

Broadly speaking a rule of law laid down in one case in order to reach a decision on the facts of the case then before the court will be binding on a lower court when that court has before it a case which raises the same legal issue. The part of the earlier decision which is binding is called the *ratio decidendi* (the rule of law expounded to solve the problem thrown up by the case). Other statements of law made in earlier cases (e.g. statements of what the result of the case would have been if the problem had been slightly different) are called *obiter dicta* and are not binding on later courts although, of course, if they have been made by eminent judges heed, in practice, will be given to them.

Decisions of courts are generally binding on courts lower in the hierarchial structure (e.g. High Court judges must follow Court of Appeal decisions). Sometimes earlier decisions of the same court can be binding.

In addition to developing case-law, of course, the courts have to decide questions raised by ambiguities in the meaning of words employed in statutes. It is impossible for Parliament to be sure that its enactments encompass every conceivable eventuality and questions will be raised from time to time as to whether the words of a statute extend to cover certain types of action or behaviour. This task also falls to the courts.

Common Law and Equity

We must finally appreciate the distinction between Common law and Equity. The term Common Law has different meanings according to the context in which it is used. (E.g. it can mean case-law as opposed to legislation or the system of law that exists in the English-speaking world as opposed to Continental systems.)

Common Law is here used to distinguish the law which owes its origin to the original King's court from that which was dispensed in the Court of Chancery. The original system of law exercised by the King's judges became rigid and inflexible and a parallel system of law dispensed in other courts grew up to palliate some of the consequent instances of injustice. The basic ideas of this system of Equity was to prevent a person exercising his legal rights (i.e. the rights enforceable by the Common Law courts) where it would be unconscionable (or inequitable) for him to do so. Suppose, for instance, that A sold a plot of land to B. At law the conveyance might be perfectly regular and this was all that was demanded. It might be, however, that B was A's parent and had exerted influence over A to make him sell the land. Equity would, in such a case, intervene to set aside the transaction.

In 1875 the two parallel systems were joined together. Now all the courts can administer both systems with all the advantages of equity where these are available. The two systems do, however, remain distinct in one sense: whereas legal rights are enforceable whatever the rest of the circumstances, equitable 'rights' are discretionary and depend on the party who needs to rely on them complying with the general principles of equity (e.g. that he should not himself be a serious wrongdoer).

The courts and the work of judges

We will discuss the structure of the courts in detail in Volume 2. The basic system may be seen from the charts in Assignments 2.4 and 2.5. We shall also present in Volume 2 detailed discussion of the judicial function, the doctrine of precedent, and the interpretation of statutes.

Summary of the legal framework

All firms are affected by accountability, whether this is self imposed or in compliance with legal sanctions. However, legal liability is seldom uppermost in the minds of those who form organisations or who already carry on business activities. But it cannot be ignored. Anyone who employs one worker or markets one product, however small his business, is subject to a formidable array of legal obligations which he ignores at his peril. The latter have expanded greatly in recent years and no organisation can afford not to be aware of the ways in which the law can hold it accountable. Law is no longer solely a matter for lawyers: it affects every aspect of the organisation's operation and its controllers and managers will be in day-to-day contact with the law whether or not they are aware of it.

Nevertheless, it is unrealistic to see the law in isolation. We have hinted that the law provides a framework within which organisations must work, but this is not the full picture. Very often the law imposes a minimum standard and simply to comply with this may not be the best way to fulfil the objectives of an organisation. Good business practice may require an organisation to go further. Similarly the framework described is not the only formal constraint on the organisation; it has also to take account of the requirement of government policy, which only sometimes finds expression in legislation, and we examine briefly below some aspects of government policy which have important implications for the relationships between organisations.

The relationships between organisations

In a mixed economy, such as the UK, the relationships between organisations are sometimes complementary and sometimes competitive.

Complementary relationships

A complementary relationship exists when one organisation supplies inputs to another. A very obvious and common example of a complementary relationship was that given above, where one organisation supplies machinery or raw materials to another. Other examples, perhaps less obvious, include the provision, by one organisation to another, of information, security services, transport facilities and waste disposal services.

Many goods and services are supplied not by one organisation to another but by organisations (producers) to consumers, individuals acting either on their own behalf or as representatives of families. But the complementary nature of the relationship is unchanged; the producer supplies what is required by the consumer – food, clothing, security services, etc. (The money paid in exchange is, of course, required by the producer.)

We have so far discussed complementarity in terms of the relationships between a supplier of goods and services and the purchasers or users of these goods and services. But complementarity also refers to the fact that different producers supply different goods and services and so together meet a wide range of needs. (We discuss this aspect in more detail below.)

Competitive relationships

By contrast competitive relationships exist when different producers supply the same (or very similar) products and compete with each other for custom. (Competition may also exist between purchasers, but we do not discuss this process.)

Complementarity, competition and the State

In a mixed economy the pattern of relationships between organisations is modified in several ways by the activity of the State. Looking first at complementary relationships, the State may itself supply products which it feels would not be supplied adequately by producers in the private sector. In the UK these products include vehicles, fuel, transport facilities, communication services, education, health and defence. These products are supplied by a number of different types of organisation, including public corporations (nationalised industries), central government departments, local authorities and the National Enterprise Board. These organisations are discussed in greater detail in Chapter 4.

Second, if the Government feels that the supply of a product is inadequate, but that it would not be appropriate for the State itself to act as a supplier, it may subsidise private sector producers. Many branches of the arts, such as orchestral music and local theatres, are heavily dependent upon such financial assistance. (Subsidies may also be given to producers primarily to help them to maintain employment, although this will also, of course, cause their output to be higher than it would otherwise be.)

The State has also modified the pattern of competitive relationships in several ways. When an industry is nationalised the degree of competition within that industry is reduced, as several private sector producers are replaced by a single public sector producer. The number of competitors in certain industries has also been reduced as a result of mergers which have been encouraged, and sometimes financially supported, by government agencies such as the Industrial Reorganisation Corporation in the 1960s and the National Enterprise Board more recently.

On the other hand the Government has introduced legislation designed to increase the degree of competition. The main basis of UK competition policy is the Fair Trading Act 1973 which built upon the Restrictive Trade Practices Act 1956, the Resale Prices Act 1964 and the Monopolies and Mergers Act 1965. This legislation (as subsequently re-enacted with amendments) is considered in greater detail in later chapters and it is sufficient to note here that it contains provisions relating to:

1. Collective restrictive practices, e.g. agreements between competitors as to what prices they should charge for their products: it is now very difficult to sustain such agreements in the UK.

2. Monopolies and mergers: in certain circumstances proposed mergers between two (or more) firms can be prevented and certain activities of monopolists (defined as firms having at least a 25 per cent share of their market) can be controlled, e.g. control has been exercised in the past over the prices charged by the major manufacturers of detergents and of cornflakes.

3. Consumer protection: government policies to control restrictive practices, monopolies and mergers are intended ultimately to benefit the consumer; in addition a considerable body of legislation exists whose primary aim is to provide direct protection for the consumer against such practices as misleading advertising and information, the supplying of faulty or defective goods and the imposition of inequitable terms or conditions.

The role of planning

In such highly centralised economies as the USSR and East Germany the activities of many organisations, and especially of producers, are specified as part of a complex planning process. A central plan is drawn up, and each producer is given a target in terms of output and the inputs required to produce this output. In a mixed economy the planning process is much more diffuse, being undertaken by a large number of independent units.

As we noted in Chapter 1, producers make their own plans in greater or less detail, relating to such things as what to produce, the volume of sales, prices, advertising and purchases of inputs. In making these plans producers try to take into account information about the requirements of consumers, the likely prices of inputs, changes in government policy, etc. However, there is always some uncertainty about these factors; some of the assumptions built into the plan will turn out to be false, and very few plans are fulfilled in their entirety. (Incidentally the consequences are not necessarily undesirable, since the deviation of performance from plan may be in either direction; for example, actual sales and profits may be either higher or lower than planned.)

Planning is also undertaken by the Government. We can make a broad distinction between macro economic planning, which is concerned with the overall level of economic activity in the country, and micro economic planning, which is concerned with individual industries and producers. Producers have been encouraged to submit their plans to the central Government in the belief that the Government would then be in a better position to take action to ensure that these plans could be fulfilled. To take one simple example, if the plans of the engineering and other metal-using industries indicated that the demand for steel would be greater than the amount that the steel producers were proposing to supply, the Government might suggest to the steel producers that they should consider increasing their capacity and indeed might provide financial assistance to help them to do so.

Planning of this type, mainly consisting of the provision and exchange of additional information, is known as *indicative planning*. Indicative planning increased in popularity in the 1960s, but there is little evidence that it helped to improve Britain's economic performance, and it has received much less emphasis since then. (The impact on organisations of Government planning is discussed in detail in Volume 2.)

Summary and conclusions

Using the term accountability in its widest sense we have shown that organisations, and especially producers, are accountable to various groups including consumers, employees and the suppliers of finance. We have also shown that this accountability is rooted partly in good business practice, partly in the provisions of the law, and partly in the requirements of government policy. In fulfilling the dual functions of supplying goods and services and providing employment, producer organisations establish a network of relationships, either complementary or competitive, with other organisations. In many instances these relationships are beneficial, but where they are not they are modified by State intervention of one form or another.

In these first two chapters we have adopted a broad-brush approach, the intention being to establish a framework for the more detailed discussion in subsequent chapters. We begin this discussion in Chapters 3 and 4, in which we define and distinguish the different legal forms of organisation in industry, commerce and government.

Assignments

2.1

By interviewing a number of people who do different jobs in any commercial organisation with which you are familiar, try to discover how they see the accountability of that organisation with respect to:

1. Employees.
2. Shareholders (if any).
3. Other sources of finance (if any).
4. Customers.
5. Suppliers.
6. The community as a whole.

2.2

Explain, in one or two sentences, the difference between each of the following:

1. Civil and criminal law.
2. The law of contract and the law of tort.
3. Fault liability and strict liability.
4. Legislation and case-law.
5. Statutes and Statutory Instruments.
6. Common law and Equity.
7. Complementary and competitive relationships between organisations.
8. Centralised and indicative planning.

2.3

The management committee of Easifit Ltd meets once a month to review the company's past performance and future prospects. At the meeting held mid-way through the last financial year the proceedings began with a report from Mr Fern, the sales director.

He reported that the picture concerning the company's three major product groups was very mixed. Helped by the fine weather, sales of the gardening equipment division had been higher than expected; sales of the furniture division were on target; however sales of the office equipment division were well below expectations.

Asked to comment on the implications of this performance Mr Woods, the finance director, pointed out that since around half of the company's profits were normally derived from the office equipment division, it was likely that – if these trends continued for the rest of the year – total profits would be substantially lower than in the previous year, and it might even be necessary to reduce the dividend paid to shareholders.

Mr Scott, the managing director, asked Mr Fern why sales of this division were so far below target, and whether there was any prospect of the lost ground being recovered in the second half of the year. Mr Fern replied as follows:

'There were really two quite distinct reasons for the sales shortfall. First, we lost some very large contracts for equipping new offices in London because our prices were undercut by competitors. Second, we have been unable to complete other contracts because of supply problems. Because of labour troubles we are way behind with our deliveries of tables, chairs and desks for European Oil's new headquarters building, and we have not started delivering filing cabinets for the Metropolitan Building Society because our major supplier of metal had a large fire in his main factory which disrupted his production schedules.

'If we can sort out these problems we should be able to make good some of the shortfall, but unless we move quickly the customers may try to cancel the contracts altogether. I know that European Oil are particularly annoyed because they have had to postpone the opening of their new headquarters, and this has led to all sorts of problems; for example, they have had to compensate staff who had to change their plans to move home, and they cannot transfer their records to the new computer. In fact I am afraid that they might sue us for failure to deliver on time.'

Faced with this prospect the committee then discussed what steps they might take to improve the situation. Some of the ideas put forward included the following:

1. Transfer workers from the furniture division to the office equipment division in order to increase the output of the latter. This would mean that deliveries of furniture to some wholesalers would have to be delayed, but Easifit could claim that they were unable to deliver on time because of labour shortages.
2. Recruit additional workers for the office equipment division. These workers would have to be laid off once the back-log of orders had disappeared.
3. Introduce overtime working in the office equipment division. Although the back-log would be cleared less quickly than by increasing the size of the work-force, this would not be a serious disadvantage because the company could claim that the failure to deliver on time was not their fault in the first place.

What do you think of these ideas? Have you any other suggestions?

Identify relationships between the various parties involved which you feel may have legal consequences should the various courses of action be adopted. What sort of restrictions do you think the law might impose on the freedom to adopt any of these courses?

2.4

The following questions relates to the chart which shows the courts which administer the civil law and the courts to which appeal lies against an unfavourable decision in such cases:

1. Your friend, Bill Banknotes, a clerk who works in the local bank, buys from Rob-U-Quick Motors Ltd a car for which he pays £3,000. After paying the money he discovers that the car is severely defective: its brakes and lights do not work, the chassis is rusty and the steering faulty. The cost of the repairs is £750. He is unable to get any satisfaction from the garage-owner and has decided to bring an action in the courts.

    In which court would you advise him to commence proceedings? Would your advice differ if the cost of the repairs were £2,250? If the judge decides in favour of the garage-owner but Bill is unsure that he agrees with the correctness of that decision what might your further advice be?
2. Find out about the distinctions between the various divisions of the High Court.
3. When we say that the House of Lords is the final appeal court what do we mean by the term 'House of Lords'? Who are the judges in this court?
4. The doctrine of precedent states that earlier decisions of higher courts and

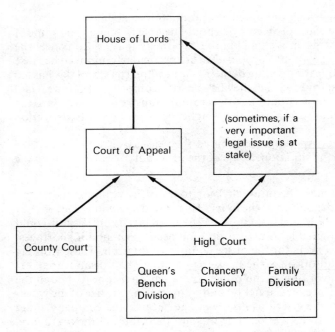

sometimes of the same court are binding in a later similar case. Find out the decisions of which higher courts (if any) bind:

(*a*) the County Court;
(*b*) the High Court;
(*c*) the Court of Appeal;
(*d*) the House of Lords.

Which (if any) of these courts are ever bound by their own earlier decision?

2.5

On page 17 is a similar chart of the criminal courts.

1. Rob-U-Quick Garages Ltd is charged by the police with offences under the Trade Descriptions Acts for having misdescribed as roadworthy very unroadworthy cars. In which court will the company be tried?
2. To which courts might the Company appeal if (*a*) it does not agree with the finding that it is guilty; *or* (*b*) it feels the sentence passed on it is too harsh?

2.6

Arrange to meet either a magistrate or a police officer who often appears in court. Ask him/her about what happens in the Magistrates courts. You might find it helpful to visit such a court yourself. Write a short account of your impressions.

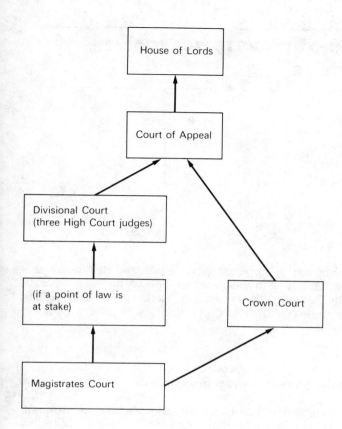

3 The forms of private sector organisations

Introduction

We shall be mainly concerned in this chapter to define and distinguish the different legal forms of organisation in private sector industry and commerce. It is, however, worth noting that individuals often join together in non-commercial groups which are also unconnected with the Government (we shall discuss State organisations in Chapter 4).

Non-commercial, non-governmental groups

We have already mentioned the family as an example of this form of organisation, and we have examined in some detail the formation of another example, our cricket club. We shall not examine in detail the legal implications of the creation of a family unit: everyone is well aware of the existence of a complex of detailed law concerning the particular bonds of husband and wife and parent and child. It might, however, be worthwhile to look briefly at the legal position of other non-commercial organisations like our cricket club.

Most such organisations are what the law designates *unincorporated associations* – sets of individuals grouped together often subject to self-imposed rules (sometimes in the form of a formal written 'constitution') and often with a particular objective. Although such groups may well be non-commercial they are very likely to need or wish to deal with money or to hold property – our cricketers, as we saw, might well want to buy their own ground. Any action which the members (or, more likely, officials appointed by and from them) carry on (like raising money by sweepstakes or buying materials to build a clubhouse) they will do as individuals though subject always to the rules upon which the members of the organisation have agreed. Should they acquire property the officers who acquire it will be recognised in law as its owners. They will not, however, own the property in quite the same sense as an individual might own his own house or car. They will be required to hold and use the property, as laid down by the rules, for the benefit of the club as a whole. They are what the law calls *trustees* of the property. Thus they must not use what they have acquired for the club (with the club's assets) to their own personal advantage.

We mentioned that trade unions are a further example of this sort of organisation. These are also unincorporated associations but this is so largely for political reasons. In many ways they are similar to companies rather than to most unincorporated associations but they are expressed by statute to be within the latter category. We shall look later in this chapter at the position of companies and, in Volume 2, at the unique position of trade unions.

Commercial and industrial organisations

The sole trader

The simplest form of business unit is the sole trader. He is, in law, the owner and only controller of the business and he is held entirely responsible for the success or failure of the enterprise. What the business earns is his income, what it loses his loss. The business and the man are, in the eyes of the law, one. The way in which he runs the business falls to be decided by him alone: he decides whether to spend or re-invest in the business any profit which it yields, and he can make the decision to stop trading altogether.

The sole trader is not, however, totally free since he would be wise to keep accounts for tax purposes (although he is not legally obliged to do so) and he may well be dependent upon banks or other financial institutions for loans should he wish to improve his business premises or to expand his business. Before lending money the institution may require information about the business and may also require the trader to provide security (e.g. the title deeds of his house) for the loan. The advantage of a lender taking security for the loan is that he will have rights over the property such as selling it if the borrower defaults (i.e. fails to repay the loan).

Nor is the position of the sole trader totally enviable. Despite his freedom to do largely as he wishes he can be held personally liable for any debts which the business incurs. This could mean that should his business fail there would follow disastrous consequences for his personal, as well as business, life.

You will be aware of many examples of sole traders, e.g. odd-job builders, your newsagent and perhaps the landlord of your local pub.

Partnerships

Often, however, individuals wish to do business in conjunction with others. A group of self-employed people may wish to carry on a business together with an agreement to share the profits or losses. We then have what the law calls a partnership. (The law also refers to such organisations as 'firms' but in this book we shall not use this term in its strict legal sense but rather, as it is used popularly, to designate any business organisation.)

A partnership is merely a collection of individuals and in many respects partners are in a similar position to sole traders. They are in a very similar position so far as raising loans is concerned, while should the partnership incur debts each of the partners will be responsible. Should there be insufficient business assets to satisfy the creditors the partners can be called upon to pay the debts from their own pockets.

Partnerships can be formed informally, although it is obviously a good idea for the partners to have a written document setting out the details of their agreement. Should the partners wish to use a name for the firm different from their own they must register it (Registration of Business Names Act 1916).

If the partners do not make a contrary agreement, certain provisions to regulate their relationship will be implied under the Partnership Act 1890:

1. Profits and losses are to be shared equally.

2. All the partners have a right to a say in the running of the business, and major decisions (like introducing a new partner) must be taken unanimously.

3. A partner who takes little part in the running of the firm from day to day (a 'sleeping partner') has the same rights and liabilities as any other partner.

4. The partners are under strict duties towards each other. They must act in good faith: e.g. a partner must not exploit the partnership property for his own benefit.

5. Each partner can enter into business contracts which bind the others.

These implied terms will often be varied by the partners in practice. For example, where an established firm takes on a new partner it may be unwilling to let him have as large a share of the profits as the partners who have built the business up over many years. The new partner may have to agree to accept a smaller share before he will be allowed to join the partnership.

Partnerships can be ended by agreement, death or withdrawal of a partner, if the time or business for which the firm was created has lapsed, or on other grounds if application is made to a court and the judge considers it 'just and equitable' (i.e. fair to everyone in the circumstances) to end the partnership. When a partnership comes to an end, the assets of the firm will be divided up between the partners.

A partnership is, then, basically a collection of individuals who continue to be treated by the law as separate persons but who have taken on certain obligations one to another. They are accountable to each other although no member of the general public has the right to investigate how they are running the business.

Most solicitors, accountants, doctors and dentists arrange their business relationships in this way.

Private companies

The most popular form of commercial or business unit is that of the registered company. While a partnership is in essence an association of individuals the company is, for legal purposes, a separate entity distinct from the individuals who set it up: it is as much a legal person as a human being. Obviously a company cannot physically buy property or make or market goods: it can function only through human agents. But the law gives to the company an existence independent from these people. Whereas in the case of a partnership the assets are owned by the individuals and it is they who reap the profits and sustain the loss, in the case of a company it is the independent corporate body which is in this position.

The notion of corporate personality is of central importance. A company is set up by promoters (who will usually become its first shareholders) who provide the initial capital either in cash or by providing premises or plant. It is in several respects of considerable advantage to be a company shareholder as opposed to a sole trader or partner in a firm:

1. Debts which are incurred in the running of the business are the debts of the company and not of the shareholders.

Whereas the shareholders own the company, it is the company that carries on the business and the company alone who can enter into contracts and can be made to pay the business debts. Once the shareholder has paid the purchase price for his shares, his liability for the company's debts is at an end. This is what is meant by a 'limited company': the liability of the shareholder (sometimes called 'members') of the company is limited to the amount if any that is still owed to the company for the purchase of his shares. Beyond that amount the shareholder cannot be called upon to pay the debts out of his own pocket. (Most companies registered under the Companies Act are of this kind; that is, they are limited by shares. It is however possible to have companies limited by guarantee in which the shareholder can be called upon to pay whatever sum he has previously agreed to pay, and also to have a company which has unlimited liability.)

The fact that a company has such limited liability is indicated by the inclusion after its name the word 'Limited' or 'Ltd'. Such limited liability is a considerable advantage: the sole trader is able, through the formation of a company of which the trader and, say, his wife are the shareholders and directors, to minimise his liability should the business fail or come upon difficult times. It is therefore extremely common for an enterprise which has begun as a sole trader concern or as a partnership to become a company.

2. A company also has distinct advantages when it comes to raising finance. Like a partnership or sole trader it can raise loans by providing some fixed asset (like a house) as security for the loan. In addition it can borrow money on a *floating charge*. Companies may use the whole of their assets as security for a loan which does not attach to any particular asset. One can see the obvious advantage of being able to use as security the assets of the company generally: if all securities were fixed assets it would be difficult for the company to function since it could not sell the assets while the loan remained outstanding. We will consider the raising of finance in more detail in Chapter 26.

3. For large commercial concerns the advantages of incorporation include the consequences of the fact that investment and ownership can be separated from control. The shareholders of larger companies often take little part in the day-to-day running of the business but use it as an opportunity for investment. The shareholders have a say in the policy decisions of the company at general meetings but in larger companies at least the ordinary running of the business is in the hands of the directors and other officers of the company who will have skill and expertise in management. In smaller companies, directors will often be substantial shareholders, with the result that they will have, additional to their day-to-day control, the ability to influence policy decisions taken by the company.

4. When an important figure in the running of the business retires or dies the company is at a further advantage over the partnership. The death or retirement of a partner means the end of the partnership. If a shareholder dies or sells his shares the company continues in existence, it being an independent entity.

5. It is also an advantage of incorporation that a shareholder can more easily transfer his interest by selling his shares than can a partner who can only cease to be a partner with the agreement of the other partners. There may be restrictions on the transfer of shares in a private company, e.g. a provision that requires a shareholder wishing to sell his shares first to offer to sell them to the directors, or the statutory restriction that shares in a private company may not be offered to the public at large; but generally speaking the shareholder is considerably more free to dispose of his shares than is the partner of his interest.

To form a company documents must be lodged with the Registrar of Companies. These are:

1. Memorandum of association which gives the company's name, its objectives and details of how the shares are organised.
2. Articles of association setting out the internal rules of the company as to how it is to be run.
3. A declaration that the legal requirements of the Companies Acts concerning the formation of a registered company have been complied with.
4. The nominal capital of the company and the way in which it is divided up into shares. It is very common to find that even a large company has a nominal share capital of £100 divided up into 100 shares with a nominal value of £1 each. If all these shares are bought by the initial shareholders the company will still only have £100 capital. It will probably raise finance to buy premises, plant and stock-in-trade and if it is successful it may well make a large profit and be able to acquire more assets. It is therefore quite possible that the actual assets owned and profits earned by the company will increase out of all proportion to the original £100 nominal value of the shares. This in turn will make the value of each shareholder's interest rise, and, as it rises, the shareholder will be able to command a higher price when he later wishes to sell. Prospective purchasers may be prepared to pay far more than the £1 nominal value of the shares in order to obtain the chance to participate in the profits of the company.

This being done, the company, owned by the shareholders and managed by its directors comes into being, thus providing the legal advantages discussed above.

Public companies

So far we have not distinguished private and public companies. Most smaller companies will be of the former variety but should their operations increase they might 'go public'. There are several main differences between the two varieties of companies:

1. A public company is open to the public in the sense that its shares are available to anyone on the open market. Any individual (generally through a broker) can then acquire an interest in such a company. A private company, on the other hand, must impose a restriction on the right to transfer shares and may not invite the public to take up its shares.
2. In a private company there may not be more than fifty shareholders. The membership of a public company is unlimited.

3. There must be at least two directors of a public company, while there need be only one of a private company.

4. Before they are formed public (but not private) companies must issue prospectuses setting out details of their directors and financial records.

Because of these extra requirements which the law imposes on public companies a small company would probably do well to remain private even though by so doing it will not achieve the advantage which having its shares on the open market gives to a public company in the raising of finance.

Large public companies may find it desirable to form *subsidiary companies*. A subsidiary company has a legal existence separate from the parent company, though the parent company will hold a substantial shareholding in the subsidiary and so be able to direct the policy of the subsidiary to correspond with the aims it has for other subsidiaries it holds or, indeed, its own business aims. Some companies, *holding companies*, exist merely to co-ordinate the policies of a whole range of subsidiaries, in which they have obtained majority shareholdings.

Companies often operate in a number of different countries (often by establishing a number of subsidiaries). *Multinational* companies which operate in the country are subject to the normal legal controls though, of course, the shifting of finance from the activities in one country to those in another can enable the company or group of companies as a whole to avoid liabilities (especially to tax) and other governmental controls. We shall examine such governmental controls in Volume 2. It remains to say only that multinational companies have great advantages. They can, for instance, manufacture their products in the country where it is most economical given the cost of labour, the sources of raw materials and the place where demand is heaviest.

Summary and conclusions

We have attempted to distinguish the various legal forms of business organisation in the private sector. In so doing we have noted some of the advantages and disadvantages of an organisation taking each of these forms. The most sensible form for an organisation will, of course, vary according to the size, needs and objectives of the organisation. Each individual or group must make a decision as to which form best suits his or its requirements. We have, however, noted the particular advantages enjoyed by the registered company, whether public or private, and made some comparison between companies and businesses run by sole traders and partnerships. In the next chapter we will look at the various forms of Public Sector Organisations.

Assignments

3.1

You are asked by Mr Jones to advise him. His son James has worked for several years as a plumber and now wants to set up in business on his own. James is hard working but has very little capital. His father has £2,000 saved up which he is prepared to put into the business as long as he can be sure of getting it back before he retires in five years' time, although he would hope to make a profit that would at least equal the amount of interest that he could obtain from a Building Society. Mr Jones also owns his own house and runs his own successful grocery business, but he is unwilling to put these at risk to support James's business. Explain to Mr Jones what sort of business unit his son would be advised to adopt so that Mr Jones's interests would be safeguarded.

3.2

What is meant by 'a limited liability company'? Why does the law allow limited liability?

3.3

What are the legal differences between a private and a public company?

3.4

Are you a member of a club or association? Does it have any assets? By whom are these owned? Is there a constitution? What matters are provided for in the rules?

3.5

You have been asked by some friends to help them in forming a football club to compete in the local football league. Write a concise note which will be passed around at the first meeting explaining what arrangements you suggest should be made before the club is formed. For example, you will have to consider whether subscriptions are to be paid and, if so, how and to whom, and what rules will need to be made.

3.6

The passage below was extracted from an article in the *Financial Times*, 18 July 1978.

    1. Drawing on this article, discuss the benefits of worker co-operatives.
    2. Say whether you think that public funds should be offered to worker co-operatives, and if so on what terms.
    3. Compare this form of organisation with any other form discussed in this chapter, stating what you consider to be the main advantages and disadvantages of each form.

    'During the past couple of years there has been a sharp change in the general attitudes towards worker co-operatives, which have not so far played a significant role in Britain's economy. The latest and most important evidence of this change has come in two recent developments. One is the creation, under new legislation, of a Co-operative Development Agency to help foster co-operatives, and the other is a decision by the Co-operative Bank to start helping to finance worker-funded enterprises.

    'Together these events could lead to a new generation of small worker co-operatives growing up in Britain, and at the same time enable the Co-operative movement to expand from the primarily consumer-oriented base.

'All the main political parties regard co-operatives with some favour, and several efforts are being made to help them. There are various reasons why this is so. First, there is the general issue of industrial democracy and employee participation which involves a debate about the individual's rights at work in relation both to management and the providers of capital. Some people, including the Liberal Party, like the idea of co-operatives because there can be greater worker influence without increased trade union power, and they regard the ideal of workers owning and running their businesses as a primary way of reducing industrial conflict.

'Next the growth of the "small is beautiful" fashion – and the current political interest in helping small firms – has concentrated people's minds on how small enterprises can be funded and organised. Then there is the interest – mainly in the Conservative and Liberal Parties – in trying to nourish the concept of individual capital ownership; which can be achieved for employees either through profit-related share-ownership schemes or through co-operatives.

'Moving further to the left of the political spectrum – where there is more interest in collectively-funded rather than individually-owned co-operatives – the subject is sometimes seen as an alternative to traditional nationalisation.

'Two recent events have given the idea a boost. The increase in recent years of company failures and factory closures at a time of high unemployment has led workers facing redundancy to consider forming co-operatives. The Manpower Services Commission's job creation scheme has helped by spending £1.1 m. in backing what it calls enterprise workshops.

'In all 33 of these co-operatives have been started, mainly in woodworking, plastics and similar trades. They have created about 300 jobs and, while only a few are likely to be viable enough to survive once the year-long job creation aid expires, others will probably be started in the future under the Commission's continuing special employment programmes.

'The other event is the "discovery" of a community of co-operatives at Mondragon in the Basque area of Spain. Two years ago hardly anyone in Britain had heard of Mondragon where, over the past 21 years, more than 70 successful enterprises with a combined annual turnover in excess of £200 m. and a labour force of 13,000 have been built up around a bank called the Caja Laboral. This bank takes in savings from the local communities and then invests in co-operatives which it also provides with essential managerial and other expertise.

'At present the few British co-operatives fall into three main camps. First there are those born out of industrial failures – Meriden and Kirkby. These have sprung from the sit-in form of defensive worker reaction to imminent redundancy and, in fact, are only co-operatives in the sense that they are worker-managed: they are not worker-owned because they are mainly State-funded, often with workers having only a £1 nominal shareholding. The job creation enterprises also fall into this category so long as they are primarily relying on Manpower Commission funds.

'Next there are about 20 older co-operatives embracing nearly 2,000 workers, mainly in the shoe and textile industries. With a turnover in 1973 of £5.6 m., they are the sole survivors of those producer co-operatives formed in the latter part of the nineteenth century.

'The third group is the most significant at present and is centred around an organisation called the Industrial Common Ownership Movement. It embraces 15 collectively-owned enterprises and has evolved from the initiatives of Ernest Bader who turned his own family-owned chemical concern in Northamptonshire over to a trust for his workforce between 1951 and 1963. Other entrepreneurs have, primarily for paternalistic or tax-avoidance reasons, taken similar steps in recent years and the reconstitution of old family concerns is regarded as a likely source of future co-operatives. But the main significance of the Movement is that it was given a fresh role by the Industrial Common Ownership Act 1976, which emerged from a private member's Bill and was backed by the Labour Government. The Act gave the movement £250,000 from the Department of Industry to spend in revolving loans to would-be co-operatives through a new organisation, Industrial Common Ownership Finance. So far £33,500 of this has been drawn and allocated to co-operatives.

'The passing of the Act and the provision of the cash gave a new impetus to the development of co-operatives and has been accompanied by regional co-operative development bodies springing up around the country in the North, Scotland (where the Highlands and Islands Development Board is also experimenting with wider community-based co-operatives), and Wales.

'This is the sort of activity on which the Co-operative Bank and the new Co-operative Development Agency can build. The agency will be charged with encouraging the spread of co-operatives in general, as well as worker enterprises. At Mondragon in Spain workers invest up to £1,000 each, sometimes borrowed and then repaid out of wages, and the Caja Laboral Bank then doubles the proceeds. The Spanish Government also provides some funds.

'Taking up this idea, which it has studied, the Co-operative Bank says that all, or nearly all, the workers in a venture should be shareholders, putting up £500 to £1,000 each. The bank would then double the amount with three- to seven-year loans at favourable rates up to a £25,000 ceiling. Because most co-operatives start with about eight to 20 people, the bank envisages that most of its loans will be nearer £5,000 than £25,000.'

4 The forms of public sector organisations

Introduction

The legal forms of organisation which we looked at in the last chapter were those available for adoption by an individual or group which operates in the private sector. In recent years the State has come to be increasingly involved in industrial and commercial as well as governmental activity. What we shall look at in this chapter are the forms of organisation which the State has utilised to carry out these roles.

Public or state-owned corporations

As noted in Chapter 2, Parliament has determined that, for political and social as well as economic reasons, certain business activities are best undertaken by the State. It is often of considerable advantage to confer corporate personality upon the institution which undertakes these activities. Acts of Parliament are passed to make such bodies public corporations.

Such corporations differ from the other companies we have looked at because of their relationship with the State. There are no shares in public corporations and so no shareholders. This means that most of the body of law which governs other companies is inapplicable to public corporations: indeed public corporations are expressly excluded from the provisions of the Companies Acts.

Yet public corporations are not merely Government departments. They enjoy a degree of self-control which is valuable since commercial and industrial concerns do not require so substantial a control over their day-to-day activities as might certain branches of government. The idea is that the Government should lay down broad objectives which the corporations are left free to pursue without governmental oversight. There is clearly a need for the management of State-run business concerns to be free to take enterprising decisions.

Whereas a private sector company is responsible to its shareholders a public corporation owes responsibility to the public. This is ensured by the supervision of the Secretary of State who is in turn responsible to Parliament.

The Minister has considerable financial control over the corporations, being able to regulate borrowing, disposal of profits, reorganisation and development, and he can make directions of a 'general character' to the corporations. The Minister appoints the Chairman and members of the boards of the corporations and is thus able to bring to bear informal pressure which has, in practice, allowed him to interfere in the running of the industries. It is in respect of this control by the Government of the day that these industries differ most substantially from private sector organisations.

The Minister is, in turn, responsible to Parliament being subject to general questions from MPs. The House of Commons has also established a Select Committee on Nationalised Industries which keeps an eye on the running of these concerns. Reports of this Committee are laid before Parliament and questions can be put by MPs.

Recently an attempt was made by the Conservative Party while in opposition to establish a Commissioner for the Nationalised Industries who would review their activities and investigate complaints. Without Government support this proposal failed to be enacted. There are, however, associated with many of the public corporations advisory councils which, among other things, make recommendations to the Minister. Additionally, public interest is very strong in this area and there is public participation to some extent in the advisory councils set up for some nationalised industries, e.g. Gas, Electricity.

While most of the public corporations are industrial concerns (e.g. the National Coal Board, British Rail, the CEGB, etc.) some, like the BBC, are rather different from the type of enterprise we should usually dub industrial or commercial. We are now about to cross the line from the commercial world (into which the State has recently made inroads) into the world of government.

We should, however, note at this point the recent growth in the number of semi-independent bodies established by government to perform a wide range of functions. Many of these are clearly carrying out functions of government outside the commercial world (e.g. the Race Relations Board set up to promote racial harmony). Others, however, have important roles in the industrial and commercial life of the country (e.g. the Manpower Services Commission). Of particular interest, however, is the National Enterprise Board, which was established to look after interests acquired by the State in private sector organisations. The National Enterprise Board holds substantial shares in many well-known companies (e.g. BL) which can in some sense be said to be partially State owned. We shall consider these organisations and their relationship to government in more detail in Volume 2.

Governmental organisations

The role played by the State in the lives of individuals has increased enormously over the last 150 years. It is easy to think of some of the wide range of services provided by the State and the variety of activity it controls: education, health, welfare, defence, environmental control, etc. We now look briefly at the institutions which carry into practice these governmental functions.

Central government

Many activities are controlled by institutions which appear more obviously as agencies of the central Government. We shall not attempt to list the considerable number of central government departments which regulate activities and provide services. Many have their offices in Whitehall (e.g. the Foreign Office). The nature of the work of other departments means that in addition to a central or head office they have regional and local offices too. Such bodies include the Inland Revenue, the Board of Customs and Excise, the Department of Employment and the Department of Health and Social Security.

Government departments, headed by a Minister who is responsible to Parliament, are often large (e.g. the Department of the Environment) and the activities which they control and/or the services which they provide increasingly diverse. In Wales and Scotland separate Ministries for those countries control many of the activities and provide many of the services which in England are regulated/provided by large (though more specialised) departments.

Local government

Many of the tasks of government are, however, carried out through a system of institutions organised locally. In non-metropolitan areas there are county councils (e.g. Avon, Oxfordshire, Norfolk) which organise, among other things, education, social services, public transport, roads, libraries. Within the county council areas are a number of districts. District councils organise housing, refuse collection, rating, public health services, etc. Some functions (e.g. town and country planning control) are shared between the two tiers of local government. There are six metropolitan counties (Greater Manchester, Merseyside, West Midlands, West Yorkshire, South Yorkshire and Tyne and Wear). These areas are divided into metropolitan districts. The metropolitan district councils have a wider range of functions than the non-metropolitan district councils, being responsible for education, libraries and social services in addition to those responsibilities undertaken by non-metropolitan districts. In London there is the Greater London Council and the various London boroughs which enjoy a relationship broadly similar to that of the metropolitan counties and districts.

Parallel to this tiered system of local government are analagous structures which carry on specialised functions. Notable among these are the health authorities which are organised at regional, area and district level and the water authorities which are organised in a tiered structure and generally divided into water, river and sewage divisions. There are also separate police authorities which are generally based on the county unit although where the counties are small or sparsely populated they may cover more than one county (e.g. the Dyfed-Powys police).

Summary and conclusions

We have surveyed the range of organisations into which the State has formed itself to deal with its industrial, commercial and governmental functions. This

29

survey was brief because we shall be discussing these organisations in more detail in Volume 2. However even this brief discussion indicated the variety of public sector organisations that exist and the wide range of activities that they undertake.

Assignments

4.1

Why do you think that the State has taken over the running of industrial and commercial concerns in recent years? Choose one of the following industries and write a short memo setting out the advantages of this particular industry being State run: (1) British Rail; (2) The National Coal Board; (3) The Electricity Industry; (4) The Gas Industry.

4.2

Try to find out which types of organisations the Labour Party may nationalise in the future. Choose to be either a Labour Party supporter who favours such further nationalisation or a Conservative Party supporter who opposes it and write a short speech attempting to defend your view.

4.3

Try to find a copy of the rates demand sent to your house or that of one of your friends or relatives. What are rates? Who has to pay them? How are they calculated?

4.4

Imagine you live in the district of Greensleeves which is in the county of Fallowshire. In Fallowshire health services are provided by the Fallowshire Area Health Authority and water services by the Fallowshire Water Authority. Because Fallowshire is a small county it shares its police force with the neighbouring county of Loamshire. Which authority will levy and collect the rates in your area? On behalf of which other authorities will it be acting? What services do each of these authorities provide? Are any of the local authorities funded mainly from sources other than the rates? If so, where do these funds come from?

5 The objectives of private sector business organisations

Introduction

In the previous chapters we have examined the various legal forms of organisations. We have seen that a broad division can be made between private and public sector organisations. Moreover, within each of these categories a further division can be made between commercial or business and non-commercial organisations. As we noted earlier, we are particularly concerned in this volume with business organisations and so in this and the following chapter we discuss the objectives of these organisations, beginning here with the objectives of private sector business organisations.

Survival

Most people who establish and run businesses hope and expect that these businesses will have a long life. The owners of family businesses hope that the next generation of the family will succeed them; the directors and managers of public companies hope to maintain the health of their businesses until they are succeeded by another 'generation' of directors and managers.

There are some exceptions to this rule. The farmer whose younger relatives are all female may resign himself to selling out when he retires (although he may also look favourably upon any romantic attachments formed between his daughters and young men of farming stock!). The directors of private companies may aim to sell their companies in order to realise a capital gain on the value of the assets. The directors of public companies may seek out other companies who are willing to take over their company; the directors may do this either because they feel that the prospects of their company will improve as part of a larger company or because they hope to be appointed to the board of the new company. (The realisation of capital gains on the value of shares may again also be important.)

However, as we have said, these are exceptions to the rule. In general the rewards of businessmen, both material and non-material, are derived from first building up and then handing on their businesses.

Profitability

Profitability is also high on the list of business objectives. Indeed it is frequently claimed that profitability is, or at least should be, the overriding objective of business organisations (but see the discussion of social objectives below).

There is, of course, a clear link between survival and profitability. A company will not survive for long if it is unprofitable. Although most established companies have built up sufficient financial reserves to enable them to withstand occasional losses, continued losses must eventually lead to bankruptcy. In the case of a public company, even if the losses are not on a scale which threatens bankruptcy, they may cause the value of its shares to fall to such a level that the company becomes vulnerable to a take-over bid. Indeed this latter possibility exists wherever a public company earns a rate of return below average.

There is, then, no conflict between the objectives of profitability and survival. The former is a means of ensuring the latter. However the argument does not always rest there. It is sometimes said that firms should aim not simply to earn sufficient profits to ensure their survival (including financing their growth where appropriate); they should attempt to maximise their profits.

Profit maximisation

Profit maximisation implies earning not the highest absolute profit, but the highest rate of return on the capital or the assets employed by the firm. A company which earned £1 m. a year from assets of £10 m. (=10 per cent), would be considered to be more profitable than one which earned £2 m. a year from assets of £40 m. (=5 per cent).

Furthermore, profit maximisation implies earning the highest rate of return not in single year, but over a period of years considered together. A given sum earned this year is worth more than the same sum earned next year, since the company can put the money to a profitable use for a year – even if only by putting it on deposit at the bank. Nevertheless this does not necessarily mean that the firm should always try to earn as high a return as possible during the current year. It may be necessary to sacrifice profits this year in order to earn higher profits in subsequent years; indeed, investment projects undertaken by firms frequently fail to make profits until two or three years after their inception.

The justification for profit maximisation

Profit maximisation is usually justified on one or other of the following grounds. First, many firms (and all companies) are owned by the shareholders, and the directors (and the managers they appoint) have a responsibility to maximise the rewards of these shareholders. These rewards mainly comprise the income from dividends plus increases in share values which give rise to capital gains when shares are sold. Both of these forms of reward depend primarily upon the profits earned by the firm.

The second justification is that the pursuit of profit maximisation is likely to lead to the most efficient use of the country's economic resources. On the one

32

hand firms will constantly search for new products, and for new markets for their existing products, in order to increase their revenue. On the other hand they will constantly search for ways of reducing the costs of making and supplying these products. (These policies are discussed in detail in Chapters 7 and 8.)

However, the advocates of profit maximisation acknowledge that in the absence of adequate legislation the search for maximum profits might not always lead to the most efficient use of the country's resources. For example, a firm which was the sole supplier of a particular product (a monopolist) might seek to take advantage of his position by charging prices which yielded very high profits; in such instances the law should make it possible for other firms to enter the market, attract customers by offering an alternative product, perhaps at lower prices, and so compete away the 'monopoly profits'.

The pursuit of profit could have other undesirable consequences unless prevented by law, e.g. pollution of the environment, unsafe or unhygienic working conditions, shoddy products. We assume that organisations fulfil their legal obligations and hence the suggestion would be that profit maximisation should be pursued within the framework established by the law.

This suggestion has certainly much to commend it. It is true that the pursuit of profit is often a spur to increased economic efficiency. Moreover – to return to the first justification noted above – it would generally be agreed that shareholders deserve a reward for the risks which they take when they buy shares. Nevertheless, the view that firms, acting within the framework established by the law, should attempt to maximise profits, has frequently been challenged.

The challenge to profit maximisation

Concern about some of the consequences of profit maximisation has led to the introduction of legislation which has tended to reduce profitability, e.g. legislation which makes it more difficult for firms to dismiss employees or, where they are dismissed, requires that they should receive financial compensation. However, since we discuss this legislation elsewhere (Chapter 29) we confine our attention here to the argument that firms ought – at least on occasion – to go beyond meeting their legal obligations, that they should pursue other objectives at the expense of profit maximisation. So, for example, if the interests of employees and shareholders conflict, the interests of the employees should sometimes take precedence.

A simple example of this conflict is where a firm has insufficient orders to keep all its work-force occupied. The interests of the workers (i.e. the rewards, both financial and psychological, from having a job) might be best served by a work-sharing agreement or by producing goods for stock, to be sold if and when demand increases. (Incidentally, the effect on national economic efficiency of these alternatives would depend very much upon whether any workers dismissed from this firm could find re-employment elsewhere.)

A more complicated example is where employees fear that a future fall in the demand for the firm's existing products might lead to redundancies, and suggest that in order to prevent such redundancies the firm should spend money in order to develop new products. In the mid 1970s this policy was advocated by employees in the aerospace division of Lucas Industries but the suggestion was not adopted, mainly because the management felt that the best way to secure the profitability and growth of the company was to develop its traditional business and especially vehicle components and accessories. (The employees had emphasised 'socially useful' products such as improved forms of transportation for invalids.) The management's assessment of the situation might well have been correct, but this would be little consolation to those workers in the aerospace division who subsequently became redundant when, as they feared, demand for the products of that division fell.

Do firms attempt to maximise profits?

This question has given rise to a long and sometimes bitter debate among economists. One of the reasons why the debate has continued for so long is that the evidence that has been produced has often been conflicting. A fair, if highly simplified, summary of the evidence would be as follows.

Firms frequently adopt policies which are intended to increase their profits. However only a minority of firms can be characterised as profit maximising. There are several reasons for this.

First, directors (and managers) do *not* always believe that they have obligations to shareholders only. They have obligations – some set by and some beyond the requirements of the law – to employees, customers and the general public. One consequence of this may be that they seek to achieve an 'adequate' rather than a maximum rate of return. Of 130 companies which co-operated in a British Institute of Management survey, 66 were in favour of firms having a code of social responsibility and 60 were against (4 were neutral). Of the 66 which declared themselves in favour, 40 had already drawn up codes and a further 13 were planning to do so within the next eighteen months.

The detailed provisions contained in these codes will, of course, vary from organisation to organisation, but in general terms they are concerned with the organisation's responsibility to: its workers (e.g. in respect of working conditions, redundancy payments, help with preparation for retirement); to customers (e.g. ensuring that products are safe, giving guarantees of perform-ance); and to society in general (e.g. minimising pollution and other unfavourable environmental effects). Sometimes organisations have legal responsibilities in these areas, as we show in later chapters, but pressure is often brought in order to persuade them to go beyond their legal responsibilities. (The activities of pressure groups are considered in detail in Volume 2.)

Second, as noted in Chapter 1, managers have their own personal objectives, and these are not necessarily compatible with profit maximisation. For example, consider the utilisation of expensive equipment. Many instances have been found where such equipment has been utilised less fully in British factories than in factories in other countries. In Britain the equipment may be run on one shift compared to two elsewhere, or two shifts as compared to three elsewhere. This is sometimes claimed to be due to the attitude of the employees who operate the machinery. However, it may sometimes be due to the fact that multiple shift working requires some managers to work less congenial hours.

Third, if a firm is to maximise profits it requires a great deal of information about the costs and revenues associated with alternative policies. The acquisition of information itself involves a cost. Perhaps the most obvious example is research into the market for a new product – market research expenditure can sometimes exceed 'scientific' research and development costs. The cost of acquiring information means that firms frequently work with less information than they need to maximise their profits.

To take a different kind of example let us assume that a firm's profits have been inadequate and that it is decided that in order to bring profits back to an adequate, acceptable, level, it is necessary to reduce the cost of production by 5 per cent. The easiest way of implementing this might be to make the manager in charge of each department responsible for a reduction of 5 per cent in the cost of his department. In practice there might be much more scope for cost reduction in some departments than in others. One manager may have to struggle to reach 5 per cent while others could (but do not) reach 8 or 10 per cent. In other words, had more information about potential cost savings been available, an overall cost saving greater than 5 per cent could have been achieved.

Certain writers who have studied in detail the decisions taken by firms have found so much evidence that firms do not seek the information that would be required to maximise profits that they have suggested the term *satisficing* to indicate their behaviour, [Cyert and March 1963]. This term indicates that firms often pursue a course of action designed to yield a satisfactory rather than the best possible outcome.

Cyert and March also stress the importance of the conflicts which, as noted earlier, may exist among the different individuals or groups within an organisation. These conflicts are often resolved by a series of compromises, which again implies satisficing rather than maximising behaviour. For example, meeting management's objective of maximum output might require that machinery be run at a very high speed, whereas maximising the worker's comfort might require that it be run at a low speed. In practice a medium speed may be agreed which maximises neither, but which is acceptable to both managers and workers.

We have considered various negative reasons or factors which may prevent firms from maximising their profits. Another, more positive, factor is that the firms themselves may have other objectives which are not necessarily consistent with profit maximisation. We now consider the most important of these.

Growth

Numerous studies of business behaviour have revealed that growth, i.e. an increase in the volume of sales, is an important objective. This is partly due to the fact that growth *may* lead to an increase in profitability, as shown in Table 5.1.

This table relates to an imaginary company whose initial performance is summarised in row A. It employs assets of £25 m. to produce 10 m. articles a year. Each article sells at £1.00 and costs 75 pence to produce, yielding a profit margin of 25 pence per article. Total profits amount to £2.5 m. representing a rate of return on the assets employed of 10 per cent. The remaining rows of the table indicate various possible forms of growth, each having a different effect on profitability.

In row B, the assets employed remaining unchanged, there is an increase in the number of articles produced (and sold) to 12 m. a year, causing a corresponding increase in total profits and in the rate of return.

In row C there is also an increase in output and sales, but now the average

35

Table 5.1 Growth and profitability

	Assets Employed (£ millions)	No. of articles sold (millions)	Price (£)	Average cost (£)	Profit per unit (£)	Total profits (£ millions)	Rate of return (per cent)
A	25	10	1.00	0.75	0.25	2.5	10
B	25	12	1.00	0.75	0.25	3.0	12
C	25	12	1.00	0.70	0.30	3.6	14.4
D	25	12	1.10	0.75	0.35	4.2	16.8
E	30	12	1.00	0.75	0.25	3.0	10
F	30	12	1.00	0.70	0.30	3.6	12
G	30	12	0.98	0.75	0.23	2.76	9.2

cost of production falls to 70 pence, causing an increase in profit per unit and, of course, in total profit and in the rate of return. (We show in Chapter 24 why an increase in output may cause average cost to fall.)

In row D the firm not only sells more than it did in A, it also increases its price. We again discuss in a later chapter the circumstances in which this may occur. One possibility is that the firm is able – by one means or another – to drive competitors out of the market, and thus increase the demand for its own products.

In the three situations considered so far, growth has been achieved without any increase in assets employed. Consequently an increase in total profits has been accompanied by a corresponding increase in the rate of return. The remaining three situations are different in that in order to increase output a (proportionate) increase in assets is required. In row E both assets employed and the number sold increase by 20 per cent. Since the profit per unit is unchanged, total profits also increase by 20 per cent (from £2.5 m. to £3.0 m.). However the rate of return remains unchanged at 10 per cent.

In situation F the increased output is accompanied by a reduction in average cost and hence an increase in profit per unit. Total profits rise to £3.6 m., as in C, but now, because of the increase in assets employed, the rate of return rises to only 12 per cent.

Finally in G the firm finds that in order to sell the increased output it must lower its price to 98 pence. Since we have assumed that the average cost remains at its initial level, the profit per unit falls to 23 pence. Total profits rise but the rate of return falls.

The various examples in Table 5.1 indicate the various ways in which growth may affect profitability. When growth occurs without any change in assets employed, total profits and the rate of return change in line. They do not do so, however, where growth requires an increase in assets employed. Indeed we showed (situation G) that total profits may rise while the rate of return falls.

Why might situations such as in row G arise? Why might a firm embark upon a growth policy which results in a fall in the rate of return? One reason is, of course, that the firm might not be aware that this would be the outcome. Firms operate in a climate of uncertainty and there are many reasons why the rate of return might turn out to be lower than expected. (In the above example price had to be reduced; profitability might also fall if an increase in sales was accompanied by an increase in average cost.)

The other possibility is that the firm might attempt to grow even though it knows that this could result in a lower rate of return. This implies that the directors do not attach primary importance to maximising the benefits of the shareholders. They are willing to accept some reduction in these benefits in order to increase the benefits obtained by other people. The growth of a firm frequently involves larger incomes for at least some employees, arising from overtime working, improved promotion prospects, increases in bonuses which are tied to the value of sales, and so forth. In addition some people may obtain greater 'psychical' rewards, such as the prestige which comes from running a bigger firm and/or the satisfaction of being in charge of more people. (These arguments have been developed in Baumol (1967) and Williamson (1964).)

The firm may be able to achieve these objectives at the shareholders' expense because shareholders have not sufficient information to be able to evaluate the firm's policies. However there must clearly be a limit to the sacrifice which they are prepared to make. If they consider that the firm's profit and dividend record has been unsatisfactory, shareholders may attempt to unseat the directors. However, the dispersed pattern of shareholding frequently makes this difficult. In many companies the largest shareholding is less than 10 per cent. Moreover the largest shareholders are often institutions – insurance companies, pension funds, investment trusts, etc. – who have traditionally been rather reluctant to make strong challenges to boards of directors.

The other reaction of disgruntled shareholders is to sell their shares. If this happens on a sufficient scale, the price of the shares may fall to such a level that the firm becomes the target for a take-over bid by another company which feels it can utilise the assets more efficiently. Since a take-over might be followed by the removal of the existing directors, this danger again limits the extent to which a firm can pursue other objectives at the cost of a *fall* in profitability. However, there may be more scope for pursuing these other objectives if the effect is simply that profitability does not increase as much as it would otherwise have done.

It is extremely difficult to measure the effect of growth on profitability and on the rewards of shareholders, partly because growth can take so many different forms and partly because profitability can be affected by so many other factors. However it is clear that growth does not always benefit shareholders. In a study of the performance of 302 large UK companies during 1968–75, it was found that growth by acquisition, i.e. by take-overs, tended to benefit management rather than other groups. The ninety-three companies classified as having a heavy commitment to acquisition performed markedly worse than unacquisitive companies in terms of the share price and the overall return to shareholders [Newbould and Luffman 1978].

Diversification

Diversification, i.e. the introduction of different types of products from those previously supplied, may be one way in which firms seek to grow, For example, Littlewoods have used their profits from football pools to develop their retailing activities. It may also be a method of preventing a reduction in the total volume or value of output. For example, when Gillette's dominant position in the market for shaving equipment was attacked by Wilkinson Sword in the early 1960s it began to diversify, with products ranging from pens to hi-fi equipment. Razors and blades which had 70 per cent of total sales in 1963, accounted for only 30 per cent a decade later.

Summary and conclusions

Business organisations in the private sector may have a number of objectives, including survival, profitability and growth. Sometimes these various objectives are compatible, sometimes they conflict. Where objectives conflict, the conflict is commonly resolved by means of a compromise. Compromise is a feature of satisficing behaviour; however, even firms which set out to maximise their profits may be forced to compromise in order to take into account the views of various groups within and outside the organisation.

Assignments

5.1

The table below shows the profits earned by each of three companies over a period of five years. Company A has assets of £100,000 while B and C each have assets of £50,000. Say which company you consider to have been the most profitable over this period, and briefly explain your answer.

Company	1	2	3	4	5
A	20	20	20	20	20
B	10	10	10	10	10
C	15	5	15	5	10

5.2

A farmer has to decide whether to buy some sheep for fattening and resale. The cost of the sheep would be £1,000 and he would incur no other expenses since he would graze them on his own land which otherwise would be left fallow. He expects to be able to sell the sheep for £1,150 in two years' time. If he does not buy the sheep he would be able to lend the £1,000 at a rate of interest of 10 per cent per annum. Say whether you consider the purchase of the sheep to be a profitable investment, and briefly justify your answer.

5.3

A series of interviews carried out in the USA revealed that International Harvester's target rate of return on capital employed was 10 per cent while General Motor's target was 15–20 per cent. List three reasons which might account for this difference.

5.4

The following assignment is adapted from F. Livesey, *Economics*, (Polytech), p. 27–28.

38

Assume that the following discussion took place in the boardroom of Jethols, a mythical tour operator. The board has met to determine the advertising appropriation for the following year, and the managing director, Jim Black, begins by asking John Turner, the finance director, to give a brief summary of the previous year's operations.

Turner reported that the number of holidays booked and taken was 50,000. At an average price of £80, this yielded a revenue of £4,000,000. However, the average cost of providing the holiday was £90, broken down as follows: administration, and salaries of senior staff £4, cost of hotels and air charter £70, advertising £16. Since the advertising budget was to be the main topic of discussion, Turner had prepared further information on this point. Last year's budget had been split between £400,000 spent on television advertising and £400,000 spent on the production and mailing of 1 m. brochures.

Black then asked marketing director Guy Durie for his views on these figures. 'Two things in particular strike me,' replied Durie. 'First we just did not spend enough on television advertising. With the spread of colour television, this is certainly the ideal way of reaching customers, and I notice that the big boys are talking about spending at least a million each on TV this year. Now I'm not saying that we should match this, but I certainly think that we should get much nearer to it than we did last year.

'The second point is that we got damn poor value from our brochures; we sent out a million brochures and only booked 50,000 holidays. I reckon that our success rate was only about half of that for the industry as a whole.'

Sales director Alec Smith commented that Durie was probably right on that point. However, if Durie was suggesting diverting some funds from brochures to television he could not agree, since it was essential that his representatives should have a well-produced brochure when calling upon travel agents. Moreover if television advertising was stepped up there would be a greater call for brochures, not less.

Durie replied that he had not been thinking of reducing the budget for brochures, but that it might be desirable to put someone else in charge of their design; someone who could come up with a better product. If there was no one in the firm at present who they felt could do this, they should find someone outside immediately. He would be quite happy to keep spending on brochures at £400,000 but he would like to see television advertising pushed up to £800,000.

At this point Turner reminded his colleagues that they had made a loss of £10 per holiday last year, that advertising on the scale Durie suggested would push up the loss to £18 per holiday if the number of holidays booked did not increase, and that this would be a very serious matter, given that the company was already at the limit of its borrowing from the bank. It seemed to him that less advertising was required, not more.

'Look,' said Durie, 'if this company is to have any future at all, we have to get more customers, and the only way to do that is to advertise. Also, don't forget that once you've got a customer, he will book his holiday with you year after year. The market is increasing very rapidly and we have to get our share of this increase now. It doesn't even matter if we don't make a profit today. Because of this repeat business, the profits will start to roll in tomorrow.'

'Yes, Guy,' mused Black, 'but I wonder if our bankers would see it like that.'

Identify the various objectives which appear to motivate the different members of the Jethols Board. Which of the several policies that are advocated would be most likely to contribute to each of these objectives?

5.5

The following assignment appeared in F. Livesey, *Economics*, pp. 28–9.

Tom Burns is sales director of Middleco Ltd, a small engineering company which makes a range of components for the vehicles industry. One day he was about to leave his office when Reg Scott, one of his salesmen, rushed in, obviously very excited.

'Take off your coat, Tom, you are not going home before you've heard this.' Scott's news turned out to be that one of the biggest car manufacturers had given them a provisional order for one of their components. Scott's excitement was due to the fact that this would be the first time that Middleco had had the opportunity to enter the 'big league'. Previously they had sold only to the small producers of specialist vehicles.

Burns left a memo on the desk of managing director Harry Sefton, saying that he wished to meet him at the earliest opportunity, and went out to buy Scott a celebratory drink.

The following day Sefton rang Burns, heard his news, and said that in view of the scale of the potential order, a meeting should be arranged with production director Walt Kerr and chief accountant Dick Symon. In the meantime would Burns please confirm the details of the order with Scott.

At the meeting later in the morning Burns reported as follows. The order was for 30,000 components, to be delivered over a period of six months, at an ex-factory price of 24p each. This was below the price usually obtained, but, Burns added, that was only to be expected given that the order was about twenty times the size of the usual order.

Sefton asked Kerr whether, given the level of orders on hand, this new order could be met. Kerr said that the main production facilities were able to cope, but that it would probably be necessary to order some additional ancillary equipment and to engage some additional labour. He added that from his point of view life would be much easier with a few large orders than a large number of small ones, and he expected that production costs per unit would fall.

Trying to draw the threads of the argument together Sefton asked Symon whether he was in a position to give them a rough estimate of the effect on profitability of the new order.

'This depends very largely', replied Symon 'upon what happens if we don't take the order. As I understand it, the current state of the market is such that we could expect to fill our factory for the next six months without any need to book business at less than our normal prices. So, even though the costs of production should certainly go down with a long production run, and even though total output might be somewhat greater than without the new order, I estimate that the overall result of taking the new order would be to reduce our profits by about 10 per cent over the next six months.'

Burns, who felt some of his earlier enthusiasm evaporating, was now impelled to break in. He pointed out that the chief buyer of the car manufacturer concerned had implied that this might well be the first of many such orders, provided that Middleco's service, in terms of delivery, etc., proved to be satisfactory. 'I am sure that Walt will ensure that we give them the service that they are after,' he added, 'and once we win their confidence, our business should reach a scale that will make what we have now look like a back-room operation.'

Do you think that Middleco should accept the order? Your answer should be written in such a way as to bring out the implications of both decisions (i.e. to accept or to refuse the order) in terms of the various objectives which the firm might wish to attain.

5.6

The following assignment is adapted from F. Livesey, *Economics*, pp. 17–19. It relates to a firm which employed several thousand workers in the heavy engineering industry. An important goal of the management of the factory was to achieve a better safety record than the other factories in the firm, and in the industry. Particular stress was placed on eliminating fatal accidents and on achieving annual reductions in the frequency of lost-time injuries.

In all the factories extensive use was made of overhead cranes, and the movement of most cranes was governed by an old type of controller. Most cranemen and supervisors preferred magnetic controllers, a newer type which had been installed on some of the cranes. Because magnetic controllers operated on low-voltage control circuits, there was less danger of severe shock or of 'flash' – visible arcing of current across contact points – than with the older type, which operated on full-line voltage. Magnetic controllers also allowed operators to direct crane movements more precisely, and thus reduced the danger of 'drift' or unanticipated movements.

The actual safety benefits that would accrue from the replacement of old-type controllers with magnetic controllers were hard to estimate precisely. Burns, shocks and eye injuries resulted from 'flash' in the older controller circuits, but they were infrequent and were not often disabling. Injuries caused by movement of cranes were usually attributable to human errors by cranemen or ground crews, but sometimes to mechanical failure of the controllers or to 'drift'.

Changeovers to magnetic controllers were being made only as the older controllers wore out, until a fatal accident in one of the factories triggered recommendations for an accelerated replacement programme. A worker was killed when an unexpected movement of a crane pinned him against a wall.

As a result of this accident a special committee was set up to consider ways in which the cranemen's control over crane movements might be improved. One of the changes that the committee recommended was that the controllers then in use 'be replaced by magnetic controllers as quickly as feasible'.

Cost estimates for the changeover were then prepared. It was estimated that the total number of replacements required, based on the proposals of the various factory managers, was 344. The chief engineer estimated that this would require an expenditure of $500,000, to be spread over a five-year programme. The execution of this programme would be the responsibility of the maintenance superintendent.

Early in the second year of the programme, the maintenance super-intendent developed a revised plan for replacements. The estimated number of replacements had been reduced from 344 to 250, the estimated total cost increased from $500,000 to $600,000, and the estimated time for completion of the programme increased from five to six or seven years. In putting forward these proposals the maintenance superintendent noted the programme's encroachment on men and facilities needed for other projects to which the maintenance division was committed.

Later in that year two divisions met adverse trading conditions, which resulted in a substantial fall in profits. On account of this worsening in their liquidity situation, further action in these diversions on the replacement programme was halted at the end of the second year. One year later almost all the divisions in the firm had reverted, for similar reasons, to the policy they were following before the accident; they were installing magnetic controllers only as the other control systems wore out.

Identify the various objectives which appear to have influenced the decisions taken, and explain why the relative importance attached to each of these objectives changed over time.

5.7

'Profit over the long term remains the principal yardstick by which the success or failure of a company should be judged.'

'A company today is concerned with a wider range of matters than in years gone by. This requires the Board to give increasing attention to relationships with employees, customers, suppliers, Government, local authorities and the general public.'

The above two quotations are taken from *The Responsibilities of the British Public Company* published by the Confederation of British Industry. Illustrate the circumstances in which these two sets of principles would (*a*) be consistent, (*b*) conflict.

5.8

The list of principles given below was contained in a report, *The Responsibilities of the British Public Company*, published in 1973 by the Confederation of British Industry. State whether you agree or disagree with these principles, outlining the reasons for your decisions.

Principles of corporate conduct

1. This summary of principles which emerges from our report is not a compendium of rules; it is a frame of reference for the judgements which individual directors and Boards must make for themselves in the light of their own circumstances.
2. Business today has to operate in a far wider context than ever before. It may be wise for Boards to see that they have authority to allow for the wider judgements involved.
3. Profit over the long term remains the principal yardstick by which the success or failure of a company should be judged.
4. A company today is concerned with a wider range of matters than in years gone by. This requires the Board to give increasing attention to relationships with employees, customers, suppliers, Government, local authorities and the general public.
5. The Board has to create a closer relationship with the company's

shareholders. It must provide all shareholders with full knowledge of the progress of the company.

6. Shareholders are owners of the business and have a responsibility that extends beyond the buying and selling of shares. They must exercise their responsibility and be provided with proper information on which they can form their judgements.

7. Institutional shareholders have knowledge and expertise not normally available to private shareholders. It is essential that institutions should fulfil their role as shareholders in the interests of all shareholders.

8. The Board has to forge closer relationships with its employees towards a common purpose. This is in the interests of its shareholders as well as its employees. The main purpose must be to secure a wider participation in the processes of decision-making on the part of all employees.

9. In any take-over or merger situation, both shareholders and employees should be presented as early as is practicable with as full information as is reasonable on the matters that affect their interests.

10. The Board of a company should normally include one or more non-executive directors. Such directors should pay particular attention to shareholders' interests and exert a monitoring influence on the Board as a whole. They should be given the necessary information and knowledge of the company to enable them to fulfil this role. This provision concerning non-executive directors may not be appropriate for all small companies.

11. The Board must give high priority to the honesty of its dealing and relationships with its customers, its suppliers and its creditors. It should ensure that all its employees observe a high standard of integrity and responsibility.

12. Within its own field of knowledge, skill, geographical concern and financial capacity, a company should be responsive to the movement of informed public opinion; it should pay proper regard to the environmental and social consequences of its business activities.

Notes

1. *J. Melrose-Woodman and I. Kverndal. 'Toward Social Responsibility: company codes of ethics and practice',* **British Institute of Management, 1976.**

References

Cyert, R. M. and March, J. G. *A Behavioural Theory of the Firm*, Prentice-Hall, 1963.
Newbould, G. D. and Luffman, G. A. *Successful Business Policies*, Gower Press, 1978.
Baumol, W. J. *Business Behaviour, Value and Growth*, New York, Harcourt Brace and World, 1967.
Williamson, O. E. *The Economics of Discretionary Behaviour: Managerial Objectives in a Theory of the Firm*, Englewood Cliffs, N. J. Prentice-Hall, 1964.

6 The objectives of public sector business organisations

Introduction

Having examined the objectives of business organisations in the private sector we now consider the corresponding organisations in the public sector. Our discussion in this chapter is much briefer; for the most part we take for granted the similarities between the two types of organisation and concentrate on the differences.

Public corporations

We noted in Chapter 4 that the major business organisations in the public sector in the UK are the public corporations (sometimes known as the nationalised industries). We also noted there that while the original intention was that the Government should lay down the broad objectives for each corporation which would then be free to decide matters of detail, in practice this intention has not been fulfilled. Ministers have frequently interfered in the detailed operations of the corporations (although less than they have with the non-commercial government departments), often in ways which have made it difficult to meet the corporations' specified objectives. For example, the profitability of the electricity supply industry was reduced when it was ordered to buy fuel from domestic producers at higher prices than those at which it could have bought from overseas producers.

Furthermore, the objectives laid down by governments have frequently changed. It is, therefore, difficult to summarise the objectives of the public corporations. However, one can say that in general they differ from those of private sector producers in three main ways.

First, profitability objectives are more likely to be expressed in terms of a rate of return which is sufficient to allow the corporation to replace its capital assets and to pay interest on its borrowings, rather than on earning a high rate of return. In earlier years the corporations were required simply to 'break even', taking one year with another. More recently specific financial targets have been laid down for each corporation and these have occasionally included a provision for the payment of a 'public dividend' to the Treasury. However, very few such payments have been made, and overall the target rates of return on assets employed have been considerably below the average for producers in the private sector. (Even these relatively modest targets have sometimes been unattainable, and industries such as steel and coal have received substantial subsidies from the Government, i.e. from taxpayers.)

Second, growth has usually been a less important objective than for private sector producers. There are some exceptions; the nationalised fuel industries – and especially gas and electricity – have spent considerable amounts on advertising in an attempt to attract new customers. But overall, public sector producers have put more emphasis on maintaining than on increasing the volume of their business. This is connected with the fact that the corporations have not been encouraged by governments to try to earn surpluses on the scale that would be required to finance major growth programmes. It is also due to the fact that the corporations have been prevented from embarking on major diversification programmes – the production of entirely new products – which are frequently the means by which private sector producers seek to grow.

Finally, producers in the public sector are specifically required to take into account non-commercial considerations. The White Paper 'Nationalised Industries: A review of economic and financial objectives', published in 1967, stated that the nationalised industries have a vital role to play 'in the development of the Government's wider social and economic policies', as well as in such objectives as increased productivity. At various times the industries have been persuaded to keep down their prices (to help the Government's fight against inflation), to provide unprofitable services (to aid the Government's regional policy) and to maintain a labour force bigger than necessary (to aid the Government's attempts to reduce the unemployment rate). On some occasions the industry has received government subsidies to compensate for the loss of profits entailed by these policies; more often it has not, especially in the early years of nationalisation.

Perhaps the best example of the attention given by a nationalised industry to social considerations is the establishment by the British Steel Corporation of a subsidiary company, BSC (Industry), with the responsibility for attracting new firms to areas in which BSC closures have created or increased unemployment.

The company seeks to attract new firms by providing two forms of assistance. The first is information concerning the various types of financial assistance from the UK Government and the EEC for which the firms might be eligible. The second is financial assistance, e.g. helping to meet the cost of training, providing land and premises at cheap rates.

Summary and conclusions

In this chapter we have indicated the major ways in which the objectives of business organisations in the public sector differ from those in the private sector. These differences are mainly in emphasis, in the relative importance attached to various objectives, rather than in the objectives themselves. Consequently when we discuss the policies of business organisations in the next chapter we do not, in most instances, need to make a distinction between organisations in the public and private sectors.

Assignments

6.1

In the light of the information below discuss the objectives of public corporations (nationalised industries). Show the ways in which these objectives (*a*) are similar to, (*b*) differ from, the objectives of private sector business organisations.

Under the Coal Industry Nationalisation Act 1946 the statutory duties with which the National Coal Board was charged included:

1. Securing the efficient development of the coal-mining industry.
2. Making supplies of coal available, of such qualities and in such quantities and at such prices, as may seem to them best calculated to further the public interest in all respects.

The Coal Industry Act 1967 stated that until 1971 the electricity industry was to use 6 m. tons of coal per annum over and above what it would have used on purely commercial considerations. The industry was to be compensated for the extra costs incurred.

Under the Transport Act 1947 the railways retained (up to 1953) their status of a 'common carrier', i.e. they were legally obliged to carry any traffic offered to them. They had to publish their rates and charges and were forbidden to discriminate against any class of traffic.

In 1955 a Modernisation Plan was published with the objectives of reducing the cost of railway operations and improving the efficiency of service so as to attract more traffic. The plan aimed specifically at improving track and signalling so as to give higher speeds, replacing steam locomotives by diesel or electric, modernising passenger rolling stock, and remodelling and speeding up the freight services, partly by reducing the number of depots and installing continuous braking on freight wagons. In 1960 the Select Committee on Nationalised Industries reported that costs and expected receipts had not been estimated for most of the proposals in the Plan. The Committee itself estimated that for the electrification of the London–Liverpool–Manchester line the rate of return was between 5 and 7 per cent, while the interest paid on the capital borrowed was between 5 and 6 per cent.

The Post Office Act 1969 laid down that 'it shall be the duty of the Post Office so to exercise its powers as to secure that all its revenues are not less than sufficient to meet all charges properly chargeable to revenue account, taking one year with another'. The Act also stipulated that 'If it appears to the Minister that the Post Office is showing undue preference to, or is exercising undue discrimination against, any person in the charges or other terms and conditions applicable to services . . . he may give it directions to secure that it ceases to do so.'

6.2

What similarities and what differences do you think might exist between the objectives of each of the following:

1. ICI Limited (Imperial Chemical Industries) and British Rail.
2. The proprietor of a hairdressing salon and a doctor (general practitioner).
3. The BBC and an independent television company?

6.3

Most nationalised industries (e.g. coal, rail) were privately owned prior to being made public corporations. The Post Office, however, was formerly a Government department until 1969 when it was made a public corporation. Identify the primary objectives of the Post Office as an organisation. How, do you think, did the Government feel that the status of public corporation (as opposed to that of Government department) might help it more successfully to pursue (and achieve) these objectives? (A comprehensive review of the objectives and operations of the Post Office is contained in *The Report of the Post Office Review Committee*, Cmnd. 6850 HMSO 1977.)

7 Policies to increase revenue

Introduction

In the previous chapters we have discussed the major objectives of business organisations. We now examine the various policies which might be adopted in order to meet these objectives. Our examination of each policy will be comparatively brief since some of these policies are discussed at greater length in later chapters.

It is convenient to make a broad distinction between policies intended to increase revenue, examined in this chapter, and those intended to reduce costs, examined in the next chapter. Both sets of policies can contribute to an increase in profitability, which has been identified as a major objective, both as an end in itself and as a means of ensuring the survival of an organisation. We also discuss the relevance of these policies to the other objectives identified in Chapters 5 and 6.

An organisation may attempt to increase its revenue either from existing or new products, and we discuss these in turn.

An increase in revenue from existing products

The revenue obtained from existing products can be increased in several ways.

A change in price

The crucial factor determining the effect on revenue of a change in price is the (price) elasticity of demand, which is defined as the percentage change in quantity demanded divided by the percentage change in price:

$$\mathrm{PED} = \frac{\dfrac{\Delta Q}{Q} \times 100}{\dfrac{\Delta P}{P} \times 100} = \frac{\Delta Q/Q}{\Delta P/P}$$

where Q is the initial quantity demanded (per period)

P is the initial price, and

Δ denotes a (small) change in these variables.

If PED>1 demand is said to be elastic.

If PED=1 demand is said to be of unitary elasticity.

If PED<1 demand is said to be inelastic.[1]

In order to increase revenue, price should be reduced if demand is elastic, and increased if price is inelastic. (If demand is of unitary elasticity, revenue is the same at all prices.) This rule is illustrated in Table 7.1 where the initial situation is shown in row A.

Table 7.1 Elasticity and revenue

	Price	Quantity	Revenue
A	10	100	1,000
B (PED=2.0)	9	120	1,080
C (PED=2.0)	11	80	880
D (PED=0.5)	9	105	945
E (PED=0.5)	11	95	1,045

Rows B and C indicate the consequences of a change in price when demand is elastic: PED=2, i.e. a 10 per cent change in price causes a 20 per cent change in the quantity demanded. In this situation a price reduction causes revenue to rise (B), while a price increase causes revenue to fall (C).

Rows D and E show the consequences of a change in price when demand is inelastic: PED=0.5, i.e. a 10 per cent change in price causes a 5 per cent in the quantity demanded. Here a price reduction causes revenue to fall (D), while a price increase causes revenue to rise (E). (The data in Table 7.1 is presented in graphical form in Fig. 7.1 where D_E indicates the elastic and D_I the inelastic

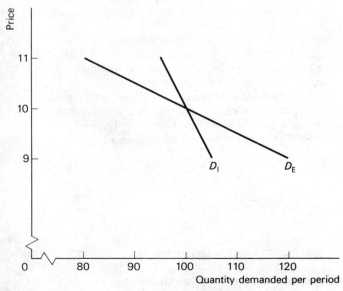

Fig. 7.1 Differing demand elasticities

49

demand curve. You can use this diagram to demonstrate for yourself the rule stated above.)

The first possibility is, then, that the firm may be able to take advantage of the elasticity of demand to increase its revenue by means of a change in price. A factor which has a very important influence on the value of the elasticity of demand is the degree of product differentiation.

Product differentiation

The product of one supplier is said to be differentiated when it is seen by purchasers (organisations or individuals) as being different from the products of other suppliers. If purchasers do not see any appreciable difference between the products of competing suppliers, a change in price by one supplier is likely to cause many purchasers to switch suppliers, i.e. demand would be elastic. On the other hand if purchasers see significant differences between products, switching is far less likely, i.e. demand would be less elastic. If you do not understand this look again at Fig. 7.1. D_E would apply where there are few significant differences between the products, D_I where the differences are more important.

A product may be differentiated in various ways. Features may be built in which are not included in competitive products; these may result in differences in performance, durability, styling, etc. The product may be advertised in order to create a belief by purchasers that it differs from other products. (Distinctive features and advertising may, of course, be combined.) The producer may attempt to differentiate not the product as such, but his total offering – product plus service. He may do this by providing early delivery, a comprehensive maintenance service, etc.

Two further points must be made concerning product differentiation. First, in order to differentiate its products a firm must utilise resources. If this causes costs to be higher than they would otherwise be, this increase in cost should be offset against any additional revenue resulting from differentiation. Where differentiation depends upon product features the cost will be incurred in research and development or in the use of different materials. The costs incurred in differentiation through advertising are obvious. In packaging both materials and design costs may be important. Finally, additional labour costs are likely to be incurred in supporting the product with a good service.

Second, if the only result of product differentiation is to cause demand to be less elastic (although we argue below that this is *not* usually so), then product differentation is desirable only if the firm wishes to increase its price. If it wished to reduce price, product differentiation would be undesirable since it makes demand less elastic.

An increase in the volume of sales

In the previous section we showed how a firm might attempt to reduce the elasticity of demand for its products. These policies might also cause the demand for those products to increase. In order to understand the implications of this, consider Fig. 7.2.

This figure shows the demand conditions facing the Hole-In-One Company, a mythical manufacturer of golf balls. In common with other

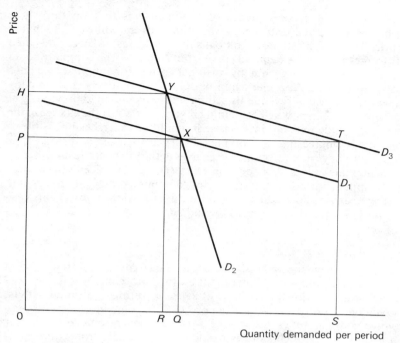

Fig. 7.2   Changes in demand

manufacturers, the company makes white balls and its initial demand curve D_1 is highly elastic. This indicates that if HIOC were to raise its price it would lose many sales to its competitors since most (although not all) consumers consider that its golf balls do not have any superior feature which would compensate for the higher price. Conversely if HIOC were to reduce its price it would win many sales from its competitors (assuming, of course, that they did not match the price reduction), since most consumers do not believe those competitive balls to have any superior features which would compensate for their higher price. Given the demand curve D_1 HIOC sets price P at which it sells Q per period, yielding revenue $OPXQ$.

Then the sales director of HIOC comes up with the idea that instead of making white balls like all the other manufacturers, HIOC will make yellow balls. He argues that a yellow ball would be just as easy to see in the grass as a white ball, and that it would have the added appeal of distinctiveness.

This proposed change might have several alternative consequences. First, consumers might have conflicting views about the yellow ball. Some, feeling the same way as the sales director, are willing to pay more for HIOC balls than for competitive brands. Others, however, perhaps because they feel that the yellow ball is *not* as easy to see as the white one, are willing to buy HIOC balls only if they are cheaper than competitive brands. In this situation the demand curve becomes less elastic, D_2 (for simplicity we have drawn the new curve so that Q is still bought at price P). Previously (D_1) an increase in price would have led to a fall in revenue. Now, however (D_2), an increase in price will – up to a certain point – lead to an increase in revenue. For example, at price H revenue is $OHYR$, which can be seen to exceed $OPXQ$.

51

The second possible consequence of the change is that on the whole consumers believe that a yellow ball has an advantage over a white one, so that at any given price HIOC can sell more golf balls than previously. This is indicated by the shift to the right of the demand curve from D_1 to D_3. The company could again achieve an increase in revenue by raising its price (for simplicity we have drawn D_3 so that at price H, R can again be sold). Alternatively the company could achieve an increase in revenue by selling more than it could previously at the existing price P. It can now sell S, yielding revenue $OPTS$. If the change in the product had only made demand less elastic it would *not* have been possible to increase revenue by increasing the volume of sales at the existing price.

In Fig. 7.2 we have assumed that the change in the product causes either an increase in demand (D_2) *or* a change in elasticity (D_3). In practice both of these things may happen. Another possibility is, of course, that on the whole consumers feel that a yellow ball is not as good as a white one. In this case demand would fall – the demand curve would shift to the left of D_1.

Channels of distribution

In the previous section we showed how policies leading to product differentiation might result in an increase in the demand for a firm's products. Another way of increasing demand, and thus the volume of sales, is to find additional outlets, additional channels of distribution for the product. In some instances this may simply involve making fuller use of the existing conventional outlets. For example, a manufacturer of chocolates would try to persuade more confectionery shops and grocers to stock his brand of chocolates. In other instances it may involve creating entirely new distribution channels outside the conventional outlets for the product concerned. For example, whereas at one time the sale of books was largely confined to specialist book shops and newsagents, it is now common to find racks of paperback books in the branches of variety stores such as Woolworths, in supermarkets, on the forecourts of railway stations, etc.

Gramophone records are another product which has emerged from the specialist shops. It has been estimated that by the mid 1970s one record in three was bought from Boots, W. H. Smith or Woolworth. (Since these multiple retailers often sell the most popular records at discount prices, specialist shops have had to rely more on sales of minority interest records for their survival.)

Sometimes the search for additional outlets takes firms into new geographical areas. The most extreme example of this is where a firm which previously confined its activities to the home market begins exporting.

Finally, manufacturers may seek to increase their sales by producing goods for sale under a wholesaler or retailer's brand. The production of such own-label products is discussed in Chapter 18.

Summary: sales of existing products

We have seen that firms may seek to increase the revenue from existing products either by changing the price or by increasing the volume of sales. (Incidentally, note that a price reduction may increase revenue but not profits, since additional costs are incurred in increasing output.)

The scope for increasing revenue in one or other of these ways depends upon the state of demand, and the degree of competition in the market (the term market is defined in chapter 14). If the product is fairly new, so that many consumers have not yet tried it and if there are few suppliers of competitive products or brands, it is reasonable to expect revenue (per period) to increase in the future. On the other hand if the market has become saturated, i.e. all potential customers have bought the product, and if there are many competitive suppliers, revenue is much less likely to increase; indeed it may well fall. In these circumstances one firm may be able to gain sales and revenue at the expense of competitors, and may even be able to drive competitors out of the market. However it is clearly impossible for *all* firms to increase their market share. Consequently, when the markets for the firm's existing products are saturated, an objective of increasing (or even maintaining) total revenue is likely to require the introduction of new products. (As noted in chapter 5, some firms may adopt a policy of diversification in order to increase the *stability* of their revenue and profitability.)

The introduction of new products

It is not always easy to draw the line between new products and changes in existing products. In the example discussed above, the production of a different colour golf ball was treated as a change in the product (product differentiation). If, on the other hand, HIOC had started to produce cricket balls this would, from its point of view, have represented the introduction of a new product. Taking another example from the field of sport, consider firms making the poles used in pole-vaulting. When these firms changed from making metal to glass fibre poles this could be considered as a change in an existing product. On the other hand one could treat it as the introduction of a new product since the new poles proved so superior in performance to the old ones that they rapidly replaced them.

Although difficulties may exist in deciding precisely what constitutes a new product, we can still demonstrate what is involved in the process of new product introductions. The first distinction to be made is between products which are new to one firm but which are already being supplied by other firms (sometimes known as 'imitative' products) and products which are entirely new ('pioneer' products).

Imitative products

Since it has already been established that a market for these products exists, the main question is whether the firm which is considering entering the market can produce a brand that is sufficiently attractive to the consumer, by way of price, product characteristics, etc., to guarantee the entrant an adequate market share. ('Adequate' refers here to the firm's objectives, in terms of revenue and profitability.) Consequently the firm has to decide whether its resources – production plant, design skill, etc. – would be suitable for the task. For example, a firm whose experience was confined to shipbuilding or heavy engineering would find it much more difficult to begin producing hi-fi equipment than would a firm with previous experience in some other branch of light electrical engineering.

53

The firm also has to take into account its reputation – or lack of reputation – in the market for the proposed new product. The initial sales of the expensive propelling pencils made by Parker were no doubt helped by the reputation built up by that company for the production of high quality fountain pens.

Finally, the firm must try to predict how the existing suppliers would react to its entry; whether they would be passive, i.e. maintain their existing policies, or whether they would change these policies in order to fight off the newcomer, e.g. by reducing their prices, increasing their advertising expenditure, improving their products, etc.

An aggressive reaction is most likely if the total market for the product is expanding only very slowly or not at all, so that the entry of a new supplier would cause a reduction in the sales of the existing suppliers. A passive reaction is most likely when the market is expanding rapidly and the existing suppliers are unable to keep up with demand.

Again, the existing suppliers will be in a better position to react aggresively in some situations than in others. They will have most scope to reduce their prices if their existing prices are high in relation to their costs, to quickly increase their advertising if they have spare cash at the bank, to improve their products if they have adequate research and development facilities.

Pioneer products

If a firm is considering introducing a pioneer product many of the questions considered above do not arise since, by definition, there is no existing supplier of a pioneer product. On the other hand, the lack of an existing supplier implies lack of information concerning the potential market for the product. The initial supplier has to try to fill this gap by conducting market research. (We are envisaging here a situation in which the firm has already formulated an idea for a new product. In other situations the need for a new product may actually emerge from the results of market research.)

This information about the potential market must then be considered together with information about the firm's capabilities, in terms of production plant, design skills, etc., as noted above. The firm will then decide whether or not the introduction of the new product would help it to meet its target revenue and profitability.

The reliability of this information is likely to be greatest when the firm has experience of supplying other products to the market for which the new product is designed, and when the new product uses the same production processes, materials, labour skills, etc., as the firm uses for existing products. However, even here considerable uncertainty may surround the estimates made on the basis of this information, and many new products fail to meet producers' hopes and expectations. Some of these 'failures' are withdrawn after a trial period; others may continue in existence for several years but without yielding an adequate return to the money invested in their production.

On the other hand, some pioneer products have achieved success beyond the expectations of their originators, e.g. the Xerox reprographic machines, Polaroid cameras and sunglasses. The primary determinant of success is, of course, that a potential market for the product should exist. But also of great importance is the ability of the initial producer to protect his position against

54

future competition. The 'body-scanner' pioneered by EMI proved to be less successful commercially than had originally been anticipated, partly because expenditure on medical care was reduced in the USA at a vital early stage in the marketing of the product, and partly because other manufacturers were able to close the technical gap established by EMI more quickly than had been expected. Sales revenue from scanners rose from £5 m. in 1974 to £93 m. in 1977, but fell back to £66 m. in 1978, resulting in a loss in that year of £13 m.

A pioneer producer may obtain legal protection for up to twenty years by taking out a series of patents. In addition (or in the absence of patent protection) he may obtain protection by means of the 'know-how' enshrined in the production process, or by establishing a good reputation with consumers.

Two case studies in product policy

We have discussed in the previous sections various aspects of marketing and product policies – product differentiation, extending the channels of distribution, new product introductions, etc. We now present detailed illustrations of how these policies operate in practice in two particular markets.

The first market is that for *primary batteries*. Experience in this market shows that to ensure its continuing success a firm may need to operate on two fronts simultaneously – increasing the sales of its existing products and preparing the way for the introduction of new products.[2]

'Events in recent weeks involving Ever Ready – the world's second largest producer of primary batteries – have highlighted a sea change which has been creeping over the battery industry throughout the 1970s and is now beginning to show through in changing production patterns and the break up of traditional trading alliances.

'As the dominant company in the UK, with 74 per cent of the market, Ever Ready is the natural spearhead and focus for the changes, which, paradoxically, have come equally from stagnation and prospects of major growth.

'The stagnation is a by-product of the very success of the zinc carbon battery, the commonest type of battery, which has been in existence for nearly a century. Its performance has certainly improved – output from today's HP2 or HP11 battery is twice the pre-war vintage – and the invention of a host of battery-powered products, not least the transistor radio, provided many years of spectacular sales growth.

'There is still further growth to come from such new products. But in the main the edge has gone off the growth in the sophisticated markets of the developed world.

'Consumption of zinc carbon batteries in Europe, the US, Japan and Britain is now fairly static, at around fourteen per person per year.

'Yet Ever Ready has just announced that it is planning to expand its main plant at Tanfield Lea by a sixth. The plant already produces 2.6 m. batteries per day and the new section will add another 800,000 per day. Nor is Ever Ready the only UK producer embarked on major expansion. Crompton Parkinson, the Hawker Siddeley subsidiary which makes batteries under the Vidor name, is also building new plant which could increase its capacity by around a third.

'What is the reason for this expansion? The lure, both for Vidor and Ever Ready, is the massive potential in the developing world. In Nigeria for instance, where Ever Ready has an established manufacturing base, consumption is a mere one to one-and-a-half batteries per person per year. The new plants in both companies will largely provide supplies for export to the Third World, though Vidor also hedges its bets by supplying the same countries with the machinery to make batteries themselves.

'The expansion of zinc carbon battery production is budgeted to account for nearly 75 per cent of Ever Ready's development programme of between £36 m. and £40 m. over the next two to three years.

'The remaining 25 per cent, however, is not insignificant, and this is going into the two new growth areas for batteries – alkaline manganese cells (whose long life and leak-proof properties make them particularly suitable for electronic equipment such as cameras and calculators) and "button" cells (a generic name which covers mercury, silver and zinc oxide products).

'So alluring is the potential growth from alkaline manganese batteries, that last month Ever Ready severed a trading alliance of thirty years' standing and sold back to P. R. Mallory of America the 25 per cent stake it had owned in Mallory's European interests in alkaline manganese batteries.

'Nearly half the £10.8 m. proceeds from this deal are to be ploughed into perfecting the pilot plant Ever Ready has set up for these batteries, which should be in full production by next autumn. The cost, between £4 m. and £5 m., seems a considerable amount to spend on a battery type which has only about 2 per cent of the UK market by volume, until one learns that in Germany its market share is 7 per cent, while in Japan it is 19 per cent, and in the US it is around 35 per cent, and possibly 50 per cent by value.

'Skilful advertising of alkaline manganese batteries, largely by Mallory, by far the market leader, is beginning to eat into the traditional zinc carbon market despite claims by the zinc carbon manufacturers that for most common usages the zinc carbon battery gives much better value for money. This encroachment has obviously intensified Ever Ready's determination to make "long life" batteries.

'In the longer term the pressure on Ever Ready must be to provide – in an increasingly sophisticated market – the full range of batteries in order to minimise the possibility of losing its UK market share to a foreign competitor.

'So far the company has had little to fear. Its own market share, 74 per cent, climbs to 83 per cent if one takes into account the batteries it supplies under "own brand" labels to Exide, the Chloride brand name, or Ray-o-Vac, the brand belonging to ESB. There is little penetration from the foreign majors: Union Carbide, the world's largest; Varta, the German Quandt company's brand which has the dominant 40 per cent share in its own country; or National, the Japanese Matsushita company's label. Together they account for only about 4 per cent of the market. Nonetheless, the fear is there.

'The same two pressures – fear of penetration by the competition and the need to maintain growth by manufacturing new types of batteries – is also stimulating Ever Ready into starting production of button cells, the main growth area for which is quartz watches and other miniaturised products, such as hearing aids.

'Ever Ready is spending £5 m. to £6 m. developing and manufacturing these cells, by the end of which it will be the sole European producer of any size (Mallory has a small plant in Switzerland) and should be able to attack the virtual monopoly at present enjoyed by Far East producers, such as Matsushita.

'The combined effect of these moves, according to Mr Lawrence Orchard, chairman of Ever Ready, should be to double turnover within five years. The bulk of this expansion is expected to come from Third World growth in zinc carbon batteries, backed up by the new types of cells.'

The second case concerns the market for *spare parts for cars*. It again shows that a firm may adopt policies designed to increase revenue from the sales of both existing and new products. It also shows how a firm whose major activity is manufacturing can increase revenue by retailing products made by other manufacturers.

'British Leyland is to sell spare parts for most of the more popular foreign cars under a scheme announced yesterday.[3] It will be competing, initially in a limited way, with both the car manufacturers and rivals among British component makers such as Lucas, Automotive Products and Motocraft.

'The company will continue to use the Unipart brand name, although about 70 per cent of the new range of parts is being imported from the countries of origin, including Japan. It hopes to turn over an additional £5 m. to £6 m. this year on the parts, which include ignition sets, filters, fan belts, radiator caps and thermostats, and spark plugs. It already covers many parts for Ford, Chrysler and Vauxhall.

'The parts division as a whole has a UK turnover target of £200 m. this year, plus £100m. in exports. The total UK parts market is estimated at £1.6 bn. a year.

'Parts for imported cars are taking an increasing proportion of the total – Leyland estimates £350 m. in 1979, more than a third being for fast-moving items rather than major engine and body components.

'The range of foreign car parts on offer is to be expanded later this year, probably taking in brake shoes and linings and other regularly replaced goods.

'Unipart expects the bulk of its early sales to be to the garage repair trade, but says that it already receives many inquiries from the public for foreign car parts and sees the do-it-yourself repair proportion growing rapidly.

'It will support local distributors with a press advertising campaign and point-of-sale material in 550 Unipart shops. The range will also be available through independent retailers.

'The Leyland parts distribution network was reorganised recently to increase from 40 to 250 the number of distributors wholesaling the full range of Unipart components. Previously, there had been more divisions along the Austin-Morris, Rover, Triumph and Jaguar ranges.

'The new "corporate wholesalers" have agreed to increase their stock-holding and put in more advanced control and handling systems. In return, they will have direct access to Leyland's central parts distribution service at Cowley, Oxford.

'They are also mounting, with the help of Leyland, a campaign in the garage repair trade aimed at increasing the share for Leyland parts.

'Packaging has been redesigned, with descriptions in three languages, and the reference catalogue has been updated to incorporate international symbols so that it can be used throughout Europe.'

Summary and conclusions

A firm may adopt a wide range of policies with the intention of increasing its revenue. These policies may relate to pricing, advertising, product differentiation, the introduction of new products, the creation of new distribution channels, etc. If revenue increases following an increase in price, profits will also increase. In all other instances, however, the increase in revenue *could* be outweighed by the increase in cost, with a consequent reduction in profits. In such instances the firm has to decide whether it is prepared to accept a reduction in profits in order to achieve other objectives, e.g. an increase in the volume of sales or in market share.

If the firm attaches the highest priority to an increase in profits, and if this objective cannot be met by means of any of the policies discussed in this chapter, the alternative approach is to try to reduce its costs. The various policies involved in cost reduction are discussed in the next chapter.

Assignments

7.1

Explain, using a numerical example, why a firm should take the elasticity of demand into account when deciding whether or not it should change its price.

7.2

'Advertising is successful if it causes demand either to increase or to become less elastic'. Discuss.

7.3

Because of the increasing popularity of cremation the demand for grave headstones has decreased substantially in many areas. What steps might be taken by the owner of a firm making headstones in order to maintain his profitability? What obstacles might he encounter?

7.4

List the most important forms of product differentiation likely to be practised by

1. a manufacturer of margarine,
2. a manufacturer of machinery used in engineering factories,
3. a one-man plumbing business,
4. the local branch of a building society,
5. a television rental company.

7.5

Explain the probable implications of each of the examples of new product introductions listed below, with reference to the marketing, production, purchasing and personnel functions:

1. A producer of broiler chickens begins rearing broiler turkeys.
2. A football pools operator opens a mail order business selling a wide range of products.
3. A television rental company opens a chain of shops hiring garden equipment.

7.6

Discuss, in the light of the following passages, the problems which may arise in introducing new products. (Pay particular attention to difficulties in predicting the future course of events.)[4]

New smoking material

'The increasing evidence of a link between cigarette smoking and ill health led a number of companies to begin research in the 1950s and 1960s into possible substitutes for tobacco. Cigarettes containing New Smoking Material (NSM) were first launched in West Germany and Switzerland. But two brands were withdrawn from the German market in 1975 and these failures led at least two companies – Bayer in Germany and Polystrep in Switzerland – to reduce their R & D expenditure.

'In the UK expenditure was halted by Courtaulds and the Scottish Co-operative Wholesale Society when the Hunter Committee published its guidelines outlining the programme of testing required by manufacturers before being able to market their products. Courtaulds, who had already spent about £1 m. on R & D over the previous ten years, estimated that it would cost a further £2 m. to £3 m. to fulfil these requirements. In addition, a further investment of £10 m. to £20 m. would be required before production could begin.

'This left only two producers when the new product was finally launched in the UK in July 1977 – the Celanese Corporation of USA, whose NSM was used by Rothmans and Gallaher, and a company formed jointly by ICI and Imperial Tobacco. Even these producers found that sales failed to match their expectations, the new brands accounting for only about 2 per cent of the cigarette market at the end of 1977. By February 1978 their share had fallen to 0.6 per cent, one producer had scrapped one million cigarettes (NSM goes stale more quickly than tobacco) and the labour force had been reduced drastically.'

The safety tyre[4]

'Dunlop is to spend £250,000 between now and the end of the year on a relaunch of its Denovo run-flat safety tyres.

'There will be a further £500,000 campaign next year, as Dunlop seeks to increase original equipment sales in line with increased production capacity and push up the replacement market to 100,000 tyres a year by 1980.

'Leyland is to make Denovo available on the Mini Clubman – it is already standard equipment on the Mini 1275 GT – and will also increase the rate of fitment to the Rover and Princess ranges.

'Dunlop has set a target of about 25 per cent for Clubman options, with about 50 per cent on the Rover 3500, but only 10 per cent on the new Rover 2300/2600. Denovo is also available on the Fiat 126 and Mirafiori models.

'Dunlop has been involved in an extensive dealer education programme on the tyre. It has built up stocks at its 740 tyre service outlets and has been helped by Leyland in making car salesmen aware of the extended option.

'Since its introduction in 1972, the Denovo tyre has been modified with a less noisy tread pattern and improved wear. Dunlop now claims that Denovo offers equal handling characteristics to normal tyres with the additional factor of drive-home safety in the event of a blow-out.

'Development of sales has been more difficult, however, and Dunlop has still to find an overseas manufacturer willing to take on a licencing agreement.'

Industrial proteins [5]

'The world population is expected to grow to more than 6 bn. by the year 2000, despite the fact that two-thirds of the present population of some 4 bn. is forced to live on a diet that is seriously deficient in proteins. The major sources of protein in the world at present are soyabean meal and fishmeal, the main protein ingredients used in compound animal feedstuffs. Fishmeal, especially, is a product that is limited by supply as fishstocks in the world's oceans become seriously depleted.

'Many companies, therefore, are convinced that a major market for industrial protein exists. British Petroleum was one of the first companies to solve the problem of producing protein on an industrial scale.

'BP started out on the costly path of protein research in 1959. A French BP research team under Alfred Champignat based at Lavera was looking for a way of taking the wax out of gas oil to make it flow more easily in low temperatures. It was experimenting with biological ways of eating the wax out with yeast bacteria, when it discovered by accident that the waste it was throwing away from the process contained a high percentage of crude protein.

'Yeasts have been used since the earliest times to produce alcoholic drinks, bread and cheese. And more recently batch fermentation processes based on yeasts and carbohydrate wastes such as molasses have been used to produce animal fodder proteins.

'But the BP breakthrough was to launch this form of protein production on a big scale, with a continuous process based on a feedstock available in really large quantities: crude oil.

'In 1963 it built a half-a-tonne per day experimental plant at Lavera near Marseilles, based on gas oil, but this process had the major disadvantage of needing a very severe purification stage when the protein was being harvested. So BP set up a parallel research project at Grangemouth, where its scientists used medicinally pure normal paraffins as the feedstock. This feedstock was readily available from the nearby BP refinery.

'By 1965, pilot plants in both locations were producing proteins for extensive independent toxicity and nutritional tests in Holland. Further development units were built with a capacity of 4,000 tonnes a year at Grangemouth and of 16,000 tonnes a year at Lavera.

'But then BP made what has turned out to be the fatal mistake. In its search for a partner with whom it could share the £40 m. costs of building a commercial scale plant with the much bigger capacity of 100,000 tonnes a year, it found Anic the chemicals arm of ENI, the Italian state hydrocarbons corporation.

'The Italian company seemed an obvious choice. Anic was both interested and had access to Libyan crude oil, which is rich in the normal paraffins needed for the protein process. It was already operating a refinery at Sarroch, Sardinia, where development land was readily available. But perhaps most important for such an untried venture, Sarroch was in an area that qualified for the maximum development grants and low-cost loans from the Italian authorities. The jointly-owned Italproteine company was born.

'The plant was finished in 1976, but it has never been allowed to enter full production. The reasons are obscure and tied into a web of political and medical intrigue with the Italian authorities.

'The decrees allowing the plant to operate were suspended in 1976 and from that day BP has never been told specifically what extra tests were needed to satisfy the authorities.

'The Italians said they had found a residue of n-paraffins in the back fat of pigs fed on Toprina at a level of 70 parts per million. BP does not dispute the finding, but questions its value. Mr Watts, managing director of BP Nutrition, points out that rice on sale in Italy has traces of n-paraffins at 1,400 parts per million. In the US, even the Food and Drug Administration, one of the toughest regulatory authorities in the world, allows an n-paraffins level of 1,500 ppm in bread and 950 ppm in meat. BP has argued consistently that there is no scientific basis for the Italians' complaint.

'The plant was allowed to operate for the commissioning stage at the beginning of 1977, but then it was closed on the further ground that dust emission from the plant was too high. In fact, says BP, the dust level was one-fortieth of that allowed for other plants such as cement works in Italy.

'Apart from passing the US and United Nations specifications, BP has had Toprina passed for use in every EEC country except Italy, as well as in Spain, Portugal, South Africa, Venezuela and Switzerland.

'Hector Watts is unequivocal in his condemnation of the actions of the Italian authorities. "It is an absolute scandal that it should be brought to nothing for reasons that do not have any scientific justification whatsoever."'

7.7

In the light of the passage below, discuss 'product innovation in the market for shaving equipment'. Say what you think are the advantages and disadvantages of innovation, and list the factors which contribute to the success of innovations.[6]

'The razor war has as sharp an edge today as it did in the early 1960s, Wilkinson Sword, which has been slugging it out for many years with Gillette, now finds itself in trouble on another front. This time it is a French company, Bic, owned by Baron Marcel Bich, whose disposable razor is having a spectacular effect on the market. Because of the intensity of the competition, Wilkinson announced earlier this week that it is cutting back employment at its Northumberland factory by one third to 850 and reducing production from 730 m. blades a year to 550 m.

'In 1961 it was Wilkinson which became the overnight sensation of the industry. Its PTFE-coated blade was superior to anything the competition had to offer; Gillette was caught flatfooted. Wilkinson's blade production went from 50 m. to 500 m. a year in the space of three years. But Gillette's resources, both in the US and outside, were such that when it finally introduced a comparable blade in 1963, its production rapidly dwarfed that of Wilkinson.

'Four years after the PTFE blade, a major innovation hit the market. It was called the "systems" blade. Instead of a traditional-type razor made up of three parts, a "systems" razor offered a light plastic handle with a cartridge head that could be inserted and discarded after four or five days.

'Gillette's model was the Techmatic, with a cartridge containing a continuous band of stainless steel. It was brought out to compete with the traditional double-edged blade and achieved instant popularity in the US and

Europe. Wilkinson's bonded twin blade in the mid-70s sparked Gillette into producing the GII which now rides in the top sales listing of the company's products. Both have the twin-blade cartridge and run at a similar price of around 25p–30p.

'Just over three years ago Baron Marcel Bich came on to the razor scene. He had already achieved fame – and fortune – from manufacturing Bic pens, and he introduced the cheap, throwaway razor that could be used for five days and then thrown away, handle and all.

'Production began first in Greece, then crept stealthily into other markets of the world. Today it claims 14 per cent of the UK wet-shave market.

'Bic spent about £200,000 on press and television advertising in the UK in 1976, £300,000 last year and £100,000 in the first quarter of 1978. The throwaway has been sold on its qualities of cheapness – a blade costs about 5p – and convenience.

'Gone are the days, says Bic, when a man has time to fiddle about with a razor in the morning. The day of disposable is here – and here to stay.

'Wilkinson reacted quickly to the threat, since the disposable was clearly going to hit the double-edged blade. They launched a modified bonded-blade razor as a disposable and though Wilkinson could not produce a cheaper product, it lost no time in telling the shaving public that "quality" was the name of the game.

'Gillette took some time to react to the successful launch of Bic's disposable. It was only after it had seen Wilkinson spend a small amount of money promoting its product in the UK and watched Bic's sales climb in the US and Europe, that Gillette was forced in January this year to launch a disposable. Again, it was a modification of its GII and like Wilkinson, Gillette promoted "quality – not quantity".

'Wilkinson also hopes to arrest Bic's rapid progress. A new disposable prototype blade is about to enter the razor war. It will first be marketed in Europe where disposables have achieved up to 50 per cent of blade sales and where monitoring will be easier. It is a choice Wilkinson has been forced into taking as double-edged blade sales have drifted back in popularity and as Gillette drives further into the systems market.

'Next month Gillette will launch a new "system" on to the UK market that has been highly successful in the US for the last two years. The pivot razor, or swivel-head, is an upmarket GII which is not only twin-bladed but is flexible enough to move closely around the contours of the face. It will be expensive, £2.00 or so, the company says.'

Notes

1. The price elasticity of demand is usually negative, i.e. a decrease (increase) in price causes the quantity demanded to rise (fall). Consequently it is conventional, for the sake of simplicity, to omit the negative sign. In Table 7.1 the elasticity should, strictly speaking, be -2 and -0.5.
2. The information used in this case was extracted from the *Financial Times*, 19 December 1977.
3. The information used in this case was extracted from the *Financial Times*, 26 January 1978.
4. The information used in this case was extracted from the *Financial Times*, 16 November 1977.
5. The information used in this case was extracted from the *Financial Times*, 20 July 1978.
6. The information used in this case was extracted from the *Financial Times*, 16 September 1978.

8 Policies to reduce costs

Introduction

Having discussed in the previous chapter policies intended to increase revenue, we now consider the alternative approach to increased profitability, namely a reduction in costs. One way of reducing costs is to reduce the volume of output. But there is, of course, no guarantee that this would increase profitability since revenue would also fall (unless the firm could increase price to compensate for the fall in sales volume). Indeed one would normally expect a fall in output to lead to a reduction in profitability. We shall, therefore, ignore this possibility and confine our attention to a reduction in cost when output (per period) is either unchanged or increasing, i.e. we are concerned with a reduction in the average cost per unit of output.

A reduction in average cost when output is unchanged

If the volume of output is unchanged, costs can be reduced by the more efficient utilisation of resources. If we consider a given resource – labour, for example – an increase in efficiency involves an increase in the ratio of output to input (in this case man-hours). Another term for this increase in the output/input ratio is an increase in (labour) productivity.

It might be possible to increase labour productivity in a number of ways, e.g. by better training, encouraging workers to work harder, simplifying the work, providing more capital for each worker.

In some instances an increase in the productivity of one resource, or factor of production, can be achieved without changing the quantity of any other factor employed. But frequently this is not possible. In the last example given above an increase in labour productivity required more capital (e.g. machines) to be employed. In such instances, although the cost of labour per unit of output would fall, the total cost, the cost of all resources, might not do so.

Exactly the same argument applies to any of the firm's resources. For example, the output produced by the existing machinery might be increased by increasing the number of workers per machine, or by running the machines for more hours per week. But this is likely to cause a *reduction* in output per man-

63

hour. Similarly it may be possible to reduce the scrap rate, and thus the total amount of material used, by reducing the speed of operation of machines. But this would, of course, reduce the output per machine. As a final example, note that savings in many areas – the use of men, machines and materials – may result from an intensification of research and development activity, but that this intensification itself involves the utilisation of additional resources.

We can see then that because of the inter-relationships which exist between different types of resources, a firm has to consider the change in the total volume of resources involved. In other words an increase in efficiency implies an increase in the ratio of output to *total* input. Since it is impossible to add together inputs with different units of measurements (men, machines, materials, etc.), total input is normally measured in terms of its cost. An increase in efficiency implies an increase in the output/cost ratio or, putting the relationship the other way round, a reduction in the cost per unit of output, the average cost.

The effect on average cost of an increase in output

We considered in the previous section a range of factors which might reduce the average cost when output per period does not change. All of these factors can apply when output increases. Moreover, additional factors may also come into operation in these circumstances. Since these are discussed in some detail in Chapter 24, we confine ourselves to a brief summary of two major factors.

First, an increase in output may enable the firm to buy inputs – especially machines and materials – in larger quantities and thus more cheaply. Second, firms often operate with some spare capacity, especially in machinery. Consequently, when output increases, a less than proportionate increase may be required in some inputs, i.e. the output/input ratio increases.

Summary: policies required to increase profitability

As the discussion in this and the previous chapter has made clear, many different policies may be adopted in order to increase profitability. As a broad generalisation we can say that when the aim is to achieve an increase in revenue, emphasis will be given to marketing policies such as pricing, product differentiation and the introduction of new products; when the aim is to reduce average cost, emphasis will be given to purchasing, production and manpower policies, e.g. work design, recruitment, training.

It follows that the relative importance of the various departments or functions within a firm is also likely to vary from time to time. At one time attention will be centred on the marketing department, at another time on the personnel department, and so forth. However, one of the factors influencing the success of business organisations – and indeed of any type of organisation – is the ability to ensure that, even though a certain objective may lead to the contribution of one department being emphasised, the policies all other departments also contribute to that objective.

For example, an objective of increasing sales may emphasise the contribution of the marketing department in searching for new outlets, identifying a need for different products, advertising, and so forth. But all of this activity will be in vain unless the purchasing department can buy additional materials at an acceptable price, the production department can re-schedule production, and the personnel department can engage and train sufficient new workers.

Assignments

8.1

Say whether each of the following statements is true or false:

1. An increase in productivity involves an increase in the ratio of output to input.
2. An increase in the productivity of one factor must be accompanied by a reduction in total cost.
3. An increase in production does not always involve an increase in productivity.
4. An increase in efficiency implies an increase in the ratio of output to total input.

8.2

In which of the situations, A–E, does labour productivity increase between week 1 and week 2?

	Number of workers		Volume of output	
	Week 1	Week 2	Week 1	Week 2
A	100	105	100	105
B	100	110	100	108
C	100	98	100	100
D	100	96	100	98
E	100	100	100	102

8.3

The information below was taken from the prospectus issued by Saga Holidays Ltd when it became a public company. On the basis of this information:

1. Identify the ways in which Saga has differentiated its product from those of its competitors.
2. Identify any other of Saga's policies which have contributed to its success.
3. Identify any other factors which have been conducive to Saga's success.

History

The activities of the Group have their origins in the hotel business started in 1950 by Mr Sidney De Haan, the present chairman. Mr De Haan wished to fill his thirty-six-bed hotel in Folkstone in the off season and recognised that retired

65

people would be the group most able to take holidays during that period.

The concept of marketing off-season holidays directly to retired people was immediately successful and by 1958 the number of holiday-makers had reached a sufficient size to warrant the chartering of special trains. This was the beginning of the close relationship still maintained with British Rail.

In 1959 the Company was formed to acquire Mr De Haan's travel business and in 1960, in order to concentrate on this business, he disposed of his hotel interests.

During the 1960s the Company's business and reputation grew steadily and contacts were increasingly developed with clubs and organisations concerned with the welfare of retired people. In 1966 for the first time the Group began to market its holidays under the name of Saga and promoted sales through its own regular publication, Saga News.

As the disposable income of pensioners gradually increased through improved pension arrangements, the Group identified a demand for overseas holidays and accordingly cruise and overseas holidays were added to the programme in 1968 and 1970 respectively.

Business

The Group's business is principally that of an operator of off-season inclusive holidays for those over the age of sixty, offering a wide range of UK, overseas and cruise holidays. It also owns and operates three hotels in the UK, two of which are used almost exclusively for holidays operated by the Group.

The Group's management has over the past 25 years built up considerable expertise in devising, marketing and operating holidays for people aged over sixty and the directors believe that, in terms of the number of holidays taken, the Group is not only amongst the largest tour operators based in the UK, but is also the predominant such operator specialising in holidays for the over sixties.

The table below shows the number of inclusive holidays taken with the Group over the past five years:

Year ended 30 June	Number of holidays
1973	39,960
1974	52,600
1975	84,830
1976	121,600
1977	162,050

Pricing

The concept of the Group's business is based upon the ability of retired people to take holidays outside the peak period and thus to benefit from the cost savings attributable to the mass availability of transport and accommodation at that time. The strength of the Group's purchasing power, coupled with its high reputation, enables it to acquire large amounts of transport and accommodation at low rates. By specialising in off-season holidays the directors believe that, whilst maintaining adequate trading margins, the Group's prices are generally lower, and in some cases substantially lower, than those of comparable off-season holidays operated by other companies.

The directors have made a comparison as at 1 March 1978 of the Group's 1978 prices of two-week overseas holidays with those shown in the latest principal summer brochures of the other tour-operator members of The Association of British Travel Agents Limited with a turnover not less than that of the Group. This comparison shows that in respect of the 86 daytime flights using London airports on holidays for which those tour operators use the same hotel during the same weeks as the Group:

1. The average price (including the amount charged for airport taxes) for the 86 departures is £142.11 per holiday, being 12.3 per cent more than the Group's average price of £126.50; and
2. in all cases the Group offers the same items in the package price as the other operators but also includes return rail fare within the UK, transport across London and holiday insurance: none of these items is stated to be included by other operators.

Marketing

The Group markets its holidays directly to the customer and as a result generally expects to receive approximately 70 per cent of its bookings direct. In this way the Group avoid much of the cost associated with marketing holidays through travel agents, bookings through which have never exceeded 35 per cent of the total holidays taken in any one year.

The Group advertises in national and local newspapers and issues brochures and other literature to people on its mailing list. Advertising and promotional costs have never been more than 3 per cent of turnover and in the Group's financial year ended 30 June 1977 amounted to only 1.9 per cent.

New links are being continually established with organisations with a view to arranging group travel. Amongst those organisations whose members have made party bookings for 1978 are The Civil Service Retirement Fellowship, Unilever Pensioners' Club, North Gas Retirement Fellowship and the Post Office Retired Staff Association.

A significant part of the Group's business is derived from the large number of film shows and lectures about its holidays which are given throughout the year by the Group's representatives. In addition, the Group's literature is displayed in many public libraries, Citizens Advice Bureaux, Tourist Information Centres and certain offices of Age Concern.

Saga Club and Saga News

As a means of establishing and maintaining contact with those over the age of sixty, a scheme was introduced in 1966 for people in this age group to subscribe to the Saga Club, through which the Group distributes to subscribers its main holiday brochures twice a year, a copy of the quarterly magazine, Saga News, and specially prepared information sheets on matters of interest to the over sixties.

Saga News, which has a circulation in excess of 500,000 copies, contains within its sixteen pages articles of general interest to retired people, up-to-date holiday information and articles on legal, financial, medical and other matters. A feature of the magazine is its 'Matchmaker' service which puts lonely people in touch with others in a similar situation.

As many subscribers receive the magazine in their capacity as representatives of associations, the directors believe that through Saga News the Group is in touch with more than 1,000,000 people aged over sixty.

Range of holidays

The table below shows the division of turnover between the group's UK, overseas and cruise holidays in the five years ended 30 June 1977:

Year ended 30 June	UK		Overseas		Cruise		Total
	£'000	%	£'000	%	£'000	%	£'000
1973	948	72	124	10	237	18	1,309
1974	1,254	64	343	18	342	18	1,939
1975	1,784	42	1,437	33	1,075	25	4,296
1976	2,813	36	3,154	40	1,829	24	7,796
1977	4,417	34	5,934	46	2,666	20	13,017

Trading figures

The Group's trading figures for the five years ended 30 June 1977 are as follows:

Year ended 30 June	Turnover £'000	Profit before taxation £'000	Number of inclusive holidays taken
1973	1,309	89	39,960
1974	1,939	129	52,600
1975	4,296	342	84,830
1976	7,796	614	121,600
1977	13,017	1,316	162,050

8.4

Discuss, with reference to any firm with which you are familiar, the contribution made by any three departments during the past year towards an increase in that firm's profitability.

8.5

Examine the newspaper files of your college or local library for the last four weeks and prepare a report on the policies listed below of any firms whose activities are reported. (You will probably find the *Financial Times, The Times, Daily Telegraph, Guardian* and *Economist* of most use.)

1. Pricing.
2. Product differentiation (including advertising).

3. The introduction of new products.
4. Increases in productivity.
5. Cost reduction (not covered in 4).

In your report you should state the main objectives that each policy is intended to achieve. You should also discuss other possible effects of the policies, e.g. the effect on employees, competitors and customers.

8.6

1. Prepare a report showing, for the town in which you live, the changes during the past ten years in the number of specialist shops – bookshops, gramophone record shops, chemists, bread shops, etc. (your local library should be able to provide information in the form of trade directories, membership of the chambers of trade and commerce, etc.).
2. Conduct interviews with the owners or managers of four or five specialist shops and prepare a brief report summarising (a) the state of competition in their markets, (b) how they are attempting to maintain or increase their profitability.

9 Organisations and the formation of contracts-I

Introduction

As noted in Chapter 2, the dealings that an organisation has with consumers, clients, suppliers and other organisations have to be seen within the context of the law. Legal rules are usually thought of as constraints that prevent individuals and organisations from doing what they want to do. This is true in many cases: the considerable amount of consumer protection law prevents organisations from evading liability for producing defective goods or marketing them in a misleading way; employment law prohibits unfair and wrongful dismissal of employees. The person who wants to carry on his own business in his own way will find himself hedged about with regulations concerning the safety of his premises, the sort of business he can operate from those premises and sometimes even the price he can charge for the products he produces on those premises.

But to treat law as a purely negative force is to see only one side of the coin. The manufacturer who complains because meeting minimum legal requirements prevents him from marketing cheaper goods will himself want to use the law for his own purposes when, for example, he wants to be sure that the supplier who has agreed to let him have the raw materials can be compelled to honour the agreement. Law is not solely prohibitive: it is a way of ordering affairs, and particularly business affairs. It provides a framework for regulating relationships, so that each party knows or should know exactly where he stands in relation to another.

In the great majority of transactions the parties will be ignorant of the fact that they are legally involved with each other until there is a dispute. Then each wants to have law on his side. Nevertheless, far more agreements are carried out than are broken, and it would be a mistake to see law only in terms of remedying disputes. In this and the next chapters we will be considering the law of contract from both these angles, seeing on the one hand how contracts are formed and used to regulate affairs and on the other what rights each party has in the event of disputes.

Contract as a voluntary bargain

Contracts are agreements that have legal consequences. They are in essence voluntary transactions which happen because the parties choose to enter into them, not because they are imposed on them from outside.

At first sight it would appear to be a simple matter to decide whether two people have reached agreement. If Smith wants to sell his car and Jones wants to buy it there is no problem in deciding that there is an agreement. At least, there is no problem if Smith tells Jones that he wants to sell and Jones tells Smith that he wants to buy. There must be outward signs of the agreement.

But let us look at a problem. X Co writes to Y Co offering to sell ten tons of scrap metal. One of the conditions included in X's letter is that the goods must be paid for in advance. Y Co writes in reply that it accepts the offer but that it will only pay on delivery. Are the parties in agreement, and if so what are they agreed upon?

The parties are obviously agreed on the sale, but when is the metal to be paid for? Is it to be paid for in advance or on delivery? We shall see shortly that failure to agree on the time of payment (or any other matter) prevents there being any agreement at all in law.

The example just given involves a contract for the sale of goods, but there are many other types of contract. Contracts are made daily in such common transactions as calling in a plumber to mend a washing machine, taking a bus ride, buying a newspaper or taking on a new employee.

Most contracts can be made quite informally. Only a few types need to be made formally. Contracts for the sale of land, for example, must have written evidence of their terms before they can be enforced by the parties.

Contracts are commonly made without any words being spoken at all. For instance, a person buying a newspaper from a stall is making a contract in law when he puts down his money and takes his paper even though nothing is said.

The common view, that an agreement is not legally binding because nothing has been written down, is a fallacy. It will often be to the advantage of the parties to have the terms of the contract written down and signed, because this will make it easier to prove what was agreed, but it is not necessary for the validity of a contract.

In one sense to say that a contract is a voluntary agreement is misleading. For the customer who has mains electricity connected to his house, there is little that is voluntary about the terms on which he agrees to pay for the electricity. Either he accepts the uniform terms on which electricity is supplied or he makes do without electricity. Similarly the firm wanting to secure a Government contract will not be free to negotiate the terms it might prefer: it may have to give way to the superior bargaining power of the Government or run the risk of losing the contract altogether. The freedom to enter into contracts on whatever terms the parties choose has also been considerably eroded in consumer protection legislation. This will be discussed in Chapter 19.

Nevertheless, even though the description of a contract as a voluntary agreement is often somewhat unrealistic nowadays, it is important to appreciate that the idea of contracts being made by parties of equal bargaining power, free to decide on the terms of their agreement, has influenced the development of the law of contract. It is these rules, as to the formation, contents and discharge of contracts, that we must look at in this and the next four chapters.

For the formation of a valid contract, the following elements must be present:

71

1. Agreement, generally demonstrated by offer and acceptance.
2. Consideration.
3. Intention to create legal relations.
4. Contractual capacity in each of the parties.
5. No vitiating factors such as duress, undue influence, misrepresentation, mistake, illegality.

We look in the remainder of this chapter at the first two of these elements.

Agreement: offer and acceptance

It is usual to analyse agreement into offer and acceptance. When an offer is accepted the contract comes into existence. It is often important, as we shall see, not only to decide whether the parties have reached agreement, but also to pinpoint the exact moment at which they did so.

1. Offer

Clearly, if it only requires an acceptance to translate an offer into a binding legal obligation, we must first be able to recognise an offer. A useful definition is that an offer is an expression by one party of his willingness to be bound as soon as it is accepted. We can see immediately that if a party is merely making inquiries or testing the other party's response he is not in law making an offer, because he is not showing any readiness to be bound. He may only be asking for information or he may be inviting the other party to make an offer to him. Such an offer to negotiate or offer to receive an offer is termed 'an invitation to treat'.

If A wishes to sell his car to B, he may say, 'What will you give me for my car?' Obviously he is not agreeing to sell the car at whatever price B names. He is merely asking B to make him an offer, to suggest a price which A can then consider. On the other hand, if A says 'I will sell you my car for £1,000', he is clearly making an offer in law. He has demonstrated in words, even though he has not used the words 'offer' or 'contract', that he is willing to be legally bound to sell his car once B says he will buy it for that price.

It is always necessary to look at the whole circumstances to decide whether a statement is an offer or an invitation to treat. Just as there may be an offer in law without the word 'offer' being used (or indeed without any words at all being used), the use of the word 'offer' is not conclusive as to the existence of a legal offer. We shall look at some examples of common situations and see how the courts approach the problem of deciding whether a statement is an offer or an invitation to treat.

Advertisements have generally been held to be invitations to treat rather than offers. In *Partridge v. Crittenden*, P placed an advertisement in a periodical which stated 'Bramblefinch cocks and hens, 25s. each'. He was prosecuted for unlawfully offering for sale a wild live bird contrary to the provisions of the Protection of Birds Act 1954. The prosecution failed. As Lord Parker said, 'I think that when one is dealing with advertisements and circulars, unless indeed they came from manufacturers, there is business sense in their being construed as invitations to treat and not offers for sale.' Mr Partridge had invited offers to buy, not offered for sale.

This is not an invariable rule, however. Advertisements of rewards for doing particular acts, for example finding a lost ring, are generally held to be offers, not invitations to treat. Similarly in *Carlill v. Carbolic Smoke Ball Co* an advertisement that promised £100 to anyone who bought and used the Carbolic Smoke Ball as directed and still caught influenza was held to be an offer which could ripen into a contract with anyone who accepted it. In this type of case, it would be unrealistic to say that the advertisement was inviting offers from the public.

It is well established that displaying goods for sale, either in a shop window or on a supermarket shelf, is an invitation to treat and not an offer. The case of *Pharmaceutical Society of Great Britain v. Boots Cash Chemists* is a good illustration of this.

In the defendant's self service shop, the customer took goods off the shelf, put them in a basket and took them to the cashier's desk where the customer paid. Under the Pharmacy and Poisons Act 1938 certain drugs could only be lawfully sold under the supervision of a registered pharmacist. A registered pharmacist was present at the cash desk, but not where the goods were on display on the shelves. If the goods were sold (i.e. contract was made) at the cash desk, Boots would not be in breach of the Act. If however the contract was made when they were taken from the shelves, they would be infringing the Act. The Court of Appeal held that the display of the goods was merely an invitation to treat. The offer was made by the customer at the cash desk.

Particular problems arise where transactions are protracted and there are many detailed terms to be agreed upon. This is often the case in contracts for the sale of land, and an example will show the difficulty of drawing the line between an offer capable of giving rise to a contract and a statement that is only part of continuing negotiations.

In *Harvey v. Facey*: A telegraphed to B 'Will you sell us Bumper Hall Pen? (a piece of land) Telegraph lowest cash price'. B telegraphed back: 'lowest cash price £900'. A replied 'We agree to buy for £900 asked by you'. A sued B to enforce the sale. It was held that there was no contract to be enforced. B's telegram was merely an indication of the minimum price should they decide to sell. It was not an offer which could be accepted.

The difficulty of deciding whether parties have passed the negotiating stage does not apply only to sales of land. It will be a problem wherever the transaction is a complex one and where an agreement on price is only one of many items to be agreed. For example, if the contract concerns the long-term hire of a very large and complex piece of custom-built machinery to be used in a factory, the hiring price may only be a minor consideration when compared with the problems involved in deciding on the precise specification for the machinery and the respective rights and duties of the parties during the period of hire.

Once an offer is accepted, a contract comes into existence. The offer must however still be there to be accepted. Offers do not last for ever. They can come to an end through the passage of time or by revocation. The length of time that an offer remains open depends on the terms of the offer. If it is stated to be open for a fixed period of time (e.g. 'Reply now. This offer closes on 31 July') at the end of that period it will lapse and can no longer be accepted. If no period of time is fixed for the offer to remain open, the law implies that it will remain open for a reasonable length of time. What is reasonable will depend on the subject matter of the contract. For example, in *Ramsgate Victoria Hotel Co v. Montefiore* an offer to purchase shares was held to have lapsed after a period of five months, so that it could not then be accepted, and it might well have lapsed much earlier. In some circumstances, for example a rapidly moving market, an offer may lapse within a period of hours or minutes. On the other hand if the parties are negotiating for a large piece of land the period for which the offer will remain open will be longer, particularly if the person to whom the offer is made shows a continuing intention to accept the offer when all other arrangements are settled (*Manchester Diocesan Council for Education v. Commercial and General Investments Ltd*).

An offer may be revoked at any moment before acceptance (*Payne v. Cave*). This is so even where it is stated to be open for a particular length of time.

The person to whom the offer is made ('the offeree') is entitled to assume that the offer is still open until he is notified that it is revoked. The person making the offer ('the offeror') must communicate the revocation to the offeree. It is not enough for him merely to change his mind. The offeror may revoke his offer by saying expressly that his offer is no longer open, or it may be implied from what he says or does; e.g. if A has offered to sell his house to B and then says that he has sold it to someone else, this will revoke his previous offer to sell the house to B. Revocation communicated by a third party will be equally effective. This does not mean that the offeree has to take notice of any scraps of gossip that he hears. For example, if B overhears A's neighbour saying that A has sold his house, this is not necessarily sufficient to revoke the offer, but being told the same thing by A's estate agent will (*Dickinson v. Dodds*).

We shall see that for an acceptance to be valid it must accept all the terms of the offer and introduce none. An acceptance which does not comply with this rule is not in law an acceptance, but a counter-offer. A counter-offer puts an end to the original offer which cannot subsequently be accepted. This is illustrated by the case of *Hyde v. Wrench*. The defendant offered to sell some land to the plaintiff for £1,000. The plaintiff said that he would give £950 for it, which the defendant refused. The defendant then purported to accept the original offer of £1,000. It was held that he was too late. In offering to pay £950 he had made a counter-offer and this put an end to the original offer and, as he had rejected it, the plaintiff could do nothing. Not every inquiry the offeree makes will amount to a counter-offer. It is only natural that he may want further information before he decides whether to accept or reject, and this will not necessarily destroy the original offer. In *Stevenson v. MacLean* the defendant offered to sell the plaintiffs some iron at a cash price per ton. The plaintiffs asked whether they could take delivery over two months at that price. It was held that this request for imformation did not put an end to the offer.

Finally, the death of the offeror probably puts an end to the offer unless the contract is one that can be carried out by the offeror's personal respresentatives, e.g. for the payment of money, and the offeree is unaware of his death. The death of the offeree brings the offer to an end.

2. Acceptance

An offer requires an acceptance to produce a binding contract. To be valid an acceptance must coincide exactly with the terms of the offer. It must accept all the terms of the offer and introduce no new ones. It is for this reason that the example given on page 71 does not produce a contract. X Co offered to sell goods, payment to be made in advance. The purported acceptance stipulated that payment was to be made on delivery. It did not accept all the terms of the original offer and it introduced a new term. For this reason it takes effect, not as an acceptance, but as a counter-offer. As we have just noted, a counter-offer destroys the original offer so that Y Co could not later accept the offer by X Co. Y Co have made a new offer which X Co is free to accept or reject as it chooses.

Thus apparently simple transactions may be more complicated than is immediately apparent. There have been a number of recent cases in which the question whether a reply constitutes an acceptance have had to be decided, e.g. in *BRS v Arthur C. Crutchley*. Here the plaintiffs delivered a consignment of whisky to the defendants for storage. Their driver handed the defendants a delivery note purporting to include the plaintiff's 'conditions of carriage'. The note was stamped by the defendant 'Received under (the defendant's) conditions'. It was held that this was not an acceptance but a counter-offer which had in fact been accepted by the plaintiffs' handing over the goods. Therefore it was the defendant and not the plaintiff's conditions which provided the term of the agreement between the parties. This was important because the defendant's conditions included a term limiting liability for goods lost while in storage.

If the offeree wants to accept the offer he must do something to indicate his acceptance: he must communicate it. The communication of acceptance will usually be by oral or written statements, but conduct can constitute acceptance too. If one acts in reliance on an offer it is sometimes the case that one's actions constitute communicated acceptance. In *Brogden v. Metropolitan Railway Co.* B regularly supplied coal to the Railway Company. A written contract between them was never concluded but the court held that the Company had accepted B's offer by conduct.

One cannot however dictate to an offeree that his silence will be taken to be acceptance. It would be clearly unfair to allow an offeror to force an offeree to notify his intention not to accept. In *Felthouse v. Bindley* F offered to buy his nephew's horse. He made an offer in a letter which said 'If I hear no more about him, I shall consider the horse mine.' The nephew did nothing and a few weeks later the horse was sold to X. F argued that the horse was his but the court held there was no contract between the uncle and the nephew.

It is interesting to note here that Parliament has recently passed the Unsolicited Goods and Services Act 1971 and 1975 to further and strengthen the position of an individual to whom a tradesman sends goods without any prior request. Although at common law the customer is not obliged to return them, if he accepts them he is bound to pay. Under these statutes a tradesman may, in certain circumstances, be treated as making a gift of the goods to the customer.

The method by which acceptance is made may be important. The offeror may stipulate that the acceptance must be made in a particular way and in no other. If he does, then for an acceptance to be valid it must be made in that way and in no other.

If the offeror states the method of acceptance but does not say that this is the only way in which acceptance may be made, the rule is that acceptance may be made in that way or any other way equally effective. For example, in *Tinn v. Hoffmann* where the offeror said 'reply by return of post', it was said that the offer could be accepted by message, telegram or telegraph, provided in each case this did not take longer than return of post. The reason that the offeror had specified a method of acceptance was the importance of a speedy reply.

It should be noted that a specified method may be implied. The sending of an offer by telegram implies that a speedy reply is wanted, so that an acceptance by second class post would not be valid.

Because the moment of acceptance will determine the time when the contract is made (and this may often be vital) we must look at the time at which the acceptance takes effect. The rule is that an acceptance takes effect only when it is received by the offeror. This applies where parties are talking over the 'phone, or face to face, or in any instantaneous or virtually instantaneous form of communication such as Telex (*Entores v. Miles Far East Corporation*).

When the parties use the post a different rule may apply, which is that the posting of a letter may constitute the acceptance (*Henthorn v. Fraser*). The contract thus comes into being not when the acceptance comes to the attention of the offeror but when the offeree posts it.

But the restrictions on this rule should be emphasised. The rule will *not* apply if it can be gathered from the circumstances that the offeree requires actual receipt or if it was not in the expectation of the parties that the post would be used.

The rule is a compromise and can work somewhat harshly. If, for example, the letter of acceptance is lost in the post, the acceptance will have taken effect and the offeror will be bound even though he does not know it. He can, of course, safeguard his own interests by making it a requirement that the acceptance must be received before it can take effect. It is probably the case that if the reason for the letter not reaching the offeror is the fault of the offeree (e.g. because he has carelessly misaddressed the letter) the 'postal rule' does not apply.

It should here be noted that there may be no contract even where there is an apparent offer and acceptance. It is for the parties to decide what they agree upon. The courts will only enforce agreements that have already been made and will not take upon themselves the task of filling in gaps that the parties have left. The danger for the contracting parties is that if they leave undecided vital parts of their contract, the whole contract may be unenforceable.

This is what happened in *Scammell Ltd v. Ouston*, where an agreement to buy a vehicle on hire purchase terms was held unenforceable. Hire purchase terms are so varied that it was impossible for the court to know what the parties had intended and so there was held to be no valid contract. A contract, to be valid, must be spelt out with sufficient certainty for an independent observer to adjudicate in the event of a dispute. This does not mean however, that the courts are anxious to strike down bargains unless every last detail is agreed. On the contrary, wherever possible they try to uphold bargains that have been made.

It may be that an apparently vague term such as the sale of timber 'at a fair specification', whilst having no meaning to the layman, is sufficiently precise within the timber trade. In such a case, the court will assume that the parties intended normal trade practice to be a term of the contract (*Hillas v. Arcos*).

In other commercial contracts the main points may be agreed at the outset, but other matters may be left to be decided at a later date. For example, the parties might agree to buy and sell 'at a price to be agreed from time to time'. This phrase is so vague as to render the whole contract unenforceable, because it is impossible to decide the rights of the parties if they fail to agree. On the other hand if they add 'or in default of agreement to be decided by X' and X is an independent adjudicator the agreement would stand. The parties have themselves provided the machinery for making certain something which was initially left vague. It may even be possible to imply that the parties intended a reasonable price to be paid, and this may be enough if there is sufficiently cogent evidence of what is a reasonable price in the particular business conerned.

Consideration

The picture we have given so far of the formation of a contract is incomplete. There is a further factor that must be present before agreements can be enforced as legal contracts. This factor is consideration.

Every promise (unless it is executed as a deed, that is, a written document that is signed, sealed and delivered) must be supported by consideration. The essence of consideration is the idea of a bargain. The law will not enforce promises that are given for nothing in return. If A promises to give his car to B and fails to do so, B can do nothing about it. If A and B agree that A will sell his car to B for £500 and A fails to do so, B can sue A. The reason is that in the second case B has given consideration for A's promise to hand over his car.

Consideration has been described as 'the price for which the promise of the other is bought' or as consisting of *either* some benefit conferred on the promisor (the person making the promise) *or* some detriment suffered by the promisee (the person to whom it is made). In each case consideration may take the form of an act or the promise of an act. The former is called 'executed' consideration and the latter 'executory' consideration.

An example will illustrate how the doctrine of consideration applies. If A agrees to paint B's house for £50 and fails to do so, B will only be able to enforce A's promise if B has given consideration for the promise, that is, if B has conferred some benefit on A or suffered a detriment himself. This is clearly satisfied here, because he has himself promised to pay £50. B can consequently sue A for any loss that B has suffered through A's failure to paint the house. If A had painted B's house and B had failed to pay, whether A could sue B would again depend on whether A had given consideration for B's promise to pay. This A has clearly done because he promised to paint the house.

Consideration must be supplied by the person to whom the promise is made. For example, if A promised to build B a shed in return for B paying him £100 there is good consideration for the promise but if A promises to build C a shed if B pays him £100 C cannot sue on the agreement if A fails to build. C has not supplied consideration.

Not every act or promise of an act will count as consideration. For consideration to be sufficient to support a contract it must be of some economic value. A promise to do something in consideration of natural love and affection, for example, is not enforceable as the consideration is not economically quantifiable.

This does not mean, though, that there must be adequate consideration in the sense of a good bargain, with a realistic price being paid. As long as the consideration has some economic value it will be sufficient in law.

Hence an agreement to sell a factory for £1 is enforceable, whereas a bare promise to give the factory away is not. But it is only in these extreme cases that the doctrine of consideration seems artificial. In most cases it will accord with common sense to enforce agreements where both parties are getting something out of the transaction and not to enforce idle promises.

Sometimes what appears at first sight to be consideration is not sufficient in law. This is so with regard to past consideration, that is when the act to be done is already past when the promise is made. An example should make this point clear. In *Re McArdle* the father of a family died and left his money equally between his children. One of them did some work on the house that formed part of his estate. Later the children got together and entered into a written agreement which provided that she should be reimbursed the money which she had spent in doing the work. The agreement was held to be unenforceable because the only consideration she had given was past. She was undertaking to do nothing new in return for the promise. There is, however, an exception to this rule where work is done at someone's request on the understanding that it is to be paid for later. Such a promise to pay is binding (*Lampleigh v. Braithwait*).

Just as past consideration is insufficient, so is a promise to do something that a person is already bound to do by a public duty or because he is already bound to do it by a contract with the promisor, e.g. if a policeman promises to prevent a breach of the peace near X's home if X pays him £10 he cannot sue for the £10 when he does so: he is already under a duty to prevent such occurrences. Likewise an employee who has agreed to carry out certain work cannot enforce a promise made by his employer to pay extra for the employee carrying out his job – something he is already contractually bound to do.

We must now look at a specific though important problem in this area of law. Imagine that A asks B to repair his car for £50. B does this but at that time A has only £20. He offers this to B, saying that it is all that he has and, being a considerate man, B accepts this in full settlement of the debt. What is B's position? Can he now, or in six months' time, sue A for the other £30?

Following on the principles we have just outlined, the answer must be that he can. A's contractual obligation was to pay £50. He has not fulfilled this because he only paid £20. B promised to accept this in full settlement of the debt, i.e. he promised not to sue for the balance. This will only be binding if A (the promisee) gave consideration. A has done nothing in return. In fact he has done even less than he was contractually bound to do. The promise is as a result worthless and B can still sue A for £30. Had A given something of economic value other than that which he was already obliged to give, or had he paid it in some way advantageous to B other than as he was supposed to under the contract, the promise would have been binding on B.

These rules were laid down in 1602 in *Pinnel's Case* and can be summarised for our purposes as follows:

(a) Payment of a lesser sum on the day due does not discharge the debt.
(b) Payment of a lesser sum on an earlier day or in a different place at the request of the creditor does discharge the debt.
(c) Payment of a greater sum at a later date discharges the debt.
(d) Payment in kind, i.e. in goods or services instead of money, does discharge the debt.

In each case except the first, the debtor is conferring some benefit, and is suffering some detriment over and above the duties under the contract.

These rules received the approval of the House of Lords in *Foakes v. Beer*. Mrs Beer sued Dr Foakes and obtained judgement under which he was bound to pay her a certain sum. A judgement debt carries interest from the date of the judgement, but it was agreed by Mrs Beer that if Dr Foakes paid back the debt by instalments, she would not require him to pay the interest. This he did, whereupon she tried to sue him for the interest due. She was held entitled to sue. He had given no consideration for her promise not to sue for the interest since she was already entitled to the full amount of the debt plus interest.

The result in *Foakes v. Beer* is particularly hard on an innocent debtor. He is no worse off legally if he pays nothing than if he pays what he can; his obligation to pay the full amount still remains. It is not surprising that there has been a development in Equity that mitigates the harshness of the operation of the law. In some circumstances, Equity will prevent a person from enforcing his strict legal rights. The circumstances can be described as follows:

Where A makes a representation to B, intending to affect the legal relations between A and B and intending B to rely on the representation, if B acts in reliance on the representation, A will be prevented from acting inconsistently with his representation.

The case which marks the start of the modern development of this doctrine is *High Trees House v. Central London Property Investment Trust Ltd*. During the Second World War the tenants of a block of flats were having difficulty in subletting the flats. They were consequently having difficulty in paying the rent that they owed to the landlords. The landlords informed them that they could pay half the usual amount of rent. At the end of the war, when the tenants had again been able to sublet the flats, the landlords claimed to be entitled to full rent again. It was held that they were entitled to the full rent for the future, but it was said that had they sued for arrears of rent they would have failed. This meant that for the period over which the concession extended (the war years) the landlords were prevented from going back on their promise not to claim the full rent even though the law would not normally recognise that promise because it was not backed by any consideration.

This doctrine is called *promissory* or *equitable estoppel* because a person is prevented (or estopped) in equity from going back on his promise provided that the other circumstances mentioned above are present.

Summary and conclusions

1. We have already noted that in terms of both structure and accountability business organisations have to be seen within the context of the law.
2. Legal rules are often thought of in terms of *constraints*, but the law is not simply probibitive – it provides a *framework* for ordering business affairs so that each party knows where it stands in relation to the other. Important in providing the framework are *contracts*.
3. *Contracts* – agreements that have legal consequences. They can be made formally and informally. For contracts to be valid there must be:

(a) Agreement (offer and acceptance).
(b) Consideration.
(c) Intention to create legal relations.
(d) Contractual capacity (each party must be capable of entering a contract).
(e) No vitiating circumstances (e.g. undue pressures).

4. The first element to be considered in detail in item 3 above was:

4.1 *Agreement:* which should be thought of in terms of:

(a Offer which is an expression by one party of his willingness to be bound as soon as it is accepted.
Note:

   (i) what constitutes an offer? (Differentiate between an offer and an 'invitation to treat'.);
   (ii) when does an offer come to an end?

(b) Acceptance: which is required to produce a binding contract. It must:

   (i) coincide exactly with the terms of the offer;
   (ii) be communicated by the offeree; and
   (iii) it determines the time when the contract is made.

Acceptance only takes place when received by the offeror (but see the postal rule exception).

5. The second element looked at in item 3 was:

5.1 *Consideration:* in essence a promise must be supported by something given in return:

(a) Consideration may take two forms: an act ('executed' consideration) or the promise of an act ('executory' consideration).
(b) For consideration to support a contract it must be of some economic value (the law does not enforce gratuitous promises).
(c) There are certain requirements to which consideration must conform (e.g. it must not be 'past' consideration).
(d) In some special circumstances a promise may be binding in the absence of consideration (promissory estoppel).

Assignments

9.1

During last week the following incidents occurred in Supamarket, a self-service shop managed by Fred:

1. Albert, a customer, emptied his shopping basket at the cash desk. The assistant picked up a packet of frozen lobster and was about to ring up the price on the till when Albert said that he no longer wanted it and did not intend to pay for it.
2. Betty, another customer, handed the cashier a box of biscuits marked at 13

80

pence. The price had been marked incorrectly and should have been marked at £2.13. Betty insisted on buying the box at the price marked.
3. Charles, another customer, when told at the cash desk what the total bill came to, found that he had forgotten to bring any money.

Fred was called in to deal with each of these incidents. What advice should he have given on the legal position in each case? Bearing in mind all his possible business objectives, what advice should he give to the assistants to help them to deal with similar problems that might arise in the future?

9.2

Barry is the buyer for a manufacturing firm. He has been told that he has £5,000 to spend on buying a new piece of machinery. He rang up a supplier that he thought could supply him with the machinery. The following conversation took place between Barry and Simon, a representative of the suppliers.

Barry: We are interested in buying your X200 machine. What price can you quote me?
Simon: The catalogue price is £4,500.
Barry: That sounds fine. We will take it. By the way, can you let me have written confirmation of the figure. We'll send in our order within the week.
Simon: Good. Our delivery time is approximately four weeks.

The following day Barry received the following letter from Simon:

Dear Sir,
   Sale of X200
   In connection with your telephone enquiry of today's date we have pleasure in confirming that our price for the X200 is £4,500. We shall be pleased to supply it on receipt of your order.

Yours faithfully,
Simon

The same day Barry wrote a reply:

Dear Sir,
   Sale of X200
   Thank you for confirming your price on the X200. I enclose our order for this machine, but as we need the machine urgently we will be grateful if you can reduce the delivery time in our case.

Yours faithfully,
Barry

The letter had just been posted when Simon telephoned Barry to say that he had just heard that his company had decided to stop making the X200, and as they had already sold the last machine in stock, they would not be able to supply one to Barry's firm.
   Advise Barry on whether there is a contract to buy the X200.

9.3

Can A sue in the following cases?

1. A agrees to buy B's car for £1,000. B refuses to hand over the car.
2. A promises to sell B his car for £1,000, payment to be made on the 1st of next month. A delivers the car to B, but when the time comes for payment, B refuses to pay.
3. B returns home one day to discover that A, his neighbour, has dug his garden for him. B promises A £20 but does not pay.
4. A is a window cleaner who offers to clean the windows of B's shop. B agrees and when window cleaner has finished, B says he will pay him £10. B later changes his mind and refuses to pay.
5. C agrees to pay £100 to B in return for B paying A £100. C pays but B refuses to.

9.4

1. Fred was a shopkeeper. Parking in the road outside his shop was restricted to 20 minutes in any hour, but several people had recently been parking there for the whole day which he thought was affecting his custom. He saw one of the traffic wardens who regularly patrolled along the street and promised her that if she would make sure that she gave a parking ticket to anyone who parked there for more than 20 minutes, he would pay her £5. Can the traffic warden enforce Fred's promise?
2. Fred, whose shop was next door to a football ground, was also worried about the possible damage to his shop that might be caused as a result of a clash between two groups of football supporters the following Saturday. He rang the Chief Constable, who said that they would provide the usual mobile patrol in the area. Fred insisted that a police constable should be on patrol for the whole afternoon outside his shop. The Chief of Constable said that he was prepared to supply that if Fred paid £20 and Fred agreed. Fred later refused to pay. Can the Police Authority sue?

9.5

Albert owed Ken £100. Albert's wife became ill and, feeling sorry for him, Ken promised that he would not enforce the debt. What is Albert's position if Ken decides to change his mind and sue for the £100?

10 Organisations and the formation of contracts – II

Introduction

In the last chapter we outlined the nature of the contract as a voluntary bargain. We noted how the law requires there to be agreement and consideration before there is a contract.

The voluntary nature of the relationship is further stressed by two rules. One requires that the parties intend to enter into a legally recognised, legally enforceable relationship. The other provides that a contracting party must be 'capable' of contracting.

Intention to enter into legal relations

The Courts are hardly able to investigate the state of mind of the parties in deciding whether the parties intended to bind themselves legally. They will however have regard to the nature of the transaction, what the existing relationship between the parties is, what they do and what they say.

The parties may say expressly that they do not intend to create any legal obligations. In *Jones v. Vernon's Pools Ltd*, Jones claimed that he filled in a football pools coupon with a winning line and sent it to Vernon's Pools, though they denied having ever received it. The coupon stated that there should be no legal relations between the sender and the company. It was held that Jones could not enforce payment of the sum he argued was due to him.

If the parties do not say whether legal relations are intended, two presumptions are used to help the court to decide.

The first is that if the transaction is a commercial one, the parties will be presumed to have intended legal relations. The presumption can be rebutted, but only by using sufficiently clear words. In *Edwards v. Skyways Ltd* the employer of an airline pilot agreed to make him an 'ex gratia' payment as part of the arrangements made when he left their employment. When he claimed the money the company denied that it was legally bound to pay it. It failed. The court held that the words 'ex gratia' were not sufficiently clear to rebut the presumption that, as it was a commercial agreement, legal relations were intended.

Where the transaction involves mere social or domestic arrangements, the opposite presumption is raised: that is, that the parties do not intend to create legal relations. This accords with common sense. Life would be almost impossible if every social activity such as agreeing to meet someone off a train or to take someone out to dinner carried with it liability for an action for breach of contract.

Problems can arise though where, even though the relationship between the parties is in nature a domestic one, all the circumstances indicate that the parties intend a formal arrangement. In one case, although the parties were husband and wife, the agreement was about how their assets should be divided between them following the break up of their marriage. The evidence was that the husband and wife had had a discussion in the husband's car which resulted in an agreement that the wife should continue to pay the mortgage in return for the husband transferring his share in the house to her. The wife refused to leave the car until the husband had recorded the terms of their agreement on a piece of paper and signed it, which he duly did. In this case it was held that all the evidence was sufficient to rebut the presumption that the parties did not intend to create legal relations and the husband was held legally bound to transfer his share in the house to her (*Merritt v. Merritt*).

Two further points should be noted concerning the question of whether or not legal relations are intended. The first concerns an important aspect of industrial relations. It was established at common law and now by statute (s. 18, Trade Union and Labour Relations Act 1974) that collective agreements between trade unions and employers or an employers' association are presumed not to be legally enforceable unless the agreement is in writing and expressly states that it *is* intended to be legally enforceable.

The second point is that the value of the subject matter of the contract is not decisive one way or another as to whether legal relations were intended. In *Esso Petroleum Co Ltd v. Commissioners of Customs and Excise* there was held by the House of Lords to be sale (i.e. a contractual relationship) by Esso of World Cup coins that were 'given away' free with every four gallons of petrol bought. This was so despite the minimal intrinsic value of the coins.

Capacity

Individuals

A human being generally has the capacity to enter into any contract he likes. He loses this full capacity only if he is drunk or of unsound mind. If someone contracts while in such a state and the other party is aware of the state then he can have the contract rendered void (the contract is said to be *voidable*) and the promises will not be enforced.

One gains full capacity to contract at the age of 18. Prior to that age one may enter into contracts but these sometimes have different consequences from contracts entered into by persons of full age. Some contracts (e.g. contracts of employment to the benefit of the infant) are valid. Some can be rendered void (or 'avoided') by the infant if he chooses to do so but will otherwise be valid (e.g. contracts to buy or rent and contracts to enter into a partnership).

Companies

For our present purposes by far the most important aspect of capacity to enter into contracts relates to companies.

We have seen that registered companies are artificial legal persons. As such they do not have the full legal capacity that humans have. With a registered company one must first look at the memorandum of association to see what the stated objects of the company are. The company has full power to enter into contracts in order to fulfil those objects, or contracts incidental thereto, but not others.

A contract that is outside these powers ('ultra vires') is void; that is, it is of no legal effect. The classic example of this rule is the case of *Ashbury Railway Carriages Co v. Riche*. The objects of the Company were to deal in railway carriages, waggons, plant, etc., to carry on business as mechanical engineers and general contractors, to deal in mines, minerals, land and buildings; and to deal also in timber, coal, etc. The directors agreed with a Belgian company to sell to it the rights which had been bought by the English company to build a railway in Belgium. It was held that since this contract related to the construction of a railway (something not included among the Company's objects) it could not be sued by the Belgian company who asserted that the Ashbury Co were in breach.

The purpose of this rule is to ensure that directors cannot suddenly commit a company to a new line of business or spend money on something wholly unconnected with what is thought to be the company's sphere of activity. This is for the protection of shareholders and creditors. But to hold that a contract is void if made ultra vires can be unfair to innocent parties, and, in fact, two recent developments have severely debilitated the rule.

First, it has become the practice to draft object clauses very widely: see *Bell Houses Ltd v City Wall Properties Ltd* where the company was authorised to carry on any trade or business which, in the opinion of the directors, might be carried on advantageously in connection with or ancillary to the main business of developing housing estates. This clause was held effective to cover any transaction that the directors honestly thought was advantageous to the company.

Second, s. 9 (1) of the European Communities Act 1972 provides:

'In favour of a person dealing with a company in good faith, any transaction decided on by the directors shall be deemed to be one which it is within the capacity of the company to enter into . . .'

Thus a company can no longer rely on the capacity rule against someone who has dealt with it in good faith.

Companies set up by statute have their powers to contract expressed in the statute setting them up as do local authorities, although in their case the provisions of other Acts which give them additional powers and duties may also be relevant.

Once it is shown that a contract was made within the capacity of a company the normal rules of contract apply.

Summary and conclusions

1. The importance of contracts as part of the legal framework had already been

established and the elements of Agreement and Consideration discussed.

2. We continued by stressing the voluntary nature of contracts via the rules requiring that:

   (a) the parties must intend entering into a legally recognisable and enforceable relationship (intention); and
   (b) a contracting party must be 'capable' of contracting (capacity).

3. *Intention* – in trying to decide whether or not the parties intend to bind themselves legally the Courts will:

   (a) consider the nature of the transactions (whether commercial or non-commercial);
   (b) look at existing relationships between the parties;
   (c) examine the actions and words of the parties involved (e.g. express statements about legal obligation);
   (d) make assumptions where matters are not fully clear (distinguishing between commercial and non-commercial situations).

4. *Capacity*
4.1 Individuals – anyone can make a contract when over the age of 18, assuming they are not insane or drunk.
4.2 Companies – these have full power to enter into contracts in order to fulfil the objects laid down in the Memorandum of Association. Contracts outside objects are void, except where section 9 (1) of the European Communities Act 1972 applies.

5. It is now necessary to turn to other factors affecting the validity of contracts even though the rules governing intention and capacity might have been met.

Assignments

10.1

The Memorandum of Association of X Co states that the objects of the company are to pursue the business of electrical contractors and any businesses incidental thereto. One of the directors, in exercise of the powers delegated to him by the board of directors, enters into a contract with Z Co for the purchase of timber. The timber is to be used by X Co in a new venture, the construction and sale of garden sheds. Z Co supplied the timber, but due to a change of policy, X Co no longer wants to extend its previous business and refuses to pay for the timber. Advise Z Co.

10.2

Lionel owns his own travel agency. After being pressurised by his wife, he offered her a job as a secretary in his office. She accepted. He then changed his mind about employing her and said that he never had any intention of entering into a legally binding arrangement. Advise Lionel's wife on whether the arrangement may amount to a contract.

10.3

The facts of *Rose and Frank Co v. J. R. Crompton and Brothers Ltd* are stated in the law reports as follows:

An english firm who manufactured and dealt in paper tissues of various kinds had for several years done business with an American firm. All goods of one kind sold in the United States, all goods of another kind sold in the United States or Canada, and all goods of a third kind wherever sold, were sold to the American firm, and that firm placed all orders for goods of the third kind with the English firm. These relations were at first made to continue for one year, but were renewed from time to time.

A great part of the tissues so sold were in fact manufactured by another English firm. In the course of time the American firm proposed a new arrangement, and a document was drawn up and signed by the three firms whereby the two English firms expressed their willingness that the present arrangements with the American firm, which were then for one year only, should be continued on the same lines for three years, and so on for another period of three years, subject to six months' notice by any of the parties. The document, after purporting to set out the understanding between the parties, including several modifications of their previous arrangement, proceeded in these words: 'This arrangement is not entered into, nor is this memorandum written, as a formal or legal agreement, and shall not be subject to legal jurisdiction in the law courts either in the United States or England, but it is only a definite expression and record of the purpose and intention of the three parties concerned to which they each honourably pledge themselves with the fullest confidence, based on past business with each other, that it will be carried through by each of the three parties with mutual loyalty and friendly co-operation.' Then followed a clause relating to prices.

The English firms having defaulted on their obligations without notice, the American firm brought an action for breach of the contract alleged to be expressed in the document.

The court had to decide whether the written document amounted to a contract, the decisive question being whether the parties intended to enter into legal relations.

How would you have decided the case? Give reasons and cite authorities for your decision.

11 Organisations and the formation of contracts - III

Introduction

Even though an agreement has been reached in accordance with all the legal rules we have discussed so far, any one of a number of factors may affect the legal validity of the contract. In this chapter we will discuss the effect on contracts of misrepresentation, mistake, duress, undue influence and conflict with a legal rule.

Misrepresentation

During pre-contract negotiations many things are said in the hope of persuading the other person to enter into the contract or of securing better terms. Everyone expects a certain amount of sales talk, and not every misrepresentation will affect the validity of the contract.

A misrepresentation which can affect the validity of a contract can be defined as *an untrue statement of fact which is calculated to and does induce the other party to enter into the contract.*

From the definition we can see that first there must be a statement of fact. Statements of opinion, intention or law do not give the innocent party any remedy. So it is not an actionable misrepresentation to say 'Brandex is the greatest washing powder on the market' because the reasonable man should take this not as a provable statement of fact but as an opinion, or merely sales talk. Nor is it a misrepresentation to say 'I intend to have my car resprayed before I sell it.' The person who buys the car on the strength of this must take his chance on whether the seller does what he says, and he will have no legal remedy if he does not. Nor is it a misrepresentation to misstate the law: everyone is presumed to know the law.

One qualification should be made. A statement that appears on the face of it to be a statement of opinion may be treated as a statement of fact if the person making the statement knows the facts to back up his opinion. In *Smith v. Land and House Property Corporation* the vendor of premises was held to have made a statement of fact when he said that they were let to a 'most desirable tenant' when in fact the tenant was, to his knowledge, in arrears with his rent.

Only a positive misrepresentation can vitiate a contract. The rule is *caveat emptor* (let the buyer beware).

The seller, even though he knows of defects in his product, is not bound to disclose these to the buyer. Keeping silent, even when the seller knows that the buyer is acting under a misapprehension, is not misrepresentation. (There may, however, be a misrepresentation even without words; for example, by a nod of the head in answer to a buyer's question.)

There are exceptions to this rule. One concerns contracts of utmost good faith ('uberrimae fidei'). Examples of these are insurance contracts, contracts between solicitor–client, doctor–patient, parent–child. Here there is a positive duty to disclose material facts and silence will constitute misrepresentation.

Another exception is the duty to speak if a statement once made subsequently becomes untrue before the contract is concluded. Thus in *With v. O'Flanagan* a doctor who was selling his practice was held liable to a purchaser when he did not inform him that the value of the practice which he stated correctly at the beginning of negotiations dropped dramatically because the doctor had suffered a long illness.

The misrepresentation must be calculated to induce the other party to contract, but this does not mean that there must be a conscious attempt to mislead. A statement simply has to be a factor which would induce a person to enter into a contract. It must also in fact have induced the party to enter into the particular contract. If he does not let it affect his mind at all he will have no remedy. It is not necessary, though, that it should be the only factor that affects him.

Clearly a person buying a particular car might be more concerned about the car's mileage than the fact that the radio works, but a statement that the radio is in working order if it is one of the factors that influences him is an actionable misrepresentation.

A person who has checked the accuracy of the statement, even if he comes to the wrong conclusion, cannot then claim that the misstatement has induced him to enter into the contract (*Attwood v. Small*). It is his own mistaken belief that has induced him. Thus if our buyer tries the radio, finds that it does not work but still buys the car, he cannot later complain.

On the other hand the person making a statement cannot escape liability by offering the other party an opportunity to check the facts if he does not take the offer up (*Redgrave v. Hurd*). The car seller would still be liable if he said 'The radio is in working order. You can try it if you like', but the buyer did not.

The rights of the injured party depend on whether the statement was made fraudulently, negligently or wholly innocently.

Fraudulent misrepresentation

The classic definition of fraud is contained in *Derry v. Peek* in which it was said that a fraudulent statement is made 'Knowingly or without belief in its truth or recklessly careless whether it be true or false.' Fraudulent misrepresentation gives the injured party an alternative. First, he may sue for damages, in the tort of deceit: The action is in tort, not in contract, because the misrepresentation will generally not have become a term of the contract. Alternatively (or in addition) he may avoid the contract.

The basic rule which applies to all types of misrepresentation is that it makes a contract voidable. A void contract is one which has never taken effect in law. A voidable contract is one that is perfectly valid until steps are taken to avoid the contract, that is to make it void.

The other technical terms that are often used in connection with voidable contracts are 'to rescind the contract' and 'rescission of the contract'. Recission is an equitable remedy and as such it is discretionary. The right to rescind a contract may be lost by the party delaying in taking steps to rescind. It may also be lost by the party affirming the contract, that is by showing that he still considers himself bound by the contract.

The way in which a contract is rescinded is by the party entitled to rescind unequivocally expressing his intention not to be bound by the contract. He may do this by words or conduct and must communicate his decision to the other party. Sometimes this may be impossible: a person who obtains property fraudulently is likely to disappear. In *Car & Universal Finance Co Ltd v. Caldwell* it was held to be enough that a person who had sold a car in return for a cheque which turned out to be worthless informed the police and the Automobile Association and asked them to find the car.

The effect of rescission is to put the parties back in the legal position that existed before the contract was entered into. Thus each party has to return to the other any property which he has acquired under the contract, as he is no longer legally entitled to it. If this is not possible, e.g. the property is a case of whisky which has been drunk, or if the property has been sold to an innocent third party, the injured party cannot rescind the contract. His only rememdy then will be to sue for damages.

Negligent misrepresentation

If the misrepresentation is not fraudulent but just careless or negligent again the innocent party may rescind the contract and/or sue for damages.

He has two ways of suing for damages. He can sue in the tort of negligence itself. This depends on there being a duty of care owed by the person making the statement. Generally, a duty of care will arise when it is reasonably foreseeable that another person will suffer from the acts or omissions of the first party. Where the loss suffered is not personal injury or damage to property but is merely economic or financial loss an additional factor appears to be necessary. The parties must be in a 'special relationship' (*Hedley Byrne & Co v. Heller and Partners*). The duty of care will only arise in these circumstances if the party making the statement makes it knowing it is going to be relied on, and can be said to have assumed responsibility for making it. This will be so where advice is given in the course of business, e.g. by an accountant or solicitor.

The other option is to sue for damages under s. 2(1) of the Misrepresentation Act 1967. This does not require a special relationship to be shown. The section states that a party will be liable in damages unless he can show that he had reasonable grounds for believing the misrepresentation made to be true and did, in fact, believe it to be true.

Innocent misrepresentation

The word innocent in this context has nothing to do with moral blame. A misrepresentation is made innocently where a person honestly believes what he is saying is true *and* has reasonable grounds for believing it to be true, e.g. person who sells a picture as a Rembrandt solely because the dealer who sold it to him sold it as a Rembrandt.

In this case, the injured party cannot sue for damages. He can only rescind the contract and this is subject to the limitations set out above. Rescission is an equitable remedy, so that the court will not grant it if it would not be equitable to do so. It may however, once it has decided that a case for rescission has been made out, award damages instead if this would be more appropriate in all the circumstances (s. 2 (2) Misrepresentation Act).

One final point about misrepresentation should be made. A party cannot exclude the liability for misrepresentation (e.g. by putting a clause in the contract) unless it is reasonable for him to do so (s. 3 Misrepresentation Act).

Mistake

Very few mistakes in the everyday sense of the word affect the validity of a contract. The person who buys a tin of paint mistakenly thinking that it matches the colour of the paintwork at home or who buys a piece of land mistakenly thinking that he can get planning permission to build a hypermarket must bear the consequences of his mistake. Such mistakes have no legal consequences, and occasions on which a mistake will vitiate a contract are few.

Sometimes both parties may be labouring under the same mistake. They may both be unaware, for example, that the subject matter of the contract does not exist or that the object of the transaction is impossible. The effect of this mistake will be to render the contract void. It may however be, even in these extreme circumstances, that one party has warranted that the thing does exist. Then the contract will be valid, and the party who did warrant the existence of the subject matter will be liable in damages for breach of contract.

In the case of *McRae v. Commonwealth Disposals Commission*, the Commission invited tenders for the purchase of 'a tanker lying off the Journand Reef'. It turned out that there was no tanker. In fact there was no Journand Reef. The Commission were held liable for breach of contract because the Commission had made a promise that there was a tanker there.

In cases where both parties are mistaken about the *quality* of the thing probably the contract is not void. For example in *Leaf v. International Galleries* the plaintiff bought from the defendant a picture which both parties mistakenly believed to be by Constable. The Court of Appeal indicated that such a contract was not void for mistake.

A second type of mistake which may render a contract void occurs when the parties are at cross-purposes, e.g. in *Raffles v. Wichelhaus* where the contract was for the sale of a consignment of cotton to arrive 'ex Peerless from Bombay'. There were in fact two ships called The Peerless, one due to leave Bombay in October and the other in December. When they entered into the contract, each party was thinking of a different ship. In this instance, the contract is void because the offer and acceptance do not match.

In the first and second types of contract that have just been mentioned, both parties are mistaken. The third type of mistake which will vitiate a contract occurs where only one party is mistaken but the other party knows or must be taken to know of his mistake. This may take two forms, mistake as to the identity of the other contracting party and mistake as to the contractual terms.

The facts that give rise to the first type of problem are commonly as follows. A rogue pretends to be a respected and well-known pillar of the community. He 'buys' goods and gives in return a cheque that turns out to be worthless. The legal problem that arises is whether his impersonating someone else affects the validity of a contract.

The question has been well discussed, and though the law is not entirely free from doubt the situation appears to be that where one party believes that he is contracting, but with a different person, the contract is void for mistake as to identity. This is easier to establish if the parties are contracting by correspondence than if they are dealing face to face. When the parties are face to face there is a presumption that each is dealing with the person in front of him, not the person being impersonated. This has the effect that the contract is not void for mistake, but the contract would of course be voidable for fraud (see Misrepresentation). The second type of problem where only one party is mistaken arises when his mistake is as to the terms of the contract. In *Hartog v. Colin and Shields* the defendants intended to offer for sale to the plaintiffs some hareskins at a certain price 'per piece'. By a slip they offered to sell them at that price 'per pound' (a far larger amount). The pre-contractual negotiations had been conducted on the understanding that the skins would be sold at so much a piece. When the plaintiffs sued on the contract the court held there was no contract. Very often, however, the courts will not deem this kind of slip sufficiently important to have the effect of rendering the contract void. Mistakes of this sort must be of material importance.

In addition to these instances a contract can be voidable in equity where parties are under a mistake as to a material fact. Exactly how wide this power is is unclear.

Finally we should note a separate ground on which signed contracts may be void. If the person signing a document thinks, through no carelessness on his part, that he is signing something radically different from the document he is in fact signing he may have the document declared void.

Duress and undue influence

Where someone is driven into making a contract by duress or undue influence the contract is voidable and may be set aside by a court.

Duress means actual violence or threats of violence to the person. Undue influence is rather wider, encompassing many varieties of improper pressure (e.g. a threat of prosecution for some criminal offence should one not agree to make a contract). In most cases it is the person who asserts that he has been subject to duress or undue influence who must prove that this was so. Sometimes, however, undue influence will be presumed because of the relationship between the parties to the contract (e.g. parent and child, solicitor and client) and the dominant person will have to prove that the other person was able freely to exercise his own will.

There have been recent attempts to hold that these rules are but part of a general rule whereby the courts will intervene to set aside any transaction made between parties in positions of unequal bargaining strength. We shall look at this idea in more detail when we examine the development of consumer protection.

Void and illegal contracts

A contract may be void or illegal because of a rule of common law or a statutory provision.

Void contracts: common law

The following contracts are void at common law:

(a) Contracts which purport to take away the rights of parties to submit questions of law to the courts.
(b) Contracts damaging to the status of marriage.
(c) Contracts in restraint of trade.

This last group of contracts is probably the most important in a discussion of the activities of business organisation. The doctrine of restraint of trade covers contracts restraining the activities of employees after they have left their employer, contracts by which the seller of a business restricts his own freedom to compete against the purchaser and certain other trade contracts. Such contracts are void in so far as they unreasonably restrict the liberty of a person to carry on his trade, business or profession as he chooses.

Contracts of the types we have mentioned are void unless they are reasonable.

An example of a restraint in a contract of employment which was held valid as being reasonable was *Forster and Sons Ltd v. Suggett*. A clause in the contract of employment of a works manager who was aware of the details of a company's confidential manufacturing process which forbade him from employment with any UK company in the same business for five years was held to be valid.

The duration of the restraint and its ambit will often be important factors in determining reasonableness both in employer restrictions and in restraints in contracts of sale of a business. Restraints of the latter variety are more often held to be valid than are restraints on the future activities of employees.

Among the miscellaneous trade contracts where the doctrine of restraint of trade has sometimes been applied are contracts embodying the rules of trade associations (e.g. *McEllistrim v. Co-op.*), agreements for exclusive services (see *Schroeder v. Macauley*) and 'solus' trading agreements, i.e. agreements which tie traders to individual suppliers in return for advances of finance or cheaper supplies (see *Esso Petroleum v. Harper's Garage*).

Void contracts: statute

The two most important varieties of contracts which are void by virtue of a statutory provision are wagering contracts (which we shall not consider) and restrictive trading agreements.

The Restrictive Trade Practices Act 1976 and the Resale Prices Act 1976 provide for the control of agreements designed to restrict the prices or the terms of conditions of supply of goods and services. We shall look at these statutes in a little more detail in Chapter 22.

Void contracts: effect

A contract is void in so far as it contravenes public policy. Parts of the contract which do not so contravene public policy may be severed from the void parts of the contract and recognised and enforced by the courts.

Illegal contracts: common law

Contracts illegal at common law include:

(a) Contracts to commit a crime on tort or fraud.
(b) Contracts damaging to the administration of justice.
(c) Contracts damaging to the country's foreign relations or safety.
(d) Contracts to promote corruption in public life.
(e) Contracts to defraud the revenue.
(f) Contracts tending to promote sexual immorality.

Illegal contracts: statutes

Very many statutes designate certain activities as illegal. Contracts to perform such acts, or contracts which in their performance involve such acts, are illegal contracts.

'Illegality' is not the same as criminality: it is not an offence as such to enter into an illegal contract, but the contract may be denied full validity in law because of the principle that the law will not encourage or enforce illegality.

Illegal contracts: effect

It is unclear whether illegal (as opposed to void) contracts can be severed (that is whether the part that is illegal can be struck out leaving a valid and enforceable contract).

Contracts can be illegal in two distinct ways. Either the contract can be illegal in itself or it may be that it is the performance of the contract which is illegal. Contracts which are of the first kind (i.e. prohibited) can be enforced by neither party except in so far as the doctrine of severance applies. Contracts of the second kind may have one (or perhaps two) 'guilty' parties (i.e. those who participate in the illegal design) while the other party (or even both parties) may be innocent. Innocent parties are able to enforce the contract.

Summary and conclusions

1. Even though agreement over a contract can be reached in accordance with the legal rules outlined in the previous two chapters, a number of other factors may affect a contract's legal validity including: misrepresentation; mistake; duress and undue influence; conflict with a legal rule. Each needs further examination.

2. *Misrepresentation* – can be defined as an untrue statement of fact which is calculated to and does induce the other party to enter the contract. *Note that:*

    (i)   it must be an untrue statement of *fact*;
    (ii) it must generally be a *positive* misrepresentation though there are limited exceptions (e.g. 'contracts of utmost good faith').
    (iii) It must induce a party to contract. It does not have to be a conscious attempt to mislead. Misrepresentations may be either fraudulent misrepresentations (i.e. deliberate) or negligent misrepresentations (i.e. careless) or innocent misrepresentations (i.e. where there are reasonable grounds for believing and the statement is believed to be true).

    Misrepresentations make a contract voidable.

3. *Mistake* – the term is not used in its everyday sense but technically; it is a rare occurrence in law.

3.1 Mistakes may make a contract void or voidable when:

    (*a*) parties are labouring under the same mistake;
    (*b*) parties are at cross purposes;
    (*c*) one party is mistaken but the other party knows of the mistake.

4. *Duress and undue influence* – duress means the threat of or actual violence. Undue influence is wider, covering various forms of improper pressure.

5. *Conflict with legal rules* – a contract may be void or illegal because it comes into conflict with existing rules of law.

5.1 The position may be summarised thus:

    (*a*) Void

        (i) Common law: e.g. contracts in restraint of trade.
        (ii) Statute law: e.g. restrictive trading agreements.

    (*b*) Illegal

        (i) Common law
        (ii) Statute law

    The validity of contracts may be affected in any of these ways.

Assignments

11.1

John owns a greengrocer's business which he wishes to sell. He has found a prospective purchaser, Malcolm, but Malcolm has heard that John is intending to move into larger premises a quarter of a mile away. Malcolm is afraid that many of John's present customers will go in future to John's new shop. Advise Malcolm on the sort of provisions he should insist on in the contract of sale in order to protect himself.

11.2

A worked for B for many years as a solicitor's clerk. When A retired B agreed to pay him £500 a year in return for A agreeing not to work for any other solicitor or accountant within ten miles of B's offices. A now wishes to take up a part-time job with C, a solicitor whose offices are nine miles away from B's. Advise A whether he will still be entitled to £500 a year from B if he takes the new job.

11.3

A wants to sell his car to B. May any of the following instances give rise to an action for misrepresentation if the statement in each case turns out to be false:

(i)   A tells B that he thinks this model is ideal for long distance motoring;
(ii) A tells B that he intends to have his car serviced before B buys it;
(iii) A tells B that the car complies with the legal requirements as to the provision of seat belts.

11.4

X bought a picture from an art dealer A for £100,000, having been told by A that the picture was an original by Constable. Two weeks later X found out that the painting was by one of Constable's pupils and was consequently only worth £10,000. Assuming that X can show that A's statement was an actionable misrepresentation advise X on what remedies are available if he can show:

1. that A knew the picture was not by Constable;
2. that A had been told that the picture was by Constable, but A could have discovered if he had examined the canvas that the painting had the signature of Constable's pupil on it;
3. that A had been sold the picture as a Constable by a reputable firm of auctioneers and, not knowing much about paintings, A believed that the painting was by Constable.

You may present your advice to X in essay form or in the form of a diagram showing the remedies available for different types of misrepresentation. In each case, you should support your decisions with authorities.

11.5

In what circumstances may a contract be rendered void or voidable as a result of

96

a mistake made by one or both parties prior to a contract? What are the results of a contract being held void or voidable for mistake?

11.6

Could the facts stated in assignment 11.4 give rise to an action based on mistake? If so, what would X's remedies be?

11.7

The following are the facts of *Re Brocklehurst*.

The deceased owned an estate consisting of a mansion house and some 3,500 acres of land which he had inherited from his father. The land included moorlands over which there were shooting rights. Those rights greatly enhanced the value of the estate. The deceased was a strong-minded, autocratic and eccentric old man who was used to commanding others and had served in the army in positions of command. He was impulsively generous. He had no male heir and did not want to leave the estate to his only male blood relation, his sister's grandson. The defendant, a former naval rating, was the proprietor of a small garage. He got to know the deceased in the 1960s. They had a common interest in shooting and the deceased permitted the defendant to shoot rabbits on the estate. After the death of the deceased's manservant and former batman the defendant frequently visited the deceased to keep him company and also performed personal services for him and did small jobs for him on the estate. Although the deceased had around him people of his own social standing with whom he discussed his personal and financial affairs and he did not discuss those matters with the defendant, he appreciated the defendant's companionship and in the last months of his life depended on him to ease the daily burden of living. The defendant always behaved subserviently towards the deceased and stood in awe of him. When the deceased was aged nearly 87, he wrote to the defendant saying that he was his best and kindest man friend, and that he wished to give him the shooting rights over the estate. The deceased was determined not to instruct his own solicitor about a lease of the shooting rights and pressed the defendant to instruct a solicitor to draw up a lease. Because of the deceased's insistence the defendant, in January 1974, instructed a solicitor to draft a lease of the shooting rights over the estate for a term of ten years rent free. Neither the defendant nor his solicitor suggested to the deceased that he should take independent advice about the lease. The defendant amended the draft lease by striking out the clauses restricting his right to assign or underlet the shooting rights and the size of gun to be used for shooting and the clause requiring him to make an annual return of the birds and game he killed.

The deceased did not want to see the draft lease, and executed the lease as amended without taking independent advice. The deceased wanted the defendant to have a longer lease and suggested one for 99 years. He pressed the defendant to get such a lease drawn up by his solicitor. After changing his will many times, the deceased finally left the estate to his sister's grandson. Subsequently the defendant instructed his solicitor to draw up another lease of the shooting rights, for a term of 99 years. The deceased executed that lease, which was dated 19 July 1974, without taking independent advice about it. The effect of that lease was to reduce substantially the value of the estate. The deceased died on 28 January 1975.

His executors brought an action against the defendant to have the leases set aside on the ground that they had been entered into because of the undue influence of the defendant on the deceased whilst in a position of confidence and trust.

How would you have decided this case? Justify your decision with reasons. You will need to consider:

1. Whether the relationship is such as to give rise to a presumption of undue influence;
2. if the answer to (1) is yes, whether the evidence would be sufficient to rebut the presumption;
3. if the answer to (1) is no, are there any considerations in the present case which would suggest to you that the transaction should be set aside in any case?

12 The contents of contracts

Introduction

The matters we have looked at so far are all concerned with the making of a valid contract.

But showing how a contract comes into being is to explain only part of the problem. It will not help the irate consumer who has bought a packet of mouldy biscuits in a supermarket to know that he has a contract with the store that was completed at the check-out, not when he took the packet from the shelf. He wants to know what he can do about it, whether he can demand his money back, whether he has to accept a credit-note or whether he has to put up with what he has got and shop somewhere else in future.

What he can do is dependent on what the contract actually contained. It may seem self-evident, but it is worth saying, that an action for breach of contract is only possible where the matter complained of is a breach of contractual obligation. Only contractual obligations can give rise to contractual remedies.

It is therefore essential to discover what matters are incorporated into the contract and what matters remain outside. We shall see that the contents of the contract are drawn both from things said and from some things that are left unsaid. We shall also see that there are various types of contractual terms.

Term or not?

Not every statement that is made before contract becomes part of the contract. A person may say a great deal during negotiations that neither he nor the other party expect to be legally obliged to honour. The task for the courts is to discover what was the intention of the parties as regards the content of the agreement. This question must be answered from an objective standpoint, and to help in making the decision there are a number of guidelines that the courts appear to use, e.g.

1. The time the statement was made. A statement that is made a considerable length of time before the contract is concluded is less likely to be held to be a term of the contract.

2. The importance of the term to one party. In *Bannerman v. White* an intending purchaser of some hops asked whether sulphur had been used in their preparation because, as he said, if it had he would not even trouble to ask the

price. The (untrue) assurance that it had not was held to be a term of the contract.

3. The relative degrees of knowledge of the parties. If one party has particular skill and knowledge on the matter and the other does not, a statement by him is more likely to be a contractual term than a statement by a party who is not an expert.

Two cases neatly illustrate this point. In *Dick Bentley Productions Ltd v. Harold Smith (Motors) Ltd* the defendant, a car dealer, sold a Bentley to the plaintiff, stating that it had only done 20,000 miles since having a replacement engine. In fact it had done nearly 100,000 miles. The statement was held to be a term of the contract, and the dealer was consequently liable in damages. On the other hand, in *Oscar Chess Ltd v. Williams* a private motorist, selling to a dealer, stated that the car was a 1948 model, when it was in fact a 1939 model. The statement did not become a part of the contract.

Collateral contracts

We have distinguished statements that become express terms of the contract from statements that remain outside the main contract. But those that remain outside are not always without legal significance. Those that fulfil the conditions for misrepresentation may give rise to rescission of the contract and/or an action for damages, either at common law or under the Misrepresentation Act 1967. Another possibility is that a statement whilst remaining outside the main contract may become a term of a collateral contract ('collateral' because it stands separately from but connected to the main contract).

A good example of a collateral contract is in *Esso Petroleum Ltd v. Commissioners of Customs & Excise.* Esso had a promotion scheme whereby anyone buying four gallons of petrol at one of its filling stations could get a free coin, specially manufactured, showing various members of the England football team that had taken part in the World Cup in that year. The way the majority of the House of Lords analysed the transaction was as follows. The sign 'World Cup coin free with every four gallons' was an offer. It was accepted when one entered into the contract to buy four gallons of petrol. It was in fact saying 'If you will enter into contract to buy four gallons of petrol, we will give you a World Cup coin'. In other words, 'in consideration of you entering into the main contract we offer you a World Cup coin'. This was a contract collateral to the main contract for the purchase of petrol.

Another example is *De Lassalle v. Guildford.* Here a prospective tenant refused to sign his part of the lease until he was assured that the drains were in order. The landlord assured him that they were – when in fact they were not. The landlord was held to be in breach, not of the lease which contained no term about drains, but of the collateral contract. This concept of the collateral contract can mean that the breach of undertakings which are not part of the main contract can still be a breach of contract. These undertakings are terms of another subsidiary or collateral contract.

Implied terms

Contracts are not made up solely of matters that are actually stated by the parties. Some terms will be implied into a contract. This may happen because the parties have thought a particular matter so self-evident that they have not bothered to mention it. If this matter must be incorporated in order to make business sense of the contract (or to give it business efficacy as it is described by the courts) the law will supply the missing term.

In *The Moorcock* the defendants were wharfingers who had contracted to allow the plaintiff to discharge and load their steamship at the defendants' wharf. Both parties knew that the ship would ground at low tide, but nothing was said about the state of the river bed. When the ship grounded, it struck a ridge of hard ground and was damaged. The Court of Appeal held that the defendants were in breach of their contractual obligation even though nothing had been said expressly. A term was implied that the defendants warranted that the bed would be reasonably safe.

The circumstances in which the court will imply a term are however rather restricted. They cannot imply terms solely on the grounds of reasonableness.

Besides the limited circumstances in which the courts may imply a term at common law, terms may be implied to give effect to trade customs, but only when such usages are universally observed by the trade and when they are not varied by express terms of the contract.

By far the most important kind of implied terms in practice, however, are those implied by statute. One of the most important groups for our purposes is that of Sale of Goods. Where the contract is for the sale of goods certain terms are implied by the Sale of Goods Act 1893 as amended by the Supply of Goods (Implied Terms) Act 1973, the Consumer Credit Act 1974 and the Unfair Contract Terms Act 1977. We will be looking at these Acts again in a later chapter to see how they deal as a whole with the question of consumer protection, but for the moment we will confine ourselves to looking at what terms are actually implied when the Acts apply.

The parts of the Sale of Goods Act we shall look at are sections 12, 13 and 14, which imply terms as to title, correspondence to description, merchantable quality and fitness for purpose.

We discuss these four matters in turn.

Title

Section 12(1)(a) provides that there is an implied condition on the part of the seller that he has a right to sell the goods. The reason for this is obvious: if X, having stolen goods, 'sells' them to Y, Y no more becomes an owner in law than X was. They were not X's goods to sell and the mere handing over of the goods from X to Y cannot invest Y with any legal right to them if X had none. The true owner can therefore claim the goods back from Y. By virtue of section 12 X is in breach of a condition. Y can therefore recover from X (if he can find him) the money which Y has paid.

Although the general rule is that no one can pass on a good title to goods unless he has one (*nemo dat quod non habet*) there are some exceptions. For example, a private purchaser who buys a car from a person who has not completed the payments under a hire purchase transaction and so has not become the owner in law would always be at risk under the general rule, but he is protected by the Consumer Credit Act 1974 if he bought the car in good faith.

Description

The implied condition that relates specially to goods sold by description is contained in s. 13(1). It provides that goods shall correspond with their description. Goods are sold by description if they are identified by labelling such as 'a cotton shirt' or 'English tomatoes', or 'timber $2\frac{1}{4}''$ thick', regardless of whether the shopper selects the item himself. Manufactured goods will almost always be sold by description.

Merchantable quality

Section 14(2) provides that 'Where the seller sells goods in the course of a business, there is an implied condition that the goods are of merchantable quality, as regards defects specifically drawn to the buyer's attention before the contract is made; or the buyer examines the goods before the contract is made, as regards defects.'

Several points should be noticed. This does not apply to private sales – only to where goods are sold in the course of a business. Goods are of merchantable quality 'if they are as fit for the purpose or purposes for which goods of that kind are commonly bought as it is reasonable to expect having regard to any description applied to them, the price (if relevant) and all the other relevant circumstances'. The goods do not necessarily have to be perfect in every way and there is considerable scope for judicial definition.

The condition does not apply if the defect is brought to the attention of the purchaser, e.g. it is common to find 'seconds' being sold marked 'slightly soiled'. If the buyer chooses to examine the goods, he cannot later complain of defects which he ought reasonably to have discovered (but ironically the buyer who ignores an opportunity to inspect the goods has his full legal rights).

Fitness for purpose

Section 14(3) provides that if the buyer makes known to the seller any particular purpose for which the goods are being bought, there is an implied condition that the goods supplied under the contract are reasonably fit for that purpose.

The buyer who says, for example, 'I want some paint that will be suitable for painting the outside of my house' is imposing the condition on the seller as he is making known the particular purpose. Often the purpose will be obvious, e.g. food is to be eaten, clothes worn, so that the food which causes poisoning, or clothes which cause dermititis, are not 'fit for the purpose' within s. 14(3).

The seller can escape liability, if he makes it clear that the buyer is not to rely on the seller's skill and judgement: s. 14(3). The seller will often have a greater knowledge of the capability of the product he is selling but if he does not know whether the goods are fit for the particular purpose that they are being bought for, the onus is on him to make it clear to the buyer.

One important factor should be noted concerning all these terms, and that is that liability is strict. That is, a person may be in breach of one of the implied conditions even though he has taken all reasonable care. This is a particular advantage of suing in contract. As we will see, liability in tort for supplying defective goods depends on the purchaser being able to prove negligence on the part of the supplier.

Conditions and warranties

Not all terms of a contract are of equal importance, and it is only common sense that breach of a relatively minor obligation should not give the injured party the same remedies as breach of a relatively major one.

The more important terms are called 'conditions', the less important terms 'warranties'. (This is the modern import of the words, though in some cases, particularly the older ones, the words are used somewhat indiscriminately.) The essential difference lies in the different remedies available in the event of a breach.

A breach of warranty gives the innocent party a right to sue for damages only. He will still be bound to perform the contract himself. Breach of condition on the other hand gives the injured party a right not only to sue for damages but also a right to treat the contract as at an end if he so wishes. He may elect to affirm, or carry on with the contract, though he may still pursue his remedy of suing for damages.

It will often be clear when the contract is made which terms are conditions and which are warranties. Where the terms concerned are terms implied by statute, statute will usually say whether it is to be a condition or a warranty, e.g. sections 12–14 SGA 1893. The parties may themselves specify whether a term is to be a condition or a warranty, and this will be strong evidence that the term was intended to be a major or a minor one. It is not conclusive, though, and the parties cannot arbitrarily describe minor terms as conditions (*L. Schuler A.G. v. Wickman Machine Tool Sales Ltd*).

It has, however, been recognised by the courts that it is not always possible to decide at the outset whether the term is a major or minor one. Take the example of a contract for the carriage of goods by sea. One of the terms will be that the ship is in a seaworthy condition. This may be broken in so many ways that it is impossible to say before breach whether the results will be so minor that the parties should be bound to carry on with the contract or whether they will be so disastrous that the innocent party should be free from his obligations. The way round this problem is to accept that it will not always be possible to predict the outcome in advance, but that the test should be applied after the results of the breach are known. The test is that if the innocent party is deprived of substantially the whole intended benefit under the contract, he may sue for damages and treat the contract as repudiated, as with a condition. If he is not deprived of substantially the whole benefit under the contract, then he is limited to suing for damages and must carry on with the contract.

Summary and conclusions

1. To date we have examined how a valid contract comes into being. Equally as important for the parties involved in business is the question: what action is possible under the contract? This obviously depends on what the contract contains and to determine this we need to look at:

    (*a*) What was said. Whether statements made become part of the contract. (Contractual terms or mere representations.)
    (*b*) What terms are implied into a contract.
    (*c*) Whether the things said were of equal importance.

2. *Contractual terms* – In trying to determine a contract's content, three criteria are used:

    (*a*) the *time* a statement was made;
    (*b*) the *importance* of the term to one party;
    (*c*) the relative degrees of knowledge of the parties.

These help to distinguish between statements that are part of the contract and those that remain outside.

3. *Mere representations* – Although terms may be 'outside' the main contract they become important when:

    (*a*) they fulfil the conditions of a misrepresentation;
    (*b*) they are part of a separate but connected (or collateral) contract.

4. *What was implied?* – Sometimes terms are implied into contracts although the parties have not stated them specifically. Such implied terms are usually restricted to:

    (*a*) giving a contract business efficacy;
    (*b*) giving effect to custom or trade use;
    (*c*) where terms are implied by Statute (e.g. under the Sale of Goods Act which implies terms as to Title, Description, Merchantable Quality, Fitness for Purpose).

5. *Were the things said of equal importance?*

    (*a*) Important terms are called 'conditions' (breach of these mean a right to sue for damages plus right to treat contract as at an end).
    (*b*) Less important terms are called 'warranties' (breach of these means a right to sue for damages only).

6. Thus, much depends on whether there is a serious or less serious breach of obligation and whether it is of terms felt to be important at the outset of the contract. Only when these more or less important areas have been investigated is it possible to say what the contract contains and what action is possible under it.

Assignments

12.1

Percy is a private motorist. He wanted to sell his car and called in at George's garage. Percy asked George what price he would give him for his car. George said that the price would depend on the age and state of the car. Percy told him that the car was a 1975 model, which he honestly believed it was because the number plate ended with the letter P. He also said that he thought that the car had had a new engine put in it shortly before he had bought it. George then said that in that case he would offer Percy £900 for the car.

    Percy looked at the cars which George had on the garage forecourt and told George that he was only interested in a car which would do at least 35 miles to the gallon. George pointed out one particular car and said that he thought this car was just what he had been looking for. Percy agreed to sell his present car to

George for £900 and buy in part exchange the car that George pointed out for £2,000.

One week later George found out that Percy's old car was in fact a 1972 model and had never had a replacement engine. Percy discovered that his new car would only do 20 miles to the gallon. Advise Percy and George on their contractual position.

12.2

Explain with examples how the courts use the device of the collateral contract.

12.3

In what circumstances will a term be implied into a contract (1) at common law; (2) by statute?

12.4

Explain the difference between (1) express and implied terms; (2) mere representations and contractual terms; (3) conditions and warranties.

13 The ending of contracts

Introduction

We must conclude our survey of the general law of contract by looking at the ways in which contractual relationships can come to an end. Many of these relationships will end by the contract being properly performed: proper performance will mean that the contract is over. Sometimes, however, the contract will be breached or frustrated. When this is the case we need also to look at the rules regulating the remedies (if any) available to the disappointed party.

Performance

Most contracts come to an end by performance: once the obligations on each side have been performed, the contract is discharged.

The performance must match the obligation exactly. If, for example, the contract provides that one party is to deliver 100 tons of coal, delivery of 99 tons does not amount to performance of the contract. If the supplier thinks that he may not be able to comply with the letter of the contract, then he must make some provision for leeway in the contract itself. Once his contractual obligations are fixed, his duty is to perform them exactly.

As we have mentioned earlier, liability for breach of contract does not depend on fault: it is what we have called strict liability, so that non-performance cannot be excused on the grounds that a party did all he could to perform the contract, unless again he had the foresight to limit his contractual obligations accordingly.

From what has just been said, it might appear that every failure to perform that is not catered for in the contract amounts to a breach of contract. This impression must be qualified. First, where one party is in breach of a condition we have already seen that the other party can treat this as a repudiation of the contract and is himself excused performance. If for example goods are to be supplied in return for payment in advance and the amount is not paid by the due date, the supplier will be excused from delivering the goods. If the rule that any non-performance amounted to a breach applied here, the supplier would also be in breach of contract! Second, the contract may have been frustrated and this will excuse the parties. We will consider this eventuality in more detail later in the chapter.

In some circumstances one side may only partly perform his side of the contract and yet still be entitled to enforce the contract. He may, for example, be able to sue for a reasonable sum if his full performance is prevented by the other party. In *Planché v. Coburn* an author had done most of the work for a series of articles which had been commissioned by a certain periodical, when the periodical ceased publication. He was held to be entitled to a reasonable sum to represent the work done.

Sometimes, however, the obligation is said to be entire, that is that the whole obligation must be completed before there is any entitlement to be paid anything. This was the case in *Cutter v. Powell* where the plaintiff's deceased husband had agreed to work as second mate on a ship travelling from Jamaica to London. He died half way across the Atlantic and his estate was held not to be entitled to a pro-rata payment as the court decided that the lump sum due to be paid to him as wages was due if and only if he completed the whole voyage. (Often, of course, contracts of service will be severable with the employee being entitled to a proportion of the amount due under the contract.)

Another example of a person not fulfilling completely his contractual obligation and yet being entitled to some payment is where the partial performance is accepted by the other party. The other party may well find it to his advantage to accept what he can, and provided he has a real choice in the matter he will be obliged to pay for the benefit he has received. The choice must be voluntary, however, and if the other party has no option but to take what he can get the exception will not apply. This rule was laid down in *Sumpter v. Hedges*. The plaintiff agreed to build two houses for the defendant on the defendant's land for a lump sum of £565, but ran out of money when the buildings were partially completed. He was not entitled to a reasonable sum for the work completed because the defendant had had no option but to accept the partial performance and complete the work himself.

Two further points must be made. First a tender or offer of performance is generally as good as performance itself. If, for example, A is due to deliver goods to B and B refuses to accept them, A is not in breach of his obligation to deliver. He has tendered performance and this is equivalent to performance itself. Where the tender is of money, though, the rule does not apply. If the offer of money due under the contract is refused, the money must be paid into court. Second, a problem that frequently arises is the effect of failure to perform at the proper time. The consequences depend on whether time is said to be 'of the essence'. Time is of the essence if the contract expressly states that it is of major importance or if this can be implied (for example, if the goods to be delivered are perishable). Even if time is not originally of the essence so that failure to perform by the agreed time would not amount to a repudiation of the contract, time may subsequently be made of the essence by one party giving notice to the other.

Frustration

As we mentioned above, a contract may not have to be performed (and, indeed, will not be capable of being performed) because it has been frustrated.

When a contract is frustrated, both parties are excused further performance. Frustration brings the contract to an end by operation of law, neither party being at fault.

As we shall see, where the failure to perform a contract arises out of the default of one of the parties, that party is in breach and he must bear the consequences of his breach. But external events sometimes occur that prevent the carrying out of the contract. The contract is then said to have been frustrated, e.g. a contract for the hire of a hall for a concert is frustrated if the hall is destroyed accidentally by fire and through the fault of neither party the contract cannot be carried out (*Taylor v. Caldwell*). The legal result is that both parties are excused further performance of the contract and neither is in breach.

The occasions on which the failure to carry out a contract cannot be attributed to one of the parties is fairly rare. The doctrine of frustration is consequently limited in its application.

A contract is frustrated if, after it has been made, either:

1. property essential to its performance is destroyed or becomes unavailable; or
2. a fundamental change of circumstances occurs; or
3. performance of the contract is rendered unlawful; or
4. a party to the contract is prevented from carrying it out when the contract is one of a personal nature; or
5. a basic assumption on which the parties contracted is destroyed.

The Law Reform (Frustrated Contracts) Act 1943 specifies the effect of frustration on most contractual relationships. Money due and paid before the frustrating event can be recovered whether or not anything has been done, while any sums which were payable before the frustration but have not been paid cease to be so. The court, however, possesses a power to grant to the person who has been (or ought to have been) paid any sum up to the amount of the sum due in respect of any expenses he has incurred in performing the contract. Compensation is also available if one party has provided the other with valuable benefit.

Breach

We have been continually aware of the possibility of contracts coming to an end by breach, but we must now collect together the points that have already been made at various points in our discussion.

Where a party has failed to perform his obligation and is not excused for any of the reasons that we have just noted, he will be in breach of contract. The remedies open to the other party will depend on whether the breach is a breach of an important term or only of a minor one. For breach of a condition (major term), the innocent party has an option. He can elect to carry on with the contract, in which case the offending party will also be bound to carry on, or he may elect to treat the contract as at an end. In either case he may sue for damages. For a breach of a warranty (minor term) he may only sue for damages. Where the term is an innominate term, dependent on whether the innocent party has received substantially the whole benefit under the contract or not, the innocent party can treat the breach as breach of condition or breach of warranty, with the appropriate consequences.

One side may not wait until the time is due for performance before indicating that he does not intend to perform his part of the contract. This is known as 'anticipatory breach'. The result of this is that the other party has immediate remedies. He can sue immediately for damages or he can treat the contract as repudiated. He may, of course, elect to wait to see whether the contract is performed in due course.

Remedies for breach

As we have indicated, then, the major remedy for breach is that of damages. There are however other remedies which are sometimes available to the party wronged and we must mention these briefly before we look in more detail at the rules relating to damages.

Specific performance

Where one party is unwilling to perform his obligations under a contract, the court may order him to carry out his contract. It does this by an order of specific performance.

Normally damages will be the prime remedy where one party has failed to complete his contractual obligations. In some circumstances damages will be an inadequate compensation for the injured party, e.g. a person who has contracted to buy a painting by an old master, or who has agreed to buy a plot of land, is not necessarily compensated by an award of money. Where he has contracted to buy a unique item the court may be willing to order that the contract be carried out, not merely that damages should be awarded.

The courts will only grant specific performance if they can compel the carrying out of the contract, e.g. they will not order the specific performance of a contract of employment.

Injunction

An injunction is a court order which orders a person to refrain from doing something. In the field of contract it will restrain a party to a contract from acting in breach of negative undertakings in the contract. It can also be used to prevent breach of a positive promise if that promise can be construed as a negative one, e.g. in *Manchester Ship Canal Co v. Manchester Racecourse Co* a promise to grant a 'first refusal' was construed as a promise not to sell to anyone else first and breach of the provision was prevented by injunction.

Like specific performance the injunction is an equitable remedy. Both remedies may be granted with or without an order for damages.

Damages

Damages will normally be the remedy that is sought. The object of the court in

109

awarding damages is to compensate the injured party for the loss that he has suffered and not to punish the party in breach.

Several consequences flow from this fact. First, although breach of contract is actionable without proof of loss, unless real loss has been suffered the damages awarded will only be a nominal amount and the party who brings such an action may have to pay his own costs. Where loss has been suffered damages will be awarded representing that loss. These are known as substantial damages, indicating not that the sum is necessarily a large one, but merely that they represent compensation for actual loss.

Second, the object of contract damages is to put the party in the position he would have been in had the contract been performed. (This must be contrasted with the corresponding principle in tort, which is that damages are to put the party in the position he would have been in if the tort had never been committed.)

Remoteness of damage

In calculating the damages that should be awarded the court must initially decide what losses are to be compensated. A breach of contract may be the start of a chain of events which can lead to exceptional loss in a particular case. We can illustrate this by an example. A hires a taxi to take him to Station B. The taxi driver by mistake takes him to Station C. The result of this is that A has to take another taxi to the correct station, finds that his train has already left, has to spend the night in a hotel and travel next morning with the result that he is late for a business appointment and loses a very valuable order which goes to his competitor with the result that A's firm goes out of business and A and his fellow workers lose their jobs. There is no doubt that the taxi driver's breach of contract in taking A to the wrong station ultimately led to A losing his job, but it would be a very harsh rule that dictated that the taxi driver was liable to compensate A and all his fellow-workers for losing their jobs, when the taxi-driver had no way of knowing what the extraordinary consequences of his mistake would be.

The principle that applies to limit liability for the consequences of breach of contract is the principle of 'remoteness of damage'. The principle accepts that some losses may be too remote to be compensated. The rule that shows how it is decided whether the loss is too remote was formulated in *Hadley v. Baxendale*. In that case, the owners of a mill sent a broken mill-shaft to be used as a pattern for a new one. The defendants were the carriers. Their delay en route resulted in loss of profits to the mill because, unknown to the carriers, the mill-owners did not have a spare shaft. This loss was not recovered.

The rule was stated as follows: 'Where two parties have made a contract which one of them has broken, the damages which the other party ought to receive in respect of such breach of contract should be such as may fairly and reasonably be considered as arising naturally, i.e. according to the usual course of things, from such breach of contract, or such loss as may reasonably be supposed to have been in the contemplation of both parties at the time they made the contract, as the probable result of the breach of it.' On the facts of this case the loss of profits was not a loss arising in the usual course of things because normally the loss of a shaft would not bring the mill to a halt; the mill owner might have a spare. Nor was this special factor that the mill would have to stop known to the carrier when the

110

contract was made, so that it could not be said to have been 'in the contemplation of both parties'.

The recent Court of Appeal decision in *Parsons v. Uttley Ingham & Co* has added a modification to this: it now appears sufficient if the *type* of loss was liable to result even though the actual loss was not or was far greater than could have been expected.

Quantification

Once it has been decided what losses are to be compensated various factors must be taken into account to decide what measure of damages will be awarded. We will consider four of the most important:

1. Mitigation   An injured party cannot merely sit back and let his losses pile up follwing a breach of contract by the other side. He is bound to take reasonable steps to mitigate or lessen his own loss. So, for example, if the seller of goods fails to deliver them the buyer is obliged to take reasonable steps to obtain them elsewhere. If the goods are freely available he may be able to obtain them at the same price or even cheaper and with little delay. Thus he will not suffer any loss, and would consequently only be entitled to nominal damages if he sued for breach of contract.

2. The market rule   If there is a ready market for the goods or services which form the subject matter of a contract, losses consequent on breach of that contract are calculated according to the market price, e.g. if X has agreed to sell goods to Y for £100 and fails to deliver, the price on the market for the goods may have risen to £110. X's damages will be £10, representing the difference between the contract price and the market price he has to pay to get the goods elsewhere. Conversely if Y tries to deliver but X refuses to take delivery and because the market has fallen Y can only sell for £90 his damages will be £10, again reflecting the difference between the contract and market prices.

Where there is no market it is more difficult to quantify the loss. One important factor to be taken into account is the supply and demand situation. For example, where the buyer defaults in circumstances in which supply exceeds demand, the seller's loss will generally be taken to be the whole of the lost profits.

A case which illustrates this is *W. L. Thompson Ltd v. Robinson (Gunmakers) Ltd*. The defendants agreed to buy a Vanguard car from the plaintiffs and then refused to accept delivery. The plaintiffs would have made £61 profit on the deal. The defendants argued that the plaintiffs could have sold the car to another customer, making the same profit and should therefore only be entitled to nominal damages. The argument failed. Because supply exceeded demand the plaintiffs had in fact sold one less car than they could have done. Their loss was consequently the whole loss of profits on the transaction.

The converse of this happened in *Charter v. Sullivan*. A buyer of a Hillman Minx car refused to accept delivery of it, but the seller was held only to be entitled to nominal damages. As demand exceeded supply he could sell as many cars as he himself could obtain.

3. Speculative damages   Mere difficulty in quantifying damages does not prevent the court from awarding a sum that it thinks fit. Often the court will have

111

to speculate on what might have happened if the contract had not been breached. In *Chaplin v. Hicks* the plaintiff had an agreement with the defendant that she would attend an audition with forty-nine other actresses at which she would have the chance of being selected as one of twelve who were to be employed. She was denied the opportunity to attend the audition and was awarded substantial damages, even though her chance of being chosen was less than one in four.

4. Taxation Damages awarded by a court may or may not be taxed in the hands of the recipient. For example, a trader who receives damages in respect of loss of profits on a business contract will have to pay tax on his damages just as he would have had to pay tax on profits actually made from the contract. An individual who receives damages for loss of future earnings will generally not have to pay tax on his damages, although had he gone on to earn the same amount of money, he would have been taxed. The rule, laid down in *B.T.C. v. Gourley*, is that where damages are awarded which are not themselves taxable but which represent items which are taxable, the incidence of tax must be taken into account when calculating the damages.

Liquidated damages and penalties

Very often the parties to a contract provide in advance what the measure of damages will be in the event of a breach. Such a clause is called an 'agreed damages' or 'liquidated damages' clause. The courts will enforce such clauses only if they are genuine attempts to pre-estimate the actual loss resulting from the breach. If the parties intended the clause not as a pre-estimate but to operate as a fine for breach this is a penalty clause. In the case of a penalty clause (though not of a liquidated damages clause) if the actual loss of a plaintiff is less than the sum specified in the clause he will recover only his actual loss.

Summary and conclusions

1. It has been established how a valid contract is drawn up and what action is possible once it is operative. We now examine the way in which contracts come to an end – either through 'proper performance' or through being 'frustrated' or 'breached'.
2. *Proper performance* – is said to be achieved when the obligations on each side of the contract are carried out so that it is at an end.
2.1 Duties must be performed exactly.
2.2 Failure to complete (or 'perform') is not always breach when:

    (*a*) the other party has repudiated the contract;
    (*b*) full performance is prevented by the other party;
    (*c*) partial performance is accepted by the other party;
    (*d*) the contract has been 'frustrated' (see below).

3. *Frustration* – is said to occur when external events create a change in circumstances that is beyond the control of the parties involved and prevents them from carrying it out. Frustration can occur in five instances.
3.1 The effects of frustration depend for most contracts on the Law Reform (Frustrated Contracts) Act 1943.

4. *Breach*

4.1 If a party fails to carry out ('perform') their obligation(s) they can be excused for the reasons listed in point 2 above; if none of these apply they are in *breach of contract*.

4.2 Breach can be of an important term ('condition') or a minor term ('warranty').

5. *Remedies* – are the actions open to an injured party and might be thought of in terms of options in relation to both breach of condition and breach of warranty. The options available are:

(*a*) continue with the contract;
(*b*) get the contract enforced (specific performance);
(*c*) get a court order preventing breach (injunction);
(*d*) obtain financial compensation (damages);

5.1 Where damages are awarded the following points are important:

(*a*) damages are 'nominal' unless there has been real (or 'actual') loss and the party bringing the action may have to pay costs;
(*b*) damages are meant to compensate so that the party is no worse off than if the contract had been performed;
(*c*) some losses may be too remote to be compensated ('remoteness of damage');
(*d*) the *amount* of damage has to be decided upon (quantified), bearing in mind:

(i) the steps taken by the injured party to limit his loss (mitigation);
(ii) the current market value of any goods or services in the contract (market rule);
(iii) the need to estimate where no clear guidelines exist (speculative damages);
(iv) any tax that might be incurred (e.g. on loss of profits or earnings).

6. This concludes the survey of the *law of contract* – a very important element in the general legal structure that helps to order business affairs. Few business organisations could obtain resources, supply goods or buy in services without the framework of rules that govern contracts; the latter also provide the basis of special legal rules which regulate the vital relationships existing between firms and their customers and workers, as we shall see later in our studies.

Assignments

13.1

Explain the difference between entire and severable obligations.

13.2

Has the contract been frustrated in the following examples:

(a) C was an English wholesale importer of fruit from Illyria. C had a contract with D, a fruit exporter in Illyria. The contract provided that D should be responsible for all costs and charges of carriage. Due to enemy action by Ruritania the Illyrian Straits were closed and Illyrian ships had to make a long detour through the Baratarian Sea to reach England. This increased D's costs considerably and he now wishes to end the contractual arrangement with C.

(b) A and B entered into a contract under which A agreed to supply £350 worth of sirloin steaks a week for B's steak house. In July, due to an outbreak of tooth and nail disease, a rare disease affecting cattle, an Act of Parliament was passed making it illegal to sell beef products. As a result A cannot supply B with steaks.

13.3

X Company sells knitting machines. Y agrees to buy one to make baby clothes which he plans to sell in his craft shop. Because of the bad winter few tourists visit Y's shop. Y decides not to buy the knitting machine and informs X that he will not take delivery. X would have made a profit of £50. Advise X as to his measure of damages against Y if:

1. X has a waiting list of customers and is able to sell the machine the next day at the same price.
2. Knitwear has become unfashionable and X is finding it very difficult to sell machines.

13.4

Explain the principle of remoteness of damage in the law of contract. Do you agree that a limit should be imposed on a person's contractual liability and if so, why?

13.5

What is the difference between an 'agreed damages clause' and a 'penalty clause'?

13.6

X agreed to ship a cargo of Y's fresh fruit to Lilliputia by 1st October. He knew that Y would sell the fruit at the local market, but did not realise that Y was hoping to make a large profit by selling the fruit in time for the local festival which was to take place on 5th October. The captain of X's ship carelessly misread his maps and as a result arrived at Lilliputia one week late, with the result that Y had to sell his fruit after the festival at a loss.

Advise Y on whether he can recover his loss from X as damages for breach of contract.

14 The market

Introduction

In Chapter 7, when discussing the policies of business organisations, we examined the various ways in which a supplier might attempt to increase the revenue obtained from the sale of a particular product. We showed that he might, for example, attempt to build into his product characteristics not possessed by other products (a process known as product differentiation). Or he might sell his product through additional channels of distribution. After discussing these policies, we noted that 'The scope for increasing revenue in one or other of these ways depends upon the state of demand and the degree of competition in the market.' We discuss demand in the next chapter, but first it is necessary to explain what we mean by the term 'market'. There are in fact several alternative definitions of a market, and we consider each in turn.

The market as a mechanism

One definition of a market is 'a mechanism whereby offers to sell, made by suppliers, are matched with offers to buy, made by purchasers'. This mechanism may take several different forms. In some instances suppliers and purchasers meet face-to-face. One example is the market stall, to be found in many towns on one or several days of each week, where the suppliers of meat, cheese, fruit, etc., personally sell to customers. Another example is the various metal exchanges where sellers and buyers meet at pre-appointed times in a limited number of international centres, such as London, and make contracts for the delivery of agreed quantities of metal on given dates. In this case the product is not present when trading takes place, and the contract will therefore carefully specify the characteristics of the product, e.g. the degree of purity of the metal.

In other instances the market comprises a series of telephone links, on a national or even an international basis. Foreign exchange is traded in such a market.

Yet another type of market is the auction sale where the auctioneer, acting on behalf of the owners of the goods being sold, is face to face with the potential purchasers (who may be acting on their own or someone else's behalf).

Trading in shares on the Stock Exchange is undertaken by stock jobbers who fulfil orders (to buy or sell) given to them by brokers who are acting as agents for the owners (or potential owners) of the shares. In this instance six people are involved in the transfer of ownership, the initial and the eventual owners, two brokers and two jobbers.

We have by no means exhausted the list of types of markets, but we can see that in every market the essential feature of the mechanism is the matching of offers to sell and offers to buy. (Incidentally there is no guarantee that these offers will exactly match. Sellers may be unable to sell, or buyers to buy, as much as they wish.)

The market as demand

We use market in this sense when we say 'How big is the market for cars likely to be in the year 2000?', or 'I doubt if there is much of a market for central heating in equatorial countries', or 'The market for home freezers is expanding by 5 per cent a year'. In each of these statements the term 'market' refers to the demand for the product in question. (In fact demand is used rather loosely here, and an economist would point out that demand should be related not only to a particular product, geographical area and time period, but also to the price of the product. We take up this point below. However, for the moment we are simply concerned to illustrate the different meanings of the term 'market'.)

The market as a group of customers

This third definition contains elements of the previous two. The offers to buy of purchasers, or customers, constitute part of the market mechanism *and* part of the demand for the product. However, note that a given number of customers may buy different quantities of the product in different time periods. Moreover customers may enter (and leave) the market between one period and another.

The market as a group of customers and a group of suppliers

Since the volume of sales is influenced by the activities of suppliers it would seem to be appropriate to include suppliers in our definition of the market. Indeed in most classifications of markets the number of suppliers is an important factor. Since it includes both suppliers and purchasers, this fourth definition comes very close to our first one. But that definition treated the market as an abstract concept (the mechanism for matching offers to buy and sell), whereas here we emphasise the institutional aspect, the actual organisations which make these offers. It is in this sense that we use the term market in the remainder of this chapter.

Market forms

Markets, defined as a group of customers and a group of suppliers, can be classified in different ways. We adopt a classification which will help us to explain certain decisions, especially those relating to price and output, made by suppliers. (These decisions are discussed in greater detail in Chapter 18.) Our classification will also help to explain how economic resources are allocated. (See Chapter 24.)

The most important features of a market are: the number of suppliers and, associated with this, the extent to which they can co-ordinate their decisions; the conditions of entry and exit; the characteristics of the product; the nature of the production process; and the number of purchasers. We examine each of these features in turn.

The number of suppliers

The number of suppliers in a market depends upon where we draw the boundary around the market. This may seem an obvious point but in fact it can give rise to considerable practical difficulties.

It may be difficult to know where to draw the geographical boundaries of a market. Is the market international, national or local (e.g. regional)? We might in fact wish to use all of these definitions. For example, it would not be sensible to discuss the UK car market without taking into account suppliers located overseas, since imports sometimes account for around half of all new cars sold in the UK. At the other extreme the Fair Trading Act extended the powers of the Monopolies and Mergers commission to include the investigation of local monopolies, i.e. situations in which one supplier accounts for at least 25 per cent of the sales of a product in one part of the country.

Even greater difficulties may arise in deciding which products constitute the market. For example, we might define the market for cars to include all types of car; on the other hand we might consider that this definition was too wide and that there are in fact a number of smaller, distinct, markets, e.g. for family saloons, sports cars, limousines. The justification for this latter view would be that at any one time there are distinct groups of purchasers for each type (although a person might, of course, move from one group to another over time as changes occur in his income, family responsibilities, etc.). The number of suppliers will clearly be greater the more types of car we include within our definition of the market.

Having mentioned some of the difficulties that may arise in practice, let us assume that we can identify the number of suppliers in a given market, and consider the significance of this factor. The most important implication is that *as a general rule* the smaller the number of suppliers the greater the discretion a supplier will enjoy in his pricing decisions.

Markets with a single supplier

In order to explain why this is so let us first consider the situation in which one supplier has an absolute monopoly, i.e. 100 per cent of the market. The market demand coincides with the monopolist's demand, and in deciding what price to set the monopolist only needs to take into account customers' reactions to price. He does not need to worry about the reactions of his competitors since there are none! So in Fig. 14.1 he can choose to sell Q_1 at price P_1 or Q_2 at price P_2. (Which combination he chooses will, of course, depend upon his objectives and upon his costs of production.)

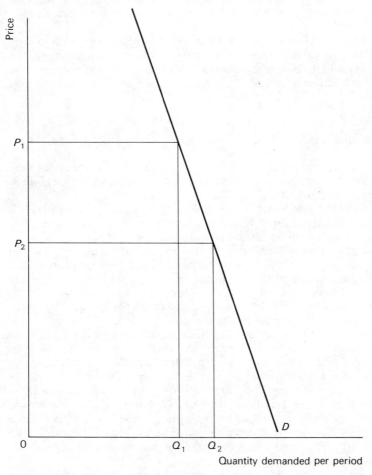

Fig. 14.1 The demand curve of a monopolist

Markets with two suppliers

Let us next consider the situation where there are two suppliers. Their market shares will depend upon a number of factors – the characteristics and, in particular, the quality of their products, the number and type of distribution channels used, their advertising expenditure, etc.

In Fig. 14.2 we assume, in order to simplify the analysis, that the net effect of these factors is that each supplier has 50 per cent of the market provided that their prices are identical. The market demand is denoted by D_M and the demand

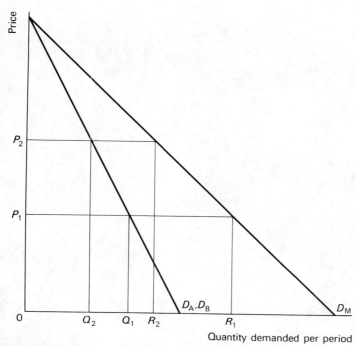

Fig. 12.2 Demand curves for the market and two suppliers

for the two suppliers by D_A and D_B. If both suppliers set price P_1 each would sell Q_1 and the total quantity sold would be R_1 $(=2Q_1)$.

If one supplier considers setting a different price he will have to take into account the reactions of the other supplier. If supplier A raised his price to P_2 and B followed suit, the original demand curves (drawn on the assumption of equal prices) would continue to apply. Each supplier would sell Q_2 and total sales would be R_2. But what would happen if B did not follow suit; if he raised his price by a smaller amount or even maintained his price at P_1?

Obviously A would be likely to lose sales to B. How many sales he would lose depends partly upon the price differential and partly upon differences in the other factors mentioned above, e.g. the quality of their products, the channels of distribution, etc. The decision facing purchasers who previously bought from A would be whether the reasons which led them to buy from A when prices were equal, were sufficiently strong as to outweigh the additional cost. (It might be useful to refresh your memory at this point by glancing back at the situation facing our imaginary producer of golf balls, discussed in Chapter 7.) The fewer the differences between the two products the greater would be the number of customers switching from A to B.

This process can be described in terms of the elasticity of demand, a concept introduced in Chapter 7.

In Fig. 14.3 we reproduce the demand curve for firm A shown in Fig. 14.2. This curve is now labelled D_1. D_2 and D_3 are two alternative demand curves for A, both of which are drawn on the assumption that B maintains the initial price P_1.

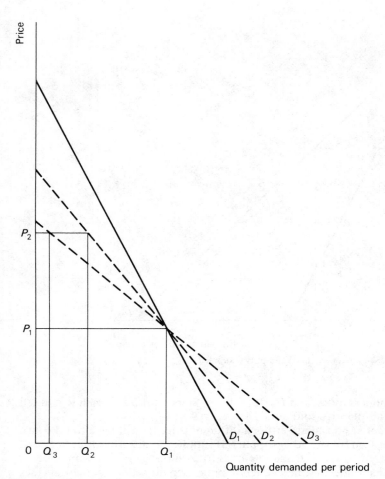

Fig. 14.3 Alternative demand curves

Let us start from this initial price and consider what would happen if A raised his price to P_2.

With demand D_2 A's sales would fall from Q_1 to Q_2. With demand D_3 the fall would be even more drastic, to Q_3. In other words the demand curve D_3 is more elastic than D_2. (Both, of course, are more elastic than D_1 which, it will be remembered, is drawn on the assumption that the prices of the two suppliers are identical.)

Pricing discretion

So far in this chapter we have considered markets with one and two suppliers, and we have seen that when there are two suppliers, each supplier has much less discretion in his pricing decisions, since he has to take into account the decisions which his competitor may make. This was especially well illustrated by the reduction in sales which A would suffer if B decided not to follow his price

120

increase and customers felt that there were few important differences (apart from price) between the two suppliers (demand curve D_3). In these circumstances A would be under very strong pressure not to raise his price.

Similarly if A was contemplating lowering his price below P_1 he would be less likely to do so if he believed that B would match the reduction, i.e. that the demand curve would be D_1 rather than D_2 or D_3.

In showing that A may have very little discretion we have, of course, made assumptions about B's reactions which are the least favourable to A, namely that B maintains his price when A raises his, but lowers his price when A lowers his. The situation would be quite different if A and B could reach an understanding whereby they would co-ordinate their pricing decisions, both raising (or lowering) prices together.

The co-ordination of pricing decisions

There are various means by which pricing (and other) decisions might be co-ordinated, but in every instance co-ordination is likely to be easier to achieve the smaller the number of suppliers. This implies that the smaller the number of suppliers, the greater the discretion in pricing enjoyed by each supplier will tend to be.

Formal agreements. The highest degree of co-ordination is likely to be achieved when suppliers can enter into a formal agreement. However, the provisions of the law mean that formal agreements concerning prices are difficult to sustain in many countries, including the UK, other EEC countries and the USA.

The creation of the Organisation of Petroleum Exporting countries (OPEC) illustrated the benefits which producers can obtain by entering into such an agreement. In the 1960s and early 1970s the price of oil had risen less quickly than that of goods in general. However, the members of OPEC were then able to agree on a series of increases that raised the price of oil six-fold. (Incidentally OPEC was formed in 1960, but its members achieved the will to act collectively and efficiently only as a result of the Arab–Israeli conflict in 1973.)

Agreement on prices implies agreement about output levels since the volume of sales will be influenced by prices. In some instances the parties to an agreement have formed a central selling organisation or cartel through which all the members' sales are made. A cartel increases the chances that the agreed prices and output will be adhered to. However, cartels are very likely to fall foul of the law. Moreover in earlier periods, when legislation was less stringent, numerous cartels broke up because individual members became unwilling to accept constraints on their activities.

Informal agreements. Informal agreements are often concerned with the same matters as formal agreements, and especially with prices and output levels. However, informal agreements are usually less detailed, of a more temporary nature, and not documented. Indeed they might sometimes be better described as understandings than agreements. (Incidentally, an agreement need not be documented to be treated as such in the eyes of the law. Under the terms of the Restrictive Trade Practices and Fair Trading Acts there is no distinction between an agreement which is set out in detail in a large manual, and one which is reached by two suppliers over the telephone. It may, however, be difficult to enforce the law in relation to the latter because of a lack of evidence.)

A typical forum for the birth of an informal agreement would be a trade association meeting at which the discussion would turn, possibly over lunch, to the fact that rising costs were hitting profits, and that in order to restore profits to their previous level a price rise of around 5 per cent would be required. In contrast to the formal agreement, suppliers do not promise that they will put up their prices; nor is there any sanction if they fail to do so. Consequently the informal agreement is a weaker method of achieving co-ordination than the formal agreement.

Information agreements.　Under these agreements, which may be formal or informal, participants agree to exchange information about various activities and decisions, especially important being information concerning costs and prices. Outside observers have expressed most concern about agreements to supply information about prices charged, especially where suppliers agree to give advance notice of impending price increases, since these are seen as an invitation to competitors to raise their prices.

Price leadership.　Price leadership is said to exist when, without any agreement, formal or informal, a change in price by one supplier is followed by all (or most) other suppliers. The price leader is usually a firm with a high market share. However this is not always so. Moreover the identity of the price leader may change from time to time.

Price leadership is the weakest of the methods of achieving co-ordination that we have discussed. However, it has sometimes proved effective in markets in which there are few changes in the balance between demand and supply.

Summary: The number of suppliers and the co-ordination of decisions

We can say that as a general, although by no means universal, rule, the pricing discretion enjoyed by a supplier increases as the number of suppliers in the market falls. We examine in Chapter 18 how this discretion may be exercised. We shall see that one of the consequences is that suppliers are able to exercise more control over their profit margins, and that they usually take costs as the starting point when setting price. We also discuss in that chapter the behaviour of suppliers who have little or no pricing discretion. In the rest of this chapter we discuss the remaining aspects of a market that we listed above.

The conditions of entry and exit

Barriers to entry

The following factors may make if difficult for a supplier who wishes to enter a market to do so:

1. Heavy financial expenditure on plant and equipment; for example, to build a modern large car assembly plant would cost over £100 m.
2. Absolute cost advantages enjoyed by existing suppliers, due to control over vital raw materials or labour skills, greater scientific and technical knowledge or simply to experience in making the product.

122

3. A high level of consumer loyalty to the brands of existing suppliers. This loyalty might be due either to the quality of the product or to long exposure to advertising.

4. Difficulty in gaining access to adequate channels of distribution. In the market for many low-value consumer products, such as groceries, retailers are often reluctant to stock new products, or additional brands of existing products, because this would mean reducing the shelf-space available for other products or brands. Also retailers may be reluctant to increase the number of suppliers with whom they deal (although some new brands and products will, of course, be produced by their existing suppliers).

The greater are the barriers to entry the greater is the freedom of action enjoyed by existing suppliers. One aspect of this freedom is discretion in pricing, discussed above. Another aspect is that existing suppliers may be willing to spend more money on research and development, since there is less chance of profits from new products being quickly eroded as new entrants 'jump on the bandwagon'. (However, it is also possible that barriers to entry may reduce the pressure on producers to introduce new products and processes in order to combat competition.)

Ease of exit

The ease of exit from a market is a rather different concept. In one sense there is no difference between one market and another, since any supplier can leave any market by closing down. However, few firms are willing to close down completely. Most firms, when withdrawing from one market, hope to utilise at least some of their assets in another market, either directly or by selling them and purchasing new assets. Consequently exit will be easiest when there is the greatest opportunity for the redeployment of assets. (Of course in some instances exit occurs because firms have insufficient financial resources to carry on, even though they wish to do so.)

A market from which (voluntary) exit has been difficult is shipping. If a supplier, i.e. a shipowner, cannot find sufficient customers who wish to travel, or transport goods, by sea, there is little else that he can use the ship for. The effect of this difficulty of exit is that when demand is depressed shipowners accept much lower prices in order to try to keep their ships occupied.

At the other extreme, if the owner of property in a city centre, such as a shop or a bank, wishes to withdraw from that area he usually has little difficulty in selling the premises for some other purpose. Alternatively the owner may himself put them to another use.

The characteristics of the product

The most important characteristic has already been referred to several times previously (see especially Chapter 7), namely whether the products offered by the various suppliers in a given market are identical (homogeneous) or differentiated in one way or another.

As we noted earlier in this chapter, cars are so different, in terms of styling, engine capacity, number of seats, etc., that it is appropriate to treat them as being sold in several separate markets. Eventually, however, we reach a point at which the products (or brands) of different suppliers are sufficiently similar as to comprise a single market, e.g. the market for family saloons. Having defined our market, we can then say that the greater the degree of product differentiation within that market the less elastic will be the demand for each supplier's products.

Other important characteristics of the product include whether it is a good or a service, whether it is an industrial or a consumer product, whether it is produced in large numbers (e.g. bread) or small numbers (power stations). Some of these points will be taken up subsequently when we discuss the importance of obtaining information about purchasers.

The nature of the production process

Production processes may differ in various ways. Some processes are labour intensive, others capital intensive. Some give rise to greater economies of scale than others. Some are more continuous in operation than others – electricity generating stations operate for more hours per week than electricity showrooms. These points are taken up in our discussion of the use of resources and the derivation of costs (Chapters 25 and 26). As far as the type of market is concerned, however, the most important aspect relates to the degree of control exercised by the producer over the level of output.

There are many factors which may prevent production plans from being achieved – a strike by the workforce, the non-arrival of vital raw materials, components or machinery, a fire in the factory, etc. Despite these uncertainties producers are often able to predict the output that they can produce.

In some industries, however, accurate prediction of future output levels is difficult and often impossible. This is especially true in agriculture, where yields are heavily dependent upon the weather, and fishing, where the supply of the major raw material can be extremely erratic. The most important consequence of this difficulty in predicting output is that there is a great deal of uncertainty surrounding the price at which the output will be sold. This point is taken up again in Chapter 18.

The number of purchasers

The decision as to where we draw the boundaries of a market affects not only the number of suppliers, as shown above, but also the number of purchasers. Furthermore, in some markets there is an important distinction between the purchaser (from the manufacturer), and the eventual user of the product. Many low-price consumer products, such as groceries, detergents, footwear, etc., are purchased by thousands or even millions of consumers. However the manufacturer of these products may have only a few hundred customers (wholesalers and retailers), some of whom account for a significant proportion of his total sales.

The number of purchasers has important consequences for suppliers' pricing procedures. If a supplier sells to a large number of purchasers he will normally have a price list or schedule which applies to every purchaser (especially if the purchasers are individual consumers). On the other hand if the number of purchasers is small, with each accounting for a significant proportion of the supplier's sales, the price is more likely to be subject to negotiation between supplier and purchaser. (This point is discussed further in Chapter 18.)

Summary and conclusions

We have suggested that the most important aspects of a market are the number of suppliers and the extent to which they are able to co-ordinate their decisions, the conditions of entry and exit, the degree of product differentiation, the nature of the production process (and in particular the extent to which suppliers are able to predict and control the level of output), and the number of purchasers. Various combinations of these factors can give rise to many different market forms. In order to simplify matters we have made, in Table 14.1, a two-fold classification of markets in accordance with the degree of pricing discretion enjoyed by suppliers.

Table 14.1 A classification of market forms

Major features	Markets in which the pricing discretion of suppliers is:	
	High	Low
Number of suppliers	Few	Many
Entry into market	Difficult	Easy
Exit from market	Easy	Difficult
Degree of product differentiation	High	Low
Ability to predict and control the level of output	Good	Poor
Number of purchasers	Many	Few

This table shows the various features which are most likely to characterise each of these two market forms. So, for example, markets in which the pricing discretion of suppliers is high are likely to have fewer suppliers than markets in which discretion is low (or, putting this the other way round, a reduction in the number of suppliers is likely to be accompanied by an increase in the pricing discretion of those suppliers).

Having examined the major features of markets we discuss, in the next chapter, the various factors that influence the level of market demand.

Assignments

14.1

Find out how the other members of your class would define the market for the following products: jeans, hairdressing facilities, shoes, cinema shows, football matches.

14.2

Say whether each of the following statements is true or false:

(a) Under the Fair Trading Act a monopolist is defined as a supplier who accounts for at least one third of the sales of a product.
(b) As a general rule the smaller the number of suppliers in a market, the less discretion each supplier enjoys.
(c) The greater the price elasticity of demand the greater the reduction in sales following an increase in price.
(d) Under the Restrictive Trade Practices Act collective restrictive agreements can be declared illegal, whether they are formal or informal.

14.3

A number of methods of co-ordinating decisions are listed below. Arrange these methods in accordance with the level of co-ordination to which they are likely to give rise. Begin with the lowest (weakest) level of co-ordination and end with the highest (strongest) level:

information agreements;
formal agreements;
price leadership;
informal agreements.

14.4

What barriers to entry do you think might be most important in:

1. the UK shipbuilding industry;
2. the manufacture of medicinal drugs;
3. the introduction of a new brand of toothpaste;
4. off-shore oil exploration.

14.5

1. Identify in the passage below the market features that influence the degree of pricing discretion enjoyed by the Readiseal Company. 2. Say which export market(s) Readiseal should attack, and justify your decision. (Your answer might take the form of a list of advantages and disadvantages for each market.)

The Readiseal Rubber and Plastic Co had been suffering from a squeeze on its profit margins because of increases in costs which it felt unable to pass on in higher prices owing to the intensity of competition. It had decided that the best way of restoring its profits to a more acceptable level was to switch some of its production from the home to the export market and the Board of Directors had met to work out the details. The company had already undertaken research designed to identify markets that offered promising opportunities, and Mr Black, the chairman, asked Mr Dixon, the marketing director, to give a brief report on the findings of this research.

'We can distinguish three broad groups of products,' Dixon said. 'First, there is a large and growing market for seals in a wide range of industrial applications. But unfortunately there are, literally, hundreds of suppliers, all cutting each other's throats.

'In industrial belting the situation is quite different. Because of the capital costs involved on this side of the business there are only a few suppliers and it seems that prices have held up well, even when the market has turned down as it did during the recession two years ago. The demand situation is not wildly exciting, but at least there are more potential customers than at home. As you know, about 90 per cent of our domestic sales of belting are to the British Minerals Board and they have really been putting the screws on us recently.

'Finally, the market for consumer products is probably the most intriguing. In some of these overseas countries parents seem to be willing to buy far more expensive toys for their kids than at home, and some manufacturers are obviously making a killing. But of course market research usually identifies the goods that are selling well. There might have been a lot of failures in the toy market that we know nothing about. The product must be exactly right in this market and I doubt if at present we have the design expertise that is required. If we want to go into the consumer market we might be better to stick to products which are less glamorous and where the margins are lower, but where we have already shown that we can produce what the customer wants. I am thinking of rubber gloves, plastic table-ware – that kind of thing.'

Mr Black said that he was struck by the fact that the market for seals was growing and would like to discuss this market in more detail. 'If at present the suppliers are cutting each other's throats, isn't it possible that a good number of them may soon leave the market, and that prices would then begin to move up?' Mr Dixon admitted that this was possible, but continued: 'I can't say that I am very optimistic. You see, most of the suppliers will try to hang on as long as possible because there is not much else they can make on their machines. Moreover, even if some producers go out of the market they will probably come back in again as soon as prices start to rise. In this part of the trade you only need a couple of thousand pounds and you are in business.'

'In that case,' said Mr Black, 'perhaps we should concentrate on the other two markets at present; but set up a programme aimed at getting us into the market for seals in two or three years time. This means that we will have to offer the customer something he cannot get at present. That, I think, is where you come in, Jack,' he said, turning to Jack Bond, the technical director.

'I would certainly like to have a go at that one,' said Bond. 'Last year the boys in R & D came up with some very promising ideas for giving our seals special properties such as resistance to corrosion, but we didn't follow these up because the home market didn't seem to be big enough to make it worthwhile.'

14.6

Complete the following statement by choosing the more appropriate word from each of the pairs of alternatives. The pricing discretion of suppliers is likely to be greatest when there are: many/few suppliers; entry into the market is difficult/easy; exit from the market is difficult/easy; the degree of product differentiation is high/low; the suppliers' ability to predict and control the level of output is good/poor; there are many/few purchasers.

15 Demographic change and the demand for goods and services

Introduction

In the previous chapter we showed that a market comprises a number of purchasers who offer to buy products (goods or services) and a number of suppliers who offer to sell these products. The volume of any product traded (bought and sold) in a given period depends primarily upon the requirements of purchasers. These requirements are in turn influenced by a wide variety of factors, and in this and the next chapter we discuss the most important of these factors.

In this chapter we confine our attention to the consequences of demographic change (changes in population). Other influences on the demand for goods and services are discussed in Chapter 16.

Changes in population

Changes in the total population of the UK during the twentieth century are shown in Table 15.1. During the first decade the population increased by about

Table 15.1 Total population, United Kingdom

	Total population (millions)	Change in decade (per cent)
1901	38.2	–
1911	42.1	10.2
1921	44.0	4.5
1931	46.0	4.5
1941	48.2	4.8
1951	50.6	5.0
1961	53.0	4.7
1971	55.7	5.1
1975	56.0	0.5*

*Change in 5 years

Source: Office of Population Censuses and Surveys

1 per cent a year (10.2 per cent over the decade as a whole). Then the growth rate fell dramatically and for the rest of the century it has increased by less than ½ per cent a year. However, even this modest growth rate results in a substantial increase in population over a long period as can be seen by comparing, say, the 1971 figure with that of 1911.

The most important determinant of population change is the *natural increase* resulting from the difference between the number of births and the number of deaths. In the UK, as in most other countries, the natural increase has usually been positive, i.e. the number of births has exceeded the number of deaths.

The second determinant of population change is *migration*. Whereas in the earlier part of the century the number of emigrants from the UK invariably exceeded the number of immigrants, the situation has been more variable since then.

Post-war changes in population

The operation in the post-war period of these two determinants is summarised in Tables 15.2 and 15.3. Table 15.2 shows that the rate of natural increase in

Table 15.2 Births and deaths, United Kingdom

	No. of births (000s)	No. of deaths (000s)	Natural increase (000s)	Birth rate (per 000 pop.)	Death rate (per 000 pop.)
1951	797	633	164	15.8	12.6
1961	944	632	312	17.9	12.0
1966	980	644	336	18.0	11.8
1971	902	645	257	16.2	11.6
1972	834	674	160	14.9	12.1
1973	780	670	110	13.9	12.0
1974	737	667	70	13.2	11.9
1975	698	662	36	12.5	11.8
1976	676	681	–5	12.1	12.1

Source: Office of Population Censuses and Surveys

population rose until the mid 1960s under the impact of a falling death rate and a rising birth rate. (The birth rate peaked at 18.8 per 000 in 1964.) Thereafter the rate of natural increase declined – mainly due to a very steep fall in the birth rate – and eventually became negative in 1976 when the number of births was exceeded by the number of deaths for the first time in many years.

Table 15.3 Population change due to migration, United Kingdom (000s)

1951–61	+12	1971	–40
1961–66	+74	1972	–10
1966	–82	1973	–50
1967	–84	1974	–85
1968	–56	1975	–42
1969	–87	1976	–31
1970	–65		

Source: OPCS and Registrar General, Scotland

Table 15.3 shows that until the mid 1960s the number of immigrants exceeded the number of emigrants. Since then the situation has been reversed, and the UK has experienced a net outflow of population each year since 1966. The major reason for this was a tightening of controls on immigration.

The structure of population

Two of the most important aspects of the structure of population are the age and the sex distribution, details of which are given in Table 15.4. We can see that the

Table 15.4 The structure of population, United Kingdom

	Percentage of total population			
	1951	1961	1971	1976
Males:				
Under 15	11.5	11.9	12.4	11.8
15–64	32.4	32.1	31.2	31.4
65 and over	4.5	4.3	5.0	5.6
All ages	48.2	48.5	48.7	48.8
Females:				
Under 15	11.1	11.3	11.7	11.1
15–59	31.6	30.0	28.4	28.6
60 and over	9.1	10.2	11.3	11.6
All ages	51.6	51.5	51.3	51.3
Total population	100	100	100	100

Source: Annual Abstract of Statistics

N.B. The totals do not always add to 100 because of rounding

number of females exceeds the number of males – the actual excess is about $1\frac{1}{2}$ m. This excess occurs despite the fact that more boy than girl babies are born. This excess of male babies is outweighed by the longer life expectancy of females (there are roughly twice as many females as males aged 75 and over).

Demographic change and changes in demand

In very broad terms we can say that a change in total population causes a change in the total volume of goods and services that producers are required to supply, while a change in the structure of population, and especially the age structure, causes a change in the types of goods and services required. These two changes frequently occur together. In the UK in the post-war period an increase in population led to a substantial increase in the total demand for goods and services, while an increase in the proportion of younger people – resulting from the rising birth rate in the first part of the period – meant that the increased demand was especially marked for such things as baby foods, toys, beds in maternity hospitals and education.

If the increasing demand for goods and services is to be met, it is necessary to employ more productive resources and/or to utilise existing resources more efficiently (i.e. to increase productivity). Let us assume for the moment that resources cannot be used more efficiently, and concentrate on the employment of additional resources.

A change in demand and in the employment of labour

In the long run an increase in demand arises from an increase in the supply of labour: 'With every mouth God sends a pair of hands.' There may, of course, be a lag on the supply side until the higher numbers of children enter the labour force. If, for this or any other reason, the labour force is insufficient to meet the demand for goods and services, immigration may be encouraged.

Germany has relied on immigrants – especially from the less prosperous parts of Europe – to man her factories when the domestic labour supply was inadequate. (One of the reasons why this was necessary was a substantial increase in demand for German exports – in this instance the increase in demand was *not* matched by an automatic increase in the supply of labour.) In the UK immigration was encouraged in the first part of the post-war period, not because the total supply of labour was inadequate to meet demand, but because it was difficult to fill certain jobs in textile factories, public transport, hospitals, etc., due to low wages, relatively poor working conditions or unsocial hours.

A change in demand and in the employment of capital

There is no automatic mechanism by which a change in demand is matched by a change in the supply of capital: each mouth is accompanied by a pair of hands, but not by a spade or a spanner. In order to provide capital – which includes not only spades, spanners and machines but also roads, hospitals and schools – resources are required which otherwise could have been used in the production of consumer products such as food, washing machines and entertainment. The sacrifice in consumption today will, it is hoped, be justified by the higher output of consumer goods and services which can be produced in future periods by the enlarged volume of capital goods.

This sacrifice of present for future consumption is not confined to situations of increasing demand, but it is likely to give rise to more acute problems than when demand is stable. To understand why this is so, consider the following highly simplified model of an economy.

Output can be divided into capital goods (designated C_A) and consumer goods (designated C_O). We assume that in one year 1 unit of capital, when combined with labour, can produce either one further unit of capital for the production of consumer goods, or 10 units of consumer goods. We start with a total quantity of 100 units of capital and we assume that one tenth of these units wear out each year. Consequently, in order to maintain the capital stock, 10 units of capital must be used to replace those which wear out. The remaining 90 units are used to produce 900 units of consumer goods. This can be formally expressed as follows:

Input $\rightarrow$ Output

year 1: $100C_A \rightarrow 10C_A + 900C_O$

Since we are ignoring here the possibility that output might be increased by using the existing capital stock more efficiently, an increase in output will require an increase in the capital stock. This in turn requires that more resources are devoted to the production of capital goods. If the units of capital used to produce capital goods increased from 10 to 11 a year, the situation would be as follows:

year 2: $100C_A \rightarrow 11C_A + 890C_O$
year 3: $101C_A \rightarrow 11C_A + 900C_O$
year 4: $102C_A \rightarrow 11C_A + 910C_O$
year 5: $103C_A \rightarrow 11C_A + 920C_O$

In order to increase the output of capital goods in year 2 a reduction in the output of consumer goods is necessary. Since in year 2 the output of capital goods (11 units) exceeds the number of capital goods wearing out (10 units), the capital stock increases to 101 units by the beginning of year 3. This increase in the capital stock is sufficient to allow the output of consumer goods to revert to its year 1 level while maintaining the higher output of capital goods. In year 4 the further growth in capital stock allows the output of consumer goods 'lost' in year 2 to be recovered. Finally, by year 5 the total output of consumer goods in the period as a whole exceeds the output that would have been produced had the initial sacrifice in consumption not been made.

The transfer of resources. It would not be appropriate to give at this point a detailed explanation of how the initial transfer of resources from the consumer goods to the capital goods industries might be brought about. But the essential mechanisms can be briefly described.

In a free market economy, with no State intervention, consumers would have to be offered a sufficiently high rate of interest to persuade them to increase their saving and reduce their consumption. The effects of this change would be two-fold. First, as the demand for consumer goods fell, some of the resources previously used for the production of such goods would become available for the production of capital goods. Second, producers would be able to borrow money from consumers to finance the building of the extra capital goods; this finance might be required because of the lag between the payments made to factors of production and the revenue earned by the machines.

If the capital goods were to be provided by the State, the State might borrow from consumers in the same way as private producers. Alternatively the State might levy taxes which would again fulfil the dual purpose of reducing the demand for consumer goods and providing finance for making capital goods.

Whichever method is adopted, consumers are required to make a sacrifice. In the above example a reduction in consumption of 10 units was required in year 2. If, under the influence of an increasing population, the demand for consumer goods is increasing, an even bigger sacrifice will be required. For example, an increase in population of 1 per cent might cause demand in year 2 to increase from 900 to 909 units, so that a sacrifice in consumption of 19 units would then be required.

In order to keep the analysis as simple as possible, we assumed in the above example that sufficient labour was available to work with the enlarged capital stock. In the short run this might be achieved by employing previously unemployed workers. Eventually, however, this source would become exhausted and further additions to the labour supply would depend upon an increase in population. This beneficial effect of an increase in population on the supply side may, therefore, modify the disadvantages on the demand side (a greater sacrifice in consumption), discussed above. However we must emphasise the point make earlier, that there may be a substantial lag between the increase in demand and the increase in (labour) supply.

An increase in demand and in productivity

Let us now consider the implications of an increase in population in a situation in which it is possible to increase output by means of an increase in the efficiency with which existing resources are utilised. To keep the analysis as simple as possible let us take the same starting point as for our previous example and assume that the increase in productivity would permit an increase in the output of consumer goods of 5 per cent a year:

year 1: $100C_A \rightarrow 10C_A + 900C_O$
year 2: $100C_A \rightarrow 10C_A + 945C_O$
year 3: $100C_A \rightarrow 10C_A + 992.25C_O$

If the demand for consumer goods were to increase by 5 per cent a year, the increased output would be purchased and the rate of resource utilisation would be unchanged. If, however, demand increased by less than 5 per cent a year – as might well happen – producers would reduce their rate of output, since otherwise they would find themselves with a growing volume of unsold stock.

One of the consequences of a reduction in the rate of output would be an increase in unemployment. Consequently an increase in population would be welcome *in the short term* insofar as the accompanying increase in demand would help to prevent this increase in unemployment. However, in the long term this advantage would be counteracted by the increase in the number of people seeking work.

Summary: demographic change and changes in demand

We have presented above two very simple models in order to explain the implications of population growth. In the first, an increase in output resulted from an increase in the quantity of resources employed; in the second it resulted from an increase in productivity. In the UK in the post-war period both mechanisms have operated simultaneously. An increase in demand has been met partly by an increase in the quantity of resources employed and partly by an increase in productivity.

The increase in population has been only one of many factors causing this increase in demand; others are considered below. We have discussed this factor at some length because the possibility that population might now have ceased to grow (and certainly is unlikely to grow as rapidly as in the 1950s and 1960s) has serious implications for the employment of resources. We can no longer rely on a growing population to absorb the additional output resulting from increased productivity, even in the short term.

To complete our discussion of the effects of demographic change we examine some of the responses, especially by public agencies, to the changes in population that have occurred in the UK in the post-war period.

The National Health Service. The increase in population led to an increase in the overall demand for medical facilities. In addition, the changing age structure led to an increase in the demand for maternity services during the first part of the period and, at the other end of the scale, for beds for geriatric patients. To meet these increased demands, the number of medical and dental staff working in NHS hospitals in England and Wales rose from 17,000 in 1960 to over 30,000 in 1976, and the number of general practitioners rose from less than 20,000 to almost 22,000.

Housing. The stock of dwellings in Great Britain increased from less than 14 m. in 1951 to more than 20 m. in 1977, representing a net gain (new dwellings minus dwellings demolished) of almost a quarter of a million dwellings a year. The increase in the number of dwellings required would, of course, have been much less had the population not increased.

Many of the houses were built for private ownership. But local authorities and new town corporations have also undertaken extensive housebuilding programmes, and in recent years have increased their share of total dwellings.

The Government's responsibility extends far beyond the provision of dwellings. They must also ensure that all the necessary services – roads, water, waste disposal, etc. – are provided. They may discharge this responsibility either directly through public agencies, or indirectly by laying down regulations which private suppliers must follow. Governments have also contributed to the housing programme in a number of other ways, including granting tax concessions to building societies and giving grants to individuals towards the cost of renovating their houses.

Education. There has been a substantial increase in the numbers undertaking education. The number of school children below the minimum school-leaving age depends mainly upon the size and structure of the population, although legislation concerning the age at which children may enter and leave school is also important, of course. The increase in the number of births up to 1964 was reflected in an increase in the number of full-time pupils under the age of 15 attending schools in England and Wales from less than 6 m. in 1950 to more than 8 m. in 1976.

The number undertaking education beyond the minimum school-leaving age also reflects the size and structure of the population. In addition it is influenced by people's desire to enjoy the various benefits of education, including an improvement in their job prospects. As national income has increased, more people have been able to sacrifice current income from employment in order to fulfil this desire. (Government grants have also helped, of course.) The number of full-time university students in Great Britain rose from 85,000 in 1950/1 to 260,000 in 1975/6, and substantial increases also occurred in other branches of higher and further education.

This increase in the number of students has been accompanied by an increase in buildings and staff. To take just one example, the number of full-time teaching staff at universities rose from 8,600 in 1950/1 to 38,000 in 1975/6. (One of the consequencies of a downturn in the birth rate is that fewer teachers are needed, at first in schools and subsequently in colleges and universities. This has already led to the closure of many of the colleges which trained school teachers.)

The main financial burden of education is borne by government, and in

1976 expenditure amounted to more than £5½ bn., one fifth of total government final consumption.

The demand for other goods and services.   We have concentrated our attention on markets supplied by public sector organisations because the effects of demographic change are particularly well documented in these markets. However, these effects have, of course, also been felt in markets supplied by organisations in the private sector. We mentioned earlier the increasing demand for baby foods and toys, and many other products could be added to this list – cosmetics, gramophone records, radios, etc. Moreover, many of the capital goods required in order to increase the production of consumer goods are supplied by private sector producers. Finally, private sector organisations produce some of the products discussed above, and especially, of course, houses.

Appendix: the optimum population

The optimum population is often defined as the size of population which would maximise the output per head of goods and services. The size of the optimum population will vary in accordance with the quantity of other resources available. In some instances there may be insufficient labour to utilise all the available capital. As we noted above, this prospect has led some countries to encourage immigration. In other instances the population may be higher than that required to maximise output per head. Such situations are usually characterised by heavy unemployment, actual or disguised, and often occur in underdeveloped countries where there is a scarcity of capital and/or land.

The size of the optimum population also depends upon the age distribution, and especially upon the percentage of the population which is of working age, since for the most part the people at work generate the nation's wealth which sustains both the working and the non-working, or 'dependent', population.

The number of people at work is substantially less than the number of working age. People of working age who do not work – or at least do not follow paid employment – include housewives, students, the sick and the unemployed.

The number of people in these various categories is influenced by a wide range of factors. But the most important single factor affecting the size of the potential – and hence also the actual – work-force is government legislation concerning the minimum school-leaving age (15 in 1951, subsequently raised to 16), and the official retirement age at which State pensions become payable (65 for men, 60 for women).

Table 15.4 reveals a tendency for the size of the dependent population to increase, mainly because of an increase in the proportion of people of retirement age.

We did not include land as a resource in the simple models of an economy presented above. This is a reasonable simplification if we are concerned with an industrialised nation such as the UK, since land is not a serious constraint upon output in general (although it may be in certain geographical areas). However, when we widen our view to consider land not simply as a productive resource but also as having alternative uses, including leisure and recreation, this might lead us to an alternative definition of optimum population to that presented above.

135

Consider the situation in which an increase in population results in an increase in demand which enables producers to take advantage of economies of scale (discussed in chapter 24), and so increase output per worker and per head of the population. According to our first definition the new, larger, population would be nearer to the optimum than the previous population.

However, using land to build factories for the production of the additional output, and houses to accommodate the increased population, would mean that less land would be available for playing fields, parks, sports grounds, etc. The loss of these amenities should be offset against the benefits of the higher output of products in assessing the desirability of the change in population. If we define optimum population as the population which maximises welfare per head, the higher population might no longer appear to be nearer the optimum. (Welfare might also be affected by other factors which sometimes accompany a rising population and a higher level of economic activity, such as increasing traffic congestion and various forms of pollution.)

Assignments

15.1

Discuss the implications of the population projections contained in Table 15.5.

Table 15.5 Projected total population, United Kingdom (millions)

	1976 (base)	1981	1991	2001	2011
All ages	56.0	55.7	56.7	57.5	57.7
Under 5	3.7	3.2	4.5	3.9	3.8
5–14	9.1	8.1	7.0	8.6	7.4
15–19	4.3	4.7	3.7	3.9	4.3
20–24	3.9	4.3	4.5	3.2	4.4
25–59	24.0	24.2	25.8	27.1	26.2
60–79	9.7	9.7	9.4	8.9	9.6
80 and over	1.4	1.5	1.9	2.0	2.0

Source: Annual Abstract of Statistics

15.2

Find out from your local council offices what are the population projections for the area, and discuss the significance of these projections for: (1) employers; (2) educational institutions; (3) the National Health Service; (4) public transport undertakings. (If you cannot obtain projections for the area, assume that the national projections, given in Table 15.5, apply.) Pay particular attention to the implications for changes in (a) the output, (b) the resources employed, by each group of organisations.

15.3

Explain the probable consequences of: (1) substantial immigration into; and (2) substantial emigration out of, the area in which you live. In your answer you should consider the implications for organisations in both the public and private sectors.

15.4

Compare and contrast the effects of an increase in population due to (*a*) an increase in the birth rate and (*b*) a fall in the death rate. In your answer you should consider the implications for organisations in both the public and private sectors.

Table 15.6 The forecast European baby products market (millions of 1976 US $)

Year	Toiletries	Foods	Nappies	Clothes	Furnishings
1979	206.8	801.2	559.9	306.7	333.3
1980	212.9	827.0	594.1	313.1	348.7
1981	221.7	866.4	640.7	323.0	368.2
1982	228.0	893.5	677.1	329.0	383.7
1983	238.2	938.8	731.2	340.5	405.3
1984	248.5	977.2	783.2	351.5	428.5
1985	248.0	978.3	802.9	348.5	432.4
1986	250.7	995.1	830.9	349.7	442.3

15.5

Table 15.6 contains forecasts of the European market for various baby products. On the basis of this data prepare a report for submission to a company that is considering entering this market. You should present the data in a form that is easy to read; for example, you might prepare a series of graphs showing, for each product, changes in the size of the market in: (1) absolute; (2) percentage terms. The implications of these changes should also be made clear.

16 Other influences on the demand for goods and services

Introduction

In the previous chapter we examined the effects of demographic change on demand. We now turn to other determinants of demand (although population change is again referred to briefly). These are: real income; the price and availability of substitutes; the price and availability of complements; advertising; tastes and technology. Each of these is discussed in turn.

Real income

Real income is defined as money income divided by an index of prices. Real income increases when money income increases more than (or falls less than) prices. An increase in real income normally accompanies an increase in population, especially when an increase occurs in the work-force. In the absence of any change in the work-force an increase in real income is most likely to result from an increase in productivity or efficiency. (In this instance there is an increase in real income per head as well as in total real income.)

The response of the demand for any product to a change in income is measured by the income elasticity of demand which is defined as:

$$\frac{\text{The percentage change in quantity demanded}}{\text{The percentage change in income}}$$

$$\text{IED} = \frac{\frac{\Delta Q}{Q} \times 100}{\frac{\Delta Y}{Y} \times 100} = \frac{\Delta Q/Q}{\Delta Y/Y}$$

where Q is the quantity demanded,
Y is real income, and
Δ is a small change in the variable

Differing values of IED are shown in Table 16.1, which assumes that income increases between years 1 and 2 by 10 per cent, and in which Q indicates the quantity of the product bought in each of the two years *at a given price*. If, in

Table 16.1 Hypothetical income elasticities of demand

	Product A		Product B		Product C		Product D		Product E	
	Q	IED	Q	IED	Q	IED	Q	IED	Q	IED
Year 1	100	–	100	–	100	–	100	–	100	–
Year 2	120	2.0	110	1.0	105	0.5	100	0.0	95	–0.5

percentage terms, demand increases more than income (IED >1) demand is said to be income elastic (product A). If demand and income increase to the same extent (IED = 1), demand has unitary elasticity (product B). If demand increases, but by less than income (0<IED<1), demand is income inelastic (product C). In all the above three situations elasticity is positive; all three products are **normal goods**. Where demand does not change (IED = 0) demand is absolutely inelastic (product D). Finally, where demand falls (IED<0) elasticity of demand is negative (product E). Product E is said to be an **inferior good**.

The value of IED for any product will vary between countries and over time, but in the industrialised countries IED tends to be higher for most consumer durable products than for necessities such as foodstuffs. (See, for example, the values for the UK given in Table 16.2.) However, it is not difficult to

Table 16.2 Estimated income elasticities of demand

Product	Income elasticity of demand
Refrigerators	0.96
Washing machines	0.74
Motor cars	0.69
Food	0.52

Source: Cramer J. S. *The Ownership of Major Consumer Durables,* Cambridge University Press, 1962; R. Stone and O. H. Rowe, 'Dynamic Demand Functions: some econometric results', *Economic Journal* Vol. 68, 1958

find exceptions to this rule. As incomes have risen in the UK in the post-war period the demand for bicycles from adults has slumped as more people have become able to afford other means of transport such as motor-cycles and cars.

The price and availability of substitutes

The extent to which products are seen by consumers as substitutes for each other is denoted by the cross elasticity of demand, which is defined as

$$\frac{\text{The percentage change in the quantity of one product demanded}}{\text{The percentage change in the price of another product}}$$

Cross elasticity of demand is $\dfrac{\Delta Q_A / Q_A}{\Delta P_B / P_B}$

where Q is the quantity demanded,
  P is price,
  A, B are two products, and
  Δ is a small change in the variable.

The higher the value of the cross elasticity of demand the closer substitutes two products are deemed to be. A pair of products which have been found to be close substitutes are butter and margarine. As butter becomes dearer, the demand for margarine increases; conversely cheaper butter causes a fall in margarine sales.

Sometimes the demand for one product falls because of the introduction of a new substitute. The spread of pocket calculators has led to a fall in the sales of slide rules; people watch television as a substitute for going to the cinema; the introduction of skateboards led to a steep decline in the sales of children's bicycles.

Finally, note that the degree of substitution may be affected by the level of income, as illustrated by the reduction in sales of adult bicycles, discussed above.

The price and availability of complements

The relationship between complementary products (complements) is the opposite of that for substitutes. Complementary products are used together; consequently a reduction in the price of one product will usually lead to an increase in the demand for that product and for any complementary products. A reduction in the price of fish sold in fish and chip shops would increase the sales of both fish and chips. Similarly, the introduction by the shop of a new complement, such as sausages, would also increase the sales of chips if it attracted people who did not like fish.

Sometimes the strength of the relationship between a pair of products is much stronger in one direction than the other. For example, while a reduction of, say, 20 per cent in the price of cars might lead to a significant increase in the sales of cars and thus of petrol, it is doubtful whether a similar reduction in the price of petrol would have an equivalent effect on the sales of cars. Similarly, the demand for oil tankers depends very heavily upon the demand for oil, whereas the converse is not true.

Advertising

Heavy advertising of a product may increase demand. Moreover the effect of a successful advertising campaign is felt more quickly than a change in population or even real income, since these aggregates change only slowly. In the post-war period in the UK real income has seldom increased by more than 5 per cent in a year, and often by much less than that, while population change has averaged ½ per cent a year, as noted in Chapter 15.

Changes in tastes

It is very difficult to determine the extent to which changes in tastes are associated with other factors, such as advertising and changes in income, and the extent to which they occur independently. What is clear is that changes in tastes can lead to

140

very substantial changes in demand for particular products. For example when, a number of years ago, the mini-skirt came into fashion it caused a fall in the demand for the yarn used for making skirt materials, but an increase in the demand for nylon yarn used in the manufacture of tights. Subsequently, as hemlines lengthened, the reverse process occurred, and the fall in demand for tights was so great that many hosiery factories were closed down.

In menswear a change in tastes to more casual fashions resulted in a fall in the sales of suits from 9.9 millions in 1973 to 6.9 millions in 1977.

The increasing importance attached to 'health self-management', which can also, perhaps, be considered under this heading, has led to an increased demand for a wide range of products, including jogging gear, tennis, squash and golf equipment, and – among the richer members of the community – home saunas.

Changes in technology

Changes in technology can affect demand in various ways. First, changes in production processes can cause increases in the demand for some products (machines, components, raw materials) and reductions in the demand for others. Second, technological changes can change the attractiveness of products, e.g. by improving their performance or by lowering their price. This is likely to increase the demand for these products, and also to cause a reduction in the demand for substitute products. Finally, technological progress leads to the introduction of new products and thus again affects the demand for substitutes.

A shift in the demand curve

It is often convenient to use demand curves to show the effects of changes in demand. In Fig. 16.1 the initial demand for the product is denoted by D_1. An increase in demand would be indicated by a shift of the demand curve to the right (D_2). This might be due, for example, to an increase in real income (but note that an increase in real income would cause a fall in the demand for an inferior good, i.e. the demand curve would shift to the left).

An increase in demand allows a larger quantity to be sold at any given price in a given period. For example, the amount that could be sold at price P_1 would rise from Q to Q_2. Alternatively, looking at the situation from a different viewpoint, any given quantity could be sold at a higher price than previously; for example, Q_1 at price P_2.

Since a demand curve relates the quantity demanded to price it is usually applied to markets for products supplied by commercial organisations. But it can also be applied to markets supplied by non-commercial organisations, including products supplied at a zero price, e.g. education and health services (the demand for these was examined in the previous chapter). Here, however, we are concerned with only a single point on the demand curve. With demand at D_1 the 'quantity' of education demanded (with price = 0) would be Q_3. As demand

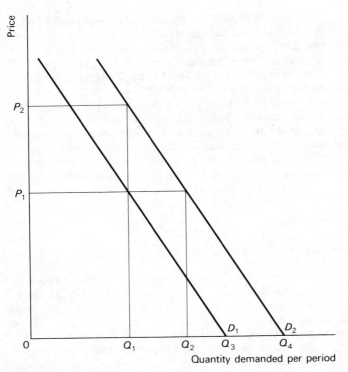

Fig. 16.1 A shift of the demand curve

increased to D_2, because, for example, of an increase in population, the quantity demanded would increase to Q_4.

Incidentally it is sometimes argued that if the Government has decided that a product should be supplied at a zero price then it has the responsibility for meeting demand at that price. If, for example, the demand for places on 'A' level courses in schools and colleges increased from D_1 to D_2, the number of such places should be increased from Q_3 to Q_4.

Whether the Government would in fact increase the number of places would depend partly upon the cost of doing so. One cannot imagine a situation in which students could not find places. On the other hand, a Government that wished to keep down its expenditure might well meet the additional demand by increasing the size of classes.

Summary and conclusions

In this chapter we have discussed a wide range of factors which affect market demand. We have not discussed each of these factors in as much detail as demographic change since changes in population have effects both on the demand and the supply of products. However, it should not be concluded from the brevity of the treatment that the effects on demand of these factors is less important. On the contrary, the demand for many products is more responsive, especially over a relatively short period, say one or two years, to changes in these factors than to changes in population.

The success of organisations, and especially commercial organisations, in meeting their objectives depends to a considerable extent upon their ability to forecast changes in demand. In the next chapter we shall examine how they might set about this task. In doing so we shall move from a consideration of market demand to a consideration of the demand for the products of individual suppliers. In preparation for this discussion, it will be useful to outline the various possible stages of the forecasting process.

The organisation may need to forecast the demand for:

1. their existing products in their present markets;
2. their existing products in new markets;
3. new products in their present markets;
4. new products in new markets.

In some instances, of course, the firm may not need to proceed beyond the first of these four stages. The demand for its existing products in their present markets may be so buoyant that the firm can easily achieve its objectives.

It has, however, been found that many products (and especially consumer durable goods) have a fairly clearly defined 'life cycle' in a given market. After a slow start, when sales are confined to a few 'early adopters' (perhaps the more adventurous or rich members of the community), sales increase rapidly. Eventually sales level off as the market becomes 'saturated', and then begin to decline.

If we take the example of the vacuum cleaner, the market would become saturated when the proportion of households possessing a cleaner approached 100 per cent. Vacuum cleaners would thereafter be sold only to new households or to replace existing cleaners. In order to avoid a decline in sales, a manufacturer might seek sales overseas; this would involve stage 2 of the forecasting process.

Eventually, as successive markets become saturated, producers may introduce new products, either in their present or in new markets (stages 3 and 4). Our manufacturer of vacuum cleaners might, for example, begin the manufacture of washing machines or floor polishers which would be sold through many of the same outlets as their cleaners. Alternatively, or in addition, they might introduce industrial products, e.g. dust extraction plant for factories. (Their familiarity with the consumer market might make demand forecasting easier for consumer than industrial products.)

As an example of the serious consequences of neglecting to monitor, and respond to changes in demand, consider the experience of Staflex International. In the 1960s its invention of fusible interlinings for shirt collars resulted in a fivefold increase in profits in five years. Growth continued in the 1970s; between 1969 and 1976 turnover rose from £12 m. to £43 m., and profits from £1 m. to £2.4 m. Unfortunately, however, instead of diversifying, Staflex went for international expansion on the basis of its existing products. This involved heavy expenditure on factories overseas, just at the time when competitive products were beginning to eat into its market. This and the textile slump at the end of 1976 led to such a rapid reversal of Staflex's fortunes that it made a loss of £6.3 millions in 1977, and went into voluntary liquidation in 1978.

Assignments

16.1

In which of the following situations does real income increase between year 1 and year 2?

	Index of money income		Index of prices	
	year 1	year 2	year 1	year 2
1.	100	110	100	110
2.	100	110	100	115
3.	100	110	100	105
4.	100	95	100	95
5.	100	95	100	100
6.	100	95	100	90

16.2

State whether each of the following statements is true or false.

1. A change in money income is always accompanied by a change in real income.
2. Real income is defined as money income divided by an index of prices.
3. Real income is likely to increase following an increase in productivity.
4. The income elasticity of demand is defined as the percentage change in income divided by the percentage change in quantity demanded.
5. An inferior good is one for which the quantity demanded changes less than proportionately to income.

16.3

Which of the data below relates to normal goods?

	Index of real income		Index of quantity demanded	
	year 1	year 2	year 1	year 2
1.	100	110	100	110
2.	100	110	100	105
3.	100	110	100	100
4.	100	110	100	95
5.	100	95	100	90

16.4

Draw a diagram to show the relationship between income and demand when the income elasticity of demand is:

1. 2.0
2. unity
3. zero
4. −0.5

16.5

State whether each of the following statements is true or false.

1. Cross elasticity of demand is defined as the percentage change in the demand for a product divided by the percentage change in its price.
2. The greater the value of the cross elasticity of demand the closer substitutes two products are deemed to be.
3. A fall in the price of one product is likely to lead to a fall in the demand for complementary products.
4. A shift to the right in the demand curve indicates that more would be bought at any given price than previously.

16.6

With reference to the discussion in this and earlier chapters, and to the information in the passage below, identify the factors that influence the demand for aluminium.

A series of price increases in 1976 and 1977 weakened the competitive position of aluminium in comparison with alternative materials for transportation work, the building industry and furnishing. Aluminium was at some price disadvantage with steel (mainly because the depressed state of the steel trade was holding prices down) but cheaper than softwood.

The persistently low price being obtained for copper has damaged aluminium's prospects for the time being in the cable and wiring market in which it was making great strides. However, the aluminium producers have continued to fight to keep their hold in the electrical market.

The four selling qualities of aluminium are its lightness, its electrical conductivity, the ease with which the metal can be formed, and its high resistance to corrosion. Having lost some of their price advantage, it is vital to the producers to go for markets when one or more of those qualities offer aluminium a special advantage over other materials.

A prime example is the car market. Design and development work is being done between British car companies and British-based aluminium companies to develop the use of aluminium alloys in car production. The aluminium companies expect the growth of the use of the metal to be fastest in the adoption of it for castings for car engines and components.

Construction and transport are two of those applications where the aluminium companies will have to look hard at their markets if they are to stick to their strategy of moving 'up-market' to seek more adequate profits. Plastics is providing growing competition in some areas of building and decorative finishes. Steel is a fierce competitor in structural applications such as commercial vehicle frames. The growth in the use of steel rectangular closed sections in both markets is at the expense of aluminium.

The consumption of aluminium foil in packaging, electrical engineering, mechanical engineering, and building reached 44,000 tonnes in 1976, growth having been most marked in dairy and confectionery packaging and foil containers for frozen foods and pre-cooked foods.

Another business which has big growth possibilities is the, as yet, small production of lithographic printing sheet from aluminium. Some tens of thousands of tonnes of aluminium are expected to be required annually for that trade. The industry is producing a specially-finished high quality aluminium plate for the printers. Some researchers in the British industry expect the use of aluminium for cans to grow from 24,000 tonnes in 1976 to more than 60,000 tonnes a year within the next ten years. Already beverage tinplate cans have aluminium tops, and Metal Box sees aluminium as an alternative material to compete on price with tinplate. The new Metal Box canning lines for making the two-piece cans – a drawn body and a separate top – are designed to run on either tinplate or aluminium.

17 The collection of market information

Introduction

Having discussed the various factors that influence demand, we now outline the sources of information that are available in respect of each of these factors. In the previous two chapters we were concerned with market demand, i.e. with the demand for the products of a group of suppliers. If a supplier assumes that his share of the market will remain constant, he can apply the change in the total market to his own product or brand. If the market is expected to grow by, say, 5 per cent a year, he can assume that his own sales will grow by 5 per cent a year.

However, many suppliers, and especially those that can afford to spend a considerable amount of money on market research, are unlikely to be content to leave the matter there. They will wish to collect information about possible changes *within* the market, changes that may affect their market share. So, for example, when they are considering the price and availability of substitutes, they will be at least as interested in the policies of competitive suppliers within their own market as in the policies of suppliers in other markets.

We should also emphasise that suppliers collect information in order to find out not what *will* happen, but what would be likely to happen if their policies remained unchanged. There are, of course, some changes whose consequences a supplier must accept, e.g. changes in population, or in government policies which affect incomes. There are other changes, however, whose consequences can be counteracted or at least modified, e.g. changes in the pricing or product policies of a competitor.

If a supplier discovers that a competitor is about to launch a new product which would threaten his share of the market, he might retaliate by launching a new product of his own. Alternatively, if he is not in a position to do this, he might try to protect his market by reducing the price of his existing products, or by increasing his advertising expenditure (in some instances, of course, the market information collected will serve to confirm that the supplier's existing policies are satisfactory and should not be changed).

Sources of information

We now discuss the sources of information concerning the major influences on demand. We discuss these influences in the order in which they were presented in the previous two chapters, beginning with population.

Population

Data on UK population is provided on a regular basis by the Office of Population Censuses and Surveys, and reproduced in several Government statistical publications, e.g. the *Annual Abstract of Statistics*. The data relates to the total population and also the age and sex structure. For many suppliers the data on the structure may be of greater interest because their products are aimed at particular segments of the population. For example, a producer of children's mouth organs might be most concerned to discover the number of boys aged 5 to 15. This data could be used on its own, or in conjunction with information relating to a sample of the population, obtained either by the organisation's own staff or by a specialist market research organisation. For example, if a questionnaire answered by a sample of, say, 10,000 boys aged 5–15 revealed that 3 per cent owned a mouth organ, and the official statistics showed that there were 5 m. boys of this age in the population, this would suggest that 150,000 (3 per cent of 5 m.) mouth organs were owned by this segment of the population. This figure could be used as the basis for estimating future sales.

Significant changes in demand due to changes in population occur only over a long period. As shown in Chapter 15, the average annual increase in UK population in the post-war period has been only $\frac{1}{2}$ per cent (although bigger changes have occurred in certain age groups). Consequently organisations may be able to ignore such changes in their short-term planning. They should, however, take them into account in decisions which have long-term implications, e.g. decisions to build and equip a new factory.

Unfortunately long-range population forecasts are subject to high margins of error, especially when birth and death rates are unstable. We showed in Chapter 15 that in 1976 there was an excess of deaths over births, mainly due to the fall in the birth rate. Starting from that date we could make three alternative, equally plausible, assumptions about future birth rates that would lead to three quite different population projections.

First, we might assume that the birth rate would continue to fall as it had since 1964. This might occur as people took advantage of the more efficient methods of contraception and the better facilities for abortion that had become available. This assumption would, of course, lead to a predication of a fall in the total population. Alternatively we might assume that people had already taken full advantage of the means of limiting the size of families and that the birth rate would stabilise at around its existing, 1976, level. This would lead to a prediction of a roughly stable population (depending, of course, upon our assumed death and migration rates).

Finally we might base our prediction on the average birth rate over a longer period, say the past ten years, on the grounds that the abnormally low rates of the mid 1970s were due, at least partly, to the unfavourable economic circumstances, including a falling standard of living, which would persuade some people to postpone having children. Since, over this longer period, the birth rate was higher than the death rate, this assumption would lead to a prediction of an increase in population – although not to the extent that would have been predicted ten years

148

previously. (In the 1960s a population of 72 m. was predicted for the year 2000; this prediction was reduced to 67 m. in 1970 and to less than 58 m. in 1976.)

Real income

Forecasts of changes in real income are published each year by the Government in connection with the preparation of the Budget, and more frequently by other organisations such as the National Institute of Economic and Social Research and the London Business School. Although the forecasts of these various organisations do not always agree, they normally point in the same direction, all indicating either a rise or a fall in real incomes.

In some years there are considerable differences in the changes in income of people in different income brackets. These differences are frequently caused by government policies, e.g. in the mid 1970s prices and incomes policies led to a substantial fall in the real income of the higher income groups while the incomes of some other groups were maintained and even modestly increased. It may be very important to try to predict such changes. For example, a supplier of a luxury product, faced with the prospect of a decline in the real income of the upper income brackets, might be able to protect his sales by introducing a cheaper version aimed at lower income earners.

The price and availability of substitutes and complements

As we noted above, it is desirable to collect information about products sold in both the supplier's own market and in other markets. This may involve obtaining information by a number of methods – by scanning newspapers, journals and trade papers, by talking to customers about any announcements of future plans made by other suppliers, by attending conferences and exhibitions, and so forth. Sometimes special enquiries have to be launched, sometimes a supplier's salesmen may obtain very useful information in the ordinary course of their business.

The more advance warning of a change can be obtained, the better position the supplier will be in to react to the change. This is especially important when he wishes to react by changing the specification of his products, or by introducing new products, since a substantial time-lag may exist between taking decisions on these matters and the eventual outcome of those decisions.

Advertising

It is not too difficult to obtain information about changes in advertising expenditure. Indeed many organisations seem very happy to have changes – and especially increases – well publicised. It is, however, more difficult to predict the content of forthcoming campaigns.

Tastes

As we noted in the previous chapter, it is difficult to decide the extent to which changes in taste are associated with other factors such as advertising, and the

149

extent to which they occur independently. In either case, however, the supplier should keep himself informed about changes in the tastes and requirements of both existing and potential customers.

Information gathered by the supplier sometimes indicates that he is satisfying the requirements of all the purchasers to whom he wishes to sell. More often, perhaps, it indicates that a change in policy would enable him to satisfy his existing customers more fully and/or gain additional customers. These policy changes might relate to his existing products. Alternatively they might relate to products which he does not at present supply, and indeed which may not yet be supplied by any producer. As noted earlier, substantial profits are often obtained by the producers of 'pioneer' products, e.g. the Xerox reprographic method, Polaroid cameras, Terylene. (For the non-commercial organisation the introduction of new products 'pays off' in terms of increased customer satisfaction.)

Technology

We showed in the previous chapter that technological change frequently results in substitution, in both factor and product markets. The more information an organisation can obtain about the likely course of technological change the better position it will be in to take advantage of its beneficial effects and to minimise its undesirable effects. However, technological forecasting often has a long time horizon and is subject to considerable uncertainty.

For example, there is no doubt that microprocessors will become increasingly used in the future and that this will cause widespread changes in our way of life. One likely change is the installation of computer terminals in houses, that will enable people to use their television sets to interrogate files of information. Whenever they wish they will be able to 'call up' the latest news, sports reports, weather reports, etc. (Already a major news service company is offering all the financial and stock market prices, both national and international, corrected every second as the markets change.)

Another likely development is magnetic tapes with all the information a customer could require about the different types of goods. This would enable her to use the domestic TV set an an instrument for ordering goods, without going outside her front door.

Other probabilities include electronic mail, taking letters anywhere on earth in seconds, the dispersal of many office jobs to the homes of the staff who would work from home via computer terminals, and the opportunity to select any of thousands of educational or informational films and view them at home.

However, although there seems little doubt that all these developments will come to pass in the foreseeable future, their precise timing is difficult to predict. For the organisations affected by these changes, and especially for the producers of goods and services, a difference of, say, five or ten years may be crucial. The consequences of entering a market either five years too early or five years too late can be very serious indeed.

Demand forecasting methods

Having discussed what information might be gathered concerning the main factors influencing demand we now examine a different (but related) aspect of the collection of market information: the main methods of demand forecasting. We begin by looking at two methods that use past, or historic, data.

Extrapolation: the projection of past trends

For some decisions it may be sufficient to obtain information on how sales vary over time. For example, if a firm is considering whether to begin the manufacture of product A or B (Fig. 17.1), it would be important to take into account the past pattern of sales. In the current period T, sales of A exceed those of B. However it can be seen that while the sales of A have begun to level off the sales of B are still growing strongly. Extrapolation of these trends suggests that sales of B are soon likely to exceed those of A, as indicated by the dotted lines. Consequently B would seem to be the more promising alternative. (The firm would, of course, also have to take many other things into account, such as the number of firms already supplying each product and the relative profits margins.)

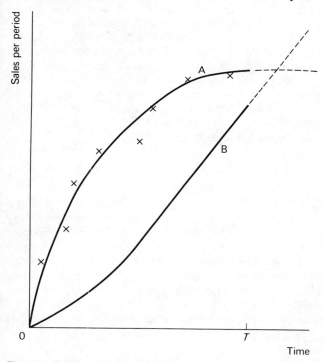

Fig. 17.1 Changes in sales over time

Firms often have to decide which of their existing products to support most strongly in terms of additional production facilities, research and development expenditure, advertising expenditure, etc. Information of the kind contained in Fig. 17.1 (but where A and B now refer to two of the firm's existing products) would again help the firm to make these decisions.

This type of information can also be obtained about sales of a given product in two different geographical markets, A and B. This information would be useful to a firm which is considering entering a new market, perhaps overseas, but wishes in the first instance to limit its expansion to one such market.

Three further points must be made concerning Fig. 17.1. First, although we are discussing demand forecasting, this figure presents data on sales. It is in fact impossible to obtain accurate data on demand, if only because some people who wished to buy the product might not have been able to obtain supplies. Consequently we use data on sales as the best available indicator of demand. Second, sales might be measured in either value or volume (quantity); each measure has both advantages and disadvantages and we cannot say which is preferable in general. Finally, the pattern of sales is unlikely to be as smooth in practice as shown in Fig. 17.1. Lines such as these are usually derived from a scatter diagram. The points marked X constitute a simple scatter diagram: these points are the actual observations, the value or volume of sales of product A in particular periods. Drawing a smooth line between these points makes it easier to see the past pattern of sales, and so to extrapolate into the future.

Extrapolation is a very simple method of demand forecasting. It shows how sales have changed over time, but it tells us nothing about why these changes have occurred. This can be a serious drawback when changes occur in any of the factors that influence sales. To illustrate this point let us consider Fig. 17.1 again.

Let us assume that sales of product A are much more responsive to changes in income than the sales of B, and that the pattern of A's sales is partly due to the fact that income increased more rapidly in the first than the second part of the period. If it seemed likely that income would begin to increase more rapidly again beyond period T, sales of A might continue to outstrip those of B. The conclusion that we reached by simple extrapolation might turn out to be incorrect. A technique which reduces this danger is regression analysis.

Regression analysis

Regression analysis can be very complicated and a full discussion of the technique would be far beyond the scope of this book. However, its basis is very simple. The objective is to discover how the behaviour of a dependent variable (sales in the above example) is affected by changes in an independent variable (income). By considering the values of the two variables for a number of periods the relationship between the two can be estimated (the greater the number of observations the more reliable the estimate tends to be). For example, if it was found that a change of £100 m. in national income was always associated with a change of £1 m. in the sales of a product, the relationship would be expressed as follows:

$$S = 0.01 \, Y$$
where S = sales (£ m.)
Y = national income (£ m.)

As we showed above, demand can be influenced by a wide range of factors and we can seldom explain changes in demand or sales by changes in only one of these factors. Regression equations normally contain several independent variables, e.g. income, the price of the product relative to the prices of other products, advertising expenditure, etc.

By including several variables it is often possible to 'explain' much of the change in sales in past periods, and to forecast future changes. However, the relationship between variables can change over time; for example, price elasticity of demand may increase because of the introduction of a substitute product. Consequently care must always be taken when using regression analysis for forecasting. Indeed when the relationships between variables are believed to be very unstable (or when the data required for regression analysis is not available) other methods, which do not rely on the use of past data, may be more useful.

Surveys of consumer attitudes and intentions

This method is used in order to gain an indication of the likely future purchasing behaviour of consumers. Its exponents believe that consumers' attitudes about, say, the future course of the economy and how this will affect income, may influence buying behaviour to a greater extent than current income levels. Similarly surveys of purchasing intentions are claimed to give an up-to-the-minute indication of probable purchasing behaviour.

This approach to forecasting was pioneered in the United States, but is now undertaken by a number of institutions in the UK, including the London Business School, Sussex University and the *Financial Times*.

When used on their own, intentions surveys have frequently predicted the future direction of changes (increase or decrease) in the purchasing of consumer durables, but have been much less successful in forecasting actual levels of purchasing. When used as a component of a model which also uses historic data they have sometimes improved the explanatory value of the model. However the improvement has been far more marked at the level of purchases of consumer durables as a whole than at the level of individual products. (The reason for this is probably that a good deal of 'switching' occurs within the total durables market, with money which it was stated was to be spent on one product actually being spent on another.) Moreover the reliability of intentions surveys is particularly low when the market has become saturated. This is presumably due to the fact that replacement sales, which form a high proportion of sales in such markets, are unpredictable, being determined largely by the rate of failure of the existing products.

Surveys of buyers' intentions may be especially useful when a firm is considering the introduction of a new product, since it cannot use past sales data. In these circumstances the survey is likely to be designed to discover not only the probable demand for the product, but also how consumers react to various styles, colours, prices, etc. – information that can guide both marketing and product policies. The weakness of this approach is, of course, that there is no commitment on the part of the consumer to follow a statement of intention to buy with a cash payment. One way of trying to overcome this problem is by test marketing the product.

Test marketing

The basic principle of test marketing is to obtain information on the reactions of consumers in a limited geographical area when confronted by the product in realistic buying situations, and to use this information as a guide in the decision whether or not the product should be sold more widely.

Unfortunately it is not always easy to ensure that the buying situation is realistic. In the first place the geographical area which is chosen for the test may not be representative of the overall market in which it is hoped to sell the product, although the firm will of course choose as representative an area as possible.

Second, the conditions in the market during the test period may not be typical of the conditions that will exist subsequently. There may, for example, be more (or less) advertising of competitive products than normal.

Third, even if the buying situation is satisfactory in the above respects, the results of the test may be difficult to interpret. For example, if the firm's information is derived from its own records or those of distributors, it will not know to what extent any given level of sales represents repeat as opposed to initial purchases. And yet this is a very important distinction since almost all successful businesses depend upon repeat purchases.

The firm may attempt to obtain this more detailed information by asking a sample of consumers about their purchasers, perhaps by subscribing to, or running, a consumer panel. However this will necessitate not only additional expense but also a lengthening of the test period, which will reduce its lead in product development over potential rival products.

Controlled experiments

Controlled experiments can take many different forms and we have room to consider only a few of these:

In the United States the Parker Pen Company was selling Quink ink at a loss-making price of 15 cents. It increased the price to 25 cents in a sample of outlets and compared sales in these outlets with sales in those outlets in which price had not been raised. At the higher price a slight fall in the volume of sales occurred, but revenue and profitability were significantly improved. Consequently Parker marketed New Quink nationally at 25 cents. The wisdom of this decision was confirmed when several competitors also raised their prices.

Another experiment conducted in the United States showed how demand can be affected by the existence of a well-known brand name (a form of product differentiation). Identical mattresses, some bearing the Simmons brand and others an unknown brand, were offered for sale at different price differentials. When prices were equal the Simmons brand outsold the unknown brand by fifteen to one; when the Simmons brand was sold at a 25 per cent premium sales were equal.

Experimentation may take place before a new product is marketed nationally. When the 'Princess' telephone was introduced in the United States the manufacturer set different prices in different geographical areas. (Since the decision to introduce the telephone had already been made this cannot be considered as test marketing, although there are clearly some similarities.) Sales were higher with an installation charge of $8.50 plus a monthly charge of 65 cents than with a charge of $29.50 plus 50 cents a month. The former price was therefore adopted on a national basis.

154

Summary and conclusions

We have outlined the sources of information on which the supplier might draw in attempting to predict changes in the demand for his products. We showed that the starting point is often the prediction of market demand, i.e. the demand for the products of a group of suppliers, but we stressed that each supplier should also take into account any policy changes introduced by his competitors which might threaten his share of the market.

We discussed information concerning the factors that influence demand; these factors were considered in the order in which they were presented in the previous chapter. We then discussed the main methods of demand forecasting. Since each method has both advantages and disadvantages the choice of method is obviously very important.

We must remember that, whichever method is used, the main purpose of demand forecasting is to enable organisations to respond as quickly and efficiently as possible to changes in demand. The response might involve changes in product policy (the modification of existing products and the introduction of new products), distribution (including seeking new markets), advertising and other forms of sales promotion, and pricing.

Assignments

17.1

Explain why demand forecasts for a market as a whole cannot always be applied directly to the demand for the products of one supplier.

17.2

'If market research shows that we are going to do well, we do not need the research; if it shows that we are going to do badly, we would prefer not to know. Consequently our company never undertakes market research.' Discuss.

17.3

Demand forecasts are often based on past patterns of sales. However this can lead to inaccurate forecasts as changes occur in economic circumstances and the behaviour of consumers. What changes might lead to errors in forecasts of demand for the following products?

1. telephone services;
2. newspapers;
3. motor cycles;
4. jeans;
5. copper.

17.4

Assume that your local college is contemplating building an extension that would enable it to provide additional places for students. Explain how you would obtain information about the future demand for education, that could be used in the decision concerning the size and form of the new building.

17.5

Assume that you are a director of a market research company and that you have been asked by clients to prepare a brief for research designed to assess the potential markets for each of the products listed below. Prepare a brief for each product, indicating the nature of the 'population' from which you would propose to draw your sample and how you would contact the members of the sample. Your proposals should also take into account the cost of the methods suggested, since if you quote too high a price, your proposals might be rejected.

1. An electrically operated small car, designed for ease of parking in city centres.
2. A series of record-albums, each containing an LP of a group, together with photographs, interviews with members of the group, etc. The important decisions to be made relate to the design of the album, its price, and the groups to be featured.
3. A new method of sound insulation designed to reduce the amount of external noise penetrating houses.
4. A new type of small yacht that can be produced more cheaply than existing models.

17.6

Discuss the ways in which the pattern of demand is likely to be affected by the widespread introduction of microprocessors, and show why it is important that information should be obtained on the likely pace of their adoption.

17.7

A company which is considering whether or not to begin manufacturing disposable cigarette lighters discovers that sales varied as follows:

1974	90,000
1975	100,000
1976	105,000
1977	120,000
1978	130,000

1. Plot this data on a graph and, by extrapolation, estimate sales in 1979 and 1980.
2. List the factors that might be included if the company wished to use regression analysis in order to forecast future sales.
3. The company believes that it could make a lighter similar to existing models for the same cost. Alternatively it could make, at a higher cost, a lighter that would have advantages over existing models in terms of a longer life and/or more attractive styling. Suggest a market research programme that would yield information that would help the company to decide between these two alternatives.

18 The determination of price and output

Introduction

In Chapter 14 we showed that various aspects of the structure of a market affect the degree of pricing discretion enjoyed by suppliers in that market. In Chapters 15, 16 and 17 we discussed the various factors that influence demand. In this chapter we build on this previous material and explain how market prices and outputs are determined under differing demand conditions.

It is useful to begin by making a broad distinction between markets in terms of the degree of pricing discretion enjoyed by suppliers. (You should look again at Table 14.1 in order to refresh your memory about the features of markets in which the suppliers' discretion is: high; and low.)

Price determination when suppliers have a high degree of discretion

The essential point about this situation is that suppliers are able to take their costs into account when setting their prices, i.e. they can adopt a procedure of cost-based pricing. Cost-based pricing is adopted by the suppliers of many manufactured goods and many services.

Cost-based pricing

In principle this procedure is straightforward. The supplier or producer estimates his cost at his expected level of output, adds to this cost a margin designed to yield his target profit and thus arrives at his target price. In Fig. 18.1, given the average cost curve AC, at the expected output Q average cost (cost per unit) is QR. To this cost is added a profit margin RS, yielding a target price $QS(=OP)$. (An alternative approach is to take average variable cost as the base, and to add a margin designed to cover fixed (or overhead) cost and to yield a profit. This so-called contribution costing approach is discussed in Chapter 25.)

However, several points must be made about this apparently straightforward procedure. First, there is an element of circularity in the reasoning. As we have

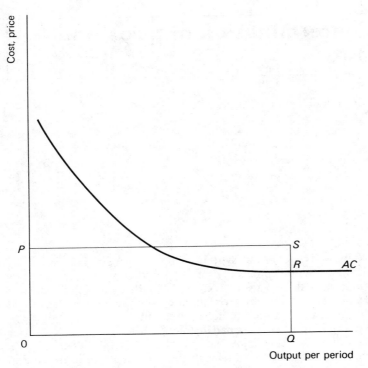

Fig. 18.1 A basic model of cost-based pricing

described it, the price-setting procedure starts from an assumption that output will be a certain volume (Q), whereas the quantity sold, and hence output, depends partly upon the price. In practice, if the producer can draw upon past experience in this market this circularity of reasoning is not too serious a matter. This experience will enable him to make reasonable assumptions about the future volume of sales. If he is producing the product for the first time the situation is subject to more uncertainty. Even here, however, market research may enable him to make a fairly accurate estimate of the price–sales relationship.

Second, the target profit depends upon the objectives of the organisation. As we noted in Chapters 5 and 6, different organisations have different objectives. These objectives may lead some organisations to adopt a low price/high sales volume policy, while others prefer a high price/low volume policy.

Third, although we are discussing markets in which suppliers have a high degree of pricing discretion, there is no guarantee that suppliers will always obtain their target revenue and profit. As we have shown in previous chapters, demand is affected by many factors, and these may make it impossible for the supplier to sell at price P. (We consider the effects of changes in demand in more detail below.)

Finally, it should be noted that, within a given market, the degree of pricing discretion may vary from one supplier to another. This is especially likely to happen when different suppliers have different cost structures. This situation is illustrated in Fig. 18.2 where firm A can produce any given output at a lower cost

158

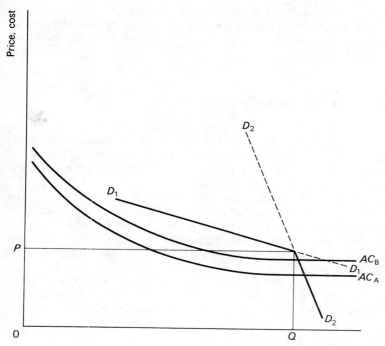

Fig. 18.2 Pricing with different cost structures

than *B*. (This might be due to greater experience, control of low-cost supplies or inputs, superior management ability, etc.)

In this situation A has considerable discretion in pricing. One option would be to set a price below B's average cost with the intention of forcing B out of the market. A would hope that his increase in sales then achieved would compensate for the small profit earned per unit. Another option would be to set a price which yielded a higher profit margin but which was also high enough to enable B to remain in the market. This price is denoted by *P* in Fig. 18.2.

Let us assume that A sets the higher price *P*, and consider the situation facing B. Although the profits earned when *Q* is sold at price *P* may be sufficient to enable B to survive, it does not follow that B would consider these profits to be satisfactory. It might well prefer a higher price and profit margin. However, it may have very little say in the matter (its pricing discretion may be extremely limited). If it attempted to increase its price it might lose a large number of customers to A. This is indicated by the demand curve D_1 which is drawn on the assumption that A's price remains at *P*.

On the other hand if B were to reduce its price below *P* in an attempt to increase its sales, it is highly likely that A would match this reduction in order to protect its market. (As the lower cost firm, A is probably in a stronger position than B to withstand a price war.) Therefore B's profits would fall, since its increase in sales volume would be insufficient to compensate for the reduction in the profit margin. This is indicated by the demand curve D_2, drawn on the assumption that A and B's prices are identical.

159

There are, then, a number of reasons why the price-setting procedure might not be as straightforward as we suggested initially. But having explored some of the complications let us put these aside and consider how market prices are determined when none of these complications exists.

The determination of market prices

We assume in this section that each supplier adopts the procedure illustrated in Fig. 18.1. We also assume, in order to keep the analysis as simple as possible, that all the suppliers in a given market have identical cost structures and identical objectives. Finally, we assume that the preferences of purchasers are such that all suppliers have an equal share of the market.

In Fig. 18.3 the left-hand diagram refers to one of these suppliers, a firm that expects to sell in a given period 250 units at a price of £10. If this expectation is absolutely accurate, i.e. if it is able to sell 250 units, but no more, we know that point X lies on the firm's demand curve. If there are ten such firms, the total sold at a price of £10 would be 2,500 units. Point Y in the right-hand diagram lies on the market demand curve.

There is no knowing in practice what other points lie on the demand curves, and so we make the usual assumption in Fig. 18.3 that demand is inversely related to price. (We have labelled the curves D_E to indicate that demand turns out to be as expected.)

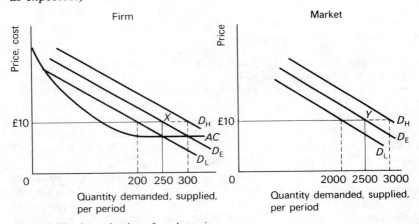

Fig. 18.3 The determination of market price

But what happens if the suppliers' expectations are not fulfilled; if they misjudge the effects of the various factors that influence demand? Demand could be either higher than expected (D_H) or lower than expected (D_L), and we consider each possibility in turn.

Demand higher than expected

If demand is higher than expected, suppliers could sell either the quantity expected at a higher price, or a larger quantity at the initial price (or it could

160

choose a point between these alternatives). Which alternative is chosen will depend upon six factors:

1. The objectives of the suppliers, and in particular the importance they attach to an increase in sales volume.

2. Whether or not the initial profit margin was satisfactory. If the profit margin was unsatisfactory, for example because demand had been depressed, it is likely that suppliers would wish to take advantage of the increase in demand to restore profit margins to a more satisfactory level. Therefore price would be raised. If, on the other hand, the initial profit margin was satisfactory, they would probably keep price unchanged, and reap higher total profits via an increase in sales volume.

3. The cost structure. Fig. 18.3, assumes that average cost remains constant as output rises beyond the expected level. As we shall show in Chapter 24 this is an entirely reasonable assumption. However, it does not always hold. In some instances an increase in output may be accompanied by an increase in average cost; for example, when the increased demand by producers for inputs causes the price of these input to rise. In other instances an increase in output may be accompanied by a fall in average cost; for example, when economies of large scale production arise. If suppliers wish to maintain their profit margins, these changes in average cost will be reflected in changes in price.

4. The amount of information possessed by suppliers about the state of demand. When we look at demand curves, such as those in Fig. 18.3, we may get the impression that suppliers are well informed about the state of, and the extent of the change in, demand. But it is most unlikely that suppliers would have as much information as is given in Fig. 18.3. In fact they would probably know, at least for some time, only that they were receiving more orders than expected. They would not know whether, or for how long, this would continue. They might believe, for example, that there had been a change in the pattern of orders over time and that the higher level of orders at the beginning of the period would be followed by a lower level at the end, leaving total orders as expected.

5. The extent to which the suppliers can co-ordinate their decisions. We are, of course, discussing markets in which co-ordination, in some form or another, may exist. But it does not follow that co-ordination is always possible.

6. The cost of changing prices. If a firm makes only a small number of products which it supplies to a few purchasers, the costs of changing prices are small. On the other hand if it sells a wide range of products to a large number of purchasers, considerable costs may be incurred in informing salesmen of the new prices, printing new price lists, changing prices on labels, etc. In these circumstances producers may decide to maintain their existing prices, especially, of course, if they believe that the increase in demand is only temporary.

A cost of a different kind may also be involved in increasing price, namely a loss of goodwill among customers. Industrial customers in particular may be annoyed by price increases which are not associated with increases in the supplier's costs. Although these customers may have to accept the higher price at first, because, for example, they need the product in order to maintain their own production schedules, they may begin to search for alternative suppliers, and this could provide the opportunity for new suppliers to break into the market. Moreover the longer the time period involved, the greater the opportunity for redesigning the product in order to use (cheaper) substitute materials and components. In other words, if prices were raised, demand might be far more elastic in the long then the short term, and this possibility might lead producers to maintain their existing prices.

Although many different factors affect pricing decisions it seems that, provided that the initial profit margins are satisfactory and that average cost remains (roughly) constant as output rises, the most likely effect of an increase in demand would be that price would be maintained, and the volume of sales increased. With demand curve D_H in Fig. 18.3 price would remain at £10, each producer would sell 300 units and the total number sold would be 3,000.

Demand lower than expected

When demand is lower than expected suppliers may be tempted to reduce their prices in order to try to increase their sales. However, a reduction in price by one supplier may lead to retaliation by competitors and to a price war which leaves all producers with lower profits. Consequently, if suppliers can co-ordinate their activities, they may maintain their price and thus minimise the reduction in their profits.

Indeed they may even be able to increase their price in order to compensate for an increase in costs. Some well publicised examples of this policy have occurred in the American steel industry. As the level of capacity utilisation fell, average cost increased, and the major steel producers took the lead in implementing price increases, their lead subsequently being followed by the smaller producers. The price increases led to profits being higher than they would otherwise have been, since only a small loss of sales occurred (the demand for steel is highly inelastic with respect to price in the short term). But on two occasions pressure from the President of the USA, who was alarmed by the inflationary effects of the price increases, caused increases to be withdrawn.

In most instances, however, suppliers would be satisfied if they could maintain their prices and prevent a price war breaking out when demand was depressed. Of course the greater the fall in demand and the longer demand remains depressed, the greater the strain put on the co-ordination mechanism. But if we assume, with reference to Fig. 18.3, that price is maintained at £10 with demand D_L each firm will produce 200 units and the total supplied will be 2,000 units.

Summary. Pricing when suppliers have a high degree of discretion

When suppliers have a high degree of pricing discretion, the market price is related to the suppliers' average costs. The relationship between cost and price is not fixed. It may vary from one market to another, depending upon differences in suppliers' objectives. Moreover it may vary with changes in demand, although we have suggested that such changes are more likely to affect the quantity sold than the price (especially when output remains within the range in which average cost is constant).

We showed that in the situation illustrated in Fig. 18.3 there was a strong probability that price would remain at £10 as demand varied within the range D_L to D_H, and that from 2,000 to 3,000 units would be supplied at that price. In other words the (market) supply curve would be horizontal within this range of output. (Supply is infinitely elastic at the going price within this range of output.)

Cost-based pricing when suppliers have a lower degree of discretion

Cost-based pricing procedures are not confined to markets in which suppliers have a high degree of pricing discretion. There are many other markets in which cost is the starting point of the pricing process. But the lower the degree of discretion the lower is the probability that suppliers will be able to adjust their prices so as to maintain their profit whenever costs change.

We can illustrate this by reference to a market in which there is only a single buyer, a situation known as *monopsony*. Let us take the example of a drug which is sold to the UK Government for use in the National Health Service. In quoting a price for the supply of this drug a producer will take into account his costs and his target profit. But the Government may not accept this price. It may consider that the profit built into the price is too high, or it may simply be concerned to buy more cheaply. Even though the supplier may be unhappy with the lower price offered, he may agree to it because the Government is the sole purchaser.

However, although the relationship between cost and price is not what the producer would wish, this does not mean that his costs have no effect on the price. If the buyer is sensible he will take the producer's costs into account; he will not drive the price down to so low a level that the producer refuses to supply the product.

Price determination when suppliers have no discretion

Finally we consider markets in which an individual supplier has no pricing discretion, no influence on the market price. These markets usually have a large number of producers supplying identical or very similar products; these suppliers are unable to co-ordinate their activities and find it difficult to predict and control the level of output. Furthermore, barriers to entry are usually low (this is, of course, one of the reasons why the number of suppliers tends to be high). We define markets having these features as open markets. Examples of open markets are to be found in the primary industries, and especially in agriculture and fishing, and we can explain how prices are determined in open markets by considering several agricultural products.

A simple model of price determination in an open market

As our first example let us consider the market for strawberries. Several factors influence the supply of strawberries. Perhaps the most obvious is the amount of land devoted to their cultivation. The amount of time and money spent on preparing the land, weeding, etc., are also important. Decisions on these matters are, of course, made by the farmer. But the farmer has no control over the weather, which also influences the supply. Indeed, if we consider the market for strawberries on any given day, the weather, and especially the amount of sunshine, will be of the utmost importance, since farmers will bring to market all the strawberries that are ripe.

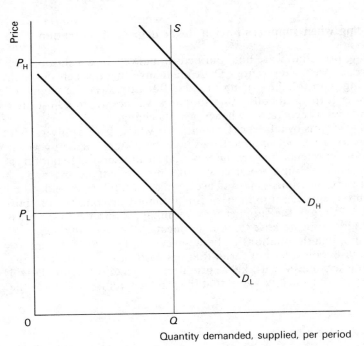

18.4 Price determination with fixed supply

This situation is illustrated in Fig. 18.4 where the quantity of strawberries supplied on a given day is Q. The price at which they are sold will depend upon the market demand. If demand is high (D_H) because, for example, the weather is fine and many housewives wish to buy strawberries for making picnic teas, the price will be high, P_H. If the demand is low (D_L – rainy weather, no picnics), price will be low, P_L.

The farmers may not be satisfied with the price P_L, but they would be better off accepting it than refusing to sell at this price; strawberries are highly perishable and any not sold on this day would be worthless. Furthermore, there would be no point in a farmer withdrawing part of his supply from the market in the hope of obtaining a higher price for the remainder. Since there are a large number of suppliers the effect on the quantity supplied, and hence on the price, would be negligible.

In the model presented above, and illustrated in Fig. 18.4, no reference was made to the suppliers' costs. This absence of a direct relationship between cost and price is a feature which distinguishes open markets from other markets. However, it would be wrong to conclude that cost has no influence on price. Cost may, in fact, influence price in various ways, as we can show by considering slightly more elaborate models.

164

An alternative model of price determination in an open market

In Fig. 18.5 AVC denotes the average variable cost, which at this stage comprises the cost of picking and transporting strawberries. (The concept of variable cost is discussed at greater length in Chapter 24.) The supply, demand and price of strawberries on day 1 are denoted by S_1 (Q_1 supplied at any price), D_1 and P_1 respectively. It can be seen that the price is below the average variable cost. On this day suppliers will accept this price. If, however, they feel that prices are likely to remain at this level on future days, it would not be worth their while sending

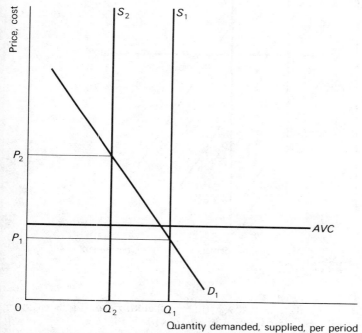

Fig. 18.5 An alternative model of price determination in an open market

strawberries to market, since the costs incurred would exceed the revenue. If, influenced by these considerations, some suppliers withdraw from the market, so that only half as many strawberries are supplied on day 2 (S_2), and if demand remains at D_1 the price will rise to P_2.

Let us now lengthen our time horizon to consider the market for strawberries during the season as a whole. Although suppliers realise that prices will vary from day to day during the season, they will form an expectation about the average price that they will receive. In Fig. 18.6 this expected price is denoted by P_E, and exceeds the suppliers' average total cost (total cost comprises all variable costs and fixed costs, e.g. the rent paid for land).

If demand and supply turn out as expected (D_E, S_E), the price will be as expected, P_E. Consequently, in the absence of any other changes, farmers will be happy to maintain the same acreage under strawberries in the following year and to supply the same quantity.

165

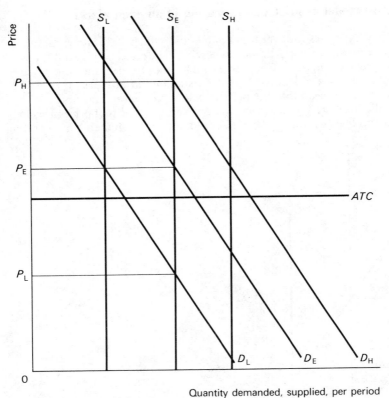

Fig. 18.6 An extended model of price determination in an open market

On the other hand, if price is lower than expected, P_L, and fails to cover average total cost and yield a satisfactory profit, it is likely that some farmers will reduce the acreage devoted to strawberries in the following year and plant another crop. This would cause the supply curve to shift to the left (S_L). (This reduction in supply would of course, result in an increase in price.)

Finally, price could be higher than expected (P_H). This price yields an extremely high profit. Consequently, if it is felt that the conditions which gave rise to the high demand are likely to recur next year, the acreage devoted to strawberries is likely to rise. The supply curve will shift to the right (S_H). (This increase in supply would, of course, result in a fall in price.)

Summary. The relationship between cost and price in open markets

We have shown that although in open markets suppliers' costs do not have a direct effect on prices, they have an important indirect effect. If the market price is considered by suppliers to be too low in relation to their costs, the quantity supplied will be reduced and this will cause prices to increase. These adjustments in supply may take place from day to day or from year to year.

Opportunity costs and price floors

In some open markets suppliers may enter into arrangements designed to protect themselves from the most unfavourable consequences of fluctuations in price. Let us consider again the suppliers of strawberries. When discussing Fig. 18.5 we said that suppliers would accept the market price ruling on any given day, because any strawberries not sold on that day would become worthless. However, let us now assume that the suppliers are able to enter into an arrangement with jam manufacturers whereby the manufacturers agree to buy at a guaranteed price any strawberries left unsold. Since the manufacturers are willing to offer a guaranteed price (P_G), this will no doubt be less than the expected average price (P_E), as shown in Fig. 18.7.

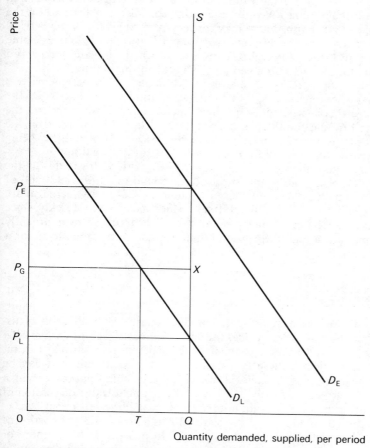

Fig. 18.7 Price determination with a guaranteed price

With supply Q and demand D_E the price is an expected, P_E. But with the lower demand D_L the price P_L would be below the guaranteed price. Consequently suppliers will sell in this market only as much as purchasers will buy at the guaranteed price. This can be seen to be quantity T. The rest of the

167

strawberries, TQ, will be sold to the jam manufacturers. (The supply curve in the market for fresh strawberries is P_GXS).

The guaranteed price acts as a floor price in the market for fresh strawberries. We can also say that the price offered by the jam manufacturers is the opportunity cost of supplying strawberries to the main market (opportunity cost is the most profitable alternative use of resources).

Price determination in other open markets

We have discussed the market for strawberries at considerable length in order to explain the working of an open market. Although all open markets have common features, they also exhibit differences of detail, frequently associated with the nature of the product. We now, therefore, consider very briefly how the market for some other products may differ from that for strawberries. (Incidentally there may also be different types of markets for strawberries. Some fruit is sold directly from producer to consumer 'at the farm gate'.) To avoid repetition we shall not discuss the similarities between the markets.

The suppliers of lettuces would find it difficult to protect themselves against the worst price fluctuations by arranging a guaranteed floor price. On the other hand, since the weather does not have such an immediate effect on the readiness of the product for sale, farmers have a little more control over the production process (however, instances have been recorded of lettuces being ploughed in because the price did not cover the cost of production.

The recent state of the weather has even less effect from day to day on the quantity of apples, pears and plums supplied (although the *total* yield will, of course, be affected by weather). Furthermore changes in capacity (acreage) are more difficult to effect. (It is especially difficult to increase capacity quickly, since more time must elapse before newly planted trees bear fruit.) Consequently profits may remain at a higher (or lower) than normal, acceptable, level for a greater length of time.

Price determination in other markets

In the previous sections we have presented models of price determination in two types of market; those in which prices are based on costs, and open markets. When we allow for the fact that in each instance particular markets may exhibit slight differences of detail, these two models of price determination can be applied to a large number of markets. However there are some markets to which neither model can be satisfactorily applied, and we conclude our discussion of price determination by briefly examining a number of these other markets.

With the growth of large food-processing firms a substantial proportion of some crops, such as peas, is grown on contract to processors for canning or freezing. The prices of these products are determined not by the interaction of market demand and supply, as in open markets, but by negotiation between purchaser and supplier. In these situations the costs of the suppliers have a more direct influence on price than in open markets although, as noted during our discussion of the market for drugs, the relationship between cost and price may not be entirely satisfactory to the supplier.

The market for shipping space has many of the characteristics of an open market. When, due to a change in the balance between demand and supply, freight rates fall, each supplier has to accept the lower rate. Since there are a large number of suppliers, the withdrawal by one supplier of part of his capacity would have a negligible effect on the price. However the market differs from that for, say, strawberries, in a number of respects.

First, when the supplier, the shipowner, has to decide whether or not to supply, he will have information on both the price (the value of the contract) and the cost of fulfilling that contract (the wages of the crew, the cost of fuel, etc.). Second, ships are not as perishable as strawberries. An owner may decide not to enter into a contract today, but to lay up his ships in the hope that he will obtain more profitable contracts in the future. However, third, he will incur costs if the ship is laid up (port dues, the wages of a skeleton crew for security purposes, etc.), and these costs should be taken into account in deciding whether or not to bid for contracts.

Some manufactured products, e.g. natural textile yarns, are sold in markets where there are a large number of suppliers who are unable to co-ordinate their activities. These suppliers frequently have price information which they can compare with information on their costs before deciding whether or not to undertake production. As with the shipping companies, and with suppliers in all open markets, their decision relates not to price but to output.

Finally, a number of products are sold on a bid or tender basis. Each potential supplier is asked to quote a price and the purchaser makes his decision on the basis of the prices quoted, together with other factors such as the reputation of the suppliers and the date by which they can fulfil the contract. In deciding what price to quote, the supplier will take into account his costs and the prices which he believes his competitors are likely to quote.

Methods of distributing goods

There are two distinct aspects of the distribution of goods that manufacturers must consider. The first is what is known technically as the mode of transportation. Manufacturers have to decide whether to transport their goods via road (and if so whether by their own fleet of vehicles or by specialist transport operators), rail, water or air. Their decisions are influenced by such things as the nature of the product (it is easier to transport watches than coal by air), the costs of the alternative methods (road transport is especially cost-effective for short journeys, air transport for long journeys), the speed of delivery (water transport would not be used for supplies required in an emergency) and the frequency of the service.

The second aspect, which applies mainly to the manufacturers of products which are eventually sold to households, is which channels of distribution the manufacturer should use. The first decision to be made here is whether to sell through wholesalers or direct to retailers. This decision must take into account the functions performed by wholesalers.

The functions of wholesalers

The wholesalers usually stock several brands of a given type of product and thus

169

make it easier for the retailer to compare the merits of these various brands. The wholesaler may advise the retailer in his choice, this advice being especially useful when new brands or products come on to the market. By holding stocks, wholesalers reduce the amount of stock that retailers need to hold. Furthermore, before transporting the goods the wholesaler will, if required, 'break bulk', i.e. he will divide large consignments received from the manufacturer into smaller consignments suited to the retailers' needs. Wholesalers also sell on credit to retailers (although they do not necessarily extend more credit than would manufacturers).

These services provided by wholesalers are of benefit to retailers and, in as much as they encourage retailers to purchase the goods stocked by the wholesalers, they benefit the manufacturers of these goods. The manufacturers benefit also because their costs of distribution are lower when they sell to wholesalers than to a much larger number of retailers (this is especially so for small manufacturers who do not produce a large enough output to justify their own sales and distribution system).

Wholesalers cover the costs of these various services by reselling goods to retailers at a higher price than they pay to manufacturers, and when manufacturers consider whether or not to sell through wholesalers they have to decide whether the advantages justify the reduction in price granted to the wholesaler. Manufacturers may decide to sell direct to retailers (i.e. undertake their own wholesaling), if they feel that they can perform these functions either at a lower cost or more efficiently from the manufacturers' point of view.

One of the problems faced by a manufacturer in selling through wholesalers is that he cannot ensure that in presenting goods to retailers the wholesaler gives greater, or even equal, preference to that manufacturer's brand. Consequently, even if the manufacturer does not expect to reduce his costs, he may sell direct if he feels that the products will thereby be promoted more efficiently to retailers. Where there is very strong competition for shelf space, as in many grocery products, some manufacturers have gone beyond the stage of selling and distributing goods to retailers; they assist in the task of shelf-filling.

In some instances the decision is taken out of the manufacturers' hands. As we show below, multiple chains have steadily increased their share of the retail trade, and many of these large retailers insist on purchasing direct from the manufacturer. Consequently in many trades manufacturers sell both direct to large retailers and to wholesalers who supply the smaller retailers.

Having examined the factors that influence the decision whether to sell through wholesalers or direct to retailers, we now consider which types of retailer the manufacturer might supply. It will be helpful in this respect to examine briefly the main features of the structure of retailing.

The structure of retailing

Table 18.1 shows the share of retail trade held by the major types of retailer. It can be seen that multiple retailers, defined here as retailers having ten or more shops (but excluding co-operatives and departmental stores), have increased their market share substantially and are now as important as the independents. The growth of the multiples is mainly due to the fact that on the whole their prices are appreciably lower than those of other retailers. Another factor that has been

Table 18.1 Share of retail sales by form of organisation

	1961	1966	1971	1972	1973	1974	1975	1976	1978
Independents	53.9	49.9	47.8	46.7	45.6	44.8	44.2	43.0	41.0
Multiples	28.2	33.0	36.5	37.4	38.4	39.1	39.6	40.1	42.2
Co-operatives	9.5	7.7	7.0	5.6	5.5	5.5	5.7	6.2	6.8
Departmental Stores*	5.9	5.7	4.8	6.0	5.9	5.8	5.8	6.0	5.0
Mail order	2.5	3.7	3.9	4.3	4.5	4.8	4.7	4.7	5.0

*Including co-operative department stores

Source: Census of Distribution, Business Monitor SD series

important, especially in recent years, is that multiples have operated very large stores – superstores, which have a selling area of at least 25,000 square feet, and hypermarkets, with a selling area of at least 50,000 square feet – that attract customers by their very wide range of goods.

The progress of the multiples has been at the expense of the independents and, to a lesser extent, the co-operatives. Independents have the best chance of surviving the competition if they can offer the consumer advantages to compensate for their higher prices, such as a convenient location or a high standard of personal attention. Many independent retailers have joined voluntary groups, sponsored either by retailers or by wholesalers. An essential feature of voluntary groups is that purchasing is centralised so that better terms can be obtained from manufacturers. The wholesaler-sponsored groups also provide the retail members with various forms of advice and assistance, and the benefits of this form of organisation can be judged from the fact that in the grocery market, where competition from the multiples has been very intense, during the period 1961 to 1976 the share of trade accounted for by retailers affiliated to groups increased from 13 to 21 per cent, while that of non-group independents fell from 40 to 16 per cent.

The loss of market share by the co-operative societies during the period 1961 to 1973, when other multiple organisations were reaping the benefits of economies of scale, may seem rather surprising, especially in view of the fact that the co-operative movement encompasses retailing, wholesaling and manufacturing. But the financial relationships which link these three activities have not led to an organisation which is fully integrated in trading terms. Each retail society has the right, frequently exercised, of buying goods on its own account from any source, within or outside the co-operative movement.

The stability of the market share of departmental stores, shown in Table 18.1, reflects a balance of conflicting forces. On the one hand these shops provide a high level of service, which may be demanded by an increasing number of consumers as incomes rise. On the other hand this level of service is reflected in higher prices, and this makes the department stores vulnerable to competition from several sources: the specialist multiple chains selling clothing, furniture, etc., variety stores such as Marks and Spencer which have gradually upgraded their image and appeal, and the superstores and hypermarkets which come increasingly close to the department store in the range of goods offered – often at lower prices and at locations more convenient to the car-borne shopper.

Mail order selling steadily increased its market share until 1974, as shown in Table 18.1. Perhaps the most important factor favouring the growth of mail order sales in the early part of the post-war period was the offer of extended credit at a time when consumers found it difficult to obtain substantial credit facilities from conventional retail outlets. Another advantage of mail order is that customers are able to try out merchandise in the privacy of their own home outside conventional shopping hours, an advantage that assumes greater significance with the increase in the number of working wives and increasing traffic congestion in town centres.

The choice of distribution channel

As we said above, the choice of distribution channel is sometimes made by the retailer rather than the manufacturer. Large retailers insist on negotiating direct with the manufacturer, and obtain better buying terms (lower prices, more frequent deliveries) than smaller retailers. Manufacturers are willing to grant these better terms partly because they are unwilling to risk losing a large amount of custom and partly because their costs are reduced by dealing with a few large customers than with many small ones.

However, manufacturers have to be careful that they do not make too many concessions to large retailers. For example, some manufacturers have found that, having granted favourable buying terms to large retailers, they still have to incur heavy distribution costs in supplying small quantities of goods to the smaller shops of these retailers. One manufacturer which found itself in this situation was Kellogg, of breakfast cereal fame,. In order to redress the situation it announced that as from 1 May 1978 it would not make deliveries of less than fifty cases, and that those small deliveries would attract a surcharge of £1.25.

In some instances large retailers (including department stores and mail order houses) and wholesalers enter into contracts whereby the manufacturer supplies goods under the brand name of the distributor, e.g. the Marks and Spencer 'St Michael' brand and Tesco's own brand. The price paid by the retailer for such 'own label' products is usually below that paid for the equivalent manufacturer brands, and this differential is explained partly by a reduction in the manufacturer's costs, e.g. for advertising, and partly by the desire to expand sales through an additional distribution channel. This latter motive is especially important for smaller manufacturers who cannot afford to spend as much as their larger rivals on advertising and other marketing activities. The production of our own label goods has been the only means of survival for some smaller firms.

The choice of distribution channel may also be influenced by the nature of the product. The manufacturers of technically complex goods, e.g. hi-fi audio equipment, may restrict supplies to retailers whose staff have technical expertise. Manufacturers who wish their goods to have a particular image may choose outlets consistent with that image, e.g. very expensive cosmetics are often sold only through department stores which offer lavish fittings, a high degree of personal attention and a general aura of opulence.

Summary and conclusions

We began this chapter by making a broad distinction between markets in terms

172

of the degree of pricing discretion enjoyed by individual suppliers. We then discussed the different pricing policies and procedures that might be adopted in these different markets (and also, briefly, in markets which do not fall into either category). In order to summarise these policies as briefly as possible it is useful to return to our initial distinction.

In some markets prices are set by individual suppliers, and changes in demand are usually reflected in changes in output rather than price. In other markets prices are determined by the interaction of market demand and supply, and the individual supplier cannot influence this price. In many markets of the latter type, price is determined only after the decision to supply has been taken, although in some instances the prices may be known in advance of the decision to supply (or not to supply).

Having discussed, in this and previous chapters, the various policies that might be adopted by organisations, and especially by commercial organisations, we now examine in the following chapters some of the legal implications of these policies, and in particular we consider how the law views the relations between organisations and consumers.

Assignments

18.1

State whether each of the following statements is true or false:

1. The term 'cost-based pricing' indicates that price bears a fixed relationship to cost.
2. In open markets products are usually highly differentiated.
3. When supply is infinitely elastic the same quantity would be supplied whatever the price.
4. A vertical supply curve indicates that the same quantity would be supplied whatever the price.
5. In open markets cost has no influence on price.

18.2

If demand turns out to be higher than expected, suppliers might increase the price or the quantity supplied (or both). Outline the factors that would influence this decision.

18.3

Why might the price elasticity of demand in the long term differ from that in the short term in the following situations?

1. The price of gas sold to domestic consumers increases relative to the price of other fuels.
2. The price of cigarettes increases.
3. The price of aluminium falls.
4. The price of natural rubber rises.

18.4

Explain the circumstances in which the market supply curve is horizontal.

18.5

'The more food farmers produce, the lower their total income is likely to be.'
Discuss.

18.6

The passage below was extracted from the *Financial Times*, 6 October 1977.

1. Draw a diagram to show how the consumer market for potatoes in 1977 differed from that in 1976.
2. Discuss the possible consequences of the guaranteed price offered by the Potato Marketing Board (you may find it helpful to draw another diagram).
3. Explain how you think the price of potatoes in 1978 might have differed from that in 1977.

'Potatoes, almost in the luxury class for the last two years, are now so cheap that farmers face catastrophic losses.

'In the wake of the price collapse the Potato Marketing Board, aided by the Government, has started buying up surpluses in an attempt to put a floor in the market.

'As a result shop prices can be expected to climb slightly in the coming days. The Board said yesterday that the cheapest potatoes, now available in some shops at 2p per pound, would probably soon go up to 4p.

'High-priced seed has pushed growing costs this year up to £600 an acre, and at present market prices growers stand to lose £170 an acre or more.

'The Potato Board is offering farmers a guaranteed price of around £45 a ton for holding their crops on the farm instead of selling them in the open market.

'Late next month, when the whole crop is harvested and consumption has been assessed, a decision will be taken on what happens to the surplus. Usually, potato gluts are fed to pigs or cattle, although they can be used for human consumption at home or abroad.

'Whatever happens the farmers are assured of their £45 a ton, compared with the present market average in England and Wales of around £33.

'At the peak of the shortages caused by drought in 1975 and last year, some farmers were earning almost £300 a ton for their crops. Then average yields fell below 9 tons an acre, but this year farmers are expecting a record 13 tons.

'The Potato Board and the Ministry of Agriculture refuse to speculate on exactly how many potatoes may have to be fed to livestock this year, restricting themselves for the moment to talk of the possibility of "a marginal surplus" from the expected crop of 6.5 m. tons.

'However, provisional figures show that last year, as shoppers stopped buying potatoes at record high prices, consumption was 24 per cent down on 1974, the last "normal" crop year on record.

'The most optimistic market experts say half a million tons of surplus potatoes may have to be bought by the Potato Board this year. The pessimists forecast a glut of up to 2 million tons.'

174

18.7

How would you explain the changes in the volume of purchases of coffee and tea, shown below? (You should refer in your answer to the elasticity and cross elasticity of demand.)

Index of price and volume of purchases of coffee and tea, UK

	Instant coffee		Tea	
	Price	*Volume*	*Price*	*Volume*
1973	100	100	100	100
1974	109	104	110	98
1975	122	109	123	94
1976	169	107	141	93
1977	322	83	269	88

Source: A.G.B. Ltd.

18.8

The passage below is based on an article in the *Financial Times* 13 March 1978.

1. Identify two changes in supply conditions and one change in demand conditions that have influenced the price of copper.
2. What factors make it difficult for copper producers to agree on cutbacks in production?
3. Do you think that the price reductions referred to in the article were desirable or undesirable? Explain your answer.

'Last week world copper prices rallied on the London Metal Exchange – partly reflecting the transport problems that threaten to cut back Zambian copper exports severely and the possible repercussions of the brief "invasion" of Zambia by Rhodesian security forces. Also boosting the market was the recent agreement, initiated by Zambia, between three of the world's leading copper exporting countries to reduce production by 15 per cent.

'But the production agreement is a sign of desperation. The three countries which are parties to it – Peru, Zaire and Zambia – are dependent on copper for the bulk of their export earnings and there seems to be little alternative to a cutback in view of the heavy losses being suffered at present price levels. On the London Metal Exchange copper last month fell to the lowest level for two years at £612 a tonne – a far cry from the all time peak of £1,400 reached in early 1974.

'By the end of 1977 world copper stocks are estimated to have risen to well over 2 m. tonnes. This compares with an annual Western world consumption of around 6.5 m. tonnes. It will take a long time for these heavy surplus stocks to be cleared. Meanwhile there is considerable competition among producers to capture a larger share of sales. Chile, which has now become the world's leading copper exporter, has refused to agree to the 15 per cent cut-back, despite being a member of the Intergovernmental Council for Copper Exporters, the producers' organisation that has been singularly unsuccessful in its efforts to stabilise the world copper market because of disagreement among its members.'

Table 18.2 Air Fares, London–New York

	SKYTRAIN (Laker)	STANDBY (BA Pan Am, etc.)	BUDGET (Major Airlines)	ABC (Advance Booking Charter)	ABC (Latesave, Jetsave)	APEX (Major Airlines) (Advance Purchase Excursions)
Return fare	**£129** £59 out, $135 back (approx. £70)	**£139** £64 out, $146 back (approx. £75)	**£149**	**£126+** £126–£139 low £184–£189 peak	**£95** £151 peak	**£153** £192.50 peak
Reservation	Day of flight	Day of flight	21 days before week of choice. You cannot choose your actual day of departure	45-plus days	During last 48 hours before 45-day deadline	50-plus days
Length of stay requirement	None	None	One week minimum	Min. 14 days, max. 45 days. Also 'long-stop' holidays available	Min. 14 days Max. 45 days	Min. 14 days Max. 45 days
Flights	One daily, two from April 1	Several daily (scheduled services)	Several daily (scheduled services)	Several weekly (charter flights)	One flight weekly until June, then several	Scheduled services
Number of seats	345 a flight	BA, Pan Am and TWA have limit of 1050 seats each a week, others fewer	As standby	All seats – but may be heavy bookings	Only the seats left unsold. About 1500–2000 expected this year	Limited – and allocations can fill rapidly
Hidden costs	Meals, films, drinks extra	Meals free, but film and drinks extra	Meals free, but film and drinks extra	Meals, drinks and films free	Meals, drinks and films free	Meals free, but drinks and films extra
Disadvantage	May fail to get on plane. Late departure to New York (5.30 pm)	May fail to get on plane, but can try luck with another airline	Advance booking and no choice of day of travel	Cannot cancel within 45 days – need to take out insurance	May fail to get on plane	Long booking, departure flight cannot be changed

176

18.2

Table 18.2 gives details of the cheap air flights that were available between London and New York in 1978. How would you account for the differences in the price of the various services? Do you think that 'the market for air travel' is a meaningful term?

19 The organisation and consumers: the civil law

Introduction

In the previous chapters we have examined various policies of organisations. We have shown that many of these policies are adopted in order to meet the requirements of consumers. The ability to meet consumers' requirements is important for successful commercial organisation.

However, the interests of organisations and consumers do not always coincide. Meeting the interests of consumers might require the organisation to spend more time and money than it would otherwise wish. Consequently there are many provisions of the law designed to protect consumers' interests, and these are discussed in this and the next three chapters.

First we will examine the protection afforded to consumers by the civil law (i.e. the law which provides remedies enforceable in the civil courts). We shall see that both the courts and Parliament have made significant contributions to the protection of consumers in this respect.

Contract: freedom of bargain

The relationship between organisations and consumers is very often a contractual one. We examined in earlier chapters the main features of the law of contract. This area of law underwent its main developments in the nineteenth century. Then the emphasis was on freedom of contract, allowing people to reach their own bargains, on whatever terms they chose, free from any intervention by the State. It was frequently said that 'the law will not mend men's bargains'. We have already seen another aspect of this same philosophy – that usually expressed by the phrase *caveat emptor*: let the buyer beware. Between the twin principles of freedom of contract and *caveat emptor*, the consumer was left to fight his own battles with little to save him from the consequences of a bad bargain.

The law did recognise that bargains should be set aside in certain circumstances, for example where there had been duress or undue influence. But, as we have seen, such doctrines are not wide-ranging in their application, and left the majority of transactions untouched.

As far as Parliamentary activity was concerned, the most important legislation was the Sale of Goods Act 1893, but even this was merely a codification of the common law rules and trade practices that had already developed.

The law of contract that developed from this approach might have been perfectly adequate to regulate transactions between people of equal standing, equal expertise and equal bargaining power. It soon became evident that the further apart the parties grew in all these respects, the more inequitable it became to leave them with only their existing common law rights. The manufacturer whose goods or services were in great demand could adopt a 'take-it-or-leave-it' attitude, not only as regards the products or services themselves but also as regards the terms on which they were sold or supplied. As the chain between the manufacturer and the ultimate consumer grew longer so the opportunity for individual bargaining gradually disappeared. And the more advanced the technology became, the less was the consumer likely to be able to assess the capabilities and defects of the product. 'Let the buyer beware', the watchword of the nineteenth century, was gradually recognised as being increasingly unfair.

The shift to paternalism

A move to paternalism can be seen in three areas:

1. *In the attitude of the courts*, with their close scrutiny of exemption clauses, their development of the law of negligence to cover the liability of a supplier of defective goods and their increased willingness to reopen unfair bargains.

2. *In the activities of the legislature*, with the prohibition and supervision of various unfair consumer practices.

3. *In the growth of administrative controls* over business organisations, the encouragement of the voluntary adoption of codes of practice and the education of the consumer.

We must now look at these various aspects of consumer protection, the original inadequacies of the common law and the different ways these have been dealt with by the courts and the legislature.

The courts

There are three main areas of activity by the courts.

Exclusion clauses

The attack on exclusion clauses (sometimes called exemption clauses) was one of the earliest overt moves towards consumer protection. Everyone is familiar with examples of exclusion clauses. Notices in car parks read 'All vehicles parked at owner's risk'. The mass of small print on the back of a booking form may read 'All conditions and warranties, express or implied, at common law or by statue are hereby excluded'. The notice at the hotel reception desk may say 'No responsibility is accepted for the loss of any valuables unless deposited in the manager's safe'.

Limitation clauses, which for most purposes are treated in the same way as exclusion clauses, are almost as common. Instead of attempting to exclude liability altogether the clause may say 'Liability is limited to £50 in respect of any one item'.

For a person to contract to do a particular thing whilst exempting himself from failure to do that precise thing is something to be wary of and should only be allowed under some sort of controls. The law has never looked kindly on a person who puts himself under a legal obligation whilst refusing to accept his legal responsibilities for his obligation.

The *ad hoc* development of the treatment of exclusion clauses set various hurdles for the person putting forward the exclusion clause in his defence to overcome. These hurdles are as follows:

1. A contractual term

The clause, as with all other terms of the contract, must have been incorporated into the contract. Where the contract is written, the signature of the party will incorporate the clause whether or not he bothered to read, or understand, the clause (*L'Estrange v. Graucob*).

If the contract is not signed, the test is whether the person seeking to rely on the clause has taken reasonable steps to bring it to the other party's notice. The usual way to do this is to display a notice where it will be seen before the contract is concluded. The more unusual a clause is then correspondingly more has to be done to bring the term to the other party's notice (e.g. if it exempts the party from liability for personal injury when all that would normally be expected is exclusion for liability for damage to property) (*Thornton v. Shoe Lane Parking*).

An exclusion clause may be incorporated into a contract by a consistent course of dealings. In other words, where the parties have over a period of time consistently contracted on certain terms, including an exemption clause, further dealings, which may be done informally because of their long relationship, will be taken to be on the same terms. But it should be emphasised that only a *course* of dealings (i.e. more than occasional dealings over a period of time), that is consistent (i.e. *always* on the same terms) is sufficient (*McCutcheon v. Mcbrayne*).

As with other terms, an exclusion clause that is brought to the parties' notice *after* the contract is made is ineffective (*Olley v. Marlborough Court Hotel Ltd*).

2. Covering the breach

As an exclusion clause is aimed at exempting the person putting it forward from liability. If he fails to perform his contractual obligation, it is vital for him to prove that the contractual obligation that he has failed in is indeed covered by the exemption clause. In other words, the courts will not permit reliance on an exclusion clause unless it is clear that the clause covers the breach that has occurred.

If the breach is a breach of *warranty*, an exclusion clause that purports to cover only breaches of *conditions* will not help, and vice versa. The court leans against the exemption clause when interpreting it.

One aspect of this attitude is that the court leans very heavily against a person who is trying to escape liability for his own negligence. In fact the House of Lords has recently gone so far as to say that in order to exempt oneself from liability for negligence, the word 'negligence' or some synonym must be used (*Smith v. South Wales Switchgear Ltd*).

A further aspect of interpretation is what has been called *the main purpose rule*. The courts will not interpret an exemption clause in such a way as to defeat the main purpose of the contract. Thus a clause that purports to allow deviation in a contract of carriage will not be allowed to stand if the deviation is so great as to defeat the object of carrying the cargo. For example, if the goods are perishable (*Glynn v Margetson*) and the (allowed) deviation means that the object of transporting the goods from point A to point B cannot be achieved because the goods have perished before delivery.

The exclusion clause, even if it has survived so far, may fail if its effect has been misrepresented or if there is an overriding oral undertaking that is inconsistent with it.

In *Curtis v. Chemical Cleaning Co* the plaintiff took a wedding dress into a shop to be cleaned. She was asked to sign a form, and when she asked what the small print meant she was informed that it exempted the cleaners from liability for damage to beads and sequins. It did in fact purport to cover all loss or damage, but the court refused to allow reliance on it when the dress came back stained. The term could only apply in the way in which it had been represented, i.e. covering damage to beads and sequins.

A party seeking to rely on an exemption clause may not have distorted the meaning of the term, but may have given an undertaking that he would perform the contract in a particular way despite the term giving him complete freedom. If he does this, he will not later be able to rely on the term if this is inconsistent with his oral undertaking (*Evans v. Merzario*).

3. Fundamental breach

We have so far treated the contract as a series of distinct obligations rather than as containing a fundamental contractual obligation. Whilst it will often be important to look at the separate terms of the contract there may be cases where the breach is so gross (or fundamental) as to amount to a complete non-performance of the contract, or a performance that is so grossly defective that it amounts to a non-performance.

An example will help to explain this. If X agrees to sell a hundredweight of beans to Y and only delivers half that amount, X will be in breach of condition and Y can treat the contract as at an end and can sue for damages. If however X delivers a hundredweight of peas, X is in fundamental breach. His obligation was to deliver beans, and he has totally failed to perform that obligation. In the same way, if he delivered a hundredweight of what had once been beans but are now a rotting mass of vegetation, his performance will have been so defective as to be tantamount to non-performance.

The importance of this appears when a party attempts to exclude liability for fundamental breach. It has been suggested in some cases that as a matter of law an exclusion clause can never operate where there has been a fundamental breach. The better view, however, seems to be that even in the case of a fundamental breach, it is still a question of construction of the clause, that is seeing whether its wording does cover the breach which has occurred. But it will

181

be very unlikely that a clause will be construed by the courts to cover an obviously fundamental breach of the whole agreement.

4. Covering the party

A person who is not a party to a contract cannot enforce the contract. This rule is known as the rule of privity of contract. The other side of the coin is that, if he is not a contracting party, he cannot rely on a provision in a contract which purports to exempt him from liability. That is particularly important where a contract is made between an employer and another. Employees or contractors who actually carry out the work are third parties for these purposes. Thus a clause in the main contract purporting to exempt employees or contractors from liability cannot be used by these classes of persons if they are sued by the person with whom the employer has agreed (*Scruttons v. Midland Silicones*).

A recent case decided by the Privy Council, *New Zealand Shipping Co v. A. M. Satterthwaite & Co Ltd*, shows that there may be a limited exception to this rule, at least so far as it concerns contracts for the carriage of goods, provided that (1) the contract of carriage makes it clear that the worker is intended to be protected, (2) the contract of carriage makes it clear that the carrier is contracting not only on his own behalf but also as agent for the worker, (3) the carrier has authority from the worker so to contract, (4) there is some consideration moving from the worker.

From the above account, it should be clear that anyone who seeks to exclude his liability for breach of contract faces many difficulties, even at common law, in trying to escape responsibility.

As we will see, Parliament has put even more problems in his way. So even if his exclusion clause passes the common law tests he may still fail.

Negligence

A second development by the courts is in the field of tort. So far we have been looking at provisions of the law of contract, but these do not provide for many common situations.

Take the following example: Mr A buys his wife a hair drier for her birthday. The first time she uses it, it catches fire and she is badly burned. How can she recover compensation for her injuries? She cannot sue in contract, because the only contract was between Mr A and the shop that sold the hair drier, and we have already seen that a person who is not a party to a contract cannot sue on that contract because of the doctrine of privity of contract.

Mr A can sue for damages for breach of contract in that the shop has supplied a defective hair drier, but the damages he will receive are limited to compensating him for the loss of the hair drier and possibly for any medical expenses that he incurs in having his wife treated. He will not be able to recover damages to compensate her for her injuries, her pain and suffering.

If Mrs A had no remedy in this case, there would be a serious gap, for she is the ultimate consumer of the goods in a very real sense.

The origins of the modern developed law in this area are to be found in the case of *Donoghue v. Stevenson*.

A young woman and her friend bought some ice cream over which was poured part of a bottle of ginger beer in a cafe in Paisley. When the girls had finished eating one of them went to pour out the rest of the contents of the bottle only to find that it contained the remains of a decomposed snail. The girl argued that she had suffered severe gastroenteritis from drinking the ginger beer and had suffered shock at seeing the snail. A majority of the House of Lords held that if these facts were true she would have a right of action against Stevenson, the manufacturer of the ginger beer.

Lord Atkin said, '*a manufacturer of products*, which he sells in such a form as to show that he intends them to reach the *ultimate consumer* in the form in which they left him with no *reasonable possibility of intermediate examination* and with the knowledge that the absence of reasonable care in the *preparation or putting up* of the products will result in an injury to the *consumer's life or property*, owes a *duty* to the consumer *to take reasonable care*.'

This statement has proved very important in clearly establishing a right of action against the manufacturer of dangerous goods by the person who is the consumer even though he is not in any contractual relationship with that manufacturer. The cases since *Donoghue v. Stevenson* have developed the ambit of the words as follows:

'*manufacturer*': this now includes repairers, assemblers, etc.

'*products*': this includes much more than just ginger beer. It has been held to include, among other things, motor-cars, underwear and hair-dye!

'*ultimate consumer*': this now includes the ultimate user and, indeed, anyone through whose hands the article may pass. It may even include anyone who is in physical proximity to the goods.

'*reasonable possibility of intermediate examination*': this means that the manufacturer may not be liable if he can prove that someone in his place would reasonably anticipate that the product would be examined (and so probably be made safe) at some stage before reaching the consumer.

'*preparation or putting up*': this covers defects in design, labels, packaging, instructions as well as the product itself.

'*consumer's life or property*': it is unclear whether the cost of repairing the defective product is obtainable.

'*a duty to take reasonable care*': it is now clear that negligence can be established from the existence of the defect and the surrounding circumstances. The injured person does not have to prove exactly how there was failure to take reasonable care.

But although this area of law would seem to provide protection for consumers who suffer injury or loss from defective products, there is an increasing lobby for imposing upon manufacturers a strict liability. Some element of strict liability has already been introduced by the Consumer Protection Act of 1978 (replacing and extending the Act of the same name of 1961) which we shall look at again later. These Acts provide for regulations to be made imposing safety requirements on classes of goods. If the manufacturer or retailer is in breach of these regulations he is liable to prosecution.

But he is also liable in tort to anyone injured simply because he is in breach of his statutory duty and not because he might be negligent. This type of action, however, is rarely brought.

It is likely, however, that a more far-ranging degree of strict liability in this area will be introduced by legislation in the near future, so that a manufacturer will always be held liable for injuries caused by his defective products without any requirement that negligence be proved.

Inequality of bargaining power

The third area in which the courts have been active, particularly recently, in unequal bargaining situations is that of the setting aside of contracts on the grounds of undue influence. A case of particular interest is *Lloyds Bank v Bundy*.

The defendant was an elderly farmer, who was not very well up in business affairs. He and his son banked at the same branch of Lloyds Bank. The son's company ran into difficulties and it was necessary to obtain an overdraft at the bank. The defendant guaranteed the overdraft and deposited the deeds of his farm, his only asset, with the bank as security.

The company ran into further difficulties. The father lent more money but the company went from bad to worse.

Eventually, the farmer received a visit from his son and the Bank Manager, who advised the farmer to enter into a further guarantee on security of his house. By this time the farmer had agreed to stand as guarantor for a larger sum than his total assets.

The son's company went into liquidation and the farmer was eventually called upon to pay. The question that arose before the court was whether the guarantee could be set aside on the grounds of undue influence.

The Court of Appeal held that in this case it could. On the evidence it was clear that undue pressure had been put upon the father to do something that was clearly in the interest of the bank and not in the interest of the father. What makes the case important from our point of view, however, is that Lord Denning propounded a principle which he suggested underlies all the cases of undue influence, whether or not there is a special relationship. He suggested that the single thread running through these is that of *inequality of bargaining power*. If this is present it permits the courts to look into the fairness of the transaction and set it aside.

Here we have a clear suggestion that the law *will* mend men's bargains if it can be shown that one party has, by his superior economic strength, taken advantage of another.

Lord Denning, in fact, has long felt that the courts have the power to set aside bad bargains made by those in a weak bargaining position. Although he has not always had the full support of other judges there are other indications that the courts might be prepared to assume this sort of power.

In *Schroeder Music Publishing Co v. Macauley* the House of Lords seemed to acknowledge this. The Lords intervened to hold void a contract for exclusive services which had been entered into by an unknown songwriter and a music company which was very one-sided in favour of the music company. In justifying this decision the House referred to the power of the courts to intervene in contracts where there is manifest inequality of bargaining power.

If applied to exclusion clauses such an attitude could have very far-reaching consequences. Lord Denning has, indeed, held that exclusion clauses contained in contracts can be held to be of no effect if they are not reasonable, given the respective bargaining positions of the parties, but in this contention he has had little support.

The extent of the courts' powers to re-open bargains should not be exaggerated. Although this may be a fruitful area for the future development of consumer protection it is as yet one of uncertain ambit. It is interesting to note, though, that this approach is rather similar to that which has been taken by Parliament in several recent statutes.

The legislature

Although the courts, by the development of Common law principles, have dealt with some problems created by inequality of bargaining power, Parliament's intervention is a more powerful weapon. A handful of Acts of Parliament in the late 1960s and 1970s have swung the balance considerably towards the consumer.

The principle of freedom of contract has been considerably eroded in statutes like the Misrepresentation Act 1967, the Supply of Goods (Implied Terms) Act 1973, the Fair Trading Act 1973, the Consumer Credit Act 1974 and the Unfair Contract Terms Act 1977. These Acts are wide-ranging in strengthening the protection of the consumer.

We will look at these Acts in detail to see what statutory protection they give the consumer in terms of safeguarding and strengthening his civil law rights. We shall discuss the protection afforded by the criminal law and administrative controls in later chapters.

Misrepresentation Act 1967

Under this Act a term which purports to exclude liability for misrepresentation has to pass the test of being fair and reasonable. The Unfair Contract Terms Act 1977 amended the test slightly to satisfy the same reasonableness test as a number of other sorts of exclusion clause.

Unfair Contract Terms Act 1977

A very broad range of contracts are within the scope of this Act.

The Act covers only 'business liability', that is where things are done a person in the course of business or arise from his use of the premises for business purposes. Some contracts are expressly excluded, e.g. those relating to insurance, land, or to patents, trade marks and copyrights.

The Act catches the purported exclusion of liability for negligence. This means the breach of the common law duty to take reasonable care or of any contractual term to take reasonable care or exercise reasonable skill in the performance of a contract.

The controls it imposes are that a person cannot by reference to a notice, exclude liability where the liability is for death or personal injuries. In the case of any other loss or damage, a person cannot so exclude or restrict his liability for negligence except in so far as the term satisfies the requirement of reasonableness.

Clauses purporting to exclude the liability of manufacturers and

185

distributors of consumer goods (under *Donoghue v. Stevenson*) are void so far as the goods cause *any* damage (not just death or injury).

The Act also places restrictions on exclusion clauses designed to excuse breaches of contract. Where one party deals as a consumer or on the other's written standard terms of business exclusion clauses are valid only if they are deemed reasonable.

A contract term will be reasonable if it 'shall have been a fair and reasonable one to be included having regard to the circumstances which were, or ought reasonably to have been, known to or in the contemplation of the parties when the contract was made'.

The Sale of Goods Act 1893 implies into contracts for the sale of goods the following broad terms:

1. the seller has the right to transfer title;
2. the goods are of merchantable quality;
3. the goods are equal to sample;
4. in sales by description, the goods will comply with the description.

The Supply of Goods (Implied Terms) Act 1973 amended these terms and applied them also to all contracts of hire purchase. This Act also made very important changes in the rules prohibiting and restricting the seller from contracting out of these implied terms.

These rules are now embodied in the Unfair Contract Terms Act. The implied term under S.12(1) cannot be excluded or restricted at all. The other terms mentioned above cannot be excluded in a contract with a consumer, though in non-consumer contracts they can be excluded if this is reasonable. These provisions (unlike those in the rest of the Act) are not confined to 'business liability'.

What the precise effect of the Act in operation will be is, as yet, unclear, but it is obvious that the protection which it affords to the consumer is considerable.

Consumer Credit Act 1974

The object of this Act is to provide a uniform approach to the control of transactions involving the supply of credit not exceeding £5,000 to individuals. It replaces the previous legislation which regulated by different methods hire purchase, credit sales agreements, moneylending, pawnbrokerage, etc., but leaves intact the terms implied into hire purchase agreements by the Supply of Goods (Implied Terms) Act 1973 (as amended).

As might be predicted with such a comprehensive Act the provisions are again complex. The transactions that are covered include bank loans and overdrafts, loans from finance companies, credit cards (e.g. Barclaycard and Access), credit sale agreements, conditional sale agreements, hire purchase agreements and hire agreements.

It would be beyond the scope of this book to investigate each of these in detail, but to see the sort of controls imposed we can take the very common example of a hire purchase agreement, although it is only one of the types of transaction covered by the Act.

186

Hire purchase agreements

From the point of view of the man in the street the hire purchase transaction is a simple one.

X wants a washing machine, but cannot afford to pay outright for it. He goes along to a shop, picks out the one he wants and tells the assistant that he wants to buy it on h.p. The assistant fills out a form, the customer signs it and is told that he will be informed in a few days whether he will be given credit. If he is, the machine will be delivered to him and he will start to pay back the purchase price of the machine, plus interest, by instalments. Eventually, when all the instalments are paid he will know that the washing machine is his.

The underlying legal framework of the transaction is, however, more complicated. In the sort of hire purchase agreement outlined above, there will generally be three parties, the dealer (or supplier), a finance company (or creditor) and the hirer (or debtor).

The dealer does not usually act as the finance company himself but sells the goods to the finance company. This is of course usually a paper transaction with the finance company rarely having sight of the goods.

It is then the finance company who agrees to hire the goods to the debtor in return for his agreement to pay the purchase price, plus interest, over a specified period of time. During the time of the hire, the finance company remains the owner of the goods, but when all the instalments have been paid the hirer can become the owner of the goods, usually by exercising his option to buy the goods on payment of a nominal amount.

The Act protects him in three ways when he enters into the agreement, during the agreement, and on termination.

Entry into a hire purchase agreement

Unless certain formalities are complied with, a creditor or owner will be unable to enforce the agreement.

1. The customer must be informed of the *true* annual cost of the credit.
2. The agreement must be written.
3. It must contain all the terms except implied terms.
4. It must be legible and comply with the regulations as to its form and contents.
5. It must be signed by the customer in person and by, or on behalf of, the creditor or owner.
6. The customer must be given a copy of the agreement.

Certain agreements may be cancelled within a period of days by the customer. Within this category are agreements which have been signed elsewhere than on trade premises. This gives the customer a 'cooling-off period' in cases where he may have been subjected to high-pressure sales techniques.

During the agreement

A debtor under a regulated agreement has the right to complete his payments ahead of time and may then be entitled to a rebate on the amount of interest due.

Where the debtor has a right of action against the supplier (e.g. for misrepresentation or breach of contract) the Act provides that the creditor is jointly and severally liable with the supplier. This gives the debtor a valuable practical advantage where the supplier has gone out of business in that he can sue the creditor.

The debtor has a right at all times to a statement from the creditor of the amount already paid and the amount owing.

Termination of the agreement

Termination of the agreement must be in accordance with the terms of the agreement. The debtor will generally exercise his option to purchase when he has paid all the instalments due. He may, however, wish to terminate the agreement before this. He has a statutory right of termination on giving notice to the creditor. Naturally he must return the goods to the owner and he must in addition pay all instalments already due, plus damages for loss caused by failure to take reasonable care of the goods, and the smaller of three amounts: (i) the amount stipulated in the agreement; (ii) the amount necessary to bring his payments up to half the total hire-purchase price; or (iii) the loss sustained by the creditor.

Frequently it will happen that the debtor runs into difficulties in making the repayments, but is unwilling to hand them back to the creditor. The Act gives him a considerable measure of protection against the creditor's repossession of the goods.

Where the creditor wishes to repossess because of a breach by the debtor, he must serve a default notice giving the debtor the opportunity to remedy the breach. If the debtor does, for example by paying off the arrears, that is the end of the matter. If he cannot or does not, he may apply to the court for a time order by which the court has very wide discretion to allow him extra time to pay off arrears due and vary the pattern of future instalments.

The debtor who has paid at least one-third of the total hire-purchase price has added protection if he subsequently breaches the agreement. The goods are then called 'protected goods' and may only be recovered from the debtor by court action unless the debtor has disposed of the goods to a third party or has abandoned them.

Even at this late stage, when the creditor sues for possession, the court has power to make a time order in favour of the debtor, though it may decide that the goods, or part of them, should be returned to the creditor. The creditor may also be entitled to damages representing his loss. (The goods will after all be secondhand now and may have to be sold at a much lower price.) Agreements generally contain a minimum payment clause stipulating this amount, but the creditor will only be able to recover this sum if it is a genuine pre-estimate of his loss and not in the form of a penalty, an excessive sum demanded in order to force the debtor to comply with the agreement.

Another important point is that the Act gives the court power to reopen an extortionate credit agreement. This is defined as an agreement which requires the debtor to make payments which are 'grossly exorbitant' or which in some other way 'grossly contravenes ordinary principles of fair dealing'.

On reopening the agreement the court has powers to vary the terms of the agreement, set it aside, order repayment of money already paid, or reduce amounts due which are in excess of what is 'fairly due and reasonable'.

This last provision is interesting in that it indicates quite how far the legislature has moved the law from the state it was in when commentators could honestly say that the law would not mend men's bargains.

Summary and conclusions

1.   Firms operate in markets where policies are designed to meet simultaneously the objectives of the firm and the needs of customers.
2.   Since a firm's objectives and consumer needs are not always compatible the relationships between the two have become increasingly affected by the law, and in particular by civil law.
3.   Traditionally many relationships between firm and consumer were contractual with considerable freedom of contract (*caveat emptor*). However, as the consumer society has become more complex there has been a positive shift to protect the consumer (paternalism).
4.   This shift can best be seen by examining:
4.1 Developments by the COURTS, especially in relation to:

   (a) *exclusion (exemption) clauses*: with strict rules that have to be observed before a party can rely on an exemption clause;
   (b) *negligence*: the right of action by a consumer against a manufacturer of dangerous goods even though there is no contractual relationship;
   (a) *inequality of bargaining power*: setting aside contracts because one party is superior (in knowledge, ability, etc.) and takes advantage of the other.

4.2. The changing activities of the LEGISLATURE – especially in the last 10–15 years – in passing Acts that give greater protection to the consumer, e.g. Misrepresentation Act, Consumer Credit Act.
5.   Thus, the law has strengthened the hand of the consumer, but the law will be of little use to him if he is unaware of them or cannot enforce them. It is to this problem of legal rights and their enforcement that we next turn before going on to consider how criminal sanctions and legal safeguards have improved the consumer's position.

Assignments

19.1

Bill goes into Dry-it-Clean Ltd's dry-cleaning shop and hands over a pair of trousers which are badly stained with beer. The assistant tells Bill that to clean the trousers will cost him £1. Bill hands over the trousers and the money. He is then given a ticket on which is printed 'All cleaning is undertaken at the customer's risk.' Bill's trousers are accidentally burned while being pressed, and Bill seeks damages from Dry-it-Clean Ltd. Can the company rely on the clause on the ticket excluding its liability? Would it make any difference if Dry-it-Clean Ltd had displayed in prominent places in its shop signs clearly indicating that dry cleaning was done only at the customer's risk?

19.2

The following are the facts of *Photo Production Ltd v Securicor Transport Ltd*. It was a factory at Gillingham in Kent. A firm called Photo Production Ltd made Christmas cards there, and the like. There was a lot of paper and cardboard about which would burn easily. The factory was shut up for the night, locked and secure. No one was supposed to go in except a man on night patrol. He came from a security firm called Securicor. He had a bunch of keys. His duty was to go through the factory and see that all was safe and secure. No burglars and no fire.

On the night of 18/19 October 1973, the patrolman was George Musgrove. He was a young man, only 23 years old, unmarried. He came of a respectable family and had satisfactory references. He had been with Securicor for some three months. Securicor cannot be blamed for employing him on the job.

At the dead of night, ten minutes before midnight, Musgrove went to the factory. He unlocked the front door and went through the factory, switching on the lights as he went. Then he lit a match and threw it on to a cardboard box. It burst into flames. He says that he only meant it to be a very small fire and intended to put it out within a minute or two. But it got beyond his control. He was terrified and dialled 999 for the fire brigade. He tried to stop it spreading. He lost his glasses and false teeth. His right hand and arm were burnt. He staggered out of the factory through the smoke and flames. By that time the firemen and police were there. They had answered the call with great promptitude. They were at the factory at three minutes past midnight. But they could not save it. There was already a wall of flame across the building. Flames were coming through the roof. The place was gutted. The damage to the building and stock was put at £400,000; the loss of business at £250,000. Musgrove was afterwards charged with arson. He pleaded guilty to malicious damage and was sentenced to three years' imprisonment.

The occupiers of the factory claim damages from Securicor for this loss. The defendants plead two exemption clauses in the contract, to the effect that 'under no circumstances are the defendants to be responsible for any injurious act or default by any employee ... unless such act or default could have been foreseen and avoided by the exercise of due diligence on the part of the (defendants) as his employer; nor in any event (are the defendants to) be held responsible for ... any loss suffered by the (plaintiffs) through ... fire or any other cause, except insofar as such loss (was) solely attributable to the negligence of the (defendants') employees acting within the course of their employment. . . .' A further clause provides that if, notwithstanding the previous exemption clause, any liability arose on the part of the defendants that liability is to be limited to a maximum of £25,000 for the consequences of each incident involving fire or explosion.

You are required to give a short judgement. Give full reasons for your conclusion.

19.3

Sell-a-van Ltd ship twenty Ford vans with Sail-a-ship Ltd at Southampton for delivery in Cape Town. In Cape Town after ten of the vans have been loaded the stevedores who are unloading them from the ship carelessly drop one into the sea. Sell-a-van Ltd want to bring an action against Sail-a-ship Ltd, but the latter has a clause in its contract with Sell-a-van Ltd stating: 'The company accepts no responsibility for any damages to cargo howsoever caused' and argues it is therefore not liable. Sell-a-van Ltd bring an action against the stevedores. There is another clause in the contract between Sail-a-ship Ltd and Sell-a-van Ltd which purports to extend the immunity for liability which Sail-a-ship enjoys to the stevedores also. What must the stevedores show if they are to rely on that clause as a defence to the action by Sell-a-van Ltd?

19.4

Mr James buys Mrs James a portable TV from Buy-a-set Ltd. The set was made by Make-a-set Ltd. When Mrs James is watching her favourite TV programme the set explodes, causing burns on her arms, maiming the family cat, Tiddles, and damaging the wall-paper near the TV. Advise: (a) Mr James; (b) Mrs James; (c) Buy-a-set Ltd; (d) Make-a-set Ltd. Would it make any difference if:

(a) the set were not new but had just been delivered back to Mr James after repairs by Repair-a-set Ltd?
(b) Make-a-set Ltd sold all its TVs in boxes with the warning 'No responsibility is accepted by the manufacturer for loss or injury howsoever caused'?

19.5

Paul is a naive 18-year-old. He signed a contract with Million Airs Ltd, a music publisher, under which he agreed that the copyright in every song that he wrote for the next ten years would belong to the company. He agreed to write songs at the rate of three a month. In return the company agreed to record and distribute any song which it in its absolute discretion chose to, and to pay Paul a percentage of the royalties on records sold. Paul was to receive no other fees. Paul has now written thirty songs for Million Airs Ltd but it has refused to record any. Paul wishes to have the contract set aside as he thinks he was pressurised into it without the benefit of independent advice. In the light of recent cases, advise Paul on his contractual position.

19.6

You write a column in the local newspaper giving advice on consumer problems. One of the newspaper's readers has written to you asking for advice on the legal protection afforded to people entering into hire purchase agreements. Prepare an article of about 600 words for inclusion in next week's edition giving as much information as possible in non-technical language.

19.7

What terms are implied by statute in a contract for the sale of goods? How far is it possible to exclude liability for breach of such a term?

19.8

'A gratifying piece of law reform' (Lord Denning). Discuss this view of the Unfair Contract Terms Act 1977.

20 The organisation and consumers: enforcing legal rights

Introduction

We have looked in some detail at the protection afforded to consumers by provisions of the civil law. Whilst many of the old inadequacies of the Common Law have been improved the fact is that the law is not self-implementing. That is, before consumers are to be able to use their rights they must know what they are and be prepared to press them.

In fact, many consumers never enforce their rights. The private law rights which we have just described may therefore be less effective than one might think.

In this chapter we shall consider the twin problems of consumer ignorance of their rights and their reluctance to pursue them. We can gain a realistic picture of the role of the civil law in protecting consumers only if we are acquainted with the system for enforcing those legal rights.

Consumer ignorance

Many individuals are unaware of the provisions of the law and so will never enforce their legal rights. Most consumer problems involve small sums of money and consumers (rightly or wrongly) do not consider taking legal action worth while. But sometimes consumers do have more serious problems. Some will take advice and might pursue any legal remedy they may have, but it is often difficult for consumers to get advice as to their legal position.

Few solicitors specialise in consumer problems or have experience in this field. A determined consumer will often do better to approach a Citizens' Advice Bureau or a Consumer Advice Centre.

Citizens' Advice Bureaux have, in recent years, improved the level of expertise of their volunteer helpers in consumer matters, while many of them are now stocked with useful guides for the layman (e.g. those produced by the Consumers' Association).

Consumer Advice Centres are now springing up all over the country. Staffed by professionals with access to technical advice and having an appearance of impartiality these Centres give considerable advice as to consumers' rights and method of redress. They also provide other useful services, such as price surveys.

Nevertheless in spite of such bodies and influential pamphlets and magazines (especially *Which?*), consumer ignorance remains a problem. Sometimes the action which consumers ignorantly take may do more harm than good. For example, many people react by refusing to pay sums due under credit arrangements. The consequence of this may be that the business organisation claims back the product rather than seeing that the consumer obtains satisfaction.

There is clearly room for more popular education in consumer matters. People should not only be appraised of their rights but also told how to enforce them.

Let us try to see why there is often a reluctance on the part of consumers to use the system for enforcing their rights.

The enforcement system

The best initial course of action is generally a direct complaint to the retailer and/or manufacturer. Very often a problem will be cleared up by such action.

Organisations may view good public relations as an important business objective and may concede even more than the law requires. Some consumers are daunted by popular impressions of hard-headed business practice which may not in fact conform with the attitude taken by modern organisations. To complain is very often the most sensible initial course of action.

Should no satisfaction be obtained a further letter either from oneself or one's adviser (e.g. a solicitor) threatening legal action is the next step. If this proves unsuccessful a claim will have to be brought in the courts. Many people are deterred from bringing action in the courts because of the idea that such proceedings are daunting and costly in terms of both time and money. To decide whether or not such an attitude is justified we must look at the relevant parts of the legal system.

Courts

The court to which the consumer must bring his problem will depend on the amount of money involved in the claim. If more than £2,000 is claimed an action can be brought only in the High Court. This court sits only in the larger cities and one needs to be represented by a barrister (unless sufficiently confident and able to present the case oneself). Solicitors cannot represent their clients in the High Court but as barristers can be approached to take cases only by solicitors. Thus the consumer must approach a solicitor who will 'brief' a barrister.

The alternative to employing these two lawyers (at risk of substantial cost) is to put your own case in the rather formal atmosphere of the High Court, probably with an experienced barrister arguing against you, since business organisations can usually afford legal representation.

It is more usual, however, that the amount of money at stake is less than £2,000. In this case the action can be brought in the County Court. This court has several obvious advantages for the consumer: there will usually be a County Court in the fairly immediate locality and solicitors have a right of appearance, so that a barrister is not a necessity. The procedure, however, is rather formal and these courts probably frighten away many potential complainants.

For actions in both of these courts the State may possibly provide financial assistance. There is a Legal Aid and Advice Scheme under which assistance with the cost of court proceedings is available for cases of this sort, provided that the applicant's means are within prescribed limits. Only the very badly-off will be provided with full aid, and many consumers will not be eligible even for partial assistance.

There is also a system for State payment of the cost of obtaining basic legal advice but this too is available only after an ungenerous means test.

But even if the finance is available problems remain. For those appearing in person the documents which they will need to understand may appear complicated and the court procedure confusing. Even with representation it can be difficult for a consumer to satisfy the court that his version of what happened is the correct one. Many consumer transactions are informal and what one said or did may be difficult to prove.

In the face of these difficulties there have been some recent attempts to provide easier procedures for consumers to enforce their rights.

Small Claims Courts

In Manchester and Westminster there have, for several years, been special Small Claims Courts. The Manchester scheme covers actions concerned with the sale or hire of products or services. There is a simple form to fill in and a small fee to pay and then a legally qualified secretary tries to mediate in the dispute. If mediation fails then the case is decided by an arbitrator. One cannot be legally represented: this would merely increase the cost. In the London scheme the system is similar though the range of cases heard is wider.

But although these schemes have been acclaimed as successes there are problems. First, there is a limit on the size of the claims which can be dealt with. In Manchester this has recently been raised to £500, though in London it remains for the moment at £250. Second, it is necessary that both sides agree to submit to the scheme: a considerable number of business organisations will not do so. Nevertheless these informal and cheaper alternatives to the County Court are of value in some consumer disputes.

The Registrar

The County Court Registrar is the chief official of that court but he is able to hear some cases himself if the sum involved is less than £200 or (if it is more than £200) if the parties agree that he can. In 1971 a system of pre-trial review of cases before the Registrar was implemented. The Registrar can help the complainant to see the real legal issues and can advise him about possible problems.

In 1973 the Registrar was given the power to refer cases to arbitration instead of to the court. Now either party can apply to the Registrar for the matter to be referred to arbitration and the Registrar will generally act as arbitrator himself (provided the claim is less than £200 or the parties agree). The procedure in the arbitration is comparatively simple, although it has not become quite as informal in some areas as had been hoped. To some extent, as well, people still see these procedures as part of the forbidding County Court system. Nevertheless this new procedure, where legal representation is actively discouraged, is a further advance.

Summary and conclusions

1. Although recent actions in the courts and through legislation have strengthened the position of the consumer, the *law is not self-implementing*. Thus private law rights are less effective than one might think.
2. There are two main problems: ignorance; enforcement.
2.1. Consumer ignorance: this is related to and affected by:

   (a) an unawareness of many provisions;
   (b) hasty actions by the consumer that often worsen the situation;
   (c) advice centres that are being set up to help consumers.

2.2 Enforcement: which is affected by:

   (a) The method of taking action, which usually follows three stages:

      (i) initial action to the retailer;
      (ii) threat of legal action;
      (iii) legal action in the courts;

      however, few go through all three stages because of shortage of time, money, expertise.

   (b) Problems encountered in taking action. Many are confused by:

      (i) which court;
      (ii) what representation is necessary;
      (iii) where there is no representation, problems of procedure and documentation;
      (iv) how costly will it be (legal aid?).

   (c) New procedures: to help ease the burden on the consumer, e.g.

      (i) Small Claims Court;
      (ii) Registrar.

3. Thus the consumer is becoming more aware of his rights and is gradually obtaining access to a system of enforcement which he is able and can afford to use. However, problems still remain and for that reason protection under civil law is now buttressed or supported by criminal law and administrative safeguards. It is to these we now turn.

Assignments

20.1

Albert has just brought a fire from Sell-a-Fire Ltd, which sells re-conditioned electric fires. He takes it home and when he plugs it in it explodes and refuses to work. The fire cost £85 and Sell-a-Fire Ltd tells him that the necessary repairs will cost at least £25. Another firm, Repair-a-Fire, tells Albert that the fault is due to poor workmanship by Sell-a-Fire. Sell-a-Fire refuse to accept that this is so. It insists that if the repairs are done it is Albert, and not the company, who must foot the bill. Advise Albert as to the steps he ought to take to process a claim against Sell-a-Fire Ltd.

20.2

Draw up a concise table (suitable for use in a Citizens' Advice Bureau) showing each of the steps which must be taken by someone who has decided that he is going to insist on enforcing his rights under the Sale of Goods Act against a shopkeeper, from the time he makes the first complaint until a judge awards him damages in the County Court.

20.3

Write short notes on (1) the High Court; (2) the County Court; (3) the Registrar; (4) Small Claims Courts.

20.4

Design a concise information sheet to be distributed in Consumer Advice Centres to those who have received defective products from mail order firms.

20.5

Design a questionnaire to determine the public's knowledge of consumer protection. Select a smaple of the public and ask them the questions. Tabulate your results for publication in a glossy magazine.

21 The organisation and consumers: the criminal law

Introduction

In the previous two chapters we discussed the provisions of the civil law which afford protection to consumers and the ways in which such rights can be enforced. Parliament has also decided that the relationship between organisations and consumers should be regulated by the criminal law. To some extent this is due to the inadequacies of the civil law and the enforcement system, but there is also a belief that the actions of business organisations can constitute wrongs not merely to the customer but to society at large. The honest trader as well as the innocent consumer has an interest in the prevention of dishonest and unfair trade practices and the manufacturer of dangerous or defective goods.

Criminal sanctions are not imposed to benefit the victim but to penalise the offender, though with the introduction of compensation orders as criminal penalties the courts can now ensure the victim of the offence can secure compensation.

There are a large number of statutes specifying criminal liability for actions or omissions by business organisations.

Consumer Safety Act 1978

The Consumer Safety Act provides for the making of safety regulations with penalties for breach of those regulations. The idea is clearly to prevent the manufacture of dangerous goods, and some of the regulations set high standards of safety. An example is the Nightdresses (Safety) Regulations. These provide as follows:

'(2) 1. A child's night-dress should comply with the requirements specified in the Schedule to these regulations.
  2. A night-dress (not being a child's night-dress or an infant's gown) shall either comply with the requirements specified in the Schedule to these regulations or have stitched to and clearly displayed inside it a durable label bearing the following words set out in legible and durable characters:
  "Warning – Keep Away From Fire".
  . . . . . .

197

Schedule

1. The night-dress shall not be made of, or trimmed below the waist or elbow with, any fabric of a kind not capable of satisfying the performance requirements specified in the British Standard Specifications "Performance Requirements of Fabrics described as of low flammability . . ."'

Food and Drugs Act 1955

The Food and Drugs legislation specifies a number of offences designed to achieve high standards of care in the supply of food and drugs. It is an offence to sell for human consumption adulterated food (that is food to which something has been added, or from which something has been taken away so that it becomes injurious to health). Again, it is an offence to sell 'any food which is not of the nature, or not of the substance, or not of the quality, of the food demanded by the purchaser'.

The legislation assumes that the best way to achieve high standards in the supply of food is to impose criminal sanctions on those who fall from the set standards. Prosecutions are normally brought by officials of local authorities so that court action is more likely than if consumers had to sue in the Civil Courts.

The standards set are high. In *Smedley's Ltd v. Breed* a consumer had bought a tin of peas which contained a small, dead caterpillar which was harmless. It was conceded that the caterpillar had only ended up in the tin because it was hard to distinguish it from the peas and that the manufacturer's system of production was of a high standard. Nevertheless it was convicted of the offence of supplying food 'not of the standard demanded by the purchaser'. Another example is *David Greig Ltd v. Goldfinch*. Here a consumer bought a pie which turned out to have a small amount of totally harmless mould. It having been found that a very small amount of this could have been present at the time of the sale, the shop was found guilty of selling food unfit for human consumption: it was no defence that the food was not dangerous to health.

Weights and Measures Act 1963

The Weights and Measures Act contains a number of offences concerned with selling goods in short or unauthorised weights or measures. Like the food laws it is enforced by local officials (nowadays known as Trading Standards Officers).

One example of the sort of standards which this legislation imposes will be of interest to those who are patrons of public houses. Gin, rum, vodka and whisky, when sold for consumption on licensed premises, are to be sold in, or in multiples of, $\frac{1}{4}$, $\frac{1}{5}$ or $\frac{1}{6}$ of a gill and there must be a notice publicly displayed, indicating in which of these quantities the liquors are offered.

The interpretation of one section of the Act has proved to mean that Guinness drinkers are less well protected: in *Marshall v. Searles* it was held that a publican is not guilty of the offence of delivering goods of short weight when he

198

serves a pint of draught Guinness, the liquid portion of which is less than a pint: apparently a consumer should anticipate that part of the pint will consist of the head!

Trade Descriptions Act 1968

The Trade Descriptions Act is probably the best known example of the use of the criminal law in the regulation of the relationship between business organisations and consumers. The provisions apply also to transactions between two commercial organisations.

Section 1 (1) of the Act states:

'Any person who, in the course of a trade or business –
(a) applies a false trade description to any goods; or
(b) supplies or offers to supply any goods to which a false trade description is applied shall . . . be guilty of an offence.'

Descriptions do not have to be written; oral statements will do. Very often, however, descriptions will consist of written statements fixed on or near goods or placed in such a position that they are likely to be taken to be referring to the goods.

S. 2 of the Act defines a 'trade description' as an 'indication, direct or indirect, and by whatever means given' of any of the large number of things which the section goes on to specify, e.g. quality, size, composition, fitness, approval, characteristics, place of manufacture, date of manufacture. Clearly the Act seeks to make criminal descriptions which are simply false: it also, however, seeks to cover those which are misleading.

A large number of the prosecutions under the Act have involved second-hand car dealers. In *Robertson v. Dicicco* a car dealer who described an unroadworthy car as 'beautiful' was held to have applied a false trade description. But the range of cases has been wide and in spite of some difficult cases most prosecutions have been of clear and obvious breaches. The following are examples of typical successful prosecutions dealt with by magistrates' courts:

(a) a garden shopkeeper was selling turf as 'fine quality lawn turf'. In fact most of the grass was coarse weed;
(b) a market trader was selling toys marked as 'Tri-ang'. They had, in fact, been made in Hong Kong;
(c) a butcher sold Australian lamb as being from New Zealand.

The Act contains other provisions relating to misleading advertisements or misleading statements as to the price of goods. An example is the labelling of goods as being at a recommended or sale price when they are not. Such goods *must* have been so offered within the last six months and for a continuous period of at least twenty-eight days unless there is an express notice to the contrary.

The Act also covers the supply of services, facilities and accommodation but is here less strict. For instance a defendant will generally be convicted whether or not he knew, or ought to have known, that the description of goods was false or misleading. With the supply of services however conviction depends on the defendant knowing the description was false or not caring whether it was true or false.

Enforcement of the Act's provisions is generally in the hands of Trading Standards Officers. Offences under the Act are punishable with fines up to an unspecified limit and/or imprisonment for up to two years. Recently the courts have also imposed compensation orders.

Consumer Credit Act 1974

We have already noted the effect of the provisions of the Consumer Credit Act on civil law rights. The Act also introduces a number of criminal offences to strengthen the position of consumers, as follows:

1. Those who supply credit under its provisions must obtain a licence from the Director General of Fair Trading. Certain criminal offences established by the Act ensure that the licensing provisions are adhered to.

2. The Act seeks to prevent unfair or misleading advertisements and modes of credit-selling. There are criminal sanctions to penalise those who break the rules (e.g. by sending circulars offering credit to children).

3. The Act controls pawnbrokers: it is, for example, an offence for them to take pledges from children.

4. Consumers are to be provided with certain written statements (for example, of their accounts) on demand. Failure to supply such statements is a criminal offence.

5. If a credit reference agency (a body which supplies credit sellers with information about the credit worthiness of consumers) refuses to disclose to a consumer any information it possesses about him or fails to make alteration in its information in the light of representations made by him it commits an offence. It is also an offence for a credit-supplier to refuse to reveal the name of any credit reference agency it uses.

Summary and conclusions

1. Parliament has decided that the relationships between organisation and consumer should be protected not only by civil but also by criminal law.
2. This line of action has been taken because of:

   (a) the inadequacies of civil law and the enforcement system;
   (b) the belief that actions by business organisations constitute wrongs against the State as well as against the consumer.

3. There are a number of statutes specifying criminal liability and among those discussed were:

   (a) Consumer Safety Act 1978;
   (b) Food and Drugs Act 1955;
   (c) Weights and Measures Act 1963;
   (d) Trade Descriptions Act 1968;
   (e) Consumer Credit Act 1974.

4. The enforcement of criminal provisions is usually more effective than civil law because:

    (*a*) the work is carried out by paid officials;
    (*b*) individual consumers do not have to spend their own time and money;
    (*c*) the offences are often easier to prove (e.g. because liability is strict.).

    However, even the criminal law is not a perfect tool although it has helped improve the lot of the consumer and encouraged higher standards amongst business organisations.

Assignments

21.1

Write a brief explanation of the distinction between criminal and civil liability, giving examples of each as they affect organisations in their dealings with customers and clients. (You will need to refer back to Chapter 2.)

21.2

Why do you think that business organisations often go to great expense in obtaining legal representation to defend themselves against prosecution for criminal offences even though the likely penalty is small? Try to identify the objective of a business organisation with which a conviction for a criminal offence might conflict.

21.3

You are a local Trading Standards Officer. Mrs Mop comes to your office in the Town Hall and reports to you:

1. that her local butcher had sold her, as high quality beef, meat which she suspects is low quality pork;
2. that her local grocer had given only 5 lbs of potatoes when she had asked and paid for 10 lbs;
3. that some cheese which she had bought from her local supermarket was green with mould when she removed it from her shopping basket at home.

    What action would you advise Mrs Mop to take and what action would you take yourself?

21.4

Try to draw up Safety Regulations to make illegal the manufacture and sale in a dangerous form of the following goods: (1) teddy-bears; (2) electric toasters; (3) car tyres.

Identify what might make this item dangerous to users and try to ensure that your regulations cover the potential hazards. What penalties would you impose? Support your decisions with reasons.

22 The organisation and consumers: administrative and other safeguards

Introduction

The legislature has sought to supplement the protection afforded by the courts by regulatory controls over the suppliers. These include requiring organisations to be licensed, by encouraging them to adopt high business standards and by the control of some trade practices.

Licensing

As an alternative to the prospect of civil proceedings or criminal prosecutions for non-compliance with set standards, Parliament has sometimes presented organisations with the choice of compliance with set standards or closure. Should certain regulations not be complied with then the organisation's licence to operate will not be granted (or, if already granted can be withdrawn). The price of non-compliance is therefore not being allowed to carry on business at all.

There are many examples of control by licensing. Everyone is familiar with signs over the doors of public houses stating 'Licensed to sell intoxicating liquors'. Other businesses required to licence include chemists, employment agencies, taxi-operators and market traders.

We shall look, by way of example, at the comprehensive licensing controls introduced by the Consumer Credit Act 1974.

The Act introduced a wide ranging licensing system operated by the Director-General of Fair Trading. Except for local authorities and a few other specified bodies, any organisation which provides credit to individuals in sums up to £5,000 must obtain a licence. This means that eventually some 100,000 organisations will have to be licensed, including those which make cash loans or grant overdrafts, those who hire out goods, collect debts or supply hire purchase facilities.

Since consumers are often in a weak position when they need to enter into agreement with these types of organisation it is felt that practices which enable these bodies to take advantage of consumers should be strictly controlled. When such organisations wish to commence operations they must now apply to the Office of Fair Trading for a licence. The Office will take into account factors like whether the applicant has ever been involved in dishonest business practices, practised discrimination, etc. Organisations are allowed to state the case in favour of their being granted a licence and, should they be unsuccessful, reasons are given.

Various sorts of licences may be granted so that an organisation can be restricted to certain types of activity. The Office of Fair Trading may, for example, decide that an organisation should be allowed to carry on the business of supplying credit in trade premises (e.g. a bank), but not to sell credit on people's front doorsteps.

Licences generally last for three years, after which time the licensed organisation has to make a further application. On breach of any of the terms of a licence the Office of Fair Trading may vary, suspend or revoke a licence though the organisation may appeal to the Minister for Prices and Consumer Protection.

The Director-General of Fair Trading

The Director-General of Fair Trading, as head of the Office of Fair Trading, occupies a central position in the protection afforded to consumers by the licensing regulations of the Consumer Credit Act. In fact the Director-General plays an important role in regard to the whole system of administrative controls on producers and suppliers.

The post of Director-General was established under the Fair Trading Act 1973. His duties are, broadly, to keep under scrutiny all commercial activities relating to the supply to consumers of goods and services. If practices are being carried on which might adversely affect the interest of consumers, he is empowered to refer such practices to the Consumer Protection Advisory Committee. The result of such a reference may be that the Prices and Consumer Protection Minister employs the power which he has under the Act to prohibit or regulate the practice. If an activity is prohibited it is a criminal offence to continue it.

In 1975 the Director-General referred the practice of selling goods without making it clear that the sale is in the course of business. This was largely due to the practice of many second-hand motor traders masquerading as private sellers. In 1977 the Minister acted to prevent this practice by making the Business Advertisements (Disclosure) Order.

The Director-General also has powers to take action himself. He can write to those who are carrying on business in a way detrimental to consumers and ask for a written assurance that the conduct will cease. Should he fail to receive a satisfactory undertaking he can take court action to secure one.

The Director-General will often, however, simply ask for co-operation from business organisations. Self-regulation has become a very important source of protection for consumers and the Director-General now has a central role to play in encouraging organisations to set their own (high) standards of business conduct.

Some businessmen, for instance, have voluntarily provided more information for consumers than it is legally necessary to do. Businesses have also launched codes of practice and the Director-General has a duty to encourage the production of such codes.

One example of such a code is that which the Electricity Boards have agreed for the servicing of domestic electrical appliances: servicing is to be done within three working days at a reasonable cost; estimates are to be given; repairs are to be guaranteed, etc. Another example is the Association of British Travel Agents Code which ensures clear and comprehensive brochures, the absence of exclusion clauses in contracts for holidays, the provision of refunds if the operators overbook, etc. Advertising standards are largely controlled by this voluntary method.

Monopolies, mergers and restrictive practices

We have mentioned at a number of points the existence of a body of law regulating monopolies, mergers and restrictive trade practices. The Director-General of Fair Trading now plays an important role in this area of law since it is for the protection of the interests of consumers that it is primarily designed.

Monopolies

As we have already noted, if at least 25 per cent of the supply of products or services specified is provided by one organisation, or if there are agreements in existence which prevent the supply of goods and services of a particular kind, then this situation can be referred to the Monopolies and Mergers Commission. Both the Minister and the Director-General have the power to make reference to the Commission.

The Commission must be asked to ascertain whether a monopoly exists and is almost invariably also asked to consider whether the existence of the monopoly may be expected to operate against the public interest. The Commission has in practice disapproved of various tactics (e.g. the making of difficulties for new organisations who wish to move into the market) and it has also sometimes made reference to high prices or excessive profits as being contrary to the public interest. In general, however, the Commission has not felt that dominance by one firm in itself necessarily operates against the public interest; indeed in some industries it is only by one firm having such a dominant position that efficiency can be attained.

Reports of the Commission are laid before Parliament. The Minister will usually seek a voluntary undertaking from the relevant firm, but he possesses wide powers to make orders to prevent or remedy the adverse effects of the monopoly indicated in the Commission's report. The Minister can, for instance, regulate a firm's prices or order a dominant firm not to amalgamate with another.

Mergers

Companies often 'merge' or join together. The simplest way in which this happens is if A Ltd buys all the shares in B Ltd. There are many other ways in which this is done, for instance, a holding company (H Ltd) might be set up and shareholders in A Ltd and B Ltd asked to transfer their shares to it in exchange for shares in H Ltd. Most mergers have little effect on competition and there are often sound commercial reasons for them. Often a merger is in the public interest; it may enable economies of scale. But sometimes mergers are a step towards a monopoly.

Under the Monopolies and Mergers Act 1965 the Minister may refer mergers to the Monopolies and Mergers Commission where (*a*) it is or may be the case that two or more enterprises have 'ceased to be distinct'; and (*b*) either the value of the assets taken over exceeds £5 m. or a monopoly relating to the supply of goods or services is created or intensified.

The Commission investigates and makes a report. It is concerned with the effects of the merger on efficiency and competition. If the Commission concludes that it is against the public interest the Minister can exercise any of the same wide-ranging powers he has over monopolies: often he will prohibit a proposed merger.

Restrictive trade practices

Business organisations sometimes enter into agreements and engage in other practices which restrict competition. This may sometimes be against the public interest. Legislative action was taken against restrictive trade practices in 1956 and most of the law on the subject is now contained in the Restrictive Trade Practices Act 1976 (as amended slightly by the Restrictive Trade Practices Act 1977). This legislation makes many restrictive trade practices subject to registration and judicial investigation.

Agreements which are covered are:

1. Restrictive agreements as to goods, i.e. any agreement or arrangement in the UK by which restrictions are accepted by two or more parties as to the prices charged or recommended for goods, the conditions of supply or processing, the quantities or description, the processes of manufacture or the persons or places to or from whom goods are to be supplied.

2. Restrictive agreements as to services, i.e. agreements or arrangements in the supply of services (except certain professional services like accounting) whereby restrictions are accepted as to charges, conditions of supply, availability or persons to whom the service is available.

3. Information agreements. The Minister can require registration of agreements providing for the furnishing of information (like the prices or charges for goods or services, or the conditions on which they are provided).

Certain agreements are exempted if, for example, their object is to improve efficiency or productive capacity in an industry.

Such agreements must be registered with the Director-General of Fair Trading before they take effect or within three months of being made or else they are void. It is unlawful for anyone to give effect to a void agreement. Registered agreements must generally be referred to the Restrictive Practices Court which decides whether or not the provisions of the agreement are contrary to the public interest.

A restriction on information provision is presumed to be contrary to the public interest unless it is shown to be beneficial in one of the ways specified in the 1976 Act (e.g. that the provision is reasonably necessary to protect the public against injury).

In the control of restrictive practices, provisions of EEC law, which are binding on the UK as a member of the European Economic Community, are of great importance. The most important provision is Article 85 of the EEC Treaty. This covers agreements and other practices which may affect trade between Member States of the EEC and which have as their object or effect the prevention, restriction or distortion of competition within the EEC.

We must finally note the Resale Prices Act 1976, which provides that, in general, condition of sale to a dealer which provides a minimum resale price is void. It is forbidden to try to circumvent this provision by refusing to supply dealers who undercut stipulated prices. The Restrictive Practices Court may exempt certain sorts of goods from these provisions and has done so in regard to books and medicines.

Summary and conclusions

1. In addition to civil and criminal law, the legislature has introduced *regulatory* controls over firms in three main ways:

   (*a*) by requiring them to be licensed;
   (*b*) by voluntarily encouraging high business standards;
   (*c*) by controlling certain trade practices.

2. Licensing: the issue of a licence to carry on a trade in compliance with set standards or be closed.

2.1 Of particular importance are the licensing controls introduced by the Consumer Credit Act 1974 as operated by the Director General of Fair Trading.

2.2 The Office of Director General is important because he:

   (*a*) keeps the licensing system under broad scrutiny;
   (*b*) has powers of reference (to the Consumer Protections Advisory Committee and the Minister) if he is not satisfied with existing practices;
   (*c*) can take action himself by writing direct to apparent offenders;
   (*d*) can refer cases to the Monopolies Commission and the Restrictive Practices Court.

3. Voluntary encouragement: greater emphasis is now being placed on organisations voluntarily setting their own standards of business conduct either through trade associations or bodies like the CBI (e.g. Electricity Boards' code, Association of British Travel Agents code, etc).

4. Trade practices: it has been the practice for some time to regulate and control monopolies, restrictive trade agreements and mergers by law. The main Acts to be considered are:

   (*a*) Fair Trading Act 1973;
   (*b*) Restrictive Trade Practices Acts 1976 and 1977;
   (*c*) Resale Prices Act 1976;
   (*d*) EEC Treaty (Article 85).

In recent years the combination of terms of the Fair Trading Act and the two above Acts of 1976 have done a great deal to influence the wide range of agreements that restrict competition (including agreements on goods, services and information).

5. Thus, the last four chapters have clearly indicated the complex body of law regulating business practices. These detailed Acts of Parliament with their complex civil, criminal and administrative enforcement procedures indicate how far we have moved from the attitude expressed in the phrase *caveat emptor*. The regulation of business behaviour not thought to be in the public interest now constitutes the most sophisticated form of consumer protection.

Assignments

22.1

List at least three sorts of trading organisations which the law requires to be licensed. In each case explain why you think this requirement is imposed.

22.2

Write an essay on the major functions of the Director-General of Fair Trading in the protection of consumers.

22.3

You are the President of the Association of Cuckoo Clock Makers and Repairers. The Director-General of Fair Trading has asked you to draw up a Code of Practice regulating the service and repair of cuckoo clocks. Try to draw up a short document specifying those undertakings you feel your members would be willing voluntarily to undertake.

22.4

Look back to assignment 19.1. Try to find out from your local Trading Standards Office or the Office of Fair Trading whether there is any Code of Practice which might help to decide upon what action Bill could expect from a dry-cleaner's in this situation. If you find a relevant Code of Practice write a short summary of its major provisions which you think would be useful to consumers.

22.5

Write short notes on: (1) monopolies legislation; (2) mergers legislation; (3) The Restrictive Trade Practices legislation; (4) Article 85 of the EEC Treaty. (You should consider the possible consequences of the legislation for (*a*) consumers, (*b*) organisations.)

22.6

The following is a list of the major methods used by statutes to protect the consumer:

1. By penalising false or misleading statements.

2. By reinforcing civil remedies for untrue statements.
3. By requiring that information be made available to consumers.
4. By regulating the content of agreements.
5. By modifying/restricting the ability to exclude remedies.
6. By prescribing standards of quality.
7. By facilitating remedies.
8. By restricting or prohibiting certain forms of commercial activity.
9. By licensing trade.
10. By regulating market forces.

The following is a list of some of the most important statutes in this area:

Food and Drugs Act
Misrepresentation Act
Sale of Goods Act
Trade Descriptions Act
Fair Trading Act
Consumer Credit Act
Consumer Safety Act
Legal Aid legislation
Monopolies and Mergers legislation
Weights and Measures Act
Unfair Contract Terms Act.

Draw a diagram to show which method(s) of protection (if any) each of these statutes employs.

23 The allocation of resources

Introduction

In earlier chapters we discussed the importance to organisations of demand. We demonstrated that certain decisions, and especially those relating to price and output, are heavily influenced by changes in demand. In this chapter we show how changes in demand lead to the reallocation of resources. This reallocation occurs within a context of scarcity, and so we begin by considering the meaning and implications of scarcity.

Scarcity

When the man in the street uses the term 'scarcity' he usually applies it to products which are difficult to obtain. However, in economics the term has a more specialised meaning. Scarcity is said to exist whenever a price is paid for a resource or a product.

When products are supplied by producers in the private sector, the price is normally paid by the consumers of the products. On the other hand many of the products supplied by agencies of the State, e.g. educational services, are provided at a zero price to the consumer; in these instances the 'price' is paid by the Government (and ultimately by taxpayers and ratepayers). Finally, there are a number of products which fall in between, where the price paid by the consumer is positive but less than the full cost of supplying the product, the difference being made up by government subsidies of one form or another (again provided ultimately by the taxpayer or ratepayer). Examples include medicinal products supplied on prescription under the National Health Service, where the cost of the prescription is frequently much less than the full cost of the product; and council houses, which are provided at subsidised rents to tenants with low incomes.

The true, non-subsidised, price of a product reflects the cost of the resources utilised in its production, and the only free products are those for which all the required resources are available at no cost. A moment's reflection will show that the number of free products is very small indeed (or, putting the matter the other way round, scarcity is widespread). Even in simple activities undertaken for charitable purposes some cost is likely to be incurred, e.g. where a

210

volunteer uses her car to transport to a charity shop items of clothing no longer required by affluent families. The fact that the volunteer does not charge for her time or the use of her car indicates that she is providing a subsidy. We return to the question of free products below, but now we consider the scarcity of resources.

Scarcity of resources

It is clear that in general labour is not a free resource, since people need to earn money in order to buy the necessities of life. If a person is willing to supply his or her labour without charge for a particular purpose, e.g. the charitable worker mentioned above, this is because the income obtained from other sources is sufficient to meet his or her needs. Capital also is not a free resource, if only because labour is involved in the production of capital assets such as factories and machines.

The third type of resource – land – differs from labour and capital in that it exists as a 'free gift of nature' (although it is often modified by the application of both labour and capital). We can find instances of land being available free. For example, a man may obtain great pleasure from walking in the countryside, breathing fresh air and, if thirsty, drinking from a mountain stream. All of these resources are classified as land and all are available free. On the other hand there are, of course, many instances in which land is not free. For example, in areas where land is needed for building houses, the cost of the land may be almost as great as the construction costs.

A comparison of these two situations, land required for recreation and for building, might suggest that what determines whether or not land is free is the amount of land available in relation to the demand. The relationship between demand and supply certainly has an important influence on price, as we have demonstrated in previous chapters. However, there is an even more fundamental factor which determines whether or not a resource is free in a particular situation; that is whether property or ownership rights in the resource have been established. To understand the significance of this factor let us examine these two situations further.

The significance of property rights

If the owner of the stream decided to establish his ownership, e.g. by fencing off the stream, he would then be able to charge thirsty walkers for a drink. How many people would actually buy is an open question; it would depend upon such factors as the temperature and the distance to the nearest free stream. But the essential point is that access to the stream would no longer be free. Similarly, walkers may sometimes have to pay to gain access to particularly attractive parts of the countryside provided, again, that property rights can be established.

Conversely, if no property rights could be established in land required for building, the land could be acquired free, on a 'first come first served' basis. This is exactly the situation that at times has applied when forests have been felled, rivers and seas have been fished, and land has been grazed by the animals of nomads. (Where no private property rights have been established, the State frequently steps in to establish such rights on behalf of the community as a whole.

211

The use of the resource is then controlled, either by charging a price or by some form of regulation. For example, the State now controls the use of rivers as a receptacle for pollutants.)

Scarcity: summary

We can summarise the above discussion by saying that resources are available free only where no property or ownership rights (private or communal) have been established – unless, of course, the owners choose not to exercise those rights. Since more than one type of resource is normally utilised in the supply of any product, it follows that very few free products exist. Indeed the best examples of free 'products' are the free gifts of nature which, without human intervention, are available for consumption – the pleasant views, the fresh air and the water from the mountain stream enjoyed by our walker.

Scarcity and prices

Whenever scarcity exists resources, and hence products, can be acquired only at a price in excess of zero. The prices that have to be paid constitute a very important source of information to the purchasers of resources and products, information that influences the decisions made by organisations as to what, how, where, when and for whom to produce. In practice decisions on all of these questions are often taken together, but in order to simplify the analysis we consider them one by one, beginning with the decision *what to produce*.

We showed in Chapter 5 that survival, profitability and growth are major objectives of organisations and, in Chapter 7, that in order to achieve these objectives, organisations adopt policies designed to increase their revenue. We have also shown that, if these policies are to be effective, the organisation should be able to estimate the quantity of a product that could be sold at various prices. Let us now consider how this information concerning the relationship between price and quantity demanded can influence the allocation of resources.

Changes in demand and the reallocation of resources

The data in Table 23.1 shows the demand schedules for tables and chairs in each of two years. For the sake of simplicity we have assumed that in year 1 the demand schedules are identical. These schedules are represented in Fig. 23.1 by the demand curve D_{T_1,C_1}. We assume that in a year producers are willing to supply from between 15,000 to 21,000 tables, and the same number of chairs, at a price of £11; this is indicated by the supply curve $S_{T,C}$. In year 1 the equilibrium position, at which the offers of suppliers and purchasers coincide, is X, denoting that 19,000 tables and 19,000 chairs are sold at £11 each.

In year 2 the supply conditions are unchanged, but a change occurs in demand conditions. As shown in Table 23.1 and Fig. 23.1, the demand for tables increases while the demand for chairs falls. The price being maintained at £11, the number of tables sold increases to 20,000 while the number of chairs sold falls to

Table 23.1 Hypothetical demand schedules

Price (£)	Year 1 Demand for		Year 2 Demand for	
	Tables (000)	Chairs (000)	Tables (000)	Chairs (000)
10	20	20	21	19
11	19	19	20	18
12	18	18	19	17
13	17	17	18	16
14	16	16	17	15

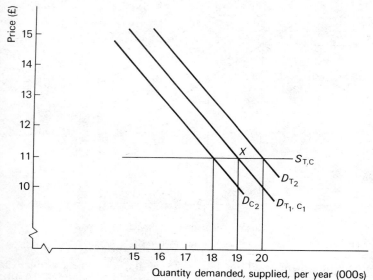

Fig. 23.1 Changes in demand and the reallocation of resources

18,000. In order to effect this change there would have to be a reallocation of resources from chair to table manufacturing. This reallocation might be made by laying off some workers and recruiting new ones or, if the skills involved in table and chair making are similar, by switching workers from one type of work to another (reallocation of other types of inputs would also be required).

As we pointed out in Chapter 18, although in many instances suppliers react to changes in demand by changing output only, they sometimes react by changing both output and price. This second response is illustrated in Fig. 23.2 in which the supply curve shows that the higher the price the more tables and chairs the producers are willing to supply. (A supply curve of this shape indicates that average cost and/or the profit margin increases as output increases. Average cost may increase because, for example, the workers employed first are more efficient than those employed subsequently; this is discussed in more detail in Chapter 24.)

In these circumstances an increase in the demand for tables from D_{T_1} to D_{T_2} results in an increase in both the price (P_2) and the sales (Q_2) of tables. Conversely a fall in the demand for chairs from D_{C_1} to D_{C_2} results in a fall in both their price (P_3) and sales (Q_3).

213

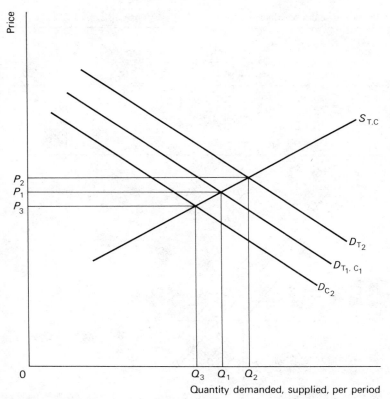

Fig. 23.2 Resource allocation with an upward sloping supply curve

A third possibility, mentioned in Chapter 18, is that, due to economies of scale, average cost falls as output increases. If the change in cost is fully or partly reflected in price, the supply curve will fall from left to right as shown in Fig. 23.3. An increase in the demand for tables now results in a fall in price (P_2) and an increase in sales (Q_2), while a fall in the demand for chairs results in an increase in price (P_3) and a fall in sales (Q_3).

In all three instances, then, a change in the demand for a product leads to a reallocation of resources, although the extent of this reallocation will depend upon the shape of the supply curve (and, of course, the extent of the change in demand). The only situation where resource reallocation does not occur is where a given quantity of the product is offered for sale regardless of the price. This situation was explored in Chapter 18 (see Fig. 18.4). We showed there that supply was most likely to be absolutely inelastic in the short term in markets for agricultural products. But even here we would expect the resources devoted to the production of a particular crop to change eventually in response to a change in demand.

A shift of the supply curve

In the above section we simplified the analysis by assuming that workers (and

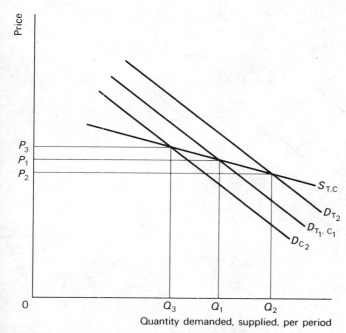

Fig. 23.3 Resource allocation with a downward sloping supply curve

other inputs) could be switched from the manufacture of one product to another without any change in the wage rates (and the prices of other inputs). This is a reasonable assumption in some situations, e.g. when, as here, the reallocation of resources occurs within a given firm. In other situations, however, an increase in output in one market may cause an increase in the input prices paid by suppliers *in that and other markets*.

This is illustrated in Fig. 23.4, where the demand and supply curves relate to the markets for new offices and houses. With demand for offices in year 1 D_{O1} and supply S_O, Q_{O1} is sold at price P_{O1}. An increase in demand in year 2 to D_{O2} results in an increase in both sales (Q_{O2}) and price (P_{O2}). The higher price reflects the fact that the supply curve slopes up, and this is partly due to the fact that the contractors who build offices have to pay higher prices in order to increase the supply of inputs, such as labour and raw materials.

These inputs are also used by housebuilders. Consequently they find that their costs have risen. It now costs more to produce any given number of houses, i.e. the supply curve shifts upwards from S_{H1} to S_{H2}. With the demand for houses D_H the change in the supply conditions leads to an increase in the price of houses (P_{H2}) and a fall in sales (Q_{H2}). We see, then, that a change in price in one market can lead to a change in the resources employed in another market even though demand conditions in this second market have not changed.

Supply conditions can change for other reasons. For example, an increase in labour productivity would cause average cost to fall and the supply curve to shift downwards and to the right. Conversely a fall in productivity would cause the curve to shift upwards and to the left. Changes in cost and supply conditions are considered again in the following chapter.

215

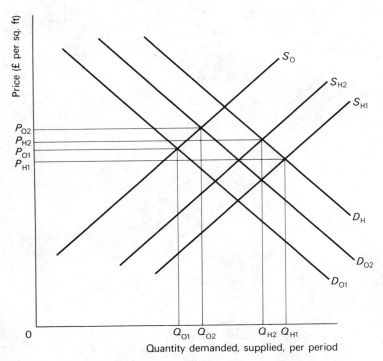

Fig. 23.4 Resource allocation with changes in demand and supply

Additional aspects of resource allocation

The analysis presented so far in this chapter has related to the question: 'What should be produced?'. We have shown that changes in the allocation of resources take place in response to changes in the demand and supply conditions. Demand and supply analysis can also be applied to the other production decisions listed earlier in the chapter.

The decision *how to produce* any product will depend partly upon technological conditions – for example, the quantity of the product that can be produced in a given period by a certain machine or a certain number of workers – and partly upon the cost per unit of the various resources or inputs. If changes in demand or supply cause the relative costs of different inputs to change, a change in the least-cost method of production is likely to follow.

In some instances the change in relative cost may occur as between broad categories of resources, such as labour and capital. For example, in the printing industry the tight control exercised by the unions over the supply of labour, together with technological developments in machinery, have caused the cost of labour, per unit of output, to increase relative to that of capital. This has resulted in the installation of labour-saving machinery.

In other instances changes in costs have occurred within a resource category. For example, the 1950s and 1960s saw a substantial fall in the price of oil relative to some other fuels such as coal. This led to a substitution of oil for coal in energy generation and especially in electricity power stations. This process was halted and to some extent reversed when the oil producers imposed substantial price increases.

In the same way, changes in demand and supply may lead to changes in the relative costs of alternative locations and so influence the decision *where to produce*. For example, in many city centres an increased demand for land for office-building has led to increases in retailers' site costs. Some retailers have responded by building new shops in off-centre or suburban locations where site costs are lower.

Decisions as to *when to produce* may also be influenced by changes in resource costs. To take an obvious example, labour is usually more expensive to employ at night or weekends than during weekdays. Some agricultural inputs vary in price from one part of the year to another (although if the product cannot be stored the decision when to produce may be influenced by the availability rather than the price of the input).

The decision when to produce may also be influenced more directly by demand conditions. For example, most entertainment is available in the evenings and on Saturdays because demand is greatest at these times. On the other hand much more electricity is demanded, and therefore generated, during the day than the evenings.

Finally, the question *for whom to produce* is closely linked with each of the other questions discussed above, in the sense that when producers supply goods they do so in response to the demands of particular groups of consumers. The major factors which influence this pattern of demand were considered earlier, in Chapters 15 and 16.

Summary and conclusions

In this chapter we have examined the meaning of scarcity and have shown that in a market economy scarcity is denoted by the existence of positive (greater than zero) prices. These prices influence the allocation of resources among various markets, i.e. they influence the decision what to produce. They also influence the decisions how, where, when and for whom to produce.

In the next chapter we continue to examine the allocation of resources. But now we narrow our focus and concentrate on the acquisition and utilisation of resources by individual organisations.

Assignments

23.2

State whether each of the following statements is true or false:

1. Scarcity exists whenever a price is paid for a resource or product.
2. The fact that a consumer can obtain a product at a zero price indicates that the product is not scarce.
3. Land, labour and capital are all 'free gifts of nature'.
4. A resource is likely to be available at a zero price if property rights in that resource have been established.

5. The prices of resources and products influence decisions as to what, how, where, when and for whom organisations should produce.
6. Resources may be reallocated following a change in either demand or supply.

23.2

Under the Clean Air Act property rights in the atmosphere can be assumed by local authorities (councils) on behalf of the local community. (1) Write a report outlining the ways in which your local authority has exercised these rights. (2) Discuss the implications of the authority's actions for (*a*) members of the general public, (*b*) producers of goods and services.

23.3

Many agricultural operations have become more mechanised in recent years. For example, an increasing number of farmers have introduced pea-picking machines. Assuming that this leads to a fall in the cost of producing peas and hence in their price, discuss the effects on the allocation of resources (*a*) in pea farming, (*b*) in the farming of beans, a substitute for peas, (*c*) in the production of cans for the canning of peas.

23.4

Explain the possible effects on resource allocation of an increase in both the demand for a product and the cost of the resources used in its production.

23.5

Obtain a list of local retail shops which have changed their locations in recent years, and find out why these changes in location occurred.

23.6

Construct a list of the products supplied in your local area for which demand has a seasonal pattern (good examples would be Christmas cards and tourist services). Find out whether the seasonal pattern of demand is reflected in a seasonal pattern of output. If it is, discuss the problems to which this gives rise; if it is not, explain why it is not.

23.7

Show how the output of entertainment in your local area varies within a given week, and discuss the implications for the local labour market.

23.8

The passage below is based on an article in the *Financial Times*, 12 June 1972. Show how the methods of steel production and the location of production facilities are influenced by the price and availability of inputs.

'This weekend, Britain's first "mini-steelworks", newly commissioned at

Sheerness on the Thames estuary, put on extra shifts in order to step up round-the-clock steelmaking from five-and-a-half days to seven days a week. Last week, two well-known private sector steel groups in the Midlands – Cooper Industries and F. H. Lloyd – announced they were forming a joint company to build a £3 m. "mini mill", only a couple of days ahead of the announcement of a similar-sized, similar-priced scheme by the Manchester wire group, Richard Johnson and Nephew.

'The idea got off the ground much faster in some other countries, including the USA. As the leading US steel companies switched progressively from the old-fashioned open-hearth furnaces to the modern BOS converters, so their appetite for steel scrap declined. Scrap prices fell, and a few individuals were astute enough to see that if they built a small steelworks in cities where a lot of scrap was being produced, they could remelt it and meet the local need for such basic products as engineering bars, or reinforcing bars for the construction industry. In the USA some industrial cities are hundreds of miles from the nearest conventional steelworks, and substantial savings could therefore be made in transport costs.

'Conditions in the UK do not coincide exactly with those in the USA. The chief executive of the Sheerness mini mill estimates that his transport costs, shipping reinforcing bar into the London market, will be only 50p–£1 a ton less than those of the British Steel Corporation which will have a huge capacity for making a similar product at the Anchor complex at Scunthorpe by the end of this year. Nevertheless Sheerness as a company believes that its circumstances are favourable with a large scrap-producing and steel-consuming area like London only 50 miles from its works. You can see, too, why the Lloyd–Cooper partnership in the Midlands is so enthusiastic. Cooper has scrap merchant interests and Lloyd steelmaking experience, and between them they can use the full output of a mini mill, so eliminating their dependence upon the British Steel Corporation or importers for supplies of billets.'

23.9

The passage below is based on an article in the *Financial Times*, 21 October 1978. Drawing on this passage, discuss the risks faced by firms in the timber industry, and the various ways in which they might seek to overcome these risks.

'This month's announcement that two major UK timber companies – International Timber and Bambergers – are planning to merge in a deal worth £7.6 m. has caused much speculation about the likely direction of the timber industry. Some people see the proposed merger as part of the rationalisation that is essential if the industry is to prosper. Others are not so convinced that this is the only solution to the underlying trading problems of the industry. They argue that the most important long-term aim is to remove the highly cyclical and speculative nature of their business through a measure of diversification, or a move into manufacturing and retailing of timber products.

'The timber companies themselves have developed from timber-importing bases, with most developing into timber wholesalers. Much has depended upon the shrewdness of the individual company's timber buying policy. Until fairly recently that meant that the timber buyer had only to assess developments in the timber market – such as the likely level of demand from its principal customer, the construction industry, which takes around 60 to 70 per cent of deliveries. But the violent movement of exchange rates in the past few years has added a new factor to a timber buyer's assessments. Forecasting the rate of exchange at the time of shipment is now as important as buying right. With interest rates as volatile as currencies, timber companies which have relied on borrowing for stock purchases have had to tread a careful path. After a bad experience in 1974 when most were caught with high stocks, the timber groups have been proceeding cautiously. In fact many have erred too much on the safe side, remaining under-bought at a time when they might have exploited an upturn in demand.

'As the timber cycle has become so susceptible to these other factors the timber groups have been searching for ways of bringing greater stability to their profits. They have tackled the problem in a number of ways.

'In the later 1960s, hardwood and softwood specialists linked up to provide a broader timber trading base. Importers have merged with groups that had a manufacturing and retail capability.

'The establishment of a wide-spread distribution/depot network has been necessitated by the decline in the number of ports used. Such a system allows stocks to be shifted quickly. The latest bid by International Timber for Bambergers is primarily a move by International to extend its distribution network. Although the timber groups seem anxious to get nearer their customers such a desire does not necessarily herald an invasion of the High Street. A strong High Street presence catering largely for the do-it-yourself market involves high costs in setting up and running such operations. New management techniques have to be learnt, marketing strategies devised, and the labour force has to be increased. The advantage of a depot network, based largely on the outskirts of town centres, is that it is essentially a low-cost, high-volume sale operation requiring little in the way of overheads and selling mainly to the building trade.

'However the new techniques and extra capital required in becoming more established in retail markets have not deterred some companies. Montague L. Meyer, the largest timber group in the UK, is developing retail units in town centres on secondary sites. The shops are selling a complete range of building materials, including some under the company's own name.'

24 The acquisition and utilisation of resources by the organisation

Introduction

We have shown earlier, and especially in Chapter 8, that organisations frequently adopt policies designed to reduce costs. We now examine costs in more detail from the viewpoint of the individual organisation. Costs are, of course, incurred as a result of the acquisition and utilisation of resources. It is therefore appropriate to take the acquisition of resources as our starting point. We first discuss the acquisition of human resources.

The acquisition of human resources

Although some workers may stay with one employer for much or all of their working lives, the relationship between employer and employee is not usually seen as being permanent. (By contrast, when a firm buys a machine it usually expects to keep it until the end of its useful life.)

External labour markets

What degree of permanence would be desirable in employer – employee relationships is an open question. (As we show below, government intervention has usually had the aim of making the relationship more permanent or, alternatively, minimising the detrimental effects on workers of a lack of permanence.) But it is clear that, given the current arrangements, both employers and employees benefit from the existence of a well developed external labour market. In such a market a worker who leaves or loses his job can make contact with numerous potential employers. Similarly a firm that wishes to recruit additional workers can make contact with many potential employees.

There are various ways of making contact, various channels of communication. Employers may advertise vacancies in the press, on television, on notice-boards outside the factory and so forth. As well as responding to such advertisements, workers may make enquiries direct to potential employers.

In addition contact may be arranged, or at least facilitated, by intermediaries of various kinds, including the Manpower Services Commission

Job Centres, private employment agencies and executive search consultants (often known as headhunters!).

However this does not mean that the efficiency of the labour market could not be improved. Indeed there are numerous obstacles or barriers which reduce its efficiency.

The first barrier is geographical. Unemployed workers may not be located in the same area as the employers who require their particular skills. In order to overcome this obstacle it may be necessary first to increase the flow of information, especially to workers about vacancies. Both private and public agencies play a part here. Second, if, having been made aware of vacancies, workers are reluctant to move, it may be necessary to provide them with financial assistance. Some employers offer assistance, and the State provides rehousing grants (of up to £600 at present), lodging allowances and the payment of fares. (In addition the State provides hundreds of millions of pounds a year to firms who are prepared to establish or expand units in areas of high unemployment; see Chapter 25.)

Another barrier is that the skills of unemployed workers may not match those required by employers. Employers provide a considerable amount of training on their own initiative, but governments have felt it necessary, especially as unemployment has risen in recent years, both to provide incentives to employers to increase the amount of training, and to supplement this training. In 1973, the first full year in which the Training Opportunities Scheme operated, 40,000 people received training. By 1976 this number had risen to 90,000, of whom 23,000 were training in government Skillcentres.

The operation of the labour market may also be impeded by the policies of the trade unions. Restrictions are sometimes imposed on the number of apprentices (e.g. in the printing trade) and this reduces the number of skilled workers. In other instances unions have refused to allow firms to recruit workers who are not deemed to have had an appropriate training. In 1978 ICI had temporarily to close a chemicals plant because the unions would not agree to the employment of workers trained in government Skillcentres. These union policies effectively reduce the supply of the particular type of labour involved, and thus, it is hoped, help to protect the jobs of the existing members and lead to wages being higher than they would be otherwise.

Internal labour markets

The above discussion referred to external labour markets. Labour markets also exist within firms. Workers may move from job to job and from department to department. An important characteristic of an internal labour market is that when the employer provides training it is normally with a view to either improving the worker's performance in his present position or preparing him for a move to a specific position, a move which will benefit both worker and employer.

The acquisition of non-human resources

Non-human resources may be acquired by several different means. They may be purchased outright (raw materials, components and much machinery), hired or leased (machinery), rented (offices and factories), or bought on hire purchase (machinery). The advantage of outright purchase is, of course, that it gives immediate ownership. The disadvantage is that it requires a greater initial expenditure than the other methods.

Where there is a choice of methods, in order to decide which would be most suitable the organisation will take into account various factors. First, the size of the initial outlay will be considered in relation to the organisation's financial reserves. Second, if one method requires the raising of additional finance the cost of this finance will be considered (this would depend, of course, upon the method of raising finance, a topic discussed later). Third, it would be important to decide whether the organisation was certain to retain the asset until the end of its useful life or whether it might wish to dispose of it before then (early disposal would be more likely for machinery than for raw materials or components). Fourth, if early disposal is anticipated, it is important to know if there is a well developed second-hand market (this would be more likely for types of machinery used by many firms than for machinery built specifically to order for the initial purchaser). Finally the organisation will, of course, consider the total costs of the various methods (account being taken of their effect on tax liability).

There are also differences in the types of markets in which various resources are acquired, due at least partly to differences in the characteristics of the resources. Many agricultural raw materials, e.g. cacoa, grains, wool, have a seasonal pattern of supply and are often subject to very violent fluctuations in price. These fluctuations are largely due to changes in supply resulting from changes in climatic conditions. Moreover, since output is in the hands of many small producers it is difficult to reach agreement on the control of supplies (see Chapter 18). However, wool producers have created their own stockpiles when supply was judged to be excessive, and the producers of natural rubber are planning the same action.

The prices of many metals and minerals have also shown considerable fluctuations, mainly because producers have found it difficult to keep supply in line with a fluctuating demand. (Fluctuations in demand arising from cycles in international economic activity have sometimes been accentuated by the tendency of producers to build up stockpiles in economic upswings and to run them down in recessions.) Attempts have been made by producers to co-ordinate supplies in a number of markets, including iron-ore, bauxite, copper and phosphates, with varying degrees of success.

By contrast the prices of machinery are much more stable (although they often tend to rise over time). In some markets, e.g. those for fairly simple machines such as lathes, there are a large number of suppliers and price competition is frequently keen. In other markets, e.g. for more complex equipment such as very large, numerically controlled machines, there may be very few suppliers. Machines are usually made to order and no two machines may be exactly alike. In such instances a market, in the sense of a meeting of a group of buyers and sellers, hardly exists.

The acquisition of financial resources

Before a firm can acquire the human and non-human resources required for production it must, of course, acquire financial resources. The various sources of finance available to new firms were referred to briefly in Chapters 2, 3 and 4 and are discussed in greater detail in Chapter 26.

The utilisation of resources

Having examined the acquisition of resources we now discuss their utilisation. In order to simplify matters we shall for much of the time conduct the analysis in terms of two broad categories of resources: labour and capital. In general, land could be substituted for capital in the analysis without changing our conclusions.

Alternative combinations of resources

Organisations invariably employ both human and non-human resources, and they can frequently choose between alternative methods of production, using different combinations of these resources. These choices are represented in a highly simplified manner in Fig. 24.1. The *equal product curve* marked 100 indicates the various combinations of capital and labour that would be required in order to produce 100 units of output per period. For example, 4 units of capital plus 1 unit of labour, or 1 unit of capital plus 4 units of labour would be required.

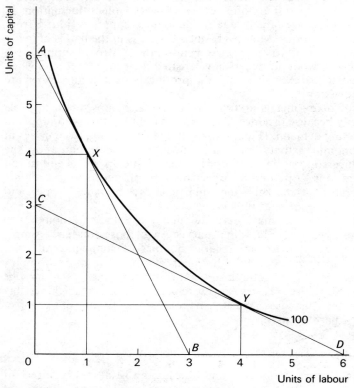

Fig. 24.1 Alternative combinations of resources

As we noted in the previous chapter the method of production, the combination of resources, chosen will be influenced by the relative prices of these resources. Two alternative *price* or *budget lines* are shown in Fig. 24.1. Line *AB* indicates that labour is twice as expensive as capital; for a given outlay the firm could acquire either 6 units of capital or 3 units of labour. This budget line touches the equal product curve at only one point, *X*. This denotes the method of production, since with any other method a higher outlay, represented by a budget line to the right of *AB*, would be required. The point of tangency *X* indicates that 4 units of capital plus 1 unit of labour would be employed.

The second budget line *CD* denotes that capital is twice as expensive as labour – for a given outlay 3 units of capital or 6 units of labour could be acquired. Now the point of tangency to the equal product curve is *Y*, indicating that 1 unit of capital plus 4 units of labour would be employed. The increase in the relative price of capital has led to a substitution of labour for capital.

As we said above, Fig. 24.1 is a highly simplified representation of the choices facing the firm. In practice there may be considerable obstacles to the substitution of one factor of production for another. Nevertheless this figure is useful in illustrating how the relative prices of factors influence the choice of production technique, especially when a producer is first starting operations or undertaking a major expansion.

Returns to scale

The equal-product curve can also be used to illustrate another point referred to

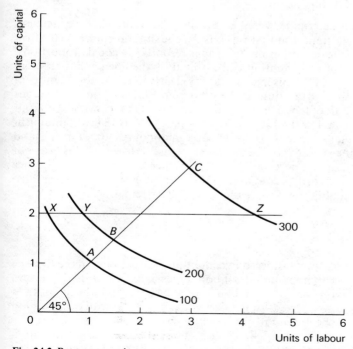

Fig. 24.2 Returns to scale

briefly in the previous chapter, namely that cost may not change in proportion to output. Figure 24.2 contains three equal product curves which indicate the combinations of labour and capital required to produce each of three levels of output. The 45° line traces the path which would result if equal amounts of capital and labour were employed (in fact this would happen only if the price of capital equalled the price of labour. The line is inserted here to help our explanation of returns to scale).

A comparison of points *A* and *B* shows clearly that a doubling of output from 100 to 200 units can be achieved with a less than proportionate increase in the quantity of resources or factors employed. If the price of the factors does not change, a reduction in the amount used per unit of output implies that the cost per unit of output (the average cost) falls.

Conversely a comparison of points *B* and *C* shows that an increase in output of 50 per cent requires a doubling of the quantity of resources employed. This increase in the amount of resources used per unit of output implies an increase in the average cost.

Within the range of output represented in Fig. 24.2, *returns to scale are non-proportional*. They increase within the range of output 100 to 200 units and decrease within the range 200 to 300 units. Incidentally the fact that returns to scale begin to decrease beyond 200 units does not mean that production should not be increased beyond this point. Even though point *C* is *technically* less efficient than B, it may still be more profitable; the increase in revenue resulting from an increase in output could exceed the increase in cost.

Diminishing returns to one factor

We show below what determines whether returns to scale are likely to increase, decrease or remain constant. But first we consider the situation in which the firm is unable to increase the quantities of the various resources in equal proportions. An extreme example of this situation is illustrated by the line passing through points *X Y* and *Z* in Fig. 24.2. This line shows very clearly that with the quantity of capital employed constant (at 2 units) the returns to successive units of labour diminish. With one unit of labour employed, output is 200 units, while with four units employed output is less than 300 units. The operation of this law of diminishing returns implies that since more of the variable factor or resource is being used per unit of output, the average cost of this resource rises. However, this does not mean that average total cost necessarily rises; the (constant) amount of the other factor is spread over a larger output and so the average cost of this factor falls. Average total cost could, therefore, either rise, fall or remain constant.

The scale of organisation

In the previous sections we considered two alternative situations. In the first the producer was able to vary the quantity of both types of resources; in the second the quantity of one type of resource, labour, could be varied but the quantity of the other type, capital, was fixed. In the first situation the scale of organisation could be changed, in the second it was fixed or given.

This distinction between a changing and a fixed scale of organisation corresponds to the distinction made by some writers between the long period or

226

long run (scale of organisation can be changed) and the short period or short run (scale of organisation given). We have not used that terminology because the phrases long and short period may be interpreted – incorrectly – as referring to fixed time periods.

We now discuss each of these situation in greater detail. We begin by examining the behaviour of costs when the scale of organisation is given.

The relationship between output and cost with a given scale of organisation

When we previously considered this situation we took capital as the factor whose quantity was fixed and this would be so in most instances; the scale or capacity of the firm would be determined by the quantity of capital inputs – land, factory space or machinery. (However it must be remembered that this is not necessarily so; some producers have spare machine capacity but are unable to increase output because of a shortage of labour with the required skills and abilities.)

When planning its scale of organisation for the forthcoming period, say a year, the firm will often instal more of the limiting factor of production than it expects to use on *average* during the period. This may seem wasteful, but can be justified on the grounds that if demand fluctuates substantially during the period the firm will be better able to meet the peak demand than if it had only sufficient capacity to meet the average level of demand. A similar argument would apply if demand turned out to be higher than expected throughout the period. The importance of being able to meet demand whenever possible should not be underestimated; it is often a very important means of defending one's share of the market, and of increasing this share by attracting customers from competitors whose capacity proves to be inadequate.

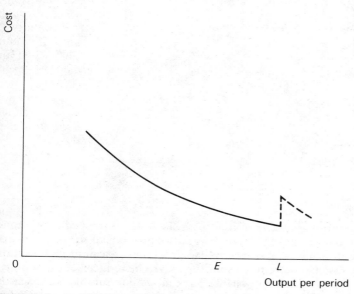

Fig. 24.3 Average fixed cost

Fixed costs

The costs incurred in acquiring and utilising resources whose quantity is fixed during the planning period are known as fixed costs. If for the moment we assume that during this period *total* fixed costs do not change, it follows that *average* fixed cost falls as output increases. This is shown in Fig. 24.3 where average fixed cost continues to fall beyond the expected level of output, E, until the limit to output, L, is reached. The broken line indicates that in order to produce more than L, the scale of organisation, the quantity of fixed factors, would have to be increased. This would cause average fixed cost to increase, but it would then start to fall once more as output increased.

Variable costs

The costs attaching to the factors or resources whose quantity can be varied at a given scale of organisation are known as variable costs. Variable factors include raw materials, the power used in operating machines and some forms of labour. The quantity of resources used increases or decreases with output. However, it is difficult to vary their use exactly in line with changes in output. This is especially true of labour; the trade unions would be most unhappy with a policy that involved the constant hiring and firing of workers (of course employers might not wish to adopt such a policy).

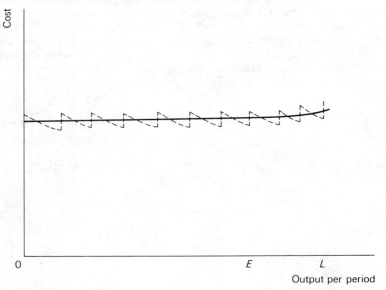

Fig. 24.4 Average variable cost

    Consequently the average variable cost usually has a stepped function as shown by the broken line in Fig. 24.4. The vertical portions of the line indicate that additional factors have to be employed in order to increase output (or that a fall in output allows the quantity of some factors to be reduced at that point).

    In order to simplify the analysis we have drawn an unbroken line which 'smooths' the cost function. This smoothed line indicates that average variable cost is constant over a wide range of output but that it tends to rise as output rises beyond the expected level. This might happen for several reasons. If the firm is doubtful as to whether demand will be maintained at this unexpectedly high level it may be reluctant to recruit additional workers, preferring instead to pay premium rates for overtime working by its existing workers. Alternatively, if it decides to recruit new workers, they may be less experienced and therefore less efficient than the existing workers. Furthermore, if other employers are producing at an unexpectedly high level of output and thus increasing their demand for workers, wage rates may rise. This might also apply to other inputs, e.g. raw materials.

Semi-variable costs

We have classified inputs in two broad categories, fixed and variable. In practice many inputs are semi-variable, e.g. indirect labour and the heating of buildings. The cost of these inputs would have a stepped function, similar to, but more extreme than, that shown in Fig. 24.4. In order to simplify the analysis we assume that we can split these costs into a fixed and a variable element. This enables us to continue to use two categories. Then, in order to obtain average total cost, we simply add together average fixed and average variable cost, as shown in Fig. 24.5.

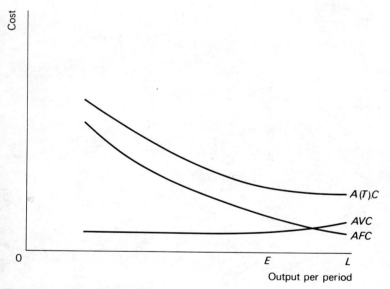

Fig. 24.5 Average fixed, variable and total cost

It can be seen that over much of the range of output, average total cost falls as output increases. Eventually, however, the fall in average fixed cost is balanced by the rise in average variable cost, and average total cost becomes roughly constant.

We showed earlier that if an increasing quantity of a variable factor is applied to a given quantity of a fixed factor the returns to that variable factor would diminish (see the line passing through X, Y and Z in Fig. 24.2), i.e. average

229

variable cost would rise. This rise in average variable cost could outweight the fall in average fixed cost, causing average total cost to rise. However this does not happen in Fig. 24.5; here the rise in average variable cost is very slight. The reason for this is that there is spare capacity in the fixed factor until the limit to output, L, is reached. The difference between the two situations can be summarised as follows. Figure 24.2 assumes that the increase in output is achieved by increasing only the number of man-hours, the number of machine-hours remaining unchanged. Figure 24.5 assumes that the increase in output is achieved by increasing both the number of man-hours and the number of machine-hours worked. Although both situations can be found in practice the second is probably far more common than the first.

The relationship between output and cost as the scale of organisation changes

We now consider how cost is likely to behave over a period which is sufficiently long to enable the producer – in order to move to a new level of output – to change the scale of organisation, i.e. a situation in which output is *not* limited by the existence of a fixed factor.

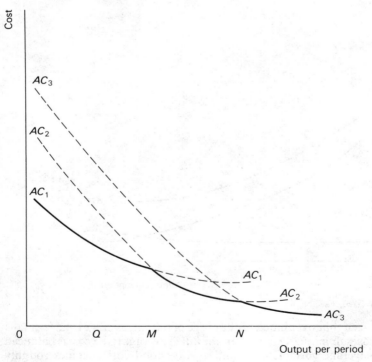

Fig. 24.6 Average cost with a changing scale of organisation

In Fig. 24.6 AC_1 is the average (total) cost curve shown in Fig. 24.5. AC_2 and AC_3 are the average cost curves that would apply at larger scales of organisation.

230

In order to simplify the analysis let us assume that the producer's choice is confined to these three alternatives. (This might happen because of *indivisibilities* in a factor of production, e.g. machinery might be available in only three sizes.)

At any output up to M the smallest scale of organisation would yield the lowest average cost (AC_1). Within the range of output MN the medium scale of organisation would yield the lowest average cost (AC_2). Finally, beyond N the largest scale of organisation would yield the lowest average cost (AC_3). The cost curve which would apply if the producer could always adopt the most appropriate scale of organisation is given by the unbroken line, composed of parts of all three cost curves.

The fact that each of the three curves falls over much of its length as output increases can be explained by the factors discussed in the previous section. But in order to explain why, beyond a certain level of output, a larger scale of organisation yields a lower average cost than a smaller scale we have to introduce the concept of economies of scale.

Economies of scale

Economies of scale can be grouped into several categories.

Technical economies.   Cost savings may arise because of increases in physical dimensions. For example, the building of bigger oil tankers can be explained by the fact that the amount of oil that can be carried increases far more than the amount of steel, etc., needed to build the tanker (and the number of men needed to operate it). The same principle applies to many production processes; the capacity of machines often increases more than proportionately to their size, and hence to the cost of purchasing and operating them.

Technical economies of scale often arise from technological progress, e.g. the development of automatic control devices – used in oil refineries, chemical plants, etc. – whose capacity can be fully exploited only at high levels of output. However, technological progress does not always imply an increase in the most efficient size of plant. In recent years the development of very small computers and microprocessors has enabled small units to adopt production techniques previously cost-effective only in the large units.

Marketing economies.   It is often possible to achieve an increase in the volume of sales with a less than proportionate increase in the costs of selling and distribution – warehousing, transport, etc. (These advantages could also be classified as technical economies applied to distribution.) Savings may also be possible in advertising costs. For example, although television advertising is more expensive than advertising in the local press, it may have a more than proportionate effect on the volume of sales, and hence result in lower advertising costs per unit of output.

Purchasing economies.   Savings in the average cost of transport and premises may also be made in relation to the purchasing function. But a far more important scale economy is the ability to buy at lower prices. Quantity discounts are frequently available when purchasing inputs – raw materials, components, machines, etc. – and larger organisations are clearly in a better position than smaller organisations to take advantage of these discounts.

231

Furthermore, very large organisations may be able to negotiate special terms, over and above those offered in the published quantity discount schedules. The Monopolies Commission found that of 624 customers of Metal Box Ltd only 45 were able to purchase on terms more favourable than those contained in the published discount schedules. However, these firms were clearly buying in very large quantities since together they accounted for 88 per cent of the company's sales.[1]

Purchasing economies are especially important in retailing, since the cost of goods purchased is by far the biggest source of expense. The benefits which can be gained by large retailers are indicated by the following extract from a report on food distribution by the Prices and Incomes Board.

'Our enquiries show that on some products the larger retailers are probably able to obtain aggregate additional discounts of between 10 and 15 per cent (calculated on the retail price of the product) beyond those obtainable by shops which can only buy in minimum case lots; that is to say that if the discount on a particular product brought in minimum case lots were, for instance, 20 per cent, the highest discount might be as much as 30 or 35 per cent.'[2] This extract referred to purchases of manufacturers' brands. Even bigger discounts may be obtained when manufacturers supply retailers' own-label products.

Financial economies.   Large firms can often obtain finance more easily and/or more cheaply than small firms. This is mainly due to the fact that large firms are usually seen, by the institutions or individuals providing finance, as being safer. In addition, savings in costs may be available in respect of some sources of finance. For example, the issue costs of raising new capital range from about 10–15 per cent of the sum raised at the lower end (say £250,000) to 3–5 per cent when the size of the issue exceeds £1 m.

Risk-bearing economies   As a general rule we can say that the larger the firm the greater the range of products produced. The biggest risk faced by small, one-product, firms is that the demand for this product may fall to such a point that the firm is forced out of business. This risk is minimised in the larger, diversified, firm. If one product becomes temporarily unprofitable it can be 'carried' by the profits made on other products, until it returns to profitability. If it becomes permanently unprofitable and is dropped, the profits earned on other products should enable the larger firm to survive. Faced with the prospect of a long-term decline in the demand for cigarettes and tobacco, many of the manufacturers have embarked upon an extensive diversification programme. For example, Imperial Tobacco has moved into retailing, food production (including J. B. Eastwood,the largest supplier of chickens and turkeys in the UK) and toiletries (e.g. Yardley).

Managerial economies.   This term is applied to a miscellaneous group of economies relating to the administration of the organisation. It includes the ability to offer the high rewards needed to attract staff of high ability in various fields – research and development, marketing, etc. It also includes the ability to utilise administrative procedures which might be too expensive for the smaller firm. (It can be seen that some of these economies could also have been included in preceding categories.)

Economies of scale and the direction of growth

As we noted above, risk-bearing economies are especially likely to arise from growth by *diversification*, particularly, of course, when the demand prospects for the firm's existing products are unsatisfactory.

Even if the *market* demand for a product remains satisfactory, a firm's survival, or at least its profitability, may be threatened by a failure to secure adequate access to the market. In order to avoid this risk, producers may adopt a policy of *forward expansion or integration* (integration involves taking over or merging with an existing firm). During the post-war period Courtaulds, Britain's largest producer of textile fibres, took over a large number of companies engaged in the processing of fibres, and in the manufacturing, wholesaling and retailing of clothing and other articles using textile fibres.

The reverse process – *backward expansion or integration* – may be undertaken in order to ensure that supplies of raw materials, components, etc., are adequate in terms of quantity, quality and price. In the early part of the post-war period all the major British car assemblers acquired their own body-pressing facilities (none of the assemblers who failed to do so survived as independent organisations). More recently they have extended their production of both mechanical and electrical components.

Forward and backward expansion (integration) are both forms of *vertical expansion (integration)*. By contrast *horizontal expansion (integration)* involves an extension of the organisation's existing activities. This clearly does little to reduce the organisation's risks. On the other hand it is likely to give rise to technical, marketing and purchasing economies.

Economies of scale and the average cost curve

We have seen that there are numerous factors which mean than an increase in the scale of organisation may lead to a fall in average cost. However it is important to note that these factors do not all have the same effects in terms of a diagram such as Fig. 24.6. Indeed some of these effects cannot be demonstrated in such a diagram.

The economies of scale represented most closely by Fig. 24.6 are the technical economies which arise during a process of horizontal expansion, i.e. when the firm installs a bigger plant in order to increase the output of an existing product.

On the other hand the risk-bearing economies considered above cannot be represented in Fig. 24.6. In order to obtain these economies the firm must increase its range of products, either by diversifying or by vertical (forward or backward) expansion. Once the firm produces more than one product it is impossible to accurately represent on a single diagram the relationship between its cost and its volume of output (although it may be possible to do so by means of a series of diagrams relating to individual products).

Economies of scale and a fall in output

Figure 24.6 shows that if the biggest plant (giving rise to AC_3) is used to produce output N, average cost is less than it would be with a smaller plant (AC_2 or AC_1). But note that if demand were to fall so that the firm produced only Q, average

233

cost would be higher than if the firm had retained the smaller plant. We can see, then, that when a move to a larger scale of organisation involves an increase in fixed costs, the position is not reversible; the firm cannot – at least for some time – revert to a smaller plant.

This contrasts with the position with respect to purchasing economies. As output expands, the organisation can buy at lower prices. As output falls, the buying prices will revert to their earlier level, but they will not be higher than they were initially, since no additional fixed costs have been incurred.

Diseconomies of scale

If you look back at Fig. 24.2 you will see that beyond point B an increase in output requires a more than proportionate increase in the quantity of inputs, i.e. diseconomies of scale arise. Careful inspection of this diagram reveals a puzzling, perhaps even a nonsensical feature. If we were to add together the lines relating to an output of 100 units and 200 units, the resulting line would lie below the 300 unit line. In other words, instead of enlarging the plant which produces 200 units, the firm should maintain the scale of that plant and build another smaller plant to produce a further 100 units. In this way the firm would avoid the (technical) diseconomies of scale.

Are there any diseconomies of scale that cannot be avoided? The most likely source of such diseconomies is the difficulty of administering a large organisation. The greater the number of employees and the more diverse the range of the organisation's activities, the more problems are likely to arise in trying to ensure that the policies of the firm are implemented efficiently. (One aspect of this situation, discussed in detail in earlier chapters, is the possibility that individuals will follow their own interests rather than that of the organisation.)

In order to try to prevent diseconomies arising many large organisations establish a number of smaller divisions, departments, or even subsidiary companies. A group of managers or directors is given the responsibility for the efficient running of each unit and in many respects this group operates in the same way as the Board of Directors of a smaller company. The main differences are first that they are responsible to the main company or group Board, rather than directly to the shareholders, and second that the access of the subsidiaries to funds for investment is normally controlled by the main Board.

Diseconomies may also occasionally arise from other sources. For example, if a company extends its sales into a new geographical area it may find that the need to establish new warehouses, etc., leads to an increase in its distribution costs per unit. However, even where diseconomies do arise, they might well be balanced or outweighed by economies elsewhere, so that average cost remains constant or continues to fall.

Summary and conclusions

Organisations can acquire resources by various means, and we outlined the most important of these, making a broad distinction between markets for human and non-human resources. Organisations also have a choice as to how they utilise these resources, and we discussed the various factors that influence this choice; the relative costs of the resources was found to be especially important.

We then considered the behaviour of costs as output changed, first at a given scale of organisation, and subsequently as the scale of organisation changed. For this purpose we found it useful to make a broad distinction between fixed and variable costs. In the next chapter we show how the behaviour of costs influences the shape of market supply curves. We also carry the analysis of cost a stage further.

Appendix: Breakeven analysis

In this and earlier chapters we have expressed the relationship between output on the one hand, and cost and revenue on the other, in terms of the behaviour of *average* cost and revenue. By comparing average cost and revenue we are able to see whether or not a firm is making a profit.

Table 24.1 A cost schedule

Output	Total cost (£)			Average cost (£)		
	Fixed	Variable	Total	Fixed	Variable	Total
10	500	100	600	50	10	60
20	500	200	700	25	10	35
50	500	500	1,000	10	10	20

This is the approach usually adopted by economists. Accountants, on the other hand, are more likely to use breakeven analysis, which requires a comparison of *total* cost and revenue. We can compare these two approaches by considering the data presented in table 24.1. Looking first at the right-hand side of the table, we see that average variable cost is constant at all levels of output. Since, as output increases, average fixed cost falls, so too does average total cost. This is shown in the right-hand diagram in Fig. 24.7. The left-hand side of Table 24.1 shows how total cost increases with output. This information is also presented in the left hand diagram in Fig. 24.7.

Turning to the revenue, we assume that the firm is able to sell up to 50 units a period at a price of £30. This means that the average revenue curve is horizontal at this price, as shown in the right-hand diagram, and that the total revenue curve is a straight line with a slope as shown in the left hand diagram.

We can see that the firm would break even at an output of 25 units: average cost and revenue would both equal £30; total cost and revenue would both equal £750. At a higher output the firm would make a profit; at a lower output it would make a loss. Although the breakeven output can be read off from either diagram, the term breakeven analysis is usually applied when total cost and revenue figures are used, as noted above. Similarly the term breakeven chart would be applied to the left-hand diagram.

We must emphasise that we have been discussing alternative forms of presenting a given set of data. Each organisation should use the form of presentation that is suitable for its own particular purposes. However the

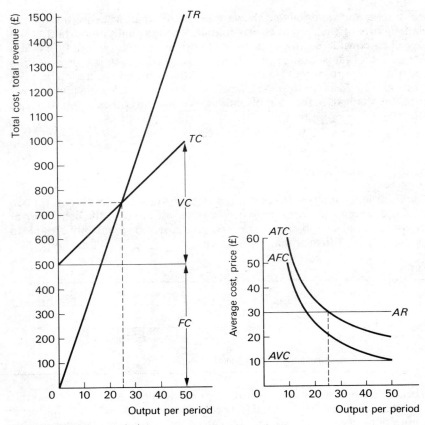

Fig. 24.7 Breakeven analysis

breakeven chart does have the advantage that it makes it easier to see the total profit or loss that would be made at any level of output. This advantage may help to explain why this form of presentation is frequently used in business.

Assignments

24.1

Make a list of the institutions which aid the operation of the labour market in your local area. Indicate which of the institutions are especially important for (1) people entering the labour market for the first time, (2) redundant workers.

24.2

Compare the methods of recruiting labour used by any six employers in your local area. (Choose your sample to include at least one employer in both the private and public sectors; one employer in both the manufacturing and the

236

service sectors; one large and one small employer.) If you can obtain sufficient information, extend your report to include a comparison of these employers' training programmes.

24.3

Say whether each of the following statements is true or false.

1. The phrase 'internal labour market' indicates that the labour market is internal to one area.
2. An equal product curve indicates the various combinations of two products that would be required to produce a given level of output.
   Statements 3 to 5 relate to Fig. 24.8.

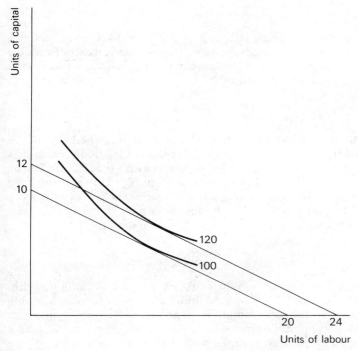

Fig. 24.8

3. One unit of labour costs twice as much as one unit of capital .
4. Given the relative prices of capital and labour shown by the budget line, an output of 100 units would be produced by equal quantities of capital and labour.
5. Within the range of output 100 to 120, returns to scale are constant.

24.4

Explain the difference between decreasing returns to scale and diminishing returns to one factor of production.

24.5

Say whether each of the following statements is true or false.

1. The operation of the law of diminishing returns implies that average variable cost rises.
2. The operation of the law of diminishing returns implies that average total cost rises.
3. Increasing returns to scale denotes that the quantity of factors employed increases more than in proportion to output.
4. A changing scale of organisation implies that the quantity of all resources can be varied.
5. Average fixed cost remains constant as output increases.

24.6

Make a list of the costs incurred by your college which are likely to be (*a*) fixed, and (*b*) variable, during a given academic year. How would you expect variable costs to change as output changes? (Before answering this question think carefully about the definition of 'output'.)

24.7

The Downunder Boomerang Manufacturing Co is considering whether or not to automate its production line. At present its fixed costs are £100,000 a year and its variable costs are £1 per boomerang. Under the new system a reduction in labour requirements would result in a fall in variable costs to 50p. However the fixed costs would rise to £200,000. Draw a diagram which would help the company to reach a decision. (In past years sales of boomerangs have fluctuated between 150,000 and 250,000 a year.)

24.8

The Curtis Weaving Co normally produces 10,000 sq. yds. of cloth a month. Each yard of cloth requires 0.2 lbs. of yarn and 0.1 hours of labour. Monthly fixed costs are £5,000. In the first six months of the year output was as planned. But for the remaining six months output was considerably higher. One of Curtis's main competitors was temporarily closed following a serious fire and, being unwilling to turn away additional orders, Curtis increased output to 12,500 sq. yds. a month.

During the first six months, the production workers were paid at a flat rate of £1 an hour for a forty-hour week. For the next three months they worked ten hours a week overtime, being paid for the extra hours at time and a half (i.e. normal rate + 50 per cent). Then the company increased its labour force by 25 per cent, and all the workers reverted to a forty-hour week at the normal rate of pay.

During the first six months Curtis bought its fibre at £1 a lb. However, as it increased the size of its orders for the rest of the year, it obtained a 5 per cent quantity discount.

Calculate the average fixed, variable and total cost per sq. yd. during (*a*) the first six months, (*b*) the next three months, (*c*) the final three months.

24.9

The cost figures below relate to a manufacturer of men's shirts. Direct labour: In general wages of production workers vary in line with output. However, at low levels of output a work-sharing agreement is put into effect which means that wages fall less than output.

Monthly output of shirts	Monthly wages of production workers (£)
1,000	800
2,000	1,000
3,000	1,200
4,000	1,600
5,000	2,000

Direct materials: The cost of materials was £1.00 per shirt, regardless of the number of shirts made.

Indirect materials, fuel and power: The cost of these inputs comprised a fixed element of £5,000 a month, regardless of the number of shirts produced, and a variable element of 50p a shirt.

Other costs: These costs, which included depreciation of machinery, rent of buildings and the salaries of senior staff, were treated as fixed during a given year, and amounted to £6,000 a month.

1. Calculate the average fixed, average variable and average total cost at monthly outputs of (a) 1,000, (b) 2,000, (c) 3,000, (d) 4,000 and (e) 5,000 shirts.
2. Plot your answers on a graph.
3. Draw a breakeven chart, assuming that the manufacturer sells all his shirts at a price of (a) £5.00, (b) £4.50. Read off the breakeven output at each price.

24.10

How would you classify each of the following economies of scale?

1. The amount of metal used in the construction of an oil pipeline increases less than proportionately to its internal volume.
2. The capacity of stone-cutting machinery is increased by adding extra cutting blades, without modifying the rest of the machine.
3. American wholesalers sold sparking plugs to garages at the following prices:

Quantity purchased	Price per plug (cents)
1–99	39
100–299	36
300+	32

4. General Motors spent a total of more than $80 m. on advertising cars, as compared to the $6.6 m. spent by American Motors. However the cost per car sold was $26.6 for General Motors and $57.9 for American Motors.

24.11

Say whether each of the following represents forward, backward, or horizontal expansion, or diversification.

1. A retailer of clothes buys a clothes-wholesale business.
2. A manufacturer begins selling direct to retailers.
3. A weaver installs more looms in order to increase his level of output.
4. A bank buys an insurance company.

24.12

What economies of scale would be likely to arise if the number of students enrolled in your college were to double? Do you think that any diseconomies of scale might arise?

24.13

Interview a number of retailers who manage or own shops of different sizes, and prepare a report on economies of scale in retailing. (The presentation of your report will be helped by a careful grouping of the economies into, say, 4 or 5 categories.)

Notes

1. Monopolies Commission, *Report on Metal Containers*, HMSO 1970.
2. National Board for Prices and Incomes, *Prices, Profits and Costs in Food Distribution*, HMSO 1971.

25 Costs and supply

Introduction

In the previous chapter we presented a classification of the various types of costs that are incurred when an organisation acquires and utilises resources. We also analysed the behaviour of costs as output changed. We now build on the results of this analysis in order to show how market supply curves are derived. We also examine some additional aspects of cost that are of relevance to the operations of organisations.

Cost curves and supply curves

In most instances profit forms the link between cost and supply. When a profit margin (profit per unit) is added to a firm's average cost curve we obtain that firm's supply curve. By adding together the supply curves of all the firms supplying a given market we obtain the market supply curve. In earlier chapters we have shown that supply curves can have several different shapes, and we can summarise that earlier discussion by means of a single diagram.

In Fig. 25.1 we show four alternative supply curves. Curves S_3 and S_4 reflect the cost conditions discussed in the previous chapter. S_3 indicates that suppliers would maintain a constant price at different levels of output. This reflects the fact that a constant profit margin is added to an average cost that is (roughly) constant over a wide range of output. (As we showed in the previous chapter, average cost would rise as output fell below a certain point. However it is difficult to impose price increases, to compensate for increases in average cost, when demand is depressed.)

S_4, which indicates that a lower average cost is associated with a higher level of output, reflects the fact that producers achieve economies of scale and pass on the benefit (at least partially) to consumers in the form of lower prices.

What about the other two supply curves shown in Fig. 25.1? As we noted in Chapter 18, S_1 indicates that supply cannot be increased during the period under consideration (which might be a single day), and is most likely to apply to the markets for primary products, e.g. fish. Supply is completely inelastic and bears no relation to the cost incurred during this period.

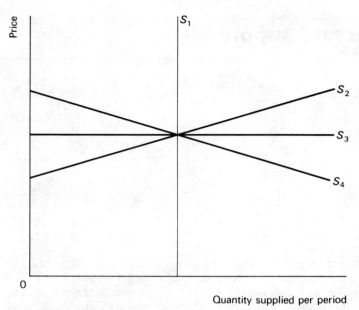

Fig. 25.1 Alternative supply curves

S_2, which indicates that more would be supplied at a higher than a lower price, may be applicable to a wider range of markets including those for manufactured goods, and we have to explain how a supply curve of this shape might relate to the cost curves that we presented in the previous chapter.

The first possible explanation has already been noted: average cost may rise at high levels of output. This could occur either because efficiency falls, e.g. if an increase in the work-rate leads to an increase in the proportion of faulty products, or because the prices of inputs rise, e.g. premium rates are paid for overtime working. If this increase in average cost is passed on in the form of higher prices the supply curve will have a rising segment.

However, this would not explain why the supply curve rises throughout its length. For this to happen all increases in output would have to lead to an increase in either inefficiency or the prices of inputs. It is most unlikely that inefficiency would always increase with output. A continuous rise in the price of some inputs is rather more likely, especially if all firms increase their demand for these inputs. But it is extremely unlikely that this increase in cost would always outweigh the fall in fixed cost which accompanies an increase in output.

It seems, then, that costs are most unlikely to behave in such a way as to give rise to a supply curve which slopes upwards throughout its length. Might the behaviour of profits provide a more acceptable explanation?

If we confine our attention to the range of output over which average cost is constant, we are able to derive an upward sloping supply curve on the (not unreasonable) assumption that firms take advantage of favourable demand conditions to add higher profit margins and, conversely, reduce their profit margins when demand is depressed. However it is by no means inevitable that firms will react in this way to changes in demand. Indeed, as we showed in Chapter 18, there is considerable evidence to suggest that firms frequently hold

242

their prices constant when demand increases and take the benefit in the form of an increased volume of sales (remember that we have identified an increase in sales as an important business objective).

Cost curves and supply curves: summary

Our examination of the relationship between costs and supply suggests that supply curves are likely to be either horizontal, when the scale of organisation is given, or downward sloping when the scale of organisation can be changed and advantage taken of economies of scale. However when the demand for products and inputs is at a very high level, prices may increase, i.e. the supply curve may turn up.

Whatever the shape of the supply curve, we have assumed so far that any supplier to a market sells to all his customers at the same price (the only exception being where discounts are given for large purchases). Later on in this chapter, as we examine the meaning of cost in greater detail, we explore the implications of dropping this assumption.

Some additional types of cost

We have so far distinguished fixed, variable and semi-variable cost, which together make up total cost. We now consider some additional types of cost, commenting on their significance for particular types of decision.

Marginal and incremental cost

These are similar concepts in that they both refer to the additional costs that are incurred when output is increased. Marginal cost is the cost of increasing output by a single unit. Incremental cost is the cost of increasing output by any number of units (including one). Since decisions on whether or not to increase output seldom refer to a single unit, incremental cost is the more useful concept. Provided that the scale of organisation remains unchanged, incremental cost comprises the addition to variable cost since, by definition, total fixed cost does not change.

The significance of this concept can be demonstrated with reference to Fig. 25.2. Average (total) cost is, as before, denoted by AC. Since fixed costs do not affect the decision with which we are concerned here, average fixed cost is omitted from the diagram. Furthermore, in order to simplify the analysis we assume that average variable cost is constant, so that marginal cost and average variable cost are equal.

Although the firm has sufficient capacity to produce N units per period it has so far received orders for only M units, at a price P_N. It then receives an enquiry from a potential customer with whom it has not previously traded. This customer offers to buy MN units at a price P_L. This price is, of course, less than

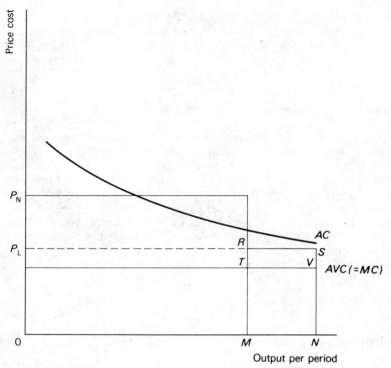

Fig. 25.2 Incremental analysis

the average cost. Nevertheless incremental analysis suggests that the firm's profits may be increased by taking the order.

The additional or incremental revenue is $MRSN$, whereas the incremental cost is only $MTVN$. Profits would therefore be higher by $TRSV$ than if the order was not taken and the firm was left with idle capacity. ($TRSV$ can be termed the incremental profit.)

Before arriving at a decision the firm should, of course, try to obtain as much information as possible about the state of demand, since it would be unwise to allocate capacity to this order if it was felt that additional orders at the normal price. P_N, would be forthcoming. Furthermore it would have to ensure that its other customers did not discover about this transaction, since if they did they might insist on buying at the lower price. The chances of discovery would be least if the new customer was in a separate market from the others, e.g. in a different country. However, although the decision is by no means straightforward, incremental analysis could clearly help the firm to reach a decision.

Note that if the order was accepted, the transaction would be represented by a point off the usual supply curve. Departures from the supply curve, orders at prices below normal, are most likely to occur when demand is lower than expected. Indeed when demand is very depressed, it may not be possible to make *any* sales at the normal price; the price for each order may be the result of a separate bargain between buyer and seller. In these circumstances the concepts of the normal price and the supply curve become meaningless.

The contribution margin

The contribution margin (or, more simply, the contribution) is defined as revenue minus variable cost. It is therefore very similar to incremental profit, as defined in the previous section.

We have shown how the concept of the contribution margin can be applied when a firm has to make a decision concerning part of its output. However, as noted in Chapter 18, the contribution approach to pricing can be applied to the firm's entire output. The fundamental principle is again that the firm should compare revenue with variable cost. Total contribution is maximised when there is the greatest difference between total revenue and total variable cost. (You will find that this approach can be used in assignment 25.8.)

Escapable cost

In contrast to the previous two types, escapable cost is the reduction in cost which would follow from a reduction in output. Its significance can also be illustrated by reference to Fig. 25.2. This time we start by assuming that the firm is selling N units per period, OM at price P_N and MN at price P_L. If the firm has to decide whether to continue to take orders at the lower price, it should compare the revenue that it would lose with the saving in cost, i.e. with the escapable cost. These two magnitudes are, of course, $MRSN$ and $MTVN$.

Sunk cost

A sunk cost is a cost that has already been incurred and therefore is not affected by a change in output. This is clearly a very similar concept to fixed cost. However, whereas a sunk cost implies that the firm incurs no current cash expenditure, some fixed costs do involve current expenditure, e.g. payments for rates and rent.

Depreciation: an imputed cost

When capital equipment is purchased, the firm hopes to recover its cost over a number of years – say five or ten – and for this purpose it includes in its cost for each of these years a depreciation charge. Once the equipment has been bought its cost becomes sunk, and the depreciation charge is an imputed cost, not involving current expenditure.

Opportunity cost

All the types of cost considered so far can be derived from the accounting data of the organisation. Opportunity cost is different in that it is not strictly an accounting cost at all. It is defined as the most profitable alternative use of the firm's assets.

Sometimes opportunity cost can be measured with a fair degree of accuracy, for example if the alternative to buying a machine is buying fixed interest securities (other examples were given in Chapter 18). In other instances measurement, or rather estimation, is more speculative. For example, in the situation represented in Fig. 25.2 the opportunity cost of utilising capacity to make items for sale at price P_L might turn out to be a revenue of $MN(P_N)$. On the other hand if no alternative customers appear the opportunity cost would be zero.

Geographical location and cost

The geographical location of an organisation, and especially of production units, influences cost in two broad ways. First, it affects the availability and cost of resources or inputs. Second, it affects the cost of access to markets.

The availability and cost of resources

In some instances the availability of a particular resource is so important that some locations are ruled out. Coal mining must take place where there are coal seams, shipbuilding where there is sufficient water to float off the completed vessel. In other instances the absence of a particular resource could be overcome, but at so high a cost as to leave the location economically unviable. For example, in the UK all major petro-chemical plants are located near to where imported supplies of oil are landed. It would be technically feasible to pump sufficient oil to an inland location, but the cost would be prohibitive.

Raw materials

In the above examples the number of economically feasible locations is strictly limited. In the majority of instances the organisation has a wider choice; however the availability and cost of resources are still important.

The availability of raw materials is especially important when they have a high weight/value ratio, since the higher this ratio the higher is the relative cost of transporting the materials. This helps to explain why the producers of pottery, bricks and tiles are normally located close to deposits of clay.

Labour

If the production process involves a large number of jobs requiring simple, repetitive operations the organisation may be most concerned with the total size of the local labour force. If, on the other hand, it involves skilled jobs, the availability of workers with these skills is more important. Even if an employer is able to persuade such workers to move to the area to join him, there is no guarantee that they will stay with him. (As noted in the previous chapter, this is the vital difference between labour and other inputs where purchase implies ownership.)

Given an adequate number of workers – either skilled, semi-skilled or unskilled – in the area, costs are determined by two factors, wage rates and productivity.

Wage rates tend to differ from one part of the country to another because of differences in the balance between demand and supply in the labour market. However, bargaining by trade unions has led to a diminishing of the differentials where the union is able to centrally negotiate wage rates for all the plants of an organisation. When Ford and Vauxhall established car assembly plants on Merseyside, the unions secured agreements that although the wage rates would initially be lower than in the 'parent' plants, these differentials would be phased out over the first few years of operation.

Differences in productivity may be due to either individual or group influences. Workers are more adept at some operations than others. For example, one of the factors which persuaded a number of engineering firms to establish plants on Merseyside in the post-war period was the fact that there was a pool of unemployed skilled engineering workers, who had previously been employed in heavy engineering or shipbuilding. However it was found that some (although by no means all) of these workers had difficulty in adapting to the different techniques required in light engineering.

Sometimes low productivity may be due more to the general attitudes of the workers towards factory operations than to a lack of skill. American employers, who were attracted to Puerto Rico by the low wage rates, found that many of the workers were unable to adapt to the disciplines of factory employment. Productivity was so low that overall labour costs were often higher than in the USA.

Productivity may also be affected by union restrictions. There has been a tendency for new textile plants to be established away from the traditional textile manufacturing areas to avoid restrictions on the introduction of more efficient methods, e.g. lower manning schedules. On the other hand, some engineering employers have found that the response of unions towards, for example, the use of semi-skilled workers in skilled jobs, has been more flexible in the traditional engineering areas such as the West Midlands than in some of the areas in which plants have more recently been established. Perhaps the differences in attitude in these two situations is due to the fact that the traditional textile areas have suffered much heavier unemployment than the traditional engineering areas, leading to a greater emphasis on job protection.

Energy

The importance of the availability of sources of energy in a particular location has gradually diminished over time. In the past, industry clustered around sources of energy – at first river valleys and later coalfields. However the development of national distribution networks for electricity, gas and oil has allowed a wider dispersion of industry. There are still some regional differences in the price of energy, but these are of minor importance.

Inherent and acquired advantages

Some regions have inherent advantages, e.g. supplies of raw materials and energy, a good harbour, a naturally skilful and adaptable labour force, and these inherent advantages are a powerful influence on the location of organisations in the early years of industrialisation. But over time these inherent advantages tend to become relatively less important and acquired advantages more important.

Acquired advantages include a pool of trained and experienced labour, educational facilities geared to the needs of local industry, a well developed infrastructure (transport, water, waste disposal systems, etc.), and a network of suppliers of components, maintenance services, financial services, etc.

The inherent advantages that initially attract industry to an area may be supplemented by the acquired advantages which subsequently arise. Consequently, even if the inherent advantages eventually disappear, e.g. if the supplies of raw materials become exhausted, the area may, by virtue of its acquired advantages, remain the lowest cost location for certain industries. A good example is the Sheffield area which has continued as the centre of the UK cutlery industry, mainly because of its skilled labour force and despite the exhaustion of the deposits of iron-ore and limestone.

External economies

Both the inherent and the acquired advantages of a region arise outside of the individual firm and benefit more than one firm. For this reason they are known as external economies (of scale), in contrast to the internal economies discussed in the previous chapter.

Access to markets

As with the availability of inputs, good access to markets is far more important in some industries than others. Several factors make location close to the market especially important. A high weight/volume ratio for the finished product means that greater savings in transport costs result from location near to the market.

For some products, such as bread, the need to deliver fresh goods on a daily basis makes location close to the market desirable. Since the market comprises individual consumers the distribution of bakeries mirrors the distribution of the total population.

In other instances quick delivery is required to highly specialised markets. For example, some heat-treatment operations are used only in the metal goods industries. Since the producers of the final product often expect the metal to be treated and returned very quickly (two or three days at the most) it is not surprising to find the heat-treatment specialists located very close to the metal goods producers.

The main markets for many financial and business services are the major cities, since they house the senior personnel who use such services. Since frequent contact between supplier and user is desirable, we find that most of the head offices of the major banks, accountancy firms, business consultants, etc., are also located in the major cities.

The ideal location

The ideal location is one at which the costs of both acquiring resources and of gaining access to the market are minimised. However in many instances this ideal cannot be attained. There is frequently a trade-off between these two sets of costs, and the organisation has to decide where the balance of advantage lies. The answer to this question will, of course, differ from one organisation to another, depending upon the type of products made, the type of workers employed and so forth.

The quantification of cost differentials

It is virtually impossible to put a precise figure on the differences in costs between alternative locations. Even though an organisation may know that productivity in one location is higher than in another it is extremely difficult to decide to what extent this is due to locational factors, e.g. nearness to suppliers, and to what extent to other factors, such as differences in the age and efficiency of machinery.

Most studies of location decisions have concluded that cost differentials are on the whole relatively small – not more than 2 per cent of total costs. However there may be a considerable dispersion around this average. On the one hand there are 'footloose' industries in which costs are unaffected by location. On the other hand there are industries in which some locations are perceived by organisations as having clear advantages over others, even if they cannot precisely quantify these advantages. There has been a marked tendency for industry to become concentrated in a 'corridor' running from the Midlands down through to South East England, at the expense of the peripheral areas (Scotland, Wales, Northern Ireland, and North and South West England). Since this tendency implies that employment opportunities are much greater in the corridor than in the peripheral areas, governments have intervened in order to try to correct, or at least moderate, this development.

Table 25.1 Incentives available to industry in the assisted areas

Regional development grants:	SDA	22 per cent DA 15 per cent
Loans	AA	On favourable terms for capital expenditure on projects providing additional employment.
Removal grants	AA	Grants of up to 80 per cent of certain costs incurred in moving an undertaking
Service industry removal assistance	AA	£800 for each employee moving his/her work
Government factories for sale or rent	SDA ⎱ DA ⎰	Two-year rent-free period if sufficient employment created
Help for transferred workers	AA	Free fares, lodging allowances and help with removal expenses

N.B. Where a given type and rate of assistance is available in all the assisted areas, this is denoted by 'AA'. Where assistance differs between the areas, the rate applying in the Special Development Areas is denoted by 'SDA', the rate (if any) in the Development Areas by 'DA'.

Government intervention

Government intervention has taken two forms, controls on development and the provision of incentives.

The basic weapon of control has been the Industrial Development Certificate, which is required for industrial developments above a certain size – at present 5,000 sq. ft. (465 sq. m.) in the South East Economic Planning Region, 10,000 sq. ft. (929 sq. m.) in other non-assisted areas, and 15,000 sq. ft. (1,394 sq. m.) in Intermediate Areas. It has always been easier for firms to obtain an IDC in areas of high than of low unemployment, and since 1972 IDCs have no longer been required in Development and Special Development Areas. Since 1965 a comparable form of control has existed on office building. Office Development Permits are now required in the South East and the Midlands.

Various types of financial assistance are available, as shown in Table 25.1. The amount of assistance provided has varied from year to year, but was running at over £600 m. a year in the mid 1970s.

Summary and conclusions

We have shown that in most instances market supply curves can be derived from the cost curves of suppliers, with the profit margin being the link between the two. In some instances, however, the link between cost curves and supply curves is more tenuous. Indeed there are certain situations in which the concept of a supply curve ceases to be meaningful. We also examined several additional types of cost which have relevance to particular decisions. Finally we discussed the importance of costs in the location decisions of organisations.

This concludes our present discussion of the economic aspects of the acquisition and use of resources.

Assignments

25.1

Explain why, although a market supply curve might have an upward sloping portion, it would be unlikely to slope up throughout its length.

25.2

This exercise relates to the following cost concepts: incremental cost, escapable cost, sunk cost, opportunity cost, depreciation. Indicate which of these concepts applies most closely to each of the following situations:

1. A firm increases its level of output.
2. A firm reduces its product range by stopping the production of two of its products.
3. A firm draws money previously on deposit at a bank in order to purchase raw materials.
4. The initial cost of a machine is spread over a number of years.
5. A firm withdraws money previously on deposit at a bank in order to purchase raw materials.

25.3

Make an inventory of the resources of the area in which you live, identifying the major raw materials, the main skills of the labour force and any indigenous forms of energy. Show how the availability of these resources has influenced the industrial structure of the area.

25.4

1. List the main economic resources of the area in which you live, distinguishing between inherent and acquired advantages.
2. Compare these resources with those in any other area with which you are familiar. (Alternatively, compare the resources of two towns or cities in your own area.)

25.5

Make a list of any firms that have recently moved into your area and outline the major reasons that led them to locate there.

25.6

Make a list of the major markets for industrial products (components, raw materials, etc.) in your area and of the areas from which these markets are supplied.

25.7

The Furness Engineering Co buys a machine which can grind aluminium and so enable a component to be made which has the advantage of being lighter than components made from steel. The machine costs £200,000 and the company plans to depreciate this over a period of five years. The company hopes to produce 15,000 units in a year of fifty working weeks and for the first three months it employs three men, each of whom produces 100 units a week and is paid a weekly wage of £60. Then an increase in the rate of orders leads the firm to recruit a fourth worker who is paid the same wage as the existing workers and who also produces 100 units a week. (The machine has a fourth grinding head that was previously not used.) However, customers then begin to cancel orders, reporting that the component proved to be too weak. After investigating these reports the company concluded that the fault could not be remedied and it closed down the production line. It dismissed the workers and was able to sell the machine for scrap. However the amount of money received was only just enough to cover the cost of removing and transporting the machine.

Assuming that no other costs were incurred, answer the following questions:

1. Had production been at the rate initially planned, what would have been the depreciation charge per unit produced?
2. What was the sunk cost incurred in starting production of the component?
3. What was the incremental cost of increasing output from 300 to 400 units a week?
4. What was the opportunity cost of increasing output from 300 to 400 units a week?
5. What was the escapable cost of ceasing production?

25.8

The Dove Rubber Company Ltd manufactures a wide range of industrial rubber and plastic products. In order to try to compensate for a decline in the sales of

251

some of its traditional products, it established a toy division whose first product was a toy for young children, the Bouncing Donkey. It set an initial price to wholesalers of £6, which it hoped would yield a satisfactory profit. Unfortunately sales were much less than anticipated and the first year's accounts revealed a loss of £5,000, as shown in Table 25.2.

Table 25.2 Extract from accounts of Dove Rubber Co Ltd

	Costs	
	Total	Per unit
	£	£ p
Labour	3,000	1.50
Materials	2,000	1.00
Selling and distribution	6,000	3.00
Depreciation	6,000	3.00
	17,000	8.50
	Revenue	
Sales: 2,000 units	12,000	6.00

Faced with such a disappointing start to the new venture the managing director of the company called in a firm of consultants to advise him as to whether they should continue to produce the Bouncing Donkey and, if so, what change in policy should be made in order to improve the division's financial performance.

The consultants began by conducting some market research. They concluded that the main obstacle to a major increase in sales was a competitive product which, although of poorer quality than the Bouncing Donkey, sold to wholesalers at £5. Their research suggested that if the price of the Donkey could be reduced to match this competitor's price, annual sales of 20,000 could be expected. If price was reduced to £5.50 annual sales of 8,000 were expected. If price was maintained at £6.00 it was unlikely that annual sales would exceed 2,500.

The consultants also obtained information about the likely behaviour of costs, from the people responsible for each cost centre.

The production director believed that the existing labour force was underemployed, and that an extra 500 units a year could be produced with no increase in total labour costs. However, if output was to be increased beyond this point additional workers would be required, and in view of the uncertainty concerning the quality of the new labour and the likelihood that training costs would be incurred, he thought that it would be prudent to assume that labour costs per unit would be the same as at present (i.e. at an output of 2,000 units).

The production director also pointed out that the existing plant and equipment was sufficient for an annual output of 20,000 units, and that the total depreciation charge would, therefore, be unchanged up to that point. Moreover there was no point in considering higher levels of output since the Board had decided that no further expansion would be undertaken in the forseeable future.

The chief purchasing officer thought that he would be able to obtain a reduction, in the form of a quantity discount, of 5 per cent of present prices, with an annual output of 5,000 units and above.

The marketing director thought that the existing rudimentary selling and distribution facilities would be able to handle sales of up to 10,000 units a year, but that higher levels would require these facilities to be duplicated, with a doubling in their total costs.

Write a report incorporating the consultants' findings. Since the managing director is a very busy man, having responsibility for many other products, your report should be easy to assimilate, and should contain clear recommendations for future policy.

25.9

Precision Instruments Ltd, a manufacturer of mini-computers, received an order from an overseas country. Until now Precision had confined its activities to the domestic market, with a normal rate of production of 250 units a month at a total cost of £30,000. These computers were sold through a limited number of dealers at a price of £150.

The overseas company offered to buy 600 computers over a six-month period at a price of £100. If Precision increased its output to the maximum level of 350 units a month, its total monthly cost would increase to £38,500. Do you think that Precision should agree to supply the overseas customer? (Your answer should make clear which factors you took into account.)

26 Resources of the organisation: finance

Introduction

As we saw in Chapter 24, every organisation needs finance to carry on its business. It must have enough to acquire premises, machinery, raw materials and so forth. Many well-established organisations can meet their financial requirements from their business activities, as we show below. However this *internal* finance is usually supplemented by *external* finance. This is either because the internal sources are inadequate or because external sources are less expensive. (The 'cost' of internal finance is an opportunity cost; this point is also discussed below.)

The organisation is likely to need external finance most when its business is growing rapidly, since there is a gap between the time when materials are bought and the sale of the resulting products.

There are legal aspects to the various sources of finance as well as economic ones for each source or form of raising finance brings different responsibilities or liabilities. We will discuss the relative importance of the various sources in recent years, and the situation in which an organisation's debts exceed its profits.

The economic aspects: internal finance

The two major internal sources of finance are depreciation allowances and undistributed profits.

Depreciation allowances relate to the cost of assests, such as plant and equipment. Although these assets usually have to be paid for at the time of purchase, it is conventional, in the accounts, to spread it out over a number of years. For example, if a firm bought a machine for £1,000,000 which it expected would have a useful life of (at least) five years, it might make a depreciation charge or allowance of £200,000 for each of these years. (This is the 'straight-line' method of depreciation, probably the method used most frequently.)

The principle underlying this procedure is that an organisation should recover the cost of its assets during their life, so that they can be replaced when they wear out. In fact if the price of machines increases, depreciation allowances related to the previous cost will not be sufficient to allow the purchase of new machines. To avoid this danger, organisations may gear their depreciation allowances to the expected replacement costs.

Undistributed profits, as the term suggests, are profits that remain after all costs and charges have been met and that are retained within the business instead of being distributed to shareholders. Profits are normally retained in order to finance the expansion of the business, although they may be partly used to supplement depreciation allowances if these prove to be inadequate.

Additional internal finance may also be generated by the sale of the organisation's assets. For example, in 1978 it was announced that Ruddle's, the family-owned brewing concern, was to sell its thirty-eight pubs. The sale was expected to yield about £1 m., and it was planned to use the receipts to improve the company's production plant. The company had insufficient capacity to meet the increasing demand for its 'real ale', and the loss of sales through its own pubs would be compensated by increased sales to other customers.

It was also announced in 1978 that Barclays Bank was to close 130 branches and reduce the size of a further 480. The money saved would be used for opening new branches in more suitable locations and enlarging other branches.

The economic aspects: external finance

There is a distinction, from an economic viewpoint, between temporary and permanent forms of finance.

Temporary finance

The most important type of temporary finance is the loan. Loans, which are of various forms (described in more detail below), may be obtained from banks and other financial institutions, from non-financial organisations or from individuals. The length of the loan may vary from a few hours (e.g. money loaned 'overnight' in specialist money markets), to several months (e.g. a bank loan made for six or twelve months) or to many years (e.g. debentures issued on the Stock Exchange).

Other types of temporary finance include trade credit and hire-purchase facilities. The renting and leasing of machinery etc., is equivalent, in some respects, to a loan, although the machinery may not, of course, become the property of the organisation.

Permanent finance

The types of permanent finance available depend upon the organisation's legal form.

Sole traders and partnerships

As we saw in Chapter 3, there is no legal separation of ownership and control in a business operated by traders and partnerships. The business is treated as

255

belonging directly to the individuals concerned. The partners or the sole trader will often supply capital to be used by the firm. The sole trader may work from his own home and he may use his own personal assets, such as a car for the purposes of his business. Partners often contribute large capital sums to the setting up or expansion of the firm that they belong to. Indeed it will sometimes be made a condition of entry into a partnership that the incoming partner contributes a certain amount of capital.

Registered companies

When companies are formed, as we have seen, it must be specified how many shares each shareholder takes and what the nominal value of the shares is. For example, a company may begin with a nominal share capital of £10,000 issued in £1 shares. There may, in the case of a private company, be only two shareholders. One may buy one share for £1, and the other 999 shares at £1 each. These he may pay for in cash, or, as will often be the case, he may transfer to the company a capital asset such as premises, plant or stock-in-trade, perhaps a vehicle or machinery.

The number of shareholders in a private company is restricted by law to a maximum of fifty not including employee and ex-employee members. This tends to limit the amount of permanent capital that can be raised by those companies. No restriction is placed on the number of shareholders in public companies. Furthermore public companies can apply for a Stock Exchange quotation and many do. This creates a much wider market for their shares and hence makes them more attractive to investors. (The function of the Stock Exchange is discussed in detail below.)

Not all shares in a company are of equal standing. They are often classified into *ordinary* and *preference* shares. Preference shares, as the term indicates, give the holder preferential rights to dividends. They may confer a cumulative right to dividends. This means that if in one year a dividend is not declared the preference shareholders' rights from that year are carried forward and must be satisfied before anything can be paid to the ordinary shareholders in future years. They may also confer priority in the repayment of capital on a winding up. The implications of this can be illustrated by a simple example.

Let us assume that a company has issued 10,000 10 per cent preference shares, and 50,000 ordinary shares, both types of share having been issued at £1. The preference shareholders would be entitled to an annual dividend of £1,000 (10 per cent of £10,000). If in one year the total amount available for distribution as dividends was £6,000, there would be £5,000 left over for the ordinary shareholders. This would represent a 10 per cent return on their investment. If profits increased and £11,000 was available for distribution the preference shareholders would still receive £1,000 (10 per cent of the issued share price), but ordinary shareholders would now have £10,000 available, which represents 20 per cent return on investment. If, however, profits then slumped and only £1,000 was available for distribution, this would all go to the preference shareholders, the ordinary shareholders receiving nothing.

Public corporations

Public corporations do not have permanent finance in the sense that we have used the term; that is, they have neither a share capital nor shareholders.

However the financial backing that they receive from the Treasury fulfils a similar function to share capital. Most of this finance is, technically, temporary (long-term loans).

Governments have sometimes been willing to reduce the burden of this long-term capital. During the period 1963–74 over £2,700 m. of capital debt was written off for the nine major public corporations – only the electricity and gas industries failed to benefit. This cancellation of debt resulted in substantial reductions in interest payments. (This reduction in capital debt should not be confused with the government subsidies that have been received from time to time by various public corporations.) Government policy towards the public corporations is discussed at greater length in Volume 2.

The Stock Exchange

As we said above, one of the benefits enjoyed by public companies (as opposed to private companies) is that they can apply for a Stock Exchange quotation which widens the market for the securities (shares and debentures) that they issue. The actual markets are made by stock jobbers who hope to make profits by selling at prices above those at which they buy. Since buying and selling orders (from stockbrokers, acting on behalf of investors) seldom coincide, and since prices may fluctuate from hour to hour, the jobber's trade is inherently risky, and his profit is mainly a reward for risk-taking.

New issues

An issue of new securities for subsequent trade on the Stock Exchange may take one of several forms:

Public issue by prospectus. The company offers, directly to the public, a fixed number of shares (or debentures) at a stated price. A prospectus must be published, setting out the nature of the company's business and giving details of its past turnover and profits.

Offer for sale. This is similar to the public issue, but the company sells the shares to an issuing house (usually a merchant bank) which in turn offers them to the general public.

Placing. The shares are again acquired by an issuing house, but instead of being offered in the first instance to the general public, they are placed with clients of the issuing house and with jobbers. When the shares are subsequently traded on the Stock Exchange, the general public is then able to buy.

Offer for sale by tender. This method is used when investors' attitudes are very volatile, making it difficult to judge which price would be likely to equate demand with supply. The stated price is the minimum at which a tender will be accepted. If investors believe that the shares are worth more than this minimum, they will put in higher bids in order to try to ensure an allocation of shares.

Rights issue. This is confined to existing shareholders, who are offered additional shares in proportion to their existing holdings. The shares are issued at a price below the existing shares, and this might be seen as a reward to shareholders.

Rights issues should not be confused with bonus or scrip issues which do *not* raise new money. Here the new shares are issued free to existing shareholders, but the increase in the number of shares issued causes the market price to be adjusted downwards.

257

The investors

In many companies the largest shareholders are now institutions – pension funds, investment trusts, unit trusts, etc. The proportion of the total value of shares held by the personal sector (individuals, executors and trustees) is less than 40 per cent, having steadily declined during the post-war period a trend that has caused concern to some observers.

Concern has also been expressed about the possibility that small and medium-sized firms may not be able to acquire sufficient capital to finance their growth. (We showed in Chapter 24 that large firms may enjoy financial economies of scale.)

The first official recognition of this problem was the establishment of the Macmillan Committee on Finance and Industry, which reported in 1931. A group of institutions intended to meet the needs of these smaller companies was set up soon after the Committee reported. But their resources were very modest, and in 1945 the clearing banks, with the support of the Bank of England, established the Industrial and Commercial Finance Corporation.

ICFC had initial resources of £45 m., with a remit to provide long-term loans and subscribe equity capital within the range £5,000 to £200,000. In 1959 the Radcliffe Committee identified a need for additional finance to facilitate the commercial exploitation of technical innovations. To meet this need ICFC established a subsidiary, Technical Development Capital Ltd.

These and other institutions have continued to expand their scale of operations, and in 1975 ICFC, along with the Finance Corporation for Industry, which supplied finance to large companies, became a subsidiary of Finance for Industry. FFI, whose shareholders are the clearing banks (85 per cent) and the Bank of England (15 per cent), has access to funds of £1,000 m., intended mainly for medium-term lending.

Equity Capital for Industry was established in 1976 with a capital of £50 m., provided by institutional investors. As suggested by the name of the institution, these funds are intended as a source of permanent finance.

In its first year of operation the government-sponsored National Enterprise Board, established by the Industry Act 1975, acquired assets in more than a dozen small companies, its smallest investment costing only £50,000, and it announced its intention of increasing the number of such companies to around seventy within the following twelve months.

However the NEB was established primarily as a vehicle through which the State could acquire a stake in large public companies. (It also took over assets that the State had acquired under the provisions of previous Acts, including British Leyland Ltd and Rolls Royce (1971) Ltd.) In December 1978, when introducing a Bill in Parliament to raise the Board's borrowing limit from £1 b. to £4.5 b., Mr Varley, the Industry Secretary, described the NEB as 'an indispensable part of Britain's industrial scene' and a 'holding company of major proportions'.

The relative importance of the various sources of finance

It is impossible to obtain comprehensive information about the relative importance of the various sources of finance. However certain broad conclusions can be drawn.

1. Internal sources have been considerably more important than external sources, accounting for more than two thirds of the funds from all sources.

2. The principal components of external funds have been long-term loans and bank borrowing, each accounting for more than 10 per cent of total funds from all sources.

3. Cash issues of ordinary shares are not a very important source of finance in terms of size. Even for large public companies with shares listed on the Stock Exchange they account for less than 5 per cent of total funds. However, new issues of ordinary shares (equity) have an importance greater than indicated by the amount of money raised. There are limits to the amount of money that a company can raise by borrowing, especially important being the company's *gearing*, that is the ratio of loan capital to equity. Issuing shares lowers this ratio and so facilitates the issue of more debt capital in the future.

4. The State has tended to become a more important source of finance for private sector firms. Assistance is given partly via institutions such as the National Enterprise Board and partly directly to firms, especially as part of the Government's regional and manpower policies.

The amounts of money raised by the various forms of finance depend upon the requirements both of those seeking and those supplying finance. These requirements relate partly to the return on each form – the rate of interest on loans and preference shares and the prospective dividends on ordinary shares – and partly upon the rights and obligations attached to each form. These rights and obligations are in the main laid down by law, and so we now turn to consider the legal aspects of raising finance.

The legal aspects

In this section we examine from a different viewpoint the major forms of finance. We discuss them in the same order as in the previous section: temporary finance (loans) first; permanent finance (shares) second.

Temporary finance

Unsecured loans

This is the term given to a simple loan of money. There will generally be a contract between the debtor (or borrower) and the creditor (or lender) under which the creditor provides finance for the debtor's use and the debtor agrees to repay the amount lent with or without interest.

The period of the loan and the rate of interest charged are for the parties to determine, although we should bear in mind the power of the court to reopen extortionate credit bargains under the Consumer Credit Act 1974 if the loan is one covered by the Act. Bank loans and bank overdrafts take this form, as well as the informal type of loan that may be given by individuals who want to supply finance for the use of an organisation.

As such a loan takes the form of a personal promise to repay, the creditor must clearly be satisfied that the debtor will be able to repay on the due date. Should the debtor fail to meet these obligations, the creditor's only recourse is to sue for the amount due. To provide an additional remedy, the creditor may insist on someone else, whose financial stability he can be sure of, guaranteeing the loan.

A guarantee has the effect of a contract to pay the amount owed by the debtor if the debtor defaults. As a safeguard against fraud, contracts of guarantee must be in writing and signed by the guarantor. The advantage to the creditor is that he can exercise his contractual right to the money against the debtor or against the guarantor if the debtor defaults.

Often private companies can only obtain loans if the directors are willing to provide personal guarantees and thus forego the privilege of their own limited liability.

Secured loans

A creditor may only be willing to lend finance to an organisation if he has some security for the loan. The advantage in taking security for a debt is that the creditor can exercise certain rights over the property used by the debtor as security if the debtor himself is unable to pay.

A debtor frequently has substantial assets in the form of a house or business premises which he owns outright. These may represent large amounts of capital. If the creditor and debtor agree, the debtor may hand over to the creditor the title deeds of the property for the duration of the loan, agreeing that the creditor will be able to exercise rights over the property, for example by selling the property, if the debt remains unpaid. This is commonly known as creating a 'charge' over the property and is one form of mortgage. Mortgages may also be created by deed, that is by a document under seal, rather than by depositing title deeds with the creditor. Whichever form is chosen, the creditor has the advantage of being able to look to the debtor's property for repayment of the loan.

Secured loans represent a valuable protection for the creditor, but as they are attended with more formalities than a simple unsecured loan they are more suited to loans of large amounts or over long periods.

Loans to partnerships

As we noted above, partners provide permanent capital to the partnership in agreed amounts. Further advances, over and above the agreed capital contribution made by the partners, are treated as loans to the firm in law, even though the firm has no separate legal existence. One of the consequences of this is that the Partnership Act provides that a partner will be entitled to interest at 5 per cent p.a. on the amount of the advance. The partners are free to vary this amount in their partnership agreement or even to provide that no interest shall be payable. Supplying a loan also gives a partner a prior claim to assets of the firm on a dissolution.

As we have seen, becoming a partner subjects an individual to certain liabilities. Although he will enter the partnership hoping that it will make profits he must accept that he will also have to bear an equal share of any losses. Often, however, an individual will be prepared to supply finance to a partnership on the condition that he does not run the same risks of bearing partnership losses as the partners. If such a loan is made, the individual may still find himself treated as a partner, with all the consequences, even though he had no such intention. Although it is provided by S. 2 of the Partnership Act 1890 that the advance of money by way of loan, with an agreement that the lender shall receive interest at a rate which varies with profits, does not of itself make the lender a partner, he runs this risk if the true nature of the agreement *is* that of a partnership, regardless of whether he is described merely as a creditor.

Debentures

A debenture is the name given to certain types of document issued by companies which indicate a debt, usually secured by a charge on property. The debenture-holder's rights are first of all the repayment of a sum lent and secondly the right to enforce that charge against the property of the company.

To explain this, it is necessary to look at another way of using personal property as security for a debt. In the same way that land may be used as security for a loan by the grant of a mortgage, which we have already considered, movable property such as machinery, equipment, may also be used as security. As with mortgages, the lender has a right not only to enforce the personal promise to repay, but also to force a sale of the property.

The difficulty in creating mortgages of personal property is that under the Bills of Sale Acts, every mortgage of personal property must be made in writing, specifying the property affected. The bill must be registered and no dealing can take place with the asset without the lender's consent. This clearly presents problems for a business with assets in the form of machinery and equipment: to create a mortgage of the property that would be governed by the Bills of Sale Acts would prevent day-to-day dealing with the assets without a good deal of time and trouble.

The advantage that the registered company has in this area (as opposed to the partnership or sole trader) is that it has long been established that a company may create a charge by way of debenture that will take effect, not as a fixed charge or mortgage relating to specific assets, but as a general floating charge over all the company's assets as they are acquired from time to time. This is desirable from all points of view. The company can borrow money on the security of its assets without the hindrance of complying with the Bills of Sale Acts; the lender knows that he has security for the amount of money he lends which can ultimately be enforced against the company's property.

The debenture-holder is therefore a supplier of finance to a company in the same way as other secured creditors. Normally, however, the debenture-holder has other rights which are very like those of a shareholder, even though he is not a member of the company as such. He may, for instance, be given a special right to attend meetings. He will negotiate special terms which entitle him to a fixed rate of interest in the same way that preference shareholders have priority in the payment of dividends. His position is, in some ways, better than that of a shareholder, for he ranks as a creditor, and therefore is first in the order of persons to be paid.

Whilst the company is doing well, the debenture-holder has no rights in law to reclaim the money he has lent, but if the company goes into liquidation, his floating charge is said to crystallise. That is, it becomes a fixed charge on the assest owned by the company and he can require these assets to be sold to repay him the amount owed. The debenture-holder, in authorising the company to deal in the meantime with its assets, runs the risk, however, that the company will trade so unsuccessfully as to dissipate *all* its assets, leaving nothing with which to repay the debenture-holders.

Debenture-holders therefore have considerable advantages over other creditors and investors in a company. To protect the latter, it is provided that certain debentures must be registered on the company's file at the Companies Registry. As this is open to public inspection, it enables a lender to discover what the company's present indebtedness is before he advances the money.

Permanent finance: shares

As we have seen, the limited company is a separate legal entity. Its existence is recognised by the law as being independent from the persons who own and regulate the company. Because the shareholders provide capital for the company, and yet are separate from it, the registered company has considerable obligations towards them. (In many ways shareholders and other creditors of a registered company are in a similar position, and many of the controls imposed on the company are designed to protect both classes.)

The share capital that is raised by the company can be seen as a fund which could be divided up between the shareholders, after creditors had been paid, thus ensuring that each would get back the amount of capital that he had put into the company. Thus, in theory at least, the rules are designed to ensure that for every £1 share issued, the company should own assets of £1.

Hence if the company wants to raise more capital and decides to issue further shares, it can only do this if it has assets equal to the value of the new shares that it issues. The reality however does not often match the theory. It is self-evident that the capital contributed by shareholders is intended to be used by the company in its business and not merely to be retained to be paid back at a later date. As the company uses its capital to further its business it will make profits or losses, and these will increase or decrease the value of the company in real terms.

To take the worst example, a company with a £1,000 issued share capital may turn out to be such a disastrous venture that after only a few months its debts exceed its assets by £1,000. In this case the actual market value of the shares may well be nil, even though they each have a nominal (face) value of £1, as there will be no surplus of assets over debts to be distributed amongst the shareholders. The law is powerless to prevent this loss falling on the shareholders, and after all, this is the sort of risk that shareholders must envisage when they buy their shares.

Nevertheless there are rules that help to prevent more obvious abuses by the company. For example, the Companies Acts prevent a company from buying its own shares, or providing loans generally for the purchase of its own shares. The *ultra vires* doctrine that we examined in Chapter 3 prevents the company from expending money on matters unconnected with the stated objects of the company. Nor may dividends be made out of capital. They are, broadly speaking, to be paid out of profits.

Nature of the individual shareholder's interests

To say that a shareholder 'owns' a share in the company, or that the shareholders together own the whole company, gives us some idea of the nature of shareholding but does not exactly correspond with the shareholder's actual position. He cannot, for example, claim his share of the company's assets whilst the company is a going concern, as might be thought. His 'ownership' is on restricted terms. The major rights that he does have are, to participate in the profits according to the nature of his shareholding, to have his say in connection with the running of the company and to realise his share of the assets if and when the company is wound up. This last point we will look at shortly. We must first consider the other rights of the shareholder as a supplier of capital that must be observed by the company.

Participation in the profits

Few people would be willing to supply finance to an organisation without some interest being paid on their investment. In the case of the shareholder, this interest takes the form of dividends, which are sums paid out of profits.

A shareholder has no legal right to dividends. How much of the profits of the company is paid out to shareholders and how often depends on the provisions in the Articles of Association. Articles generally give the discretion to declare dividends to the directors, who announce the dividend at annual general meetings. Once a dividend is declared, it has the effect of a debt owed by the company to the shareholder.

Control over the running of the company

As we have seen the limited company is a very flexible legal unit. It is possible, by using this legal form, to cater for simple organisations such as the sole trader who wants to take advantage of limited liability and yet remain to all intents and purposes the absolute controller of how the business is run. This he can do by forming a limited liability company with himself as the majority shareholder and himself and, say, his wife as the directors. On the other hand, the limited company is equally adaptable to the needs of a large company, where there are several hundred shareholders and where the directors and other officers hold their positions by virtue of their special expertise rather than substantial shareholding. It should therefore be obvious that the degree of influence that a particular shareholder has on the running of the company will depend to a large degree on the nature of the company concerned.

It is nevertheless possible to isolate some of the basic rights that a shareholder has by virtue of his status and to consider how far any company must take these rights into account.

In the same way that shareholders have no legal right to dividends, they have no legal right to participate in policy decisions of the company. Nonetheless, the general practice is to confer on shareholders the right to vote at meetings of the company at which the major policy decisions will be taken. These rights will be found in the Articles of Association.

By statute, there is a minimum number of meetings that must be held by a company. The Annual General Meeting is the most important of these. At this meeting, the shareholders have an opportunity to question the actions of the Board of Directors and to vote on the composition of the board. Auditors must be appointed at the Annual General Meeting and generally this will be the occasion for the discussion of the annual reports, directors' reports, and accounts of the company.

Other meetings may be convened during the year, such as Extraordinary General Meetings, and to ensure that every shareholder has notice of intended meetings, and of certain resolutions to be proposed, there is a rigid procedure laid down for the calling of meetings, so that the shareholder may attend in person or arrange for his vote to be recorded.

Even in a small company, there are clearly potential sources of conflict between shareholders. There are consequently provisions that determine how far the majority in General Meeting of the company can override the wishes of a minority. Generally, the wishes of the majority will succeed, but certain alterations in how the company is run (for example, an alteration in the Articles of Association changing the voting rights of the shareholders) must be carried under special formalities designed to protect the minority. Certain resolutions, such as the one just mentioned, must be passed with a two-thirds majority.

Thus the company, which cannot, being an artificial legal entity, make personal decisions, and which makes its decisions in General Meeting, or by its Board of Directors exercising powers delegated by the General Meeting, or by the Articles or Memorandum, is subject to considerable control by the shareholders.

Where the majority are using their powers to perpetrate a fraud on the minority, the courts will intervene. The circumstances are limited and it is only in clear cases where, for example, the company's property is being expropriated, or where the action is clearly to the detriment of the company as a whole, that there will be any intervention.

Insolvency and its consequencies

We have examined the ways in which an organisation can raise finance, either from outside agencies or from the participants in the organisation. We must now consider the results of an organisation's failure to raise sufficient finance for its needs. If the organisation is not making sufficient income to pay its creditors, it may eventually be forced to cease business.

The decision may be a voluntary one of the organisation itself. Those involved may decide that it would be better to put an end to the business and distribute what assets remains amongst those entitled rather than to risk losing everything in trying to make an unprofitable business profitable.

Often, however, creditors of the organisation will instigate the action, with the aim of compelling the organisation to realise its assets and satisfy its debts so far as possible. We must bear these two possibilities in mind as we look at the ways in which an organisation can be brought to an end through insolvency, which is the failure to be able to meet financial liabilities as they occur.

There are two distinct consequences of insolvency: bankruptcy and liquidation. The law of bankruptcy relates only to individuals, and hence to those organisations run by sole traders and partnerships. Liquidation (or 'winding-up') is applicable only to registered companies who have a legal existence separate from those who own and control it. We will examine these in turn.

Bankruptcy

The law of bankruptcy is contained in the Bankruptcy Acts. The object of the legislation is to rescue an individual's assets for the benefit of his creditors and to ensure that the bankrupt cannot dissipate these assets once proceedings have been started to make him bankrupt.

The procedure that applies on a bankruptcy is broadly as follows. Bankruptcy proceedings can only be brought once the individual has committed an 'act of bankruptcy'. This may take several forms. It may be by the individual fraudulently transferring his property to another with the object of defrauding his creditors, or leaving the country with similar intent.

The widest category is that the debtor, or his creditors, file a declaration in the court of his inability to pay his debts. The debtor may also file a bankruptcy petition on his own behalf. Any creditor who is owed at least £200 may bring a petition.

Once an act of bankruptcy has been committed, the next step is that a bankruptcy petition is presented within three months to the court. This may be by the individual himself or by his creditors. The petition will ask for a receiving order to be made.

The receiving order must be advertised in the press by the petitioner. Its effect will be to appoint an Official Receiver and to place the individual's affairs under the control of the court via the receiver. From this moment, the individual, though not yet declared bankrupt, must account to the receiver for all dealings that he has with his property. The receiver must deal with any assets received for the benefit of the creditors. The receiver convenes a meeting of creditors to consider whether a scheme can be drawn up for the payment of creditors. Such a scheme needs the approval of the court. The debtor must present a statement of his affairs to see what assets are available for payment of his creditors, and the receiver fixes a time and place for public examination of these.

If at this stage the creditors are paid, or the court approves a scheme as being for the benefit of all the creditors, the proceedings will be discontinued. Failing this, the individual will be adjudicated bankrupt. (If it is the debtor himself who presents a petition for bankruptcy, he may immediately be adjudicated bankrupt.)

Adjudication of bankruptcy is done by court order. The effect of this is to vest the bankrupt's property in a trustee in bankruptcy. This will generally be the same person as the official receiver. He has control over the bankrupt's property which he will exercise for the benefit of the creditors.

As far as the creditors are concerned, they can look to the trustee in bankruptcy for the payment of what is owed to them. The trustee, who is an officer of the court and must therefore exercise his duties in the light of this duty, has power to sell the bankrupt's property and to sue for any debts owed to the bankrupt. He may carry on the bankrupt's business if this is necessary for the benefit of the creditors. He may also divide actual property up and distribute it amongst the creditors. The priority as between the creditors is laid down by statute. Rates and taxes must be paid first. Next come salaries and wages, then secured and unsecured creditors. Any creditor whose debt is secured has priority over unsecured debts.

From the bankrupt's point of view, the results of bankruptcy can be harsh. He loses control over his own property and stands to lose everything if his debts are large as compared with his assets. He incurs certain disqualifications from public office, such as standing as a local or parliamentary candidate, for five years from his ceasing to be bankrupt. Even more important for an individual who has been running a business is that he must disclose in the future that he is a bankrupt unless he trades in his own name. Neither may he obtain credit of more than £50 without disclosing his status.

A bankrupt may, after being adjudged bankrupt, apply to the court for an order of discharge. The court will take into account the official receiver's report as to the bankrupt's conduct of his affairs and may within its discretion order that he be discharged. The effect of this is that the bankrupt is released from the debts that were provable against him in his bankruptcy. He may then commence business contracting freely and obtaining credit without disclosing that he has been adjudicated bankrupt.

As we have seen, bankruptcy proceedings may be taken against sole traders or partnerships. As far as partnerships are concerned, bankruptcy may affect either the individual partner or the partnership. When an individual partner becomes bankrupt, his share of the partnership is treated as one of his assets, so that it can be brought under the control of the official receiver or be vested in his trustee in bankruptcy. It may be, however, that the partnership as a business unit becomes insolvent. In this case, proceedings may be brought against the partnership in the same way as they are brought against an individual. Where an action is brought against a partnership, the action will be brought against the partners in their own names.

Partnerships may be brought to an end in any of the ways specified in sections 32–34 of the Partnership Act 1890. We noted some of these ways in Chapter 3. Another way, that is particularly relevant here, is that a partnership can be dissolved by order of the court, on the application of a partner that it is just and equitable to order dissolution. Creditors of a partnership must be satisfied first, but after they have been paid, there may remain assets of the firm to be distributed. The Partnership Act lays down the order in which the surplus assets are distributed amongst the partners. Broadly speaking capital advances and contributions by partners are repaid and the remaining assets distributed in the same ratios as profits were divisible.

Liquidation

A company cannot die as an individual does. It can only cease to exist by being wound-up or by being struck off the Register. The most common way in which companies cease to exist in practice, even though they may still continue on the Register of Companies, is by liquidation following insolvency. (We use the terms 'liquidation' and 'winding-up' interchangeably.)

As with the bankruptcy of individuals, the liquidation may be instigated by the owners of the company or by its creditors. The procedure is largely the same in each case, though with certain modifications reflecting the needs of each. We will look at the procedure first as regards compulsory winding-up and secondly as regards voluntary winding-up.

Compulsory winding-up

Any of the company's shareholders, or any of its creditors, or the company itself,

266

may petition that the company be wound up. The grounds of petition are contained in s. 222 of the Companies Act 1948. The most common of these are that the company is unable to pay its debts and (a separate ground) that it is just and equitable that the company should be wound up.

The second ground requires some explanation. Petitioning that the company be wound up on the ground that it would be just and equitable to do so bears a strong resemblance to one of the grounds on which a partnership may be dissolved. Many small companies, with perhaps two or three directors who are also majority shareholders, are almost identical in practice to partnerships. Bearing this in mind, the courts have adopted the same attitude to winding-up on this ground as they would to a partnership. Thus, a dissolution will be granted if the shareholders are deadlocked, or if relations have so totally broken down between them that the carrying on of the business has become virtually impossible.

Following the petition to the court, a liquidator will be appointed by the court. He will be supervised by a committee of inspection set up by creditors and shareholders.

Voluntary winding-up

A company in its general meeting may pass a special resolution to the effect that it cannot continue its business and that the company should be wound up. If the directors state at the general meeting that they have formed the opinion that the company will be unable to pay its debts within a specified time, then after the resolution the liquidation follows the procedure of a voluntary (members') winding up, and the members have control of the appointment of a liquidator.

If at any time it becomes clear that the company will not be able to pay its debts, a meeting of creditors must be called and the liquidation proceeds as a creditors' voluntary winding up, with the creditors appointing the liquidator and, if necessary, a committee of inspection.

Subsequent procedure

The rules affecting the winding up of a company are extremely detailed, but a general outline is as follows.

Liquidator

The position of the liquidator is very like that of the Official Receiver following a petition of bankruptcy. He does not become the owner of the company's assets but he has control and management of them. He is under a fiduciary duty to control them both for the benefit of the company as a whole and also for the benefit of the creditors. He generally ousts the Board of Directors in the control of the company in a compulsory winding-up. In a voluntary winding-up, it may be agreed that the directors will continue to exercise their functions. This is particularly likely when it is a members' voluntary winding-up.

Control on officers of the company

There are various controls on the officers of companies once a winding-up has

267

commenced, because of their special position of control over the company's assets. If they abuse their position and dispose of the company's property in such a way as to defraud creditors, the directors may be made personally liable.

Other controls

In a compulsory liquidation, the liquidator is subject to the control of the court. In a voluntary liquidation the liquidator will be responsible to the creditors' committee of inspection if a creditors' winding-up, or to the committee of inspection of creditors and members in other voluntary liquidations.

Disposal of the assets

The assets of the company must be utilised for the benefit of the creditors and members of the company. There is an order of priority for payment comparable to that applying to bankruptcy. Thus rates and taxes must first be paid, then payment of wages and salaries, followed by the payment of secured debts (e.g. debentures) and then unsecured debts (e.g. ordinary shares).

Receivership

A receiver may be appointed at the instigation of the debentureholders if the terms of the debenture give such a power or if the debentureholders' position is in jeopardy. The primary task of a receiver is to safeguard, and if necessary realise, the company's assets that are charged by the debentureholders. He is often appointed manager of the company as well, which enables him to sell assets, sue for money owed and even to sell the company as a going concern. Appointing a receiver is a common preliminary to liquidation, though liquidation does not inevitably follow: the company may be able to continue to trade once the claims of the debenture-holders have been met.

Summary and conclusions

In this chapter we considered the various sources of finance available to different types of business organisation. We made a broad distinction between internal and external sources of finance, showing that overall the former is considerably more important than the latter.

Internal finance mainly comprises depreciation allowances and undistributed profits, although in some instances substantial sums can be generated internally by the sale of assets. External finance can be either temporary or permanent, each of these categories being capable of further sub-division.

We showed that the relative importance of the various forms of finance depends upon the requirements of both those seeking and those supplying finance. Those requirements relate to both the financial return on each form and the rights and obligations attached to each form. We examined these rights and obligations in considerable detail.

We concluded by looking briefly at the consequences of insolvency as they relate to sole traders, partners and registered companies.

It was clearly evident from earlier study that a firm must have sufficient finance to carry on its business. To examine how this money was obtained, and used, a three-pronged attack was suggested to consider:

The economic aspects	The legal aspects	The failure to match raising and spending objectives

1. *Internal finance* was based on
 	
 (a) depreciation allowances
 (b) undistributed profits
 (c) sale of assets
	Note the importance of:
	 Companies Acts (for registered companies).
	 Finance Acts (for tax and profit regulations).
		Insolvency – the failure to meet financial liabilities as they arise.
		 It has two direct consequences:
		 bankruptcy;
		 liquidation.
		
		 Bankruptcy:
		 (a) relates only to individuals or organisations run by individuals (e.g. sole traders and partnerships).
		 (b) The objectives of the Bankruptcy Act are to rescue an individual's assets for his creditors, when it appears insolvency is more than temporary.
		 (b) *Procedure* follows a given pattern:
		   (i) the act of bankruptcy;
		   (ii) petition to the court;
		   (iii) receiving order made and official receiver appointed;
		   (iv) on being judged bankrupt property passes to a Trustee in Bankruptcy to be administered.
		 (d) Effects of bankruptcy on the individual are harsh (p. 265).
		 Liquidation:
		 (a) relates to companies and takes the form of winding up of the company under the terms of the Companies Acts.

2. *External finance* based on the distinction between: (a) *Temporary finance* principally in the form of LOANS ⟶ (Trade credit and hire purchase finance come into the same category in practice.)	taking on various legal forms: (a) *Unsecured*, i.e. a personal promise to repay, and the lender must be satisfied this can be done; the only recourse is to sue for damages if anyone defaults. (b) *Secured*, i.e. lender only offers if there is security to repay the loan. (c) *To partnership*, i.e. an advance over and above capital but liability is *unlimited*. (d) *Debentures*, i.e. a loan to the company and chargeable against its property.	
(b) *Permanent finance* which varies according to the Legal Structure of the company: (i) Sole traders and partnerships ⟶	Money supplied by owners with no legal distinction between ownership and control.	

The economic aspects	The legal aspects	The failure to match raising and spending objectives
(ii) Registered companies Private } Public } shares (iii) Public corporations State loans ⟶ NOTE: looking at the problem from another angle there are different types of investors: (i) personal investors } (ii) institutional investors } (iii) private and semi-government bodies supporting investment in medium and small firms, e.g. FFI 1975 } NEB 1975 } ECI 1976 }	in the form of ordinary or preference shares and giving shareholders certain ownership rights, e.g. to participate in profits; to have a say in company affairs; to realise their share when the company is wound up. And balanced by company obligations not to: buy its own shares; pay individuals out of capital, etc. The importance of *new issues* (five types, p. 257). The equivalent of private industry share capital. ⟶ Covered by the Companies Act. ⟶ Covered by specific pieces of legislation.	(b) *Compulsory* winding up – becomes necessary when petitioned by the shareholders and/or creditors on any of the grounds listed under 1948 Act. Following the petition a liquidator is appointed. (c) *Voluntary* winding up. A members' winding up if the company can pay its debts and directors file a declaration of solvency. Otherwise it proceeds as creditors' winding up. (d) Important in the procedure of winding up are: (i) the role of the liquidator; (ii) the controls of officers of the company; (iii) the controls of the court; (iv) the disposal of assets.

Thus obtaining and using money is an important and complex part of the business operation but forms only one aspect of the way the firm uses its resources.

Assignments

26.1

List the various sources from which the firm might obtain finance in each of the situations below, and justify your choices in one or two sentences.

1. A retailer wishes to increase his stocks in anticipation of a buying spree at Christmas.
2. Joe Smith decides to leave his paid employment and set up in business on his own account making toys in his garage. He needs money to purchase tools and materials, and he would like to buy a van in which he could transport the toys to his customers.
3. The Brightside Engineering Co Ltd, a private company, has patented a new product which it estimates could lead to a doubling of its total sales within two years. This would require massive investment in plant and equipment.
4. Daniel Booth, a farmer, has recently bought some additional land, and it would now be worth his while to purchase a combine harvester. Unfortunately the purchase of the land took the last of his cash reserves.

26.2

Refer back to Assignment 3.1. Reconsider the sort of business unit that you would now recommend and explain, in the light of what you have read in the chapter how Mr Jones's interests could be safeguarded.

26.3

Compare and contrast the following:

(*a*) shares and debentures;
(*b*) ordinary shares and preference shares;
(*c*) internal finance and external finance;
(*d*) permanent finance and temporary finance.

26.4

John Brown has been running a joinery business for some years as a sole trader. He is also a local councillor, and because he has devoted so much time to council business his firm is now in severe financial difficulties. He has received a letter from one of his suppliers, who is owed £200, saying that if John Brown does not pay within one month, steps will be taken to make him bankrupt. Advise John Brown on what procedure will have to be followed if he is to be made bankrupt, and what the consequences of bankruptcy will be for him.

26.5

You are a union shop steward. Your members have become very worried recently about reports in the newspaper that your company may have to go into liquidation and are anxious to know what effect this will have on the company. During your next union meeting you intend to explain, in layman's terms, what effect liquidation will have on the way the company is run. Prepare a personal note of what you will say at the meeting.

26.5

The Board of the Piltdown Sand and Gravel Co had met to discuss the company's capital expenditure programme for the coming year. At their previous meeting they found that the requirements submitted by the various operating divisions exceeded their financial reserves, and the Board had asked Mr Pritchard, the finance director, to prepare a paper summarising the situation. The first part of Mr Pritchard's paper read as follows:

'The major proposed items of expenditure are:

'1. A purpose-built extraction plant to be imported from Germany at a cost, at present exchange rates, of £250,000.
'2. Three grading machines. These are produced by several British manufacturers at prices ranging from £25,000 upwards, but to obtain a machine of proven reliability we would need to pay £30,000.
'3. Three dumpers. These will replace six of our smaller dumpers which are to be scrapped, and so will yield a considerable increase in labour productivity, but at a price. The big dumpers are currently being sold at £45,000, and we have tried unsuccessfully to find any second-hand vehicles.
'4. Extensions to the site-premises. These are required partly because we have to meet stiffer Health and Safety Regulations. We have had estimates for this work from three contractors and the lowest estimate is £150,000.

'The total expenditure under these four headings is £625,000, and there is no doubt that we need to spend this amount during the coming year if we are to continue operating efficiently. Moreover, there are several more items whose purchase cannot be delayed much longer. In fact a good case can be made out for a total capital expenditure programme during the coming year of £800,000, especially when we remember that in the current inflationary conditions prices are likely to be about ten per cent higher next year.

'The problem is, of course, that if profits turn out as anticipated and if we wish to pay the same dividend rate as last year, our reserves will not be sufficient to finance more than half of this programme. I must admit that we have been caught on the hop, somewhat, by the combination of inflation and a failure to anticipate all the items on which expenditure would be required.'

Write a report outlining the various ways in which the company might solve the problem identified in Mr Pritchard's report.

27 Resources of the organisation: intellectual and industrial property and goodwill

Introduction

As we noted in Chapter 7 business organisations will often be producing or supplying goods which possess some unique improvement or innovation and it may be important to prevent their competitors copying these ideas. Design and research work is expensive and the law recognises that the results of it can constitute a resource of an organisation in a very real sense.

Another important asset of a successful organisation is its reputation and the goodwill which it has built up. We shall look at these matters in this chapter.

Patents

If an article is essentially improved in some respects or if it has been made in a better way a patent may be granted to protect it from exploitation by others. The law of patents is now laid down in the Patents Act 1977.

When an organisation makes an advance in design or technology, it can apply to the Patent Office for it to be patented. To be patentable an invention must be capable of industrial application. On application the officials of the Patent Office examine a description of the invention to ensure as far as they can that no such description has previously been published. If it has then a patent will not be granted.

If, however, the Patent Office officials are satisfied as to novelty a patent may be granted on payment of fees. This means that for a twenty-year period other individuals or organisations will not be permitted to use the innovation commercially.

Of course, patents may be bought and sold, for a patent is a form of property. Patent owners may also wish to grant licences for the manufacture, import, sale or use of a patented article. Thus they can make the invention earn money for them even though they do not wish to be sole makers of, or dealers in, the new product. The names of the owners of a patent are kept on a register at the Patent Office.

Owning a patent gives an organisation the right to stop others using the device and to decide whether others are to be allowed to imitate it. If a patent owner thinks that his patent is being infringed he can challenge the imitator in the Patents Court. It is irrelevant to the question of infringement that the infringing organisation was unaware of the patent. In practice, however, an organisation will be aware of most existing patents in its area of operations and will rarely dare to infringe them. Furthermore if the owner of a patent once successfully defends his patent in a court action it will be very unlikely that there will be any further infringements. Actions for infringement can be costly for the loser and it is generally only the most valuable patents or those which appear open to challenge which are in fact infringed.

If an action for infringement is brought by the patent owner the court first has to decide whether the patent is valid. The most important ground upon which invalidity may be asserted is that the invention is not a patentable invention, e.g. because it is not novel in some respect. Should it be held valid the court then has to decide whether the patent is sufficiently wide to cover the alleged infringement. If the patent owner succeeds in his action he may be granted an injunction to prevent further infringement and/or damage. Ownership of a patent for an invention made by an employee is given to the employer if the invention was made in the normal course of the employee's duties.

Recently a system of European patents has been created and in the future this system will, no doubt, come to be of considerable importance. For the moment, however, the British system alone need concern us.

Copyright

Unlike patents, copyrights come into existence without registration or the payment of fees or any formalities. They arise automatically when 'works' are produced. Copyright arises only in 'works' but the meaning of that term is extremely wide: it covers literary works, speeches, scripts, artistic words, designs, etc. Copyright belongs to the author or creator of the work and generally lasts for the duration of his life plus fifty years.

From the point of view of most business organisations the most important aspect of copyright is that in industrial design. The Design Copyright Act 1968 provided for copyright of industrial designs. (This lasts for fifteen years from the date of the marketing of the first articles based on the design.) Since this Act organisations have realised that the general law of copyright (that is, the provisions of the Copyright Act 1956) might itself afford protection to such designs, and this has the advantage of generally longer periods of protection.

If a copyright work is copied to a substantial extent there is an infringement unless one of the exceptions listed in the Act applies (e.g. if the copying of the 'work' is for individual research or private study).

Reputation

The purpose of both patents and copyrights is to protect the fruits of work. It may be that an organisation's assets consist not so much in its research as in its reputation. We now look at the ways in which the law prevents unfair exploitation of another's reputation, or goodwill.

Passing-off

The law forbids a business from misleading customers into thinking they are dealing with the business or goods of another. A trader who suffers financial loss in such a way can bring an action in the tort of passing-off. If he is successful he may be granted an injunction and/or damages.

Most cases of passing-off occur after a trader has been using a sign or 'get-up' which people have come to associate with that other business organisation. More often it will be a misleadingly similar one.

There will not always be a successful action; however, even though a similar name is used. For example if an organisation is using a name which merely describes the sort of business it does, it cannot complain if another organisation in the same field uses a very similar name.

Trade marks

An action in passing-off does not always afford sufficient protection of an organisation's reputation or goodwill. It is often difficult to prove that there has been or will be actual misleading of anyone. For this reason trade marks are important. Moreover, while a passing-off action requires proof that a reputation has been established, an action for infringement of a trade mark can be brought as soon as a mark is registered.

Passing-off actions are today brought only where an organisation has omitted to register a trade mark, or the imitation is of something that cannot be registered as a trade mark (e.g. a business name).

Almost anything which changes the appearance of goods is a 'mark'. But to be registrable under the Trade Mark Acts a mark must be in use or intended for use as a trademark. It must also be distinctive in the sense of distinguishing its owner's goods from those of others.

The first registered trade-mark was the now familiar Bass red triangle. Registration takes place at the Patent Office. The trade mark can be renewed on payment of fees after seven years and thereafter every fourteen years. The Registrar considers whether to accept the mark. He can reject on a number of grounds (e.g. that it is misleading or immoral). It must then be advertised so that any interested parties may challenge it should they so wish.

Like patents, trademarks can be sold and licences over them granted. If the owner retains the trade mark, however, only he can use it. If anyone else employs the same mark, or one which so closely resembles it that it may cause confusion, the owner has an action for infringement under the Acts.

Injurious falsehood

An alternative method of unfair competition consists in attempting to 'do down' another reputation. The law prevents this sort of behaviour by the tort of injurious falsehood, or slander to goods. An action in the tort lies against one who injures another in business by making, out of some dishonest or spiteful motive, a false statement which occasions financial loss or the real risk of it.

Summary and conclusions

1. When marketing its products a firm needs various forms of legal protection and in this section we considered the protection of non-tangible property such as:

   Research and development work.
   Reputation and good will.

2. *Research and development work*
2.1. *Patents*

   (a) New ideas and products need to be protected but to be patented an invention must be capable of industrial application. Such innovations may be patented under the 1977 Patents Act.
   (b) Owning a patent gives protection for a twenty-year period and allows the organisation:

      (i)   to stop others using it without permission;
      (ii) to grant licences for manufacture, and distribution;
      (iii) to challenge imitators in the Patents Court.

   Patents may be bought and sold like other property.

2.2. *Copyright*
The protection of 'words' produced by the firm in whatever form, e.g. speeches, scripts, designs, etc. Especially important to the firm is industrial design and the Industrial Design Act 1968.

3. *Reputation and goodwill*

   (a) Goodwill is regarded as an asset of the business; it implies that consumers will continue to purchase goods for a variety of reasons (e.g. a quality product, service, etc.).
   (b) If firms attempt to imitate others and the original firms lose as a result, they can take legal action (in the tort of 'passing-off') against the offenders to seek an injunction and/or damages.
   (c) Trade marks help to protect goodwill, as it is illegal to copy another person's trade mark and thus usurp his goodwill.
   (d) Any attempt deliberately to make false statements about another firm's product can be prevented through the tort of 'injurious falsehood'.

Assignments

27.1

Compare and contrast the following:

1. patents and copyright;
2. copyright and trademarks;
3. trademarks and patents;
4. passing-off and injurious falsehood.

27.2

Bill Oilspill, a council road worker, uses his spare time to repair cars in his garage at home. In the course of this part-time work he discovers a substance which he thinks will, when mixed with petrol, reduce fuel consumption by 50 per cent. He wishes to protect this idea from being 'stolen' by commercial organisations.

(a) Outline the steps he should take to obtain protection for this idea, and
(b) Show the various ways he might exploit his idea should he succeed in getting it legally protected.

27.3

Fred Fauna has discovered a chemical substance which makes roses grow twice as fast as normal. He obtains a patent to protect his invention. Gro-a-Rose Ltd develops a very similar chemical by testing a sample of Fred's substance and imitating it.

(a) Assume you are Fred. What action might you take?
(b) Assume you are Gro-a-Rose Ltd's legal adviser. How might you try to defend Gro-a-Rose Ltd, against this action?

27.4

Rock-it-all-Over Ltd has produced a record written and recorded by Wailing Walter Williams, a pop star. In a contract with the company, Wailing Walter has transferred all his rights in the songs in return for £10,000. A rival record producer has now made a cheaper version of one of Wailing Walter's more successful songs which is selling well. Advise the company.

27.5

The Managing Director of Bite-and-Break Biscuits Ltd has found out that a rival firm, Choc-O-Bisc Ltd, has developed a new jam-filled biscuit called 'Cartwheel'. Eager to cash in on the popularity of this idea he orders Bite-and-Break Ltd to start making similar biscuits which he plans to call 'Cart-O-Wheel'. Advise Choc-O-Bisc Ltd as to any legal action it might take if the sales of its biscuit begin to fall. Would it be appropriate to take the same action if its sales did not fall?

27.6

Mr Green, a village grocer, displays a notice in his shop window saying 'Do not buy from the new supermarket: it is owned by foreigners who sell shoddy goods.' Some of the villagers take notice of the sign and the supermarket's grocery trade falls off noticeably. What action might you advise the supermarket to take?

27.7

Discuss the possible consequences of the patents system from the point of view of (a) a firm which is granted a patent in respect of a particular product, (b) the competitors of that firm, (c) the consumer buying that product. (In answering, you should draw upon the information contained in earlier chapters, as well as this chapter.)

27.8

Explain and discuss the following statement: 'The benefits conferred upon an organisation by the granting of a patent are similar to the benefits which organisations seek to obtain through their marketing activities.'

27.9

The passage below is based on an article in the *Financial Times*, 27 November 1978. What light does it throw on the problems that can arise in trying to decide what measure of legal protection should be afforded to organisations?

'For much of the past 100 years innovators were protected and encouraged by laws designed to ensure that the time and expense needed to develop a new product could be recouped with profit, provided the market approved of the product. The legal machinery serving this end consisted of patent, copyright, and industrial design laws protecting inventors and creative artists; of trade mark laws protecting those who took the trouble to market goods of a quality worth remembering; and of laws protecting industrial and business secrets, enabling those who would or could not rely on a patent to bring a new product to the market well ahead of imitators.

'Recent legal developments have put a brake on the pace of innovation. They include the gradual erosion of the patent system by the ease with which chemical or electronic innovations can be modified to enable those with money for litigation to frighten off the genuine, but financially weak, inventor. The restrictions of patent licensing already put into effect by the EEC Commission, or proposed by the Commission and by the developing countries, further diminish the rewards of innovators.

'Moreover the two latest trade mark decisions of the European Court allowing, under certain conditions, the repacking of trade-marked products by dealers not authorised to do so by the manufacturer, provided a legal mantle under which dishonest operators could sell imitation products under the trade-mark owner's label.

'Product liability legislation, if enacted as proposed by the European Commission, would make innovation very risky by making innovators responsible for defects of products which could not be foreseen or detected at the time the product was placed on the market. In this connection, one can ask whether the public interest in innovation should not be reflected in a public responsibility for damages exceeding a certain percentage of the innovator's turnover.

'The increasing restrictions on the use of patent and trade mark rights and the erosion of copyright by new reproduction devices diminish the advantages so far enjoyed by innovators, and a stricter product liability imposes new burdens on them. But the increasing volume of product safety legislation provides imitators with an important advantage which further reinforces the change in the economic climate to the detriment of innovation. The safety of drugs legislation has been for a long time a feature of all civilised legal systems. But the time and outlay required for the completion of biological and clinical tests to satisfy health authorities is constantly increasing. Expensive and time-consuming tests are also required before obtaining approval for insecticides and all sorts of plant protection products – and quite rightly so, as these can be even more dangerous to human health and environment than medicines. Numerous other chemical, electrical and radiation products have to be proved safe before their marketing is allowed. The same applies to new types of motor cars and other automotive machines and to building materials.

'Approval can take two forms. First, as is often the case with new building materials or chemicals used in agriculture or industry, a general authorisation will apply to the new material and anybody may start making it or selling it without having to go through the long and costly process preceding an authorisation. The innovator may try to salvage as much as he can of the advantage of having been first, by means of trade mark rights. But this may be of little avail if the imitators are either financially stronger or have a better distribution network.

'Second, as is mostly the case with pharmaceuticals, insecticides and electrical devices, the approval will apply only to the specific product of the enterprise applying for it, so that others wishing to market an imitation will have to apply again. Even here, however, the imitator starts with the tremendous advantage of having bypassed internal development costs and will be betting on a probable winner. The approving authority will approach his application with the knowledge that a product of this type can be harmless. Depending on the variations introduced by design or in the course of the production process, it will require only supplementary tests or none at all. The benefit of the knowledge which cost the innovator much time, effort and money will be obtained by the imitator free of charge. There is, however, no chance that the imitator could be made to pay compensation on the grounds of "unjust enrichment". He did not receive anything, in the legal meaning of that word; he was merely saved further expense and loss of time.'

28 Resources of the Organisation: land and buildings

Introduction

We have seen that land is one of an organisation's most important resources. In this chapter we aim to look at the ways in which organisations can acquire land. We will distinguish between freehold and leasehold land and consider how these forms may be used to satisfy the particular needs of an organisation. We will then look at the ways in which organisations are restricted in their use of land. We shall see that restrictions are often imposed for the benefit of other individuals but that sometimes they are for the benefit of society as a whole.

We must first of all examine some basic ideas in land law.

'Land'

The word 'land' has an extended meaning in law. Not only does it mean a plot or area of land but it also includes objects such as houses and factories on the land. Even though they start off as bricks and mortar, once these become part of a fixed structure they become land and are governed by the law that relates to land rather than the law which relates to movable (called 'personal') property.

'Ownership' of land

Lawyers rarely use the phrase 'owning land'. They prefer to speak of people or organisations owning 'estates' or 'interests' in land. The reason for this is historical. Ever since the Norman invasion in 1066 when William I became king by conquering the English, the only person capable of owning land has been the sovereign. In theory everyone else owns merely an estate or interest in land, that is rights over the land owned by the sovereign. In practice the sovereign's ownership is of minimal importance, but it helps to explain how the two major forms of land holding, the freehold estate and the leasehold estate, are defined. These we will now consider.

Freehold and leasehold estates

The word 'estate' signifies the rights which a person has in land held from the sovereign. Estates are classified according to the length of time for which they may continue. The estate in land which most closely approximates to absolute ownership is the *fee simple absolute*.

This is an estate which can last indefinitely. A person who owns a fee simple absolute can sell it as he wishes or leave it to whoever he wishes by his will. If he dies without leaving a will it will pass to the next of kin who are entitled to inherit. A list of such relatives is included in the Administration of Estates Act 1925. It is only if there are no next of kin to inherit it that the fee simple will come to an end and revert to the Crown.

It is rare for this to happen, so that for all practical purposes the fee simple absolute can be regarded as lasting for ever.

The term fee simple absolute is what is meant by the term 'freehold' in common usage.

The other estate in land that is of great importance for the organisation is the leasehold estate. A lease is an interest in land that lasts for a definite length of time.

A lease, like a fee simple absolute, can be sold ('assigned') or left by will but the purchaser or legatee only gets an interest in the land lasting as long as the unexpired duration of the lease. The person granting the lease is known as the lessor (or landlord); the person to whom it is granted is called the lessee (or tenant).

More than one estate can exist in one piece of land at any one time. This fact can be illustrated by an example. B, the owner of a fee simple, grants a ten-year lease to A at a rent of £1,000 p.a. By granting a lease, B does not cease to own the fee simple but as he has granted a lease to A for ten years, it will only be at the end of this time that the land will revert to B. A may also grant a lease of the land ('a sublease'), to X, but as A's estate is only for ten years he cannot grant a lease exceeding that period. He may choose to grant a lease to X for five years at a rent of £1,200 per annum. During the currency of the sublease, X is bound to pay rent to A at £1,200 p.a. but as A is himself a tenant under a lease from B, A will continue to pay the rent due under that lease, i.e. £1,000. When the sublease ends, A will be able to take possession of the land again. This illustration shows how by defining estates in terms of time, it is possible for the 'ownership' of land to be split between several people.

There is a third way in which an organisation may choose to hold land, and that is by a periodic tenancy. As its name suggests, the periodic tenancy still involves the relationship of landlord and tenant but its duration is not fixed at the outset. It may run from year to year, quarterly or weekly or for any other period that the parties choose, and can be terminated by either party giving notice to quit.

The choice for the organisation

There might therefore seem little difference between an organisation buying the fee simple in certain land or buying a lease of that land for 999 years. Nevertheless there are considerations which may make one form of estate preferable to the other.

Covenants

Frequently when land is being sold, the seller will wish to impose obligations on the purchaser's use of the land. A builder, selling houses on a housing estate, will commonly impose a restriction on the use of the houses for business purposes. A freeholder granting a lease will commonly impose restrictions on the demolition of existing buildings or on the erection of new ones. The reason for this is to ensure that the land retained by the seller will maintain its character and value.

These obligations can be made to bind a purchaser by being incorporated in the contract of sale. The seller will then have the normal contractual remedies on breach of the obligation. A difficulty arises, however, when the purchaser of land sells. The original owner will not have the same contractual remedies against subsequent purchasers because of privity of contract. The law does however recognise that restrictive obligations ('restrictive covenants') should be enforceable against subsequent owners where they are entered into for the benefit of land retained by the owner. In freehold land, however, positive covenants, for example to build a wall or to pay a sum of money, are enforceable only between the original parties. They cannot be made to bind subsequent purchasers.

In leasehold land, the range of covenants that can be enforced is wider. If they are the original parties, both lessor and lessee can enforce the lease in the same way as they would enforce a contract. If however either the lessor or the lessee sells his interest, all the covenants contained in the lease can be made to be enforceable by and against the new owner.

The commonest covenant found in almost all leases is a positive covenant. This is the covenant by the lessee to pay rent. Other covenants on the part of the lessee that are frequently found are to keep the premises in good repair, not to use the premises for certain trades or businesses, not to demolish buildings, to build boundary walls, not to sell his lease without the lessor's consent.

In order to protect himself and give him a valuable remedy if any of these covenants are broken, the lessor will generally include a forfeiture clause in the lease. This will state that he has the right to terminate (or forfeit) the lease on the breach of a covenant. We will look shortly at the statutory restrictions on the exercise of this right in relation to business tenancies.

Not all the obligations under a lease fall on the tenant. It is up to the parties to negotiate their own bargain and they can decide for themselves what their rights and duties should be. For instance it is quite common in short leases for the lessor to agree to be responsible for structural repairs to the premises whilst the lessee is liable only for internal decoration. The lessor will generally also covenant that the tenant will be free to use the premises unhindered by acts of the lessor or his other lessees. This is the covenant for quiet enjoyment.

Cost

The financial aspect of acquiring business premises will be a major factor influencing the organisation. There are financial advantages in buying freehold land as any increase in the value of land will belong solely to the organisation and not to any landlord. The organisation will not have to pay rent and will not have to observe the wider range of covenants under a lease.

On the other hand outright purchase of a site for even a small factory may be too expensive. And to borrow money to finance the purchase may involve disproportionately large interest payments in the short term, even though in the long term the organisation may be acquiring a valuable capital asset.

The purchase of a lease shows corresponding advantages and disadvantages. A tenant taking on a lease, say for ten years, may merely pay rent at intervals throughout the term. Or may pay a lump sum at the beginning together with a smaller, or even nominal, rent throughout the term. But because he is only entitled to a limited term his interest decreases in value as the years go by (it is a 'wasting asset'). Thus he is not investing his money in something which will bring him a large capital return in the future. The amount that he has to spend initially however will be correspondingly smaller, because he is only buying the use of the land for a short period. And if he has been able to negotiate reasonable terms in his lease the obligations imposed on him may be no more demanding than the obligations that a reasonable freeholder would in any case observe.

Statutory protection

Whether they own freehold or leasehold land organisations using premises will often have to spend a considerable amount of money in adapting them to their own particular needs. If an organisation has direct contact with clients and customers its actual location will be of prime importance; a change of address might lose the organisation some of its best customers. This type of organisation, if it takes a lease, is in a vulnerable position. If compelled to leave when the lease comes to an end it will risk losing the benefit of the money already spent on the property. And if it *could* negotiate a new lease of the premises, the landlord would be in a strong position to demand a higher rent. Tenants of business premises have therefore been given statutory protection both as regards security of tenure and as regards the rent which can be charged under a new tenancy.

The relevant legislation is the Landlord and Tenant Act 1954 Part II. To gain the protection of the Act at least part of the property leased must be occupied by the tenant for business purposes. Certain tenancies are excluded. For example those residential tenancies which have protection under the Rent Acts, agricultural tenancies (which have a separate system of protection) and short tenancies, that is those for less than six months unless they provide for extension. 'Business' is defined very widely under the Act and includes virtually all the organisations that we are considering in this volume.

Security of tenure

The scheme of the Act provides machinery for a business tenant to apply to the court for the grant of a new lease which will take effect when his current lease comes to an end. There is a detailed procedure to be followed consisting of notices and counter notices to be served. This varies slightly as to whether it is the tenant who takes the initiative to request a new lease or the landlord who wishes to terminate the current tenancy. The end result is however the same: the tenant has a right to apply to the court for the grant of a new lease and the landlord can only oppose the grant of a new tenancy if he can establish one of seven grounds laid down in the Act.

Three of these grounds relate to failure by the tenant to observe the terms of his current lease in respect of failure to pay the rent or repair the property, or the breach of other covenants in the lease. Three other grounds relate to the landlord's needs. He can oppose the grant of a new lease if he owns other property which could be let together with the tenant's premises for a substantially greater rent, if the landlord intends to demolish the premises or to reconstruct them substantially which cannot be done with the tenant still in occupation, or if

283

the landlord requires the premises for his own occupation. Additionally the landlord can oppose the grant on the ground that he has offered and is willing to provide suitable alternative accommodation.

The parties may agree on the length of the new lease. If they fail to agree, the court may grant a lease of whatever length it sees fit, subject to a maximum of fourteen years.

Even when the landlord successfully opposes the grant of a new lease, he may have to pay compensation to the tenant. Where he opposes on the ground that he wishes to demolish or reconstruct the premises, or where he requires the premises for his own occupation or for letting the property together with other property (of his), the landlord must pay to the tenant a sum equal to the rateable value of that property, or twice that amount if the tenant or the tenant and his predecessors in the business have occupied the premises for fourteen years.

Rent control

Unlike the position with respect to residential tenancies, there is no restriction on the rent which may be agreed between the parties during the original lease, but if the tenant succeeds in obtaining the grant of a new tenancy under the Act, the rent under the new tenancy is subject to the court's approval. The new rent is to be that which the premises 'might reasonably be expected to be let on the open market by a willing lessor'. Such rent will be fixed disregarding the fact that the present tenant might himself be willing to pay a higher rent in order to remain in the property.

Restrictions on the use of land

The law imposes restrictions on the way in which organisations and individuals make use of their land and premises. The reasons for this are not difficult to appreciate. Industrial organisations in particular are likely to carry on activities which are potentially dangerous to a wide range of individuals and other organisations – employees, visitors, neighbours and even whole populations. Retail organisations are less likely to create such obvious dangers by their use of their premises but they (like any organisation or individual) can carry on activities which neighbours or others find annoying or distressing – like making excessive noise at night – and there is always a possibility of employees or visitors sustaining an injury, if only as a result of slipping on an over-polished floor.

The law has long intervened to limit the danger and distress which inconsiderate or merely careless use of premises can lead to, and in recent years statutory provisions have strengthened the protection afforded to all those groups of people who might suffer. We shall now look at the legal protection afforded to them, distinguishing the common law restrictions on use from examples of more recent statutory intervention.

Common law restrictions

These largely provide compensation for damages or injuries caused by the wrongs (torts) of those owning or occupying land or premises.

The tort of trespass

The tort of trespass protects those with a sufficient interest in land against interference in the form of physical intrusion by another upon that land.

Thus if an organisation uses its property in a way that involves people coming into direct contact with another's land that other may have the right to bring an action in trespass. This would aim to gain an injunction to prevent the activity being so carried on and/or to obtain damages for any loss he has suffered. This is provided that the trespass was done intentionally and not just carelessly or negligently. Both freeholders and leaseholders may bring such actions, as probably can anyone who has exclusive possession of land.

Thus in its activities an organisation must ensure that there is no interference of this kind with the land of another. An industrial concern, for example, must avoid deliberate dumping of waste on another's land. A retail organisation must ensure that its employees do not need to cross another's land, for instance to reach lorries awaiting unloading.

The tort of nuisance

The tort of nuisance also prevents damage to, or interference with, the use or enjoyment of another's property. A material physical injury to person or property justifies an action in nuisance, e.g. if the activities of a factory shake a neighbouring house causing the chimneys to collapse or if fumes from a smelting works mean that a neighbouring gardener's exotic plants are destroyed.

If it is merely interference with the enjoyment of property that is alleged then *substantial* interference must be proved. An example is *Bridlington Relay Ltd v. Yorkshire Electricity Board*. The Board's power line interfered with the Relay Co's ability to provide a television relay service to subscribers. But because interference with the recreational amenity of watching television was held not to be substantial they did not succeed in a nuisance action.

Among the factors which are taken into account when deciding whether an interference is substantial are:

1. Duration of the interference – the longer it goes on the more likely it is to be substantial, although a temporary interference can also be substantial.
2. The locality where the act is performed – interference substantial in one setting may not be so in another.

But even if an interference is substantial, to be actionable it must also be unreasonable. Amongst others the following factors may be relevant:

1. The sort of business the organisation causing the nuisance is carrying on: is the activity worthwhile to society?
2. Whether the nuisance is merely a side-effect of a proper activity or is motivated by spite or malice.
3. Whether the locality is a suitable one. Certain industrial activities might be unreasonable if carried on in suburbia while being perfectly reasonable on an industrial estate.
4. How difficult it is to prevent the interference. If it could have been easily prevented then the interference is more likely to be held to be a nuisance.
5. The extent and character of the interference.

The tort we have been discussing so far is more properly referred to as private nuisance. There is another distinct tort (which is also a crime) called *public nuisance*. This tort is concerned with interference, not with the rights of another property owner, but with the rights of the population at large. Examples of public nuisances include obstructing the highway, keeping property in a state of collapse, etc. One can sue the creator of such nuisances, however, only if one has suffered some particular damage beyond that suffered by the rest of the community, e.g. physical injury, or being delayed or inconvenienced more than everyone else.

The tort of *Rylands v. Fletcher*

In the case of *Rylands v. Fletcher* some landowners hired contractors to build a reservoir. Unfortunately the site contained some old mine-shafts which the contractors failed to block up. The consequence was that when the reservoir was filled, water flooded through the shafts and into the mine owned by the plaintiffs. The result of this case was that a new tort was created which places further restrictions on the use one may make of one's land. In this case the landowners themselves had not been negligent (although their contractors had). For the new tort, however, this does not matter. The rule laid down in *Rylands v. Fletcher* imposes a strict liability when the following circumstances are present:

1. *The defendant brought on to his land and kept there certain 'things'.*
   This is usually known as *accumulation*. The strict liability imposed by this rule does not apply if the 'thing' is naturally on the land.
2. *These 'things' must be likely to do harm if they escape.*
   The 'things' do not have to be normally dangerous: in *Rylands v. Fletcher* the offending substance was water.
3. *The use of the land must be 'non-natural'.*
   Whether use of the land is non-natural is a decision for the court in the light of all the circumstances. The court can take into account at this stage the social desirability or otherwise of the activity, and attitudes can change.
4. *There must be an 'escape' from the place where the thing was to the outside.*
   The case of *Read v. Lyons* illustrates this requirement. A worker in a munitions factory was injured by an explosion in the factory's shell filling shop. The House of Lords held that she could not recover damages under the rule in *Rylands v. Fletcher* because there had been no escape from the factory.

The torts we have looked at so far in the main impose restrictions on the use of land in order to protect neighbouring property interests. But the range of persons likely to be affected by commercial or industrial land use is wider than just neighbouring property-owners. It is through the tort of negligence that the common law protects this wider range of people.

The tort of negligence

In our discussion of product liability we saw that the modern law of negligence dates from the case of *Donoghue v. Stevenson*. Although that case was concerned specifically with negligently manufactured products Lord Atkin made a statement which has shaped the development of the whole area of law on liability for careless action. He said:

'You must take reasonable care to avoid acts or omissions which you can reasonably foresee would be likely to injure your neighbour. Who, then, in law is my neighbour? The answer seems to be – persons who are so closely and directly affected by my act that I ought reasonably to have them in contemplation as being so affected when I am directing my mind to the acts or omissions which are called in question.'

This general statement applies to everyone, including those who carry on activities on land or in premises, though there have developed, special, more detailed, formulations of the relationship between landowners and those persons who come on to their property.

The *general* law of negligence, however, governs the relationship between the owners and users of land and premises and other groups of persons – notably those people who live or work in the vicinity or who merely pass by. We shall therefore look briefly at the general law of negligence.

If we wish to know whether someone who suffers injury, damage to property or other form of loss might succeed in an action of negligence we have to ask the following three questions:

1. *Is there a duty of care?*
2. *Is there a breach of duty?*

If a duty of care is owed then the person who owes it must act as a 'reasonable man in the circumstances'. Among the factors which must be considered are:

(a) whether the plaintiff knows of hazardous circumstances and is aware of the danger;
(b) the degree of risk of harm;
(c) the seriousness of the potential harm;
(d) the expense and effort which would have been necessary to avoid the risk.

The question is whether, in all the circumstances, a careful man of full age and normal intelligence would have acted as the defendant did. If not then the defendant is in breach of his duty.

3. *Did the breach of duty cause the harm?*

If the answer is 'yes', and provided that *sort* of harm was *reasonably foreseeable* then the plaintiff will have proved the elements of the tort.

Of course the *plaintiff* may have acted so as to indicate that he knew of and accepted the risk. If this is so then he will fail to recover damages for this harm.

Even if a plaintiff does not accept the risk he might act in such a way that he, too, is negligent. If this is so, under the Law Reform (Contributory Negligence) Act 1945 he may have his damages reduced.

Having looked at the bare elements of this very important tort we examine in more detail the way in which it applies to an owner or occupier of premises.

Liability to those outside the premises

There are many examples of highway users succeeding against the occupier or owner of land or premises on which activities which have caused injuries have been carried on, e.g. *Holling v. Yorkshire Traction Co.*

The plaintiff was killed as the result of an accident caused by smoke which poured out of a nearby factory. A successful action in negligence was brought against the factory owners.

Liability to those on the premises

The other obvious category of persons protected by the law against the actions of occupiers of land consists of those who are injured while on the premises.

The law has long drawn a distinction between the duty owed to visitors (those expressly or impliedly invited on to or allowed on to land or into premises) and others. The law designates the latter category *trespassers* but this term should not be allowed to conjure up a picture of prowling thieves or poachers. Most of the very many, innocently-motivated, young children who play in fields or on building sites will fall into this category since they cannot be said to have been invited on to the land in any sense.

The common law rules concerning the duty owed to visitors have now been replaced by statutory rules enacted by the Occupiers Liability Act 1957 so that we shall leave consideration of these until later. We must, however, look at the law relating to trespassers which is still governed by Common Law rules.

The courts, until recently, took a harsh line towards trespassers. In *Addie v. Dumbreck* (1929) the House of Lords laid down that the occupier of property owes no duty to a trespasser other than that of not inflicting damage intentionally or recklessly on a trespasser actually known to be present. Remembering that the term trespasser covers not only the wicked but also the innocent and inquisitive, this was a hard decision especially as it is sometimes difficult to distinguish trespassers from some types of visitors to whom the law accorded much wider protection.

In *Herrington v. British Railways Board* (1972) the House of Lords declared *Addie* to be obsolete in modern social conditions and declared that a 'duty of common humanity' was owed by occupiers to those trespassers whom the occupier knew to be present, and also to trespassers whose likely presence would have been clear to the reasonable man.

The nature of the 'duty of common humanity' is less demanding of the occupier than his ordinary duty of care in negligence owed to others (such as neighbours), but it is unclear quite how much is to be expected. It seems that one very important relevant factor is the financial resources of the occupier: less is to be expected of a householder than a large industrial organisation in this context.

Although the new law affords a higher degree of protection to trespassers, it does not place an intolerable burden on those occupiers of land or premises who cannot because of poverty, weakness or age be expected to take stringent action.

Statutory restrictions

The restrictions imposed on the use of land by statute fall into two broad categories. The first set of restrictions either fills gaps in the scheme of protection afforded by the common law, or impose a wider range of duties or higher standard of care in specific cases. The second set seeks rather to effect control over the use of land and premises for the benefit of society at large: it attempts social control of land rather than the provision of private law remedies.

Occupiers Liability Act

One leading example of the first type of statutory intervention is the Occupiers Liability Act 1957. This sets out the obligations owed by occupiers to visitors.

An occupier is the person to whom one points when one asks the question 'Who has control of the property?'.

Visitors include:

1. Those who come on to the premises or land to satisfy some material interest of the occupier (e.g. an electrician to do re-wiring).
2. Those who come for pleasure (e.g. guests to a birthday party).
3. Those who come in exercise of a right conferred by law (e.g. a policeman with a search warrant).

There is imposed on occupiers by the Act a duty 'to take such care as in all the circumstances is reasonable to see that the visitor will be reasonably safe in using the premises for the purposes for which he is invited or permitted by the occupier to be there'.

To decide whether an occupier has fulfilled this duty we must look at all the facts of the case. The Act gives an indication of some factors which might be relevant, e.g.:

1. An occupier must be prepared for children to be less careful than adults.
2. An occupier may expect that specialist workers called on to the premises to do specific jobs will be aware of special risks which the job entails, e.g. a chimney-sweep may be taken to know the dangers arising from flues: *Roles v. Nathan.*

The Act, then, envisages variation in the standard of care required of occupiers according to the circumstances.

An occupier will generally not be liable for injuries caused by independent contractors working on his land or premises provided that he has taken all steps reasonably necessary to satisfy himself that the contractor is competent and the work properly done. If, however, an occupier is an employer and damage or injury is negligently caused by one of his employees who is acting in the course of his employment then the occupier will be liable to the party who has suffered loss.

This is because of the doctrine of *vicarious liability*: an employer is held liable for torts committed by his employees while at work whether or not he has committed a tort himself. An employee can be distinguished from an independent contractor by asking the question 'Is he part of the enterprise?'. An employee is part of the organisational set-up, whereas an independent contractor has generally been hired to do a specific job. The normal rules about the injured party having consented to the risk of injury or having been contributorily negligent apply here as in other cases of negligence liability.

Defective Premises Act

Under the common law the liability of an owner for the creation of danger on his premises ended when he sold or leased the land. Doubt was thrown on this rule in *Dutton v. Bognor Regis* and recently, in *Anns v. Merton London Borough Council* the House of Lords also disapproved the rule.

The rule has in fact been largely eroded by s. 3 of the Defective Premises Act 1972 which provides that 'Where any work of construction, repair, maintenance or any other work is done . . . any duty of care owed . . . shall not be abated by the~subsequent disposal of the premises by the person who owed the duty.'

The Act also imposes a duty on builders to build properly (s. 1) and, by s. 4, imposes duties on landlords for injuries caused by the state of leased premises.

So far we have been concerned with statutes of the first of the two types which we distinguished. We now move into statutory intervention of the second, more far-reaching kind.

Public health legislation

As early as the fourteenth century there were attempts to promote public health by legislation. There were, for example, criminal sanctions placed on, among other things, the throwing of garbage into rivers. With the growth of urbanisation the range of intervention was greatly increased. The restrictions which we discuss briefly here are contained in the Public Health Acts of 1936 and 1961, the Clean Air Acts 1956 and 1968 and the Control of Pollution Act 1974. We shall look briefly at these controls on the use of property under several headings.

Sanitation and waste on land

Building regulations have been made by the Secretary of State for the Environment and organisations which are undertaking work within the scope of these regulations must submit plans to the local authority. The local authority must reject them if they do not make adequate provision for drainage, sanitary accommodation, the removal of refuse, etc.

If an existing building has no satisfactory drainage system or if it is insufficient, defective or a health risk, the local authority can require the owner or occupier to carry out remedial work.

The Control of Pollution Act 1974 prohibits the disposal of waste on to land unless a licence to deposit has been granted. Licensed dumping is controlled by the local authority. These controls mean that the disposal of industrial waste can be supervised for the benefit of the public's health.

Dangerous buildings

Not only does legislation try to ensure that such obvious dangers to public health are kept under control but it also controls less obvious sources of danger to life. There are, for instance, regulations to ensure that buildings are reasonably safe in the event of a fire. These apply to many buildings owned by commercial and retail organisations (e.g. shops and hotels under the Fire Precautions Act). If a building is actually dangerous the local authority has power to order remedial work or to demolish the building.

Atmospheric pollution

There are statutory controls over the pollution of water and, indeed, the atmosphere generally. The Control of Pollution Act provides, for instance, that the Secretary of State may make regulations concerning, among other things, the content of motor fuels and the amount of sulphur in oil fuel. Noise has long been recognised as a problem and those organisations who carry on noisy industrial processes are subject to regulations as to the area in which such activities are permissible.

Planning legislation

The other way in which the use of land has been extensively restricted by statute is by the Planning Acts. Thus it may well be that an organisation will have to seek permission in order to develop its land.

The law in this area is now largely contained in The Town and Country Planning Act of 1971 (as amended).

The basis of planning control lies in the powers of local planning authorities to grant or refuse permission as they see fit. This is primarily the task of the District Council though the County Council must prepare a structural plan (essentially a written statement of policy) based on a survey of the area. This plan involves the Council formulating its general policy and stating general proposals for development in the area. The plan must be subject to examination in public and be approved by the Secretary of State. District Councils can then make local, more detailed plans.

These plans will give some indications as to whether planning permission is likely to be granted for a certain type of development in a particular area. Section 22 of the 1971 Act states that to 'develop' property is to carry out 'building, engineering, mining or other operations in, on, over or under land, or . . . to make . . . any material change in the use of any buildings or other land. . . .'

A wide range of exemptions is provided by General Development Orders and Use Classes Orders. The former exempts, among other things, certain alterations to dwellinghouses, e.g. building on extensions of less than a prescribed size. The latter permits any change from one use to another within the same class. For instance, the change from one kind of shop to another (with certain exceptions) is permitted. Where the development is covered by one of the exceptions in a General Development Order or Use Classes Order, no planning permission is required.

No development that requires planning permission may lawfully take place without the permission either of the local planning authority or the Secretary of State. When the local authorities decide on planning permission they must have regard to the development plan and 'any other material consideration'.

If an industrial organisation wishes to build or extend its factory it must also obtain an industrial development certificate from the Department of Trade and Industry stating that the building can be carried out consistently with the proper distribution of industry.

Applicants for planning permission who are refused planning permission or who are granted it subject to unwelcome conditions may appeal to the Secretary of State. We shall consider the position of a person who feels aggrieved at the determination of Government departments in greater detail in Volume 2. For the time being it suffices to say that in certain circumstances these decisions may be reviewed in the High Court. As well as the right of appeal, provided that the owner is able to show that the land has become incapable of reasonably beneficial use in its existing state he may serve a 'purchase notice' on the local authority requiring it to purchase his interest in the property.

Should a development take place without consent the authority may serve an enforcement notice which requires the land to be restored. Rights of appeal are provided in certain circumstances to the Secretary of State. If such a notice is not complied with the authority can enter the land or premises and restore it, charging the cost to the owner. The High Court has the power to grant an injunction to prevent persistent breach of an enforcement notice. Very often there may be a criminal prosecution in the Magistrates' Court.

The statutory provisions which we have so far looked at are concerned with planning control in the sense that they are negative, consisting in the ability to prevent changes taking place where these are thought objectionable. Public authorities also have a more positive role. They possess powers enabling them to devise and implement projects designed to improve land.

To achieve this, local authorities, the Secretary of State and certain other public bodies have specific powers enabling them compulsorily to acquire land for certain purposes (e.g. to build a new school). The procedure for making compulsory purchase orders is laid down by statute. The procedure is broadly that the authority draws up a compulsory purchase order and advertises this fact in the local press and by serving notices on the owners of the land. The compulsory purchase order is then submitted to the Secretary of State, who considers the objections to the order and decides whether it should be confirmed.

If an order is confirmed the relevant authority acquires the land, though subject to a duty to compensate the landowner. This compensation has generally to include the 'market value' of the land plus a sum representing other losses directly consequent upon the acquisition (e.g. a fall in value of remaining land held by the landowner).

Certain statutes afford authorities (generally local authorities) more general powers. Under the Town and Country Planning Act 1971, for instance, local authorities (subject to governmental supervision) are empowered to acquire land 'in connection with development and for other planning purposes'. Under the Community Land Act 1975 certain authorities (again *generally* local authorities subject to governmental approval) have the power to bring land available for development under public control.

Summary and conclusions

1. In addition to finance and intellectual and industrial property, land is a very important resource of an organisation. Before we look at the detail of the legal problems of land as a resource, it is important to be clear about certain definitions:

    (*a*) land;
    (*b*) ownership of land;
    (*c*) freehold, leasehold estates, periodic tenancies.

2. Although different types of holding often have similar consequences for the firm, the *choice for the organisation* is important and there are various considerations that make one form of estate preferable to another:

292

(a) covenants (obligations imposed on the purchaser's use of the land; may be wider on leasehold than freehold);

(b) costs (different financial advantages in buying freehold or leasehold land);

(c) security of tenure (machinery whereby business tenant can apply to the court for the grant of a new lease, taking effect when current lease ends;

(d) rent control (control over rent paid under new tenancy).

3. There are *restrictions* on the way *firms use their land* and which on the one hand allow the firm to be protected from intrusions by the public and on the other protects the public from dangerous conditions caused by firms. Such restrictions fall into two categories:

3.1. Common law restrictions: which include,

(i) trespass;

(ii) nuisance (distinguishing between private and public);

(iii) *Rylands v. Fletcher;*

(iv) negligence (is there a duty of care? Is there a breach of duty? Did the breach of duty cause harm? Liability to those outside the premises; Liability to those inside the premises).

3.2. Statutory restrictions – which fall into two main categories:

(a) either filling gaps in the common law scheme or imposing a wider range of duties and a higher standard of care in specific cases (illustrated by such Acts as Occupiers Liability Act; Defective Premises Act);

(b) attempting control over the use of land and premises for the benefit of society as a whole (social control) illustrated by Public Health legislation and Planning legislation).

4. Thus the law will protect those who hold limited interests in land to safeguard them from unscrupulous treatment but it also imposes restrictions on the activities which may be carried on. Although land and premises are often the most expensive outlay for a firm, the organisation has to appreciate that society does not allow the use of such property without any control.

Assignments

28.1

Distinguish between

1. leasehold and freehold estates;
2. restrictive and positive covenants;
3. leases and periodic tenancies.

28.2

Stick-it-Tight Ltd, a firm of glue manufacturers, wishes to acquire a site on which to build a large factory. If built, the factory should be running at a profit after about five years. Stick-it-Tight is not in a very strong financial position at the moment but envisages business improving steadily over the next five to ten years. It is probable that manufacture of the new glue which it envisages carrying on in the factory will be an economically viable enterprise for about twenty years. After that, it is likely that, because of new developments just beginning in Japan, the demand for this sort of glue will fall off. It is unlikely that manufacture of these products will require large factory space. Advise the managing director of the company as to the advisability of buying freehold or leasehold land on which to build the factory.

28.3

A owns a large plot of land on an industrial estate. He has built a factory on part of its land and he wishes to sell the remainder (which is suitable for industrial development) in order to raise money at once to buy machinery for his factory. A manufactures precision optical instruments. He is concerned that any use of the rest of the land should not cause vibrations which might affect his business. He also wishes to make it a requirement that the purchaser build secure boundary fences and that the purchaser and subsequent owners should be entirely responsible for the upkeep of these fences. Advise A on the ways in which he can achieve his objects when he sells the land.

28.4

Explain the statutory protection in respect of security of tenure and rent control afforded to tenants of business premises. Why is such protection necessary?

28.5

The following are the facts of *Halsey v. Esso Petroleum*;

The plaintiff occupied a house in Rainville Road, Fulham, which was a road zoned for residential purposes. The defendants, Esso Petroleum Co Ltd, operated an oil distributing depot at premises adjoining Rainville Road which were situated in an area zoned for industrial purposes. In this industrial area there were other premises dealing with oil. The defendants' depot dealt with fuel oil in its light, medium and heavy grades, the oil being pumped from river tankers on to the depot and from the depot into road tankers. It was necessary to heat the medium and heavy grades of oil for the purpose of pumping them and these grades were kept hot throughout their transportation, including the time while they were at the depot. The through-put of oil at the depot had increased from 30,414,000 gallons in 1953 to 56,607,000 gallons in 1957. In 1956 night shift working was reintroduced. On the depot and opposite to the plaintiff's house there was a boilerhouse with two boilers heated by burning oil and used for producing steam to heat the fuel oil. Two metal chimneys projected from the roof of the boilerhouse. From these chimneys acid smuts containing sulphate were emitted and were visible falling outside the plaintiff's house. There was proof that the smuts had damaged clothes hung out to dry in the garden of the plaintiff's house and also paintwork of the plaintiff's car which he kept on the highway outside the door of his house. The depot emitted a pungent and nauseating smell of oil which went beyond a background smell and was more than would affect the sensitive person but the plaintiff had not suffered any injury to health from the smell. During the night there was noise from the boilers which at its peak caused windows and doors in the plaintiff's house to vibrate and prevented the plaintiff sleeping. The defendants had attempted to reduce this noise by soundproofing the walls of the boilerhouse but it remained and was more than trivial. Further, during the night shift from 10 p.m. to 6 a.m. there was noise from road tankers which arrived at and left the depot at points close to the plaintiff's house. The tankers were enormous vehicles and made a very loud noise. Up to fifteen tankers came to and left the depot at different times during the night shift and sometimes up to four tankers arrived or left together. The noise from the tankers was made partly in the public highway outside the depot, as they manoeuvred on entering or leaving the depot, and partly in the depot itself.

You are required to advise the plaintiff as to what he might do. Consider the various legal arguments he might advance and his chances of success.

28.6

X runs a textile factory for which he requires two large reservoirs of water for treating the cloth. He has just had the two reservoirs built. One has been defectively constructed by normally reputable contractors and when filled with water overflowed and caused damage to a neighbouring farm. The other reservoir has been properly built but water escaped because X's employees carelessly forgot to close the valves. This time some neighbouring houses were flooded. Advise the farmer and the householders concerning their legal rights.

28.7

Two young children strayed into the garage of a private bus company which had carelessly been left open. While inside, one of the children climbed under some dangerous machinery and was injured when the other child, unknowingly, started up the machine by pressing a button. As he rushed out to get help for his injured friend, the other child tripped in a hole in the floor and grazed his knees. Advise the bus company about its liability towards the children.

28.8

Sylvester, a salesman, came (as he did every Tuesday) into Fred's shop to inquire whether Fred needed any supplies of sweets. He slipped on the highly polished floor, broke his leg and damaged his new briefcase. Advise Sylvester on whether he can sue Fred.

28.9

James saw some empty accommodation which he thought would be very suitable for his latest business venture, which is assembling toy ducks. Until it became empty the accommodation was used as offices. Advise James on how to find out whether or not he requires planning permission to use the offices for his business. What steps would James have to take to apply for such permission? What factors would the planning authority take into account in deciding whether to grant permission? What steps could James take if (*a*) permission was refused, (*b*) permission was granted provided that he operate the business only between 10 a.m. and 3 p.m. and this would be unsatisfactory for James?

29 Resources of the organisation: labour

Introduction

The final important asset of a business organisation which we discuss is its workforce. The law no longer allows employers ruthlessly to exploit the human resource of labour and there has developed in recent years a complex body of legal rules and principles designed to regulate employer/employee relationships on both the individual level and more generally.

The legal relationship between an individual worker and the organisation which employs him is a contractual one, although contracts of employment cannot be fully understood simply by reference to the general law of contract. In this chapter we look first at the legal rights and responsibilities which arise from contracts of employment, both when the employee is at work and also when the contract of employment is brought to an end. We then look generally at the aims of workers as a group and the law governing those organisations into which workers have formed themselves in order to pursue those aims. We begin by looking at the relationship of the individual worker and the employer.

Contracts of employment

Someone who contracts to work for another may be employed either as an employee (under a contract of employment) or as an independent contractor (under a contract for services). If a worker is an independent contractor he is self-employed and cannot claim most of the legal rights discussed in the chapter since these legal rights arise from duties owed by employers, and the contractor is his own employer. The distinction between contracts of employment and contracts for services is therefore very important.

Recently the courts have decided whether or not an employment relationship exists by answering the question: 'Is the worker in business on his own account?' If so, he is a contractor: if not he is an employee. Relevant factors include whether the person provides his own equipment, whether he hires other workers, whether he undertakes financial risk, etc. In *Ferguson v. Dawson Ltd* a building worker was held to be an employee because, among other things, the company could move its workers from site to site; the workers were provided with tools; the company told the workers what to do; the workers received an hourly wage.

If there is a contract of employment the major question is clearly as to what its terms are. Many contracts of employment are written but, like other contracts, they may also be oral and informal. In principle the general contractual rules as to the contents of contracts apply. Thus, the contract may contain both express and implied terms.

Express terms

The worker and his employer may have expressly stated the terms which form the basis of the contract, e.g. relating to pay, hours of work, holidays, sick pay, and the courts will generally give effect to such terms.

Implied terms

Occasionally, however, the courts may be prepared to imply a term where the parties did not expressly cover a particular contingency. Trade usage and practice may give rise to the implication of terms though strong evidence of the existence of such customs will be required, e.g. in *Sagar v. Ridehalgh* a deduction from the wages of a cotton weaver for bad workmanship was upheld because of a long-standing custom in the trade.

An important source of terms is the *collective agreement*. A collective agreement is an agreement made between an employer (or an association or group of employers) and trade unions as to terms and conditions of employment. Often the terms of such agreements are expressly incorporated into the contracts of employment of individual workers, but they can also be impliedly incorporated if no express provision has been made. As well as implying particular terms into individual contracts the law considers that certain terms are to be implied into all contracts of employment. These cast duties on both employers and employees.

Employers' duties

1. The employer has a legal duty to treat his employees with due respect, e.g. the employer may not act in a deliberately provocative way towards an employee.

2. The employer may *sometimes* be under an obligation to provide the employee with work. This is so, for instance, where failure to provide work can lead to a loss of reputation and where it might mean a reduction in the employee's actual or potential earnings (e.g. if he is on piece-work an employee must be given a chance to earn a reasonable sum).

3. The employer is generally liable to pay the wages of employees if they are available for work but none is provided by the employer unless the contract expressly or impliedly provides otherwise.

4. Employers are under an obligation to take reasonable care to ensure the safety of their workers. This is ensured by both common law and statutory rules which we look at in more detail later.

Employees' duties

The fundamental duty of an employee is that of serving faithfully his employer. Any serious or persistent action which contravenes this duty (e.g. persistent lateness, theft of the employer's property) will thus place the employee in breach of contract.

The following are some more specific examples of action which is deemed to be necessary for the employee to fulfil this duty.

1. The employee must obey all lawful and reasonable orders of his employer.

2. He must not accept bribes, nor gifts from persons other than his employer in respect of his work.

3. He must not disclose confidential information relating to his employment.

4. He must carry out his job with proper care.

Written particulars

Under sections 1–4 of the Employment Protection (Consolidation) Act 1978 an employee is to be given, within thirteen weeks of commencing his employment, a written statement of certain of the terms and conditions of his employment. This statement must refer to hours of work, pay, holiday arrangements, sickness and injury arrangements, pension schemes and length of notice to be given. The statement must be accompanied by a note stating any disciplinary rules and outlining grievance procedures.

Statutory protection of those presently employed

Having noted, among other things, the obligations and duties on the part of an employer to which contracts of employment give rise it is now time to look at the further protection afforded to workers by statutory provisions.

Wages

Under the Employment Protection (Consolidation) Act 1978 every employee has the right to be given by his employer an itemised statement of wages or salary, specifying the amount of and reasons for any deductions and the net amount of payment. This provision is one part of an attempt by the legislature to protect the financial interests of workers from unscrupulous employers. This is traceable back to the Truck Act 1831, which requires that the entire amount of the wages of a manual worker are to be paid in current notes or coins thus preventing abuses current at the time (e.g. payment in credit to be exchanged at the employer's shop). Although this rule has now been relaxed to some extent it is an interesting example of legislative intervention to protect wages earned from not carrying their full value to the employee.

Wages councils

Although legislation affords these forms of protection there has never been a general attempt to fix minimum wages by law. In certain traditionally poorly paid industries, however, wages councils have been established to fix rates of pay (and also holidays, etc.) as a first step towards establishing collective bargaining machinery. The wages councils consist of representatives of both sides of industry plus three independent members. An employer who fails to comply with a wages council order may be prosecuted and the court may award back pay to his employees.

Fair Wages Resolution 1946

Those who have contracts with Government departments are required, by the Fair Wages Resolution of the House of Commons 1946, to pay wages and observe hours and conditions not less favourable than those established by collective bargaining for the trade or industry locally.

General conditions and terms

Under the Employment Protection (Consolidation) Act 1978 any employers' association or trade union can make out a case that a particular employer is observing terms or conditions of employment which are less favourable than recognised terms (e.g. terms settled by collective bargaining for workers in comparable jobs) or the general level observed for comparable workers. The *Advisory, Conciliation and Arbitration Service (ACAS)*, a body set up by the Government to encourage the development of collective bargaining machinery, tries to settle claims. If it cannot settle the issue the *Central Arbitration Committee (CAC)* may hear the case and, if it finds the case well founded, it can make an award that the employer observe the relevant terms and conditions.

Discrimination

Racial discrimination

The Race Relations Act 1976 makes discrimination on racial grounds unlawful. It is specified to be unlawful for a employer to discriminate directly or indirectly against job applicants or presently employed workers unless being a member of a particular racial group is a real qualification for a job (e.g. for employment in a Chinese restaurant). Any complaints concerning racial discrimination in employment must be made to an *industrial tribunal*, a body consisting of a legally qualified chairman and two lay members sitting in regional centres to hear, in a relatively informal way, a large number of industrial law issues. (Appeals from industrial tribunals lie to the Employment Appeal Tribunal which is more formal and consists of a judge of the High Court and two or four other members.) The Commission for Racial Equality keeps the legislation and its operation under review and can assist individuals in complex or important cases.

Sex discrimination

It is also unlawful for an employer to discriminate on the grounds of sex. He must not discriminate either directly or indirectly in terms of the arrangement which he makes for determining who shall be employed, or on what terms, nor in the way in which he offers opportunities for promotion, transfer, training or other benefit, facilities or services. Neither must an employer dismiss workers merely on grounds of their sex. There are exceptions to these provisions of the Sex Discrimination Act (if, for example, the sex of the person is a genuine occupational qualification for the job). Again complaint is to be made to an industrial tribunal which can declare the rights of the parties, award damages and/or recommend that the employer remedy the discrimination. The Equal Opportunities Commission fulfils a role analogous to that of the Commission for Racial Equality.

The Equal Pay Act 1970 provides that where men and women are employed on equivalent jobs, an equality clause is read into contracts of employment. This means that if a woman is employed on the same job as men she is not to be paid less or treated in any way worse than are the men and any benefits which the men enjoy is to be extended to cover her too.

Employment protection

The Employment Protection Act 1975 (the provisions of which are now consolidated in the 1978 Act) introduced a number of new statutory rights for those in employment. The more important of these include:

1. The right to a statutory guarantee in respect of working days when the employee is not given work.
2. The right to maternity pay and the right to return to work after absence through pregnancy.
3. The right not to be penalised for membership of or pursuing the activities of a trade union.
4. The right to time off work for trade union duties and activities and public duties (e.g. as a magistrate).

Health and safety at work

One of the relationships that from very early on was recognised as giving rise to a duty of care for the purposes of the tort of negligence was that of employer and employee. The employer owes to workers a duty to take reasonable care for their safety. This duty has often been said to comprise three duties: to select competent fellow-workers; to provide proper and adequate machinery; to provide a proper system of working. If this duty is not carried out and an employee is injured as a result he will be able to bring a claim for damages. Indeed, the Employers' Liability (Compulsory Insurance) Act 1969 requires that every employer (except a nationalised industry or a local authority) must insure against such a loss.

But to supplement the protection to workers afforded by the Common Law Parliament has enacted a whole range of statutes over the years. In many of these provisions an action for damage in the tort of breach of statutory duty lies for a worker who is injured as a result of the employer's non-compliance with the standards set (e.g. if a factory-worker is injured as a result of his employer's having failed to instal guards on dangerous machinery).

In 1974 Parliament enacted the Health and Safety at Work Act which will eventually regulate this whole area of law, although at the moment many of the specific statutes (especially the Factories Act 1961) remain important. The new Act lays upon employers a general duty to ensure, so far as is reasonably practicable, the health, safety and welfare of his workers. Most employers are required to have a written statement of safety policy and to consult with safety representatives from the employees who can ask for the setting-up of a safety committee.

The Act also provides for the gradual replacement of the old law with a system of Codes of Practice and regulations made under the Act and designed to maintain and improve standards of health, safety and welfare. The Act is to be enforced by the Health and Safety Executive who have the function of assisting in the raising of standards as well as the bringing of prosecutions for breach. Inspectors of the Executive can stop the carrying on of dangerous activities or insist on improvement in safety standards.

Ending the contract of employment

We have now looked at the principal rights and duties arising out of the employment relationship at common law and by statute. We need next to look at the consequences of termination of that relationship. The employment relationship may come to an end by the employee resigning or retiring, by the contract being frustrated (we looked at the doctrine of frustration of contract in Chapter 13: a contract of employment might be frustrated if, for instance, a worker is absent for a long period of time and is unlikely to return – perhaps because he has been sentenced to life imprisonment for the murder of his wife) or by the employee being dismissed. It is with this last eventuality that we are mainly concerned and we shall consider it in more detail. We might note, first, however, that an employer may wish to take action against one of his workers because of some misconduct on that worker's part though he may not wish to dismiss him. How far can employers discipline members of their workforce?

Discipline

The practice of firing an employee for misconduct usually depends for its legality on an express term in his contract of employment. An employer does not need contractual power to give warnings or reprimands. Often, however, the power to warn or reprimand will be dealt with in work rules which may specify the procedure to be adopted. A Code of Practice states that management should ensure that fair and efficient disciplinary procedures exist in all but the smallest establishments and that these should be worked out with the employees. If a contract expressly or impliedly so provides an employer may be allowed to suspend an employee on disciplinary grounds.

Dismissal

Often an employer will wish, for one or more of many reasons, to bring the contract of employment to an end. The common law rule was that every contract of employment was terminable by reasonable notice when the contract provided for a certain period of notice. The Employment Protection Act, however, lays down minimum periods of notice, the periods being determined by the employee's length of service, though where certain grounds are present an employee may be summarily dismissed (i.e. dismissed without *any* notice). This may be the case, for instance, if an employee commits gross misconduct, if he wilfully refuses to obey a lawful and reasonable order, if he is dishonest or grossly negligent.

Wrongful dismissal

If an employer dismisses an employee with shorter notice than he is contractually obliged to give, or without notice in circumstances in which summary dismissal is not warranted this is a *wrongful dismissal* for which the employee can bring an action for breach of contract. The employee can sue the employer for damages and may recover for the time he would have served had the appropriate notice been given (subject, of course, to the rule requiring mitigation of damage). The court will generally not grant the remedy of specific performance of a contract of employment.

Unfair dismissal

Even if an employee is not wrongfully dismissed he may under certain circumstances have an action for *unfair dismissal* provided that he has been continuously employed for fifty-two weeks or more and provided that he is not employed under a contract for a fixed term of two years or more having agreed to exclude any claim in respect of unfair dismissal.

An employee who feels he has been unfairly dismissed can present a complaint to an industrial tribunal. The employee must show that he has been dismissed. A dismissal takes place only:

1. *Where the contract of employment is terminated by the employer.* Thus there is no dismissal if the employee resigns voluntarily though the fact that the employer invited the employee to resign may constitute a dismissal.

2. *Where the employee is employed for a fixed term and that term expires without being renewed under the same contract.*

3. *Where the employee terminates the contract where he is entitled to do so because of the employer's conduct* ('constructive dismissal'). Whether the employee can so do depends upon whether the employer was guilty of conduct which was a significant breach going to the root of the contract of employment or which showed that he no longer intended to be bound by its essential terms.

Once an employee claims he was dismissed it is for the employer to show that the dismissal was fair. It may be fair if:

(*a*) It was done because of the capability or qualification of the employee for performing work of the kind which he was employed to do.

(*b*) It was done because of his conduct.

(*c*) It was due to the redundancy of the employee.

(*d*) It was done because the employee could not continue to work without contravention of some statutory provision.

(*e*) It was due to some other substantial reason such as to justify the dismissal of an employee holding the position which he held.

Whether a particular dismissal based on one of these five grounds will be held to be fair or unfair depends upon whether or not the employer satisfies the industrial tribunal that in all the circumstances he acted reasonably in treating that reason as a ground for dismissal. Thus the employer has to show not only that one of the above grounds existed but also that it was reasonable for him to regard it as a ground for dismissal. If, for instance, an employer has dismissed a worker because of that worker's incapacity the tribunal will act whether the employer did everything possible to discover (and if possible rectify) the cause of the lack of competence and to bring the accusation of incompetence to the worker's attention so that he could himself try to improve his performance. Again, if an employer has dismissed a worker on the grounds of bad conduct he must show, for instance, that he investigated the relevant incident promptly and thoroughly, and considered the gravity of the conduct and its effect on the employment.

If an industrial tribunal finds that the employee has been unfairly dismissed it may, with his consent, make an order that he be re-instated or re-engaged though the tribunal must consider whether this is practicable. Very often it will make an award of compensation. This will usually consist of two elements: the basic award – usually something between one half and two weeks pay plus a compensatory award. This latter element will be such amount as the tribunal considers just and equitable in all the circumstances up to a maximum of £5,200. Appeal on legal points lies to the Employment Appeal Tribunal.

Redundancy

If an employee is dismissed for reason of redundancy he may be eligible for redundancy payments. A dismissal is due to redundancy if wholly or mainly attributable to:

1. The fact that the employer ceases (or intends to cease) business.

2. The fact that the employer ceases (or intends to cease) carrying on business at the place where the employee was employed.

3. The fact that the employer requires fewer employees for executing work or there is (or is about to be) less work.

The Redundancy Payment Act 1965 (most of the provisions of which are now included in the 1978 Act) sought to compensate long-serving employees in these cases. The sums payable are designed to compensate the loss suffered: receipt of this is not dependent on an inability to find a new job.

Claims are made to industrial tribunals. The employee must have been continuously employed for two years and the amount of redundancy payment is determined by the age of the employee, e.g. for each year of employment between the ages of 18 and 21 he is entitled to one half of a week's pay; between the ages of 22 and 40 to one week's pay, etc.

If an employer 'recognises' a trade union he is required to meet with officials of that union. It is unclear quite when there is 'recognition' for these purposes and generally the trade union has to show that there is some formal agreement for the purposes of collective bargaining. If an employer fails to negotiate as the law requires the trade union can make a protective award specifying a period for which every employee involved shall be entitled to pay. An employer also has a duty to notify certain large-scale redundancies to the Minister.

Organised labour

We have looked so far at the relationship of an employer with his individual employees. It must be appreciated that we have thereby looked at only part of the whole picture of the employment scene. When an organisation employs a workforce it is doing more than employing a number of separate, individual workers: it is employing a group of people which will have ideas and objectives which may well conflict with the ideas and objectives of the organisation or perhaps even those of every similar organisation. Business organisations wish to obtain labour at a price which enables them to maximise their business objectives (especially the realisation of profits for investment and the payment of dividends). Thus employers will want available the resource of qualified workers just when needed, at reasonable cost, and without the possibility of expensive industrial disputes.

Aims of organised labour

The workforce will, generally, be unlikely to share this set of priorities. Employees will expect a reasonable and increasing real level of wages in order to enhance their living standards. They will expect a degree of stability in their jobs so that they can plan their lives and those of their families in the long term. Workers will expect safe and reasonably comfortable working conditions. Many workers will be concerned not only that they enjoy the fruits of the furtherance of their objectives, but that their fellows do likewise; thus they will generally be opposed to unemployment.

It can readily be seen that employers (as a group) and the forces of organised labour may come into conflict and some of their objectives may often clash. In order effectively to pursue their objectives workers have organised themselves into organisations known as trade unions.

Trade unions

A trade union is an organisation made up of workers, the principal purposes of which include the regulation of the relations between workers and employers or employers' associations. Under the Trade Union and Labour Relations Act 1974 a trade union is not a corporate body so that it is really an unincorporated association but it can make contracts and sue and be sued in its own name.

Every trade union has a statutory duty to keep proper records of its accounts. In conducting the affairs of the union its officials can work only within the confines of the rules of the union and the courts will enforce the rights of members which are granted to them by the rules. There are special rules

305

concerning the setting up of political funds by unions. These must be kept separate and must be approved by a majority of the members voting in a ballot: no member can be forced to contribute.

The rationàle of trade unions is the furtherance of the objectives of the membership. The law seeks to create a framework in which the union can further the aims of their members by means of collective bargaining. We have already seen how the terms of collective agreements may be incorporated into individual contracts of employment. We look now at the ways in which the law ensures that employees carry on collective bargaining in the first place.

If an employer is unwilling to negotiate issues with trade union representatives the union can refer the matter to ACAS, who will examine the issue and consult the interested parties. It will try to settle the matter by negotiation or make recommendations which then in effect make collective discussion between employer and unions in the ways specified and on the topics listed virtually obligatory. If a recommendation is not followed the Central Arbitration Committee can make an award specifying terms and conditions which the employer must observe provided that the union can show that the employer has not taken such action towards negotiation 'as might reasonably be expected to be taken by an employer ready and willing to carry on such negotiations as are envisaged by the recommendation'.

At all stages of collective bargaining the employer has a duty to disclose, on request, all relevant information without which the union would be impeded to a 'material extent' and which the employer should disclose in accordance with good industrial relations practice.

In the case of protracted bargaining – a highly sensitive issue – it is clear that the strength of the union's case lies to some extent in its ability to withdraw its members' labour. With the establishment in recent years of a framework of institutions like ACAS and CAC to which difficult and acrimonious points of dispute may be referred there is hopefully less need for a conflict of objective between organisations and their employees to result in strikes. Nevertheless it is clear that if they are to be as effective as is at least sometimes necessary trade unions must enjoy a right to advocate the withdrawal of labour. What is equally clear is that a trade union cannot effectively carry out this role without committing torts for which it could be sued in the courts. It is, for instance, a tort to induce another to break a contract. As employees have contracts of employment with their employers, if a trade union called on its members to strike in furtherance of a dispute with the employers it would be inducing them to break those contracts and so it would be liable in the tort of inducing breach of contract. Again, there is a tort of conspiracy which is committed whenever people plan together to perform an act which is a tort. This would be another tort of which unions (being by nature groups of people with a concerted plan) would fall foul.

The Trade Union and Labour Relations Act grants listed trade unions (those which have included their names on a list kept by the Certification Officer) certain immunities from action in these torts provided that they are pursuing legitimate objectives: the immunity extends only to acts done in furtherance or contemplation of a trade dispute. Section 29 of the Act defines a trade dispute as a dispute between employers and workers, or amongst workers concerned with things like terms and conditions of employment, engagement, suspension or dismissal of workers, disciplinary matters, negotiation or consultation. An act is done in contemplation of a trade dispute if the dispute is imminent, although it has not begun. To come within the immunity the act must be in furtherance of the dispute and not any other issue.

Section 13 of the 1974 Act (as amended) gives immunity to those calling strikes or other industrial action and those threatening to call such action from legal action in inducing breach of contract, conspiracy, etc. Section 14 makes it clear that trade unions are liable only in torts like negligence, nuisance, etc., and then only provided the act was not done in contemplation or furtherance of a trade dispute.

Picketing usually accompanies industrial action. Section 15 of the 1974 Act makes peaceful picketing (picketing 'for the purpose only of peacefully obtaining or communicating information, or peacefully persuading any person to work or not to work') lawful. But pickets have no power to do anything else – like stopping traffic or preventing free passage.

Summary and conclusions

1. The workforce is probably a firm's most important asset and there exists a complex body of legal rules (based on the law of contract) to regulate employer–employee relationships.
2. *General relationship between employer/employee*
2.1. *Duties:* i.e. terms implied in all contracts and arising out of the special relationships that have developed over time. They apply to both employer and employee.

Employer	*Employee*
(*a*) Due respect.	(*a*) Serve faithfully and work with care.
(*b*) Provision of work.	(*b*) Obey lawful and reasonable orders.
(*c*) Liable for wages.	(*c*) Resist bribery.
(*d*) Reasonable care and safety.	(*d*) Non-disclosure of confidential information.

2.2. *Contractual obligations*

    (*a*) The common law duties outlined above are considered so important that they affect *all* contracts of employment. They are an example of 'implied' terms, i.e. terms that are enforced though not specifically stated.
    (*b*) There are also 'express' terms, i.e. special conditions written into the contract. Under the Employment Protection (Consolidation) Act 1978 an employee must be given a written statement of the terms and conditions of his employment (within thirteen weeks of starting work).

3. *Employer's Statutory Duties (or Employee's Statutory Protection)*
    It would be impossible to cover all the Statutory duties brought in by the wave of labour law in the recent past. Here we concentrate of four areas: Wages; Discrimination; Employment Protection; Health and Safety.
3.1. *Wages*

    (*a*) Every employee must be given an itemised statement of wages or salary and can opt to be paid in coin or by cheque (1978 Employment Protection (Consolidation) Act.).

(b) Wages Councils fix pay in traditionally low paid industries. (1959 Wage Councils Act; 1975 Employment Protection Act).

(c) Government contractors must not go below standards set by an established collective bargain for the industry (1946 Fair Wages Resolution).

(d) Any Union (or employer) can bring a claim before ACAS that an employer (or employee) is not observing existing terms and conditions of employment (1978 Employment Protection (Consolidation) Act).

3.2. Discrimination

(a) *Racial discrimination*: It is unlawful for an employer to discriminate directly or indirectly against job applicants or current workers (1976 Race Relations Act).

(b) *Sex discrimination.* It is unlawful for an employer to discriminate directly or indirectly between the sexes (note the exceptions) (Sex Discrimination Act 1975). Where men and women are employed in similar jobs they are to receive equal pay (1970 Equal Pay Act; 1975 Sex Discrimination Act).

3.3 Protection in employment

A number of new statutory rights were introduced in 1975 (Employment Protection Act) of which four were particularly important.

3.4. Health and Safety at Work

We noted above that safety was a common law duty of the employer and the duty is said to comprise three aspects: to select competent fellow workers; to provide proper and adequate machinery; to provide a proper system of working. To supplement this general protection Parliament has added a wide range of statutes, the most important of which are:

(a) 1961 Factories Act; 1969 Employers Liability (Compulsory Insurance) Act;

(b) 1974 Health and Safety at Work Act.

The latter act is particularly important as it aims to:

(a) replace previous legislation and provide a uniform system of regulation;

(b) place on employers general responsibility for health, safety and welfare;

(c) provide a written statement of safety policy;

(d) provide codes of practice.

4. *Ending a contract of employment*

A contract can be brought to an end if the contract is 'frustrated', if the person resigns or if he is dismissed. We shall concentrate on the last.

4.1. Disciplinary procedures: are important when they are invoked, as they indicate dissatisfaction between the parties that might lead to dismissal.

4.2. Dismissal:

(a) Summary dismissal: i.e. without any notice and applicable in relation to gross misconduct, gross negligence.

(b) Dismissal with notice: i.e. within the terms laid down by Employment Protection Act and related to an employee's period of service – usually on grounds of incapacity or misconduct (e.g. disobedience, lateness, rudeness).

(c) Wrongful dismissal: i.e. dismissing an employee in breach of the contract of employment.

(d) Unfair dismissal: when there is disagreement over the fairness of dismissal and once an employee has been dismissed it is up the employer to prove that it was fair. Cases are heard by an industrial tribunal.

4.3. Redundancy

(a) A dismissal is in order when a firm stops work, changes location, reorganises work.

(b) Under such conditions redundancy payments are available (1965 Redundancy Payments Act).

(c) Disputed claims are made to industrial tribunals.

5. *Organised labour*

Contracts of employment must not be thought of simply in terms of individual employees, as generally speaking labour is organised in unions.

(a) *Aims of organised labour*: increasing level of real wages; job stability; safe working conditions; protection from unemployment.

(b) *Trade unions*: in law unincorporated bodies with power to make contracts, sue and be sued (1974 TULR Act). They are important in relation to:

(i) Collective agreements, being responsible for negotiating and supporting them (with reference to ACAS in dispute).

(ii) Legal immunity: from certain torts (e.g. inducing breach of contract, conspiracy) under the 1974 TULR Act when they are pursuing legitimate objectives.

(iii) Strike action and *peaceful* picketing.

Assignments

29.1

In *Ready Mixed Concrete v. Minister of Pensions* it had to be decided whether certain drivers were employees of a firm or were self-employed. The following were some of the more important features of the drivers' work arrangements. Prepare a short judgement sorting out the arguments on both sides, weighing them against each other, and give a reasoned decision.

The firm owned a number of lorries which the drivers used to drive. A new scheme was devised whereby the drivers were voluntarily dismissed and the lorries were sold off to them. The drivers were re-engaged under new contracts with the firm. The drivers now had to pay the running costs of the lorries. If they wanted they could hire substitute drivers to work the lorries and any one driver could, if he was able to afford it, own more than one lorry. The drivers had to pay their own income tax and national insurance contributions. When driving the lorries a company uniform had to be worn and the lorries were not to be used for any purposes but those of the company. Use of the lorries had to be placed at the company's disposal for a certain number of hours, though the drivers had no set hours of work. The drivers had to obey orders of the foreman employed by the company but could take their own decisions about the routes they took while engaged on the company's work and could take meal-breaks when and where they wanted. If the company so required, the drivers had to sell the lorries back to the company at an agreed price related to their current market value.

29.2

You are the personnel officer of Make-a-Bed Ltd, a company which employs a large number of skilled carpenters. Make a list of (*a*) as many of the terms which you think it advisable for the company expressly to include in the contracts of employment of such workers, and (*b*) those terms which the law requires you to give notice of to new workers within thirteen weeks of their commencing employment.

29.3

Distinguish clearly between:

1. contracts of employment and contracts for services;
2. express and implied terms in contracts of employment;
3. implied duties of employers and implied duties of employees under contracts of employment.

29.4

Assume you are Sheila.

1. You apply for a job in an office of a club for retired gentlemen. The advertisement says 'Male clerk wanted'. You are turned down because you are a woman.
2. You apply for a job in a shop selling wallpaper run by a male chauvinist. His advertisement said, 'Only bald candidates with beards need apply'. You are rejected because you are not bald and you do not have a beard.
3. You work for a firm which always sends men on a training course in their fourth year of employment. You are not sent on the course because the management feel it is a 'waste of time' training women who will only 'leave to have babies'.

What action would you, as Sheila, take? What arguments might you put forward in pursuing that action? Try to find out from the relevant legislation the whole range of possible defences which your employer might have in order that you can be ready to give convincing replies.

29.5

You work in a factory where ball-bearings are produced on dangerous machinery. Your employer has failed to provide the necessary safety-guards on the machinery and you are injured by metal shooting off the machinery which hits you in the leg. What legal action can you take?

29.6

Has there been a dismissal in the following cases?

1. A lorry driver decides that driving a large lorry is too hard and so says that he does not wish to go on working.
2. A lorry driver who usually drives a lorry is told that the manager feels that, because of his ill-health, he would be better off driving a smaller van at the same rate of pay. He is told that this involves no demotion.
3. A lorry driver crashes his lorry and is told to 'resign or be dismissed'. He resigns.
4. A lorry driver who has crashed his lorry is called an 'incompetent fool'. He is told that he will not be paid for six months, and that he will never be allowed to drive a lorry outside the depot. He resigns.

29.7

How do you think that an employer could try to convince an industrial tribunal that the following dismissals were fair?

1. A worker on a production line assembled a large number of items incorrectly. He had done this on several occasions before and had been given formal warnings, and an indication that continued bad work would result in dismissal. There was evidence to suggest that although this worker had been given the usual training he was incapable of mastering the necessary skills. He was dismissed.
2. A school teacher had been convicted of indecent assaults on young children in a public park after a session of football coaching which he organised. The court had given him a heavy fine and a suspended prison sentence. He was dismissed.
3. An employee of a small butchers firm had been ill for two and a half years and a replacement had been engaged. There seemed no prospect of the original employee returning for at least another year and then only on a part-time basis. The firm had taken the trouble to find out all these details from the employee but now feel bound to dismiss him.
4. A lecturer was employed to teach law at a technical college provided that he obtained an external LL.B. degree within a year. In fact he failed the degree and despaired of ever achieving it. He was dismissed.
5. A night security guard got drunk while on duty at a large factory. He started a small fire to keep himself warm. The fire got out of control and burned down a large part of the factory. He was dismissed.
6. In order to keep their factory running efficiently a firm had to introduce Sunday working. One employee refused to work on Sundays because she wanted to go to Church. The other employees agreed to the changes and they threatened industrial action if the one employee was allowed not to work. The management replied by dismissing that employee.

29.9

Explain the following terms:

1. trade union;

2. collective bargaining;
3. the tort of inducing breach of contract;
4. picketing.

29.10

The officers of NAPOL (the National Association for the Protection of Overworked Lecturers) plan a strike to mark their annoyance at the foreign policy of Illyria, a right-wing state in Central Europe. They advise all their members not to give lectures although the contract of employment of a lecturer requires that he 'give such tuition as the Head of Department requires'. Bill Boneshaker, a strong-minded radical, organises his colleagues into a picket line outside Broombury College of Further Education preventing anyone from going in and preventing the traffic from moving down Broombury High Street. Discuss any points of legal interest arising from these facts.

30 Overview

In this book we have examined several different aspects of organisations. In the earlier chapters we discussed the various factors that might lead to the formation of different types of organisations, and to the major objectives of these organisations. We showed that the individuals and groups within an organisation might have different objectives and that it might be necessary to effect a compromise between them.

We then examined in Chapters 7 and 8 the various policies and activities that might be adopted in order to achieve an organisation's objectives (we concentrated our attention here on business organisations). These policies usually involve an organisation in contractual relationships with other organisations and individuals and these relationships were examined in Chapters 9 to 13.

Having examined these two aspects of an individual organisation – what we might call the internal and external relationships – we widened our horizons to consider the relationships among groups of organisations. One of the definitions of a market that we consider in Chapter 14 was a group of suppliers (organisations) and a group of purchasers (organisations and/or individuals).

This led to a discussion in Chapters 15, 16 and 17 of the factors affecting demand. As far as any single organisation is concerned, the demand for its products is influenced partly by external factors, including demographic changes, changes in income and changes in policies of other organisations, and partly by internal factors, i.e. the policies of the organisation itself. Consequently during this discussion we referred back to the outline of business policies presented earlier, and especially in Chapter 7. We then went on to consider in greater detail in Chapter 18 those policies relating to the determination of price and output.

These policies have very important implications at two levels. The first is the relationships between organisations and consumers, examined in Chapters 19 to 22. The second is the allocation of a country's resources examined in Chapter 23.

In order to implement these policies and thus to attain its objectives an organisation must acquire resources of various kinds, and various aspects of the acquisition and utilisation of resources were examined in the final chapters. During this discussion we paid particular attention to the obligations of organisations towards the individuals and institutions who supply these resources.

This book has shown that a modern economic and social system is extremely complex. Each organisation is involved in a web of relationships with suppliers, customers, etc., and these relationships are influenced by a variety of external factors. (Further external factors are examined in Volume 2.)

Many people working in organisations may see only a very small part of this system; they may be concerned at any one point in their career with only one or two types of relationships. But the further up the organisation one moves, the more relationships one usually becomes concerned with. We conclude, therefore, with a number of assignments which require you to apply what you have learned at various points during the course (and in some instances in other courses) and which give an indication of the complexity of the economic system and the variety of an organisation's relationships.

Assignments

30.1

Bill Greenfingers, a keen amateur gardener, had won several prizes at local flower shows for his roses. This generated a great deal of interest in the area, and he began to sell cuttings and plants to other gardeners. Demand eventually grew to such an extent that he bought, out of his savings, the freehold of a field behind his house, and cultivated it for use in growing and propagating roses.

Although this solved one problem it created another, for Bill now found that he had not the time that was needed to look after the larger area of land. So he gave up his job and began to work full-time in the business. He also took on Alfred Moss, the son of a former colleague, as a full-time worker.

Bill was happiest when he was out in the garden. He enjoyed the fresh air and he had succeeded in producing several new varieties of rose that were liked by his customers. He was also happy when out in his van delivering plants, especially to the local shops which he supplied on a regular basis.

On other occasions, however, he was less happy; for example when he received a letter from the Inland Revenue asking for financial details of the business. Bill did not wish to avoid paying tax, but he had not bothered to keep a regular note of his receipts and payments, and it would require quite a lot of time to get all the necessary information together.

Bill also tended to become frustrated when he thought of all the things that he could do with the business if he had more capital. He would like to buy two greenhouses and install heating in them. These would be useful in the growing of both roses and other plants that Bill wished to introduce in order to reduce the seasonal nature of the business. Another idea was to set up a 'garden centre', which would sell a wide range of products, including young trees, bushes, peat and fertiliser. He also thought that he might be able to get contracts to supply some of the larger shops located in towns further away than those he currently supplied.

Bill also had some worries about the existing business. Although Alfred was a good worker his health appeared to be affected by cold or wet weather. He had been off work on several occasions during the past year, including one spell of three weeks at a very busy time. This had made it difficult for Bill to meet all his orders, and he felt that he ought to dismiss Alfred and take on a replacement.

Another source of worry was that Mrs Mitchell, one of his private customers, had written to him to say that some of the 'Red Devil' roses that she bought had produced white blooms, and that she wanted her money back. Mrs Mitchell was the president of the local Women's Institute and had a reputation of being something of a gossip.

Moreover, Morgans Ltd, one of the shops that he had supplied regularly for the past few months, had refused to pay him for some of the flowers, saying that they were not up to his usual standard and had sold very badly. Bill had delivered the flowers on a Friday and Mr Morgan had rung him the following Monday, saying that most of the flowers had been left on his hands and that he could take them back because Morgans did not want them. Bill did not know what to do because he did not have a formal arrangement with Morgan. He normally said, when delivering the flowers, 'Same again next week?' and Morgan replied, 'Yes', or 'OK' or merely nodded his head.

Finally, Chemco Ltd, a chemicals manufacturer, had bought the plot of land adjoining Bill's garden, and Bill had heard that it intends to build a factory on it. Bill is worried that the fumes from the factory will damage his roses.

One evening Bill was discussing his business with a number of friends at the local pub. One of these friends, Donald Clarkson, had recently left industry after a highly successful career. He had built up his own business which he had then sold to a large multinational company. The multinational had offered to retain him as managing director, but he had declined the offer, since he felt that at the age of 55 he should start taking things more easily. However he had soon tired of a life devoted to playing golf and bridge and was looking for an opportunity of investing some of his time and money in a business 'as a hobby'. He knew of Bill's business; in fact he had bought some roses from him earlier in the year, and so he was very interested in what Bill had said. The following day he called on Bill and made the following proposal:

'After listening to you last night I think we ought to consider the possibility of getting together. I don't know any of the financial details of your business but if they turned out to be satisfactory I might be prepared to invest £20,000 in your business. I think that I could also be a help on the sales and administration side. I used to be the president of the local Chamber of Trade, and I have a lot of contacts that might be useful. My wife Mollie might also be interested in coming in. She was telling me the other day that none of the local florists supply really good flower arrangements for weddings, parties, etc., and she believes that she could do a better job. She also has some spare capital and might put in up to £5,000. Of course if we did come in we would want to form a company or partnership.'

Bill was somewhat taken aback by Donald's proposal. Although he had often thought about the expansion of the business he had not expected to have to make a decision yet. Furthermore he was not sure that he wanted to share control so soon after becoming his own boss. On the other hand he knew that he was a gardener at heart and lacked interest in certain aspects of the business in which Donald was very experienced. Also he had always got on very well with Donald and he thought that they would be able to work well together.

'I am certainly interested in your proposal,' he said, 'but I would like to think it over. When do you want an answer?'

315

'I am off on holiday next month,' replied Donald, 'and I would like to know before then. Look, I will ask some people from my old company to come down next weekend to get some information that should help us both to make up our minds. I will get someone from the finance department; I expect that the figures he produces will also be suitable for sending to the Inland Revenue. I will ask one of our lawyers to come round; it looks as though you could use some free legal advice. It might also be useful to have a chat with one of the chaps from the marketing department; I always brought them in at a very early stage when we were considering expanding the business.'

Not being a man to look a gift horse in the mouth, Bill accepted Donald's suggestion, and the three men duly visited him to see what more he could tell them that would help in the preparation of their reports. Bill produced the following details:

Payments during year (£)

Freehold land	10,000
Van	3,000
Wages (A. Moss)	2,000
Purchases of rose trees and bushes	3,500
Purchases of fertilisers, stakes, twine, etc.	300
Van expenses	200
Other expenses (telephone, stationery, electricity, etc.)	500
	19,500

Receipts during year (£)

Sales of rose trees and bushes	2,000
Sales of cut flowers	8,500
	10,500

Bill also estimated that he had taken £3,000 out of the business for his own use.

The greenhouses, complete with heating systems, would cost £5,000. The initial cost of the garden centre was estimated at £30,000, comprising £15,000 for the construction of the display house, office and stores, £10,000 for the laying out and initial stocking of the gardens and display house, £3,000 for the construction of a car park and £2,000 for a security fence. It would also be necessary to purchase a light truck at a cost of £6,000 for the delivery of larger items such as large bushes and small trees. This truck could also be used to supplement the van for deliveries of smaller items.

Questioned by the marketing man, Bill said that he thought that people who bought roses are influenced by the scent, colour, size, resistance to disease and length of the flowering season of the different varieties. However he had no idea about the relative importance of these factors. Nor did he know why customers bought from him rather than from other suppliers.

On the basis of the above information:

1. Prepare a profit and loss account for the year and a balance sheet at the year end, stating carefully your assumptions.
2. Specify the steps that would have to be taken if Bill were to form either:

   (i) a company or
   (ii) a partnership, together with

(a) Mr Clarkson,

(b) Mr and Mrs Clarkson.

Carefully specify the respective obligations, rights and responsibilities of each person.

3. Prepare a financial plan for the next year of the business's operations on the assumptions that:

(a) the greenhouses are purchased and the garden centre is constructed and stocked,

(b) Mr and Mrs Clarkson invest the maximum amounts mentioned by Mr Clarkson. Make a clear recommendation as to whether or not the company should seek external finance and, if so, indicate what sources it might use.

4. Prepare a programme of market research to provide information that might:

(a) help to increase the profitability of the existing business;

(b) guide the company in the decision as to whether it should construct a garden centre;

(c) guide the company as to what new types of plant it should grow in the greenhouse.

The programme should specify the topics on which information is required and how this information might be collected. Since it is unlikely that the company would be able to spend a large amount of money on research, you should take into account the likely costs of the various methods of data collection.

5. Advise Bill concerning his legal rights and obligations in connection with:

(a) his decision to sack Alfred Moss;

(b) the complaint from Mrs Mitchell;

(c) the refusal of Morgans to pay for all the roses he delivered; and

(d) Chemco Ltd's plan to build a factory adjoining his garden.

30.2

Outline the advantages of a well-developed external labour market. Show what economic, social and legal factors might impede the working of such a market.

30.3

The passage below, which was extracted from the *Financial Times*, 1 February 1978, relates to an overtime ban imposed by tanker drivers in an attempt to obtain a wage increase. Drawing on this passage discuss:

(a) the factors influencing the size of the wage increase demanded by the tanker drivers;

(b) the factors influencing their chances of obtaining this increase.

'From today Shell drivers are joining the overtime ban already imposed by the delivery staff of Esso, British Petroleum, National and Texaco. Between them these companies account for 23,000 of the 30,000 filling stations in Britain. The companies say that deliveries could be cut by between 25 and 40 per cent, causing considerable disruption of road transport and, to a lesser extent, trouble for those industrial, commercial and domestic users of oil products who rely on tanker drivers for their deliveries.

'Now that the dispute – about a wage claim exceeding the Government pay guidelines – has spread to Shell, one of the main British oil suppliers, the alternative sources of supply are virtually closed. There is little scope for the other companies to step into the breach, even assuming that their own trade union employees would allow it. What is more, it is quite possible that the overtime ban will spread to a number of the second tier petrol companies.

'There is no scope for switching oil products from road to other forms of distribution. Even if the unions countenanced such a switch (which they would not) oil companies would quickly run into unsurmountable difficulties. Although rail, pipelines and water-borne transport play an important part in the movement of oil from refineries to distribution centres, power stations and large industrial complexes, road tankers are invariably used to deliver products to petrol stations, homes, factories and commercial premises. The Institute of Petroleum's figures for 1976 (the last full year for which data are available) show that some 50 m. tonnes of the 80.3 m. tonnes of refined products were moved by road.

'It is expected that as the overtime ban takes effect, perhaps with panic buying accentuating the impact, many retailers will devise their own means of meeting the pressure. As in the 1973–74 energy crisis, when petrol and other fuel products were also in short supply, retailers could restrict sales to a few gallons per customer. They might even give priority service to their regular cutomers. Some might open garages for a limited period each day; others might sell their restricted stocks as quickly as possible and shut down until the next delivery.

'Following the energy crisis some four years ago the Government has armed itself with the Energy Act. By means of orders the Energy Department can quickly restrict the sale and use of certain oil products. One option being considered in the event of major disruption is to limit severely sales of petrol to private motorists in order to maintain as far as possible deliveries to public transport, industry and commerce.

'The oil companies have offered increases of about 15 per cent including 5 per cent for productivity. The drivers' attempt to wrest more from them is not simply the action of a relatively powerful group intent on disregarding pay guidelines by pursuing a "greedy" claim. Officials of the Transport and General Workers' Union, to which the men belong, say the claim reflected the anger of drivers about the way in which successive years of pay policy have eroded the rewards they received for working productivity arrangements agreed in the 1960s. Moreover recent settlements for non-tanker drivers have been running at about 15 per cent, in breach of guidelines. That in itself has helped to steel the tanker men to push for a little more. According to the oil companies, the improvements that have been sought by the drivers would mean an overall advance of about 20 per cent.

'Mr Jack Ashwell, the TGWU transport secretary, said yesterday that fears about the level of employment in the industry was now "a big worry" for the tanker men. Shell has already announced that within the next few years it will be ending its contracts with one-fifth of the filling stations selling its petrol. Their sales are so small, Shell says, that it loses money supplying them. Union officials say the oil companies are not replacing the tanker drivers who leave their jobs, and that there is a growing tendency to use outside contractors rather than to require overtime from staff drivers during peak supply periods.'

30.4

Universal Toys Ltd manufactures teddy bears. Due to extensive imports of electronic toys from abroad, the sale of teddy bears has dropped dramatically. The company made a loss of £100,000 last year and expects to make an even bigger loss this year. The increase in imports has led to severe price cutting in most of the markets for traditional toys, and market research has failed to reveal any profitable alternative uses for the company's production facilities. Consequently, the Board of Directors has decided that it is impossible to maintain the company at its present size and that plans for a reduction in activity will have to be introduced. It is felt that the demand for traditional toys, such as teddy bears, will eventually revive, but that this will probably not happen within the next three years. The Board believes that the plans for a reduction in activity should take into account the following factors:

1. The decline in demand has been particularly marked in the section that produces de-luxe teddy bears. These are made mainly by hand, and all the workers in this section are female. If this section were closed, and its remaining work transferred to other sections, it would be possible to retain all the remaining workers.
2. These women are not members of a union. However, many of them have been with the company for many years. On average they are not as highly paid as the workers in other sections, and have perhaps been willing to accept lower wages because their job is intrinsically more interesting.
3. Since this section is in a self-contained unit, it might be possible to let the unit to another firm to be used for production and/or warehousing.
4. The alternative to closing one section would be to reduce the level of output of all the sections. This would involve, for each section, either making some workers redundant or introducing a work-sharing scheme.
5. The Directors have identified two other ways in which the costs of production could be reduced. The company is proud of its strict system of quality control. However this has proved to be very expensive and could be made less complex. The company could also begin to use less expensive fabric, although some doubts have been expressed about the flammability of the material under conditions of extreme heat.
6. It would be possible to reduce the costs of distribution by restricting sales to large buyers (wholesalers or retailers). This would cause some further loss of sales, but it is expected that even so profits could be increased since it is very expensive to supply large numbers of small buyers.
      In the light of this information:

(*a*) Discuss the relative merits of reducing the level of output by

    (i) making workers redundant and
    (ii) introducing a work-sharing scheme.

(*b*) If it was decided that some workers should be made redundant, discuss the relative merits of dismissing workers only from the de-luxe section or from all the sections.

(*c*) Outline the disadvantages of the methods of cost-reduction discussed in paragraphs 5 and 6 above.

(*d*) If Universal Toys Ltd was a public company whose shares were quoted on the Stock Exchange, what consequences might follow from its lack of profitability? Would the consequences be the same if Universal was a private company?

(*e*) If you thought that the demand for teddy bears would never revive what steps, other than those already discussed, would you advise Universal to take in order to try to protect the interests of its shareholders?

(*f*) Assume that the Directors have decided that some workers will have to be declared redundant and that the workers have heard rumours about this decision. The personnel officer is visited by a representative of the women in the de-luxe department and by a union official representing the workers in the other department. Outline the arguments that each of these workers might put forward in order to protect the interests of the workers in her (his) section.

30.5

The following statements include pairs of alternative words or phrases. Choose the more appropriate word or phrase in each statement.

1. A patent lasts for a 40/20 year period.
2. Copyrights must be/need not be registered.
3. A trade mark may be renewed initially after 7/10 years.
4. The Bass red triangle is a patent/trademark.
5. Injurious falsehood is also known as passing-off/slander to goods.
6. A freehold/leasehold estate is of limited duration.
7. The covenant to pay rent is a restrictive/positive covenant.
8. Actions for personal injuries can/cannot succeed in the tort of *Rylands v. Fletcher*.
9. Trespassers/visitors are protected by the Occupiers' Liability Act 1957.
10. From a refusal of planning permission by a local authority, appeal lies to the Secretary of State/Court of Appeal.
11. The change in cost that arises when output is increased is known as incremental/escapable cost.
12. A good for which the income elasticity of demand is positive is known as a(n) inferior/normal good.
13. A fixed cost is one that does not change when a change occurs in the output/scale of organisation.
14. The Post Office is/is not a public company.
15. The level of government assistance to firms is more/less in Intermediate than in Development Areas.
16. Some/All contracts must be in writing.

320

17. Intention to create legal relations is/is not presumed in commercial contracts.
18. Breach of condition does/does not give a right to repudiate the contract.
19. Misrepresentation renders a contract void/voidable.
20. Specific Performance is an equitable/legal remedy.

30.6

Objective Test Questions

In questions 1 to 14 give the correct answer, A, B, C, D or E.

1. A company sells 100 articles a day at a price of 10 pence. It then raises the price to 11 pence. If the price elasticity of demand for the article was (—)3 the firm's daily revenue would fall by (pence)

   (A) 10
   (B) 30
   (C) 100
   (D) 230
   (E) 300

2. Which of the following conditions must exist in any market?

   (A) Suppliers and purchasers meet face to face.
   (B) The goods traded are available for inspection by purchasers.
   (C) The offers of suppliers exactly match the offers of purchasers.
   (D) All participants in the market act on their own behalf.
   (E) None of the above.

3. A shift in the demand curve for books would be likely to follow from all of the following *except*:

   (A) A change in the price of books.
   (B) An increase in advertising by publishers.
   (C) A substantial increase in the television licence fee.
   (D) A fall in population.
   (E) An increase in the real income of consumers.

4. An open market usually has all of the following features *except*:

   (A) A large number of suppliers.
   (B) Suppliers are able to co-ordinate their activities.
   (C) Suppliers find it difficult to predict and control the level of output.
   (D) Suppliers supply identical or very similar products.
   (E) Barriers to entry are low.

Questions 5 to 9 are based on Fig. 30.1 which refers to the market for strawberries. The unbroken lines indicate the initial demand and supply conditions and the broken lines indicate new demand and supply conditions that might apply after the changes listed below have occurred. Starting each time from the initial equilibrium position X, indicate the new equilibrium position A, B, C, D or E. (Each letter may apply once, more than once, or not at all.)

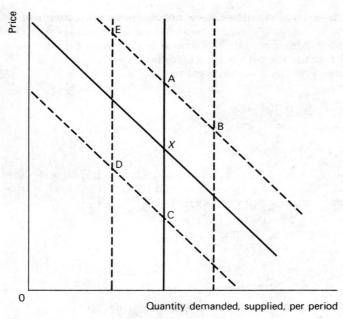

Fig. 30.1

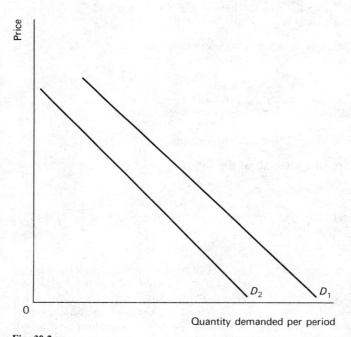

Fig. 30.2

322

5. Fine weather increases the demand for strawberies and the number of ripe strawberries.
6. The price of raspberries, a substitute for strawberries, falls.
7. The beginning of the school holidays means that more children are available to pick strawberries; the price of raspberries rises.
8. A popular newspaper runs an article giving a number of receipes for using strawberries.
9. Attacks by weevils reduce the strawberry crop; a medical report is issued which demonstrates that eating fresh fruit is conducive to good health.
10. The shift of the demand curve from D_1 to D_2 in Fig. 30.2 could have been due to all of the following *except*:

   (A) An increase in the price of a complementary product.
   (B) A fall in the price of a substitute product.
   (C) A fall in income, if this product is a normal good.
   (D) A fall in income, if this product is an inferior good.
   (E) A reduction in advertising expenditure on this product.

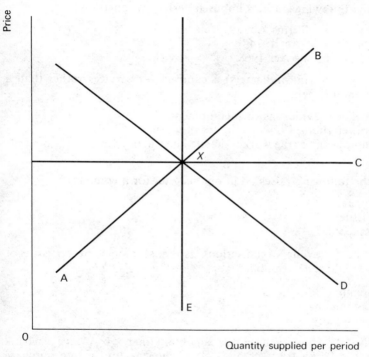

Fig. 30.3

Questions 11 to 14 refer to Fig. 30.3 which comprises a number of alternative supply curves. Indicate which supply curve would be most likely to apply when the initial equilibrium, denoted by point X, is disturbed by each of the following changes:

11. As output increases in response to an increase in demand, average cost rises.

12. As output increases, economies of scale arise which are passed on to the consumer.
13. There is no change in the quantity supplied in response to a fall in demand.
14. A reduction in demand leads to a reduction in price and profit margins.

In questions 15 to 20 there are three responses. Answer:
(A) if responses 1, 2 and 3 are correct.
(B) if responses 1 and 2 only are correct.
(C) if responses 2 and 3 only are correct.
(D) if response 1 only is correct.
(E) if response 3 only is correct.

15. The statement 'The demand for refrigerators was 60,000' is imprecise because it does not specify:

(1) the price of refrigerators;
(2) the time period involved;
(3) the geographical boundaries of the market.

16. Which of the following statutes impose(s) criminal sanctions?

(1) Unfair Contract Terms Act 1977.
(2) Consumer Credit Act 1974.
(3) Trade Descriptions Act 1968.

17. Which of the following indicate(s) a contract for services rather than a contract of employment?

(1) The worker provides his own equipment.
(2) The worker chooses his own hours of work.
(3) The employer gives the worker detailed instructions as to how to do the work.

18. Which of the following raises additional capital for a company?

(1) rights issue;
(2) bonus issue;
(3) scrip issue.

19. Which of the following organisations can raise money by an issue of debentures to the general public?

(1) partnership;
(2) private company;
(3) public company.

20. Which of the following organisations can obtain finance by means of a bank loan or overdraft, by trade credit and by entering into a hire purchase agreement?

(1) partnership;
(2) private company;
(3) public company.

Table of Cases

Index